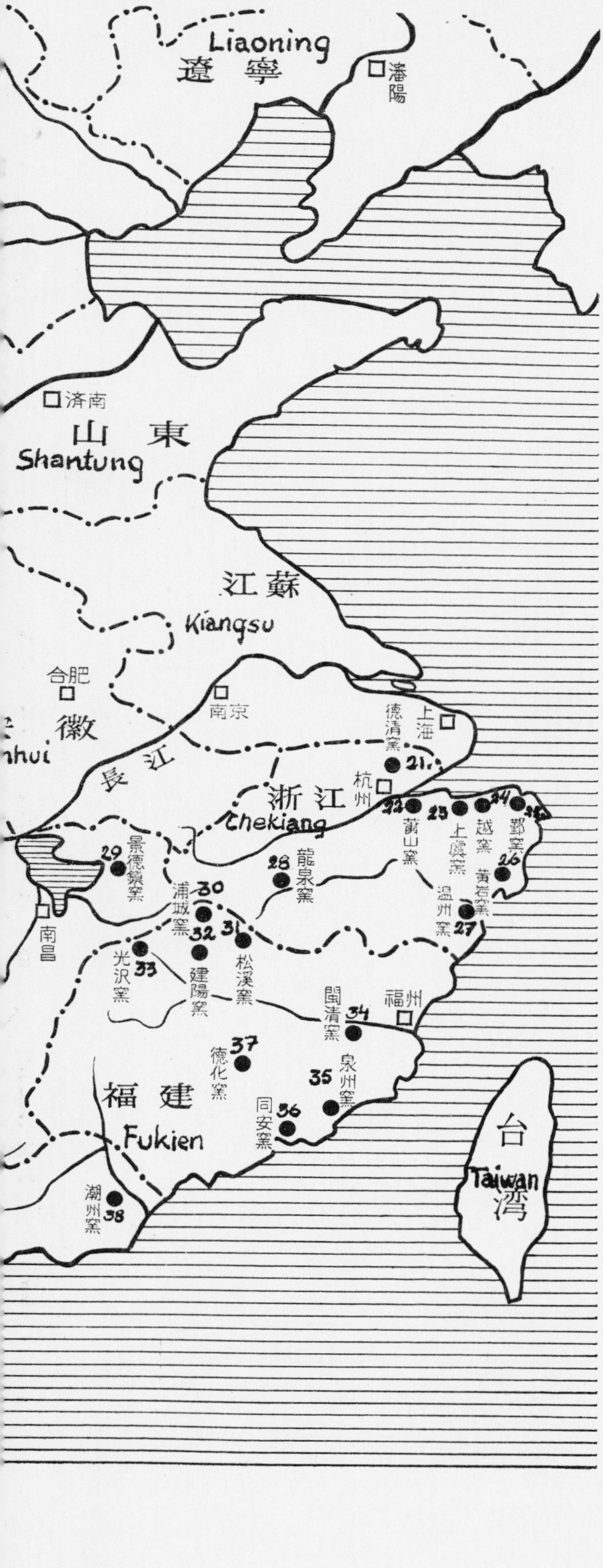

1. Ting yao
2. T'ai-yüan yao
3. Chieh-hsiu yao
4. Tz'u-chou yao
5. An-yang yao
6. T'ang-yin yao
7. Hsiu-wu yao
8. Kung yao
9. Hsin-an yao
10. Yao-chou yao
11. T'ien-shui yao
12. Teng-feng yao
13. Mi yao
14. Chün yao
15. Lin-ju yao
16. Chia yao
17. Pao-feng yao
18. Lu-shan yao
19. Kuang-yüan yao
20. Ch'iung yao
21. Te-ch'ing yao
22. Hsiao shan yao
23. Shang-yu yao
24. Yüeh yao
25. Yin yao
26. Huang-yen yao
27. Wen-chou yao
28. Lung-ch'üan yao
29. Ching-te chen yao
30. P'u-ch'eng yao
31. Sung-ch'i yao
32. Chien-yang yao
33. Kuang-tse yao
34. Min-ch'ing yao
35. Ch'üan-chou yao
36. T'ung-an yao
37. Te-hua yao
38. Ch'ao-chou yao
39. Chi-an yao
40. Chang-sha yao
41. Canton yao

Sung Ceramic Designs

Jan Wirgin

London, 1979

Originally published in
The Museum of Far Eastern Antiquities
Bulletin No. 42, Stockholm, 1970

Publisher:
Han-Shan Tang Ltd
P.O. Box 101
London WC2E 9DX
U.K.

ISBN 0 906610 01 X

Printed in Great Britain by
Biddles Ltd, Guildford, Surrey

SUNG CERAMIC DESIGNS

BY

JAN WIRGIN

CONTENTS

Foreword 3
Introduction 5
Northern celadon 20
    List of designs found on the Northern celadon ware 45
Ch'ing-pai 48
    List of designs found on the ch'ing-pai ware 72
Lung-ch'üan yao 74
    Early Chekiang celadon 77
    Lung-ch'üan celadon 80
    List of designs found on the Lung-ch'üan celadon 85
Tz'u-chou yao 86
    The enamelled group 118
    List of designs found on the Tz'u-chou ware 122
Ting yao 124
    List of designs found on the Ting ware 162
Some principal motifs 166
    Peony 166
    Lotus 170
    Chrysanthemum 173
    Prunus 175
    Other flowers 176
    Bamboo 177
    Pomegranate 177
    Melon 179
    Boys among floral scrolls 179
    Other human representations 184

Dragon 186
Phoenix 190
Lion and ch'i-lin 193
Tiger 195
Hsi-niu (Rhinoceros) 196
Tortoise 198
Deer 199
Other animals 201
Ducks and other water-fowl 201
Other birds 203
Fish 205
A tentative chronology 208
Northern Sung 210
Chin 219
Southern Sung 228
List of abbreviations 233
Chinese characters 234
Bibliography 236
Western literature 236
Catalogues 239
Japanese literature 240
Chinese literature 242
Chinese periodicals 243
Figure index 249
Plate index 255
Cross index from plates to types 273
Corrigenda 278
Figures
Plates
Map of kiln sites

FOREWORD

An investigation of this kind would not have been possible without extensive travels and thorough studies of museums and private collections all over the world. My thanks are due to all those various Funds and Institutions which on several occasions have helped me to finance those travels. I also wish to thank all my colleagues abroad and all collectors and connoisseurs who have shown me their collections and have generously let me share their knowledge.

My first studies of foreign collections took place in England, and I have always felt especially indebted to all my British friends who with great friendliness and hospitallity have guided me through the rich ceramic collections both public and private which are found in that country.

My first visit to Japan, in 1961, was a great experience and I am most grateful for getting the access to all the collections I was able to study there and for the most obliging helpfulness of my Japanese colleagues. My studies of ceramic collections in China, Hong Kong, Iran and Turkey have been comparatively short but none the less of great importance to me.

I am very glad to have been able to see most of the main collections of Oriental Art in the United States and I am greatly indebted for all kind assistance given to me when studying those important collections. It was also a most rewarding and interesting experience to be able to stay a year in Honolulu as a visiting professor and I am most grateful to all friends and colleagues in Hawaii.

To my teacher in European art-history, Professor Sten Karling, I am deeply grateful for all the help and the support he has given me in my studies. Although Far Eastern art-history has not been included among the subjects taught in the University of Stockholm, he has in all possible ways tried to facilitate my work and has encouraged me to continue my studies in this special field. His own stimulating teaching in art-history and art-theory has been most valuable to me and has given me the foundation for the methods of research in these subjects.

To my teacher in sinology, Professor Bernhard Karlgren, I owe a great debt of gratitude. I have had the privilege not only of his excellent and stimulating teaching and his constant encouragement but since I, in 1957, became his assistant in the Museum of Far Eastern Antiquities I have permanently received his help and advice. His scientific method, profound knowledge of Far Eastern linguistics, history, archaeology and culture in general has been a never-ceasing source from which I have profited greatly. He has urged me to conclude this academic paper, and he has spared no pains in going through the text, and with his usual generosity he has offered me to have it published in the Bulletin of the Museum of Far Eastern Antiquities.

To my present chief and colleague Dr. Bo Gyllensvärd I wish to offer a warm thank for his constant interest and support, and for everything I have learned from him since for the first time he introduced me into the fascinating field of Chinese ceramics. His own academic paper about T'ang gold and silver has been one of the most important starting-points for this work and it was he who originally suggested to me to make a similar investigation of the designs of the Sung dynasty such as they are found on ceramics.

I wish likewise to give my warm thanks to my colleague Dr. Tien Lung for all help he has given me in the arduous and time-consuming work of translating the Chinese texts and excavation reports. He has also kindly taken upon him to write the Chinese characters in the word-list and the Bibliography.

I am also grateful to Miss Lilly Kling for her kind help with the editorial work. With painstaking exactitude and many years' experience from her work with the Bulletin she has helped me to arrange and correct the text, and with the lay-out and the proof-reading.

My thanks are also due to Mr. Sven Nilsson for all the trouble he has taken in the photographic work and for his great patience and carefulness in this task and also for his help in the arrangement of the plates.

I would also express my gratitude to the Friends' Association of the MFEA who with a generous grant enabled me to include a colourplate among the illustrations of this paper.

INTRODUCTION

Since at the beginning of this century the interest in older Chinese ceramics became prominent in the West it has continuously increased, and a very rich flora of books and articles on this subject has appeared in Western languages. The wares of the Sung dynasty have been considered by collectors and scholars in agreement to represent perhaps the finest achievement ever obtained in the history of world ceramics. It has in particular been the undecorated stoneware the beauty of which is dependent on form and glaze alone that has been praised the most, and which seems to have made a special appeal to modern aesthetic ideals. The decorated wares have not been appreciated to the same extent even if large and important collections of such wares have also been formed, and the rustic charm of the Tz'u-chou type ware has been stressed by many connoisseurs. It is, however, rather surprising that, considering the whole body of works hitherto published on Sung ceramics, very little attention has been given to the designs found on the different wares of this period. A closer study of this subject will reveal the fact that one of the most important changes that took place in the history of Chinese ceramics, the development towards more richly and freely decorated specimens, occurred during Sung.

During the T'ang dynasty the ceramic is as a rule very sparsely decorated and the designs found are mostly stiff and heraldic, and they are often obviously loans from other materials. It is mainly through its rich glazes and its variety of vigorous and swelling shapes that the pottery and stoneware of the period are characterized. The majority of T'ang wares found in collections all over the world are tomb wares, never intended to be used by the living. It is mainly through the white porcelain of the type which, with a somewhat inappropriate term, is labelled *Hsing yao* and the celadon wares of *Yüeh* type that we are able to get an idea of the daily wares of T'ang. Regarded from the point of view of design, the Yüeh yao is undoubtedly the most interesting, and it forms a most important link between T'ang and Sung. The Yüeh yao is often richly decorated, and the new free treatment of the designs found already in this ware is a major achievement which became of fundamental importance to the later development of ceramic designs.

In the present study I have tried to give a survey of some of the designs found on different Sung wares. One of the main difficulties in making such a study is the abundant richness of the material available. It is necessary to make a selection among the materials which can offer us a representative body of designs and at the same time avoid our being overwhelmed by the variety found. In order to restrict the volume of material I have selected only the main groups of wares with a rich décor *Northern celadon, ch'ing-pai, Tz'u-chou yao* and *Ting yao* and also presented a few decorated types of *Lung-ch'üan* and other Chekiang celadons, but have neglected all other more provincial wares. The wares of Liao and the decorated wares from the Chi-chou kiln I have already discussed in earlier papers,[1]) and even if it would have been interesting to make a more thorough study of the Liao group based on the material excavated since the article was published, it has not been possible to do so because of a lack of space. The two wares mentioned will, however, be referred to on several occasions. A study of the Yüeh yao is also outside the scope of this work, and several writers have already issued important publications on this subject from which we can select the comparative material needed.

Within each group of ceramics discussed I have tried to select a representative body of the most frequent designs found, but have also included more rare and unusual patterns especially when they can help us to understand the development of certain motifs or in other ways are able to enlighten our knowledge of the subject. A selection of this kind must, in the nature of things, be rather personal and I have no pretensions to be exhaustive. There will no doubt be many designs missing and some which could with equal right have been exchanged for others, but on the whole I hope the material will give a fairly accurate picture of the designs found on Sung ceramics.

The designs presented have been selected from ceramic specimens in the main museums and private collections in Europe, North America, China and Japan. It has sometimes been impossible to obtain illustrations of all specimens I had wished to show, but the majority of design types discussed are illustrated either with a plate or a text figure. Because of the abundance of the material it has been necessary to make many of the illustrations rather small, but I have preferred this arrangement to leaving them out completely. To those specimens that I have not been able to illustrate there have as a rule been given references to other works where they can be seen, but this has not always been possible as some pieces have not been previously published.

The selected material has under each main ware been divided into a certain number of types. Those types are mostly formed by objects with the same design, but sometimes it has been necessary to let objects with a certain shape[2]) or a certain arrangement of the design constitute a specific type. Even if this arrangement could be considered somewhat arbitrary, I have judged it to be the most surveyable.

---

[1]) *Some notes on Liao ceramics. BMFEA* 32, 1960.
Some ceramic wares from Chi-chou. BMFEA 34, 1962.

[2]) Shape is undoubtedly a very important criterion when judging a ceramic specimen, and several authors have worked with the form aspect in connection with dating. Unfortunately none of the works so far published on this subject are sufficiently comprehensive or reliable. It has not been possible in this paper to deal at any length with the form problem, but I have constantly referred to shapes as a help to dating.

Most types have also been given a date, those dates are sometimes only tentative, when the material available does not give enough evidence of a more certain date, but I have tried to make the dating as close as possible considering all the different criteria available. A summary of the reasons for the dating and a tentative chronology is found in the last chapter.

In some wares I have also tried to assign, when possible, the objects discussed to specific kilns, but in many groups this has not been achievable because of the lack of a sufficient amount of scientifically excavated material. The dating and attribution of the different wares is of course of great interest to anybody working with Sung ceramics, but the main purpose of this paper has been to present a rich selection of designs and to co-ordinate some of the widely scattered objects into specific groups, in order to find out what is typical of the Sung decorative style as it is manifested in the ceramic art and what achievements in this field were made during the period. Special emphasis has been laid upon the dating of some of the ceramic production to the *Chin* dynasty and to show that the main kilns, including the Ting kiln, were still active during that period. A discussion of some of the main floral and animal motifs is found in a special chapter.

A large amount of the material used in this study has been examined by the author in different collections, but it has not been possible for me to see or handle the whole body of material, and it has to a certain extent been necessary to depend on photographs and publications. Luckily enough very good catalogues are available of Sung ceramics from the pioneer works of Hobson, Hetherington and Honey to the recent excellent catalogues by John Ayers, Michael Sullivan and others. The different publications published by the Oriental Ceramic Society and all exhibition catalogues from different countries have been most valuable sources of information. Many excellent publications have also appeared in Japan, the majority of them having been written under the supervision of Fujio Koyama, the foremost ceramic expert in that country. Among Chinese publications the works of Ch'en Wan-li have been of great value, and the recent archaeological periodicals *K'ao ku hsüeh pao*, *Wen wu* and *K'ao ku* have been of the utmost importance for our knowledge of the new excavations carried out in China, which have given us an abundance of material that has thrown light upon several obscure points in the development of Sung ceramics and also solved many problems concerning the location of kilns. Unfortunately not all the excavations carried out have been adequately published, and the quality of the illustrations leaves much to be desired. It also seems that some of the excavators have not been experienced enough, and datings and descriptions are not always to be trusted; the material must be handled with care and read with a critical mind. Even with these shortcomings duly calculated, the extensive excavation work carried out in China during recent years and the reports published are highly admirable, and the material has been of fundamental value for this study.

A comparison between the designs found on Sung ceramics with those found on other kinds of applied arts, as well as the sculpture and painting of the period, would undoubtedly have been of great interest. But the abundance of the ceramic material alone is so great that a more detailed study also of other branches of Sung art would have been an impossible and overwhelming undertaking. I have, however, when it has been of fundamental value for the explanation of a certain design referred to other materials, especially such as come from scientifically excavated and datable tombs. A further study of the decorative ornaments of the Sung time especially based on ornaments and objects from tombs would be of great interest, and I hope to be able to make an investigation of this kind in a coming paper.

But the problem of comparison with other materials also has other aspects. When it comes to such materials as bronze, jade and silver, the material available is extremely poor. There is a number of bronze vessels in archaic style that has been attributed to the Sung dynasty, but there is not one single piece which has been found in an excavation, and very few that can be proved to derive from the period in question.[1]) The principal bronzes found in Sung tombs are the mirrors, and the decoration of those is usually composed of the same kind of floral scrolls that we find on the ceramic. Jade pieces datable to Sung are also extremely scarce; they are almost all dated according to stylistic reasons, and as the material itself reveals very little of the age, this kind of dating is most unreliable. The silver ware of Sung is also rather meagre, even if we in this field can be much more confident of the dating thanks to the thorough study of the gold and silver work of T'ang that has been carried out by Gyllensvärd.[2]) Sung painting is a field where the surviving material is somewhat larger, but here too we have the problem of authenticity. Its influence on the decoration of ceramics is unquestionable, especially the Tz'u-chou ware often shows close parallels with compositions found in contemporary painting.

If we sum up what has been said above of other types of Sung art it would seem that the selection made would somewhat restrict the possibilities to understand and date the patterns on Sung ceramics. But the case is not quite so difficult. It has to be considered that the conditions obtaining during the Sung dynasty were quite different from those found, for instance, during T'ang. Whereas during the T'ang dynasty the influences and loans from abroad were a distinctive feature in the art of the period, and the possibilities of following a certain design from the source to its development on different materials are great; the initial conditions at the beginning of Sung were entirely dissimilar. The majority of the designs used in Sung art were already introduced to China much earlier, and with the

---

[1]) For a further discussion of this problem see pp. 15–17 below.

[2]) Gyllensvärd, Bo, *T'ang gold and silver*. Stockholm 1957 (hereafter *Gyllensvärd*).
Gyllensvärd, Bo, *Chinese gold and silver in the Carl Kempe collection*. Stockholm 1953 (hereafter *Chinese Gold and Silver*).

increasingly deteriorating relations with its neighbours, which is significant of the period, very few impulses from abroad were received. The Chinese Empire retired into its shell, and under the beneficial influence of imperial patronage its art developed with little influence from abroad; but instead it was absorbing and recreating the achievements of preceding periods. The Sung dynasty thus became a period of "sinization". It is accordingly not so much the motifs themselves that are new and innovative but mainly the way they are treated and with which preference they are selected; and those features can be studied on ceramics perhaps better than in any other branch of art with the exception of painting.

* * *

Before we start to give a survey of the designs found on Sung ceramics it is necessary to give a very brief account of the historical and cultural background to this classic age of Chinese culture.

When the Sung dynasty was founded in 960 it marked the end of half a century of anarchy and partition, known in the history of China as the period of the Five Dynasties. Once more the main provinces of China were all united under one ruler.[1]) But the State that now arose differed considerably from the large and mighty T'ang Empire. All possessions outside China were now irretrievably lost, and at the border of the new empire new states had formed which threathened its domains. In the north-west the Tibetan-Tangut Kingdom of Hsia cut off Sung China from the traditional commercial routes to Central and Western Asia. In the south-west the T'ai Kingdom of Nan Chao was a powerful and dangerous neighbour. But most dangerous of all states around the Chinese borders was the Liao Empire in the north-east. At the beginning of Sung the Liao Empire (907–1125) had already consolidated its position by conquering several neighbouring states and had also incorporated the northern parts of Hopei and Shansi, and was thus in dangerous proximity to the Sung capital of Pien-liang (modern K'ai-feng). After some years of war the Sung Emperor was forced to make a peace treaty in A.D. 1004. But it was a peace on hard terms and large annual subsidies had to be paid by the Chinese. The following century was, except for minor border conflicts, on the whole peaceful, and it became the Golden Age of the Liao Empire, Chinese customs and culture were adopted, and the state became more and more sinisized, but also more weakened. In 1114 one of the vassal tribes of Liao, the Ju-chen, encouraged by the Sung, revolted against Liao supremacy and after only ten years of fighting

[1]) The submission of the last independent states was not received until 979. Among these were the states of *Wu Yüeh* [1] in Chekiang, where the Yüeh ware was produced.
Figures in brackets refer to Chinese characters listed immediately preceding the Bibliography.

the whole empire was forced to surrender to its enemy. The new State, which called itself the Chin Empire (1115–1234), took possession of the conquered land. The fall of the Liao was naturally witnessed with great delight by the Sung Emperor, and he now believed the right time had come to recapture at least the territories within the Great Wall. This decision proved to be disastrous and started a new war between the victorious armies of Chin and the weakened and untrained Sung forces, which ended in a complete defeat of the latter. The Emperor, Hui-tsung, abdicated in favour of his son, who tried to make peace with the enemy, but through an unwise policy the Chin armies were soon again turned against China. The capital, K'ai-feng, was captured in 1126 and the emperors and more than 3000 of their retinue were taken prisoners and carried off to the north, and they were never to return.

This marked the end of the Northern Sung Empire (*Pei Sung*) and it seemed like the termination of the whole dynasty. But in the south a younger son of the captured Emperor Hui-tsung had been proclaimed emperor. After more than a decade of war, in which the Chinese benefited by the obstacle that the densely populated flat country, with all its canals and rice fields on the other side of the Yangtze, offered the foreign cavalry, peace was at last concluded in A.D. 1141. By this peace China was divided between the two empires of Southern Sung (*Nan Sung*) and Chin. Shansi, Shensi, Hopei, Honan and Shantung remained in the hands of the Chin, Central and South China were still under the domain of Sung, and with Lin-an (present Hang-chou) as capital the dynasty lasted until 1279.

The political power of the Sung Empire was broken, but still the country was rich and fertile with a dense population, and a period of peace and cultural prosperity followed. This relatively peaceful state of affairs went on until the Mongols made their appearance on the Chinese scene after their victorious progress through Central Asia. The Chinese campaign, however, turned out to be a lengthy and troublesome affair and the Chin Empire offered hard and courageous resistance. But in the long run the Mongol forces were too superior, and after the sack of K'ai-feng in 1233 the end of the Chin Empire was certain. In the last phase of the war the Sung Empire had joined forces with the Mongols in their attempt to break the last stronghold of the Chins in Honan, and this unwise policy was the beginning of the end. When the Mongols, after their victory, retired to assemble their forces the Sung Emperor thought the time had come to reconquer the old domains on the other side of the River. This immediately resulted in the return of the Mongol army and the beginning of the final conquest of China. A long and bloody war followed, and the Chinese resistance was amazingly violent and brave, but again the end was certain. Hang-chou was captured in 1276 and the Emperor was taken prisoner. This event marked the actual end of Southern Sung even if the official overthrow of the dynasty is not reckoned until A.D. 1279, when the last Pretender tragically lost his life by drowning in a last fruitless attempt to escape capture.

This short recapitulation of the political state in China during the period usually referred to as the Sung dynasty has been necessary in order to emphasize the fact that the time we are dealing with is actually covering four different periods, *Liao*, *Pei Sung*, *Nan Sung* and *Chin*. The Liao period has already been sufficiently covered by different authors and the stylistic nature of its art is so characteristic that we have no reason to study it further in a paper concerned with Sung ceramics.[1]) The Liao material is, however, most valuable for comparative reasons and will be used in this capacity in the stylistic analysis of the ceramics of the period. We will accordingly concentrate our study on the Sung and Chin periods, and it is necessary to give a short cultural background to these periods and the internal state of affairs.

A most characteristic feature of Sung China is the new importance of the civil administration. During the foregoing periods the actual power had been in the hands of the generals and the military governors, but after the consolidation of the Sung Empire most of the army was disbanded and the forces still kept at the borders were subordinated to the civil servants. The power of the civil administration thus became more mighty than ever before, and its organization was extremely well organized and controlled. To enter the civil service it was necessary to have a competent knowledge of the national literature, especially the Confucian classics, and the traditional examination system was strictly maintained. The consequence of this rigorous demand for learned examinations was that the severely national and conservative philosophy of Confucianism gained a very strong position which it held throughout the entire dynasty.

Buddhism, which already during the end of T'ang had lost much of its importance and especially its political and financial power, now further decayed. But it still kept a strong grip over the people and even many intellectuals of the time held the faith in high esteem. During the Southern Sung period its philosophy had a short new time of prosperity through the *Ch'an* sect, the influence of which was a major source of inspiration for the art of the period. Among the more popular sects the worship of *Amitabha* and *Kuan-yin* was especially prominent, as can be seen from the contemporary Buddhist sculpture. Taoism, which like Confucianism was a purely national faith, succeeded in maintaining its position and exerted an important influence during the reign of some emperors.

The internal history of Northern Sung China is characterized by the antagonism between radical and conservative parties among the civil servants, which embittered the lives of many scholars of the time. From the middle of the 11th century to the end of the dynasty this strife between the two factions went on continuously. Some of China's finest and most celebrated scholars belonged to the conservative party, but unfortunately it was only during short intervals that they had any possibility of influencing the official politics. The disastrous "new laws" introduced by the leader of the radicals, Wang An-shih, and which have been explained as

[1]) Wittfogel, K. — Feng, C. S.: *History of Chinese Society. Liao.* Philadelphia 1949.
Tamura, J. — Kobayashi, Y.: *Tombs and mural paintings of Ch'ing-ling.* Vol. I–II. 1952–53.

a kind of State socialism, brought poverty and suffering to the people and seem to a great extent to be responsible for the downfall of the dynasty. The inner struggle, which became particularly pronounced and malignant at the end of the period and resulted in the degradation and exile of a great number of scholars, deprived the administration of some of its most able civil servants and proved disastrous to the country, also because it turned away the attention from the dangerous political situation abroad.

But in spite of these inner disturbances the dynasty on the whole represents an epoch of progress and development. It is not until now that South China gets its importance felt, its rich soil was brought under cultivation, its trade was steadily growing and it became densely populated. The population of the empire was steadily increasing, as can be learned from the census. It seems almost to have doubled between 1060 and 1126, when it had reached the figure of 100,000,000 persons. During the Southern Sung period the importance of the south part of the country logically became especially pronounced and the capital, Hang-chou, was at the time the biggest city in the world with a population of over one million.

The Sung period is the classic age of Chinese culture, famous for its literature, art and intellectual activity in general, and many of China's greatest poets, essayists, historians, philosophers and artists lived during this time. The method of printing, which now came into general use contributed considerably to the spread and development of literature.

Among the greatest scholars of Northern Sung were Ssu-ma Kuang and Ou-yang Hsiu, both celebrated essayists and historians, and the universal genius Su Tung-p'o, statesman, essayist, poet, calligrapher and painter and perhaps the most beloved scholar in Chinese history.[1]) It would lead too far to discuss the works of these scholars, but it might be noted that they combined profound learning and interest in the past with a strong feeling for nature and a scientific curiosity for everything in the world around them. All these features seem to be also significant for the Sung culture in general.

Important encyclopedic works were also compiled during this time; one of the largest and also earliest of these *ts'ung-shu* is the *T'ai-ping yü lan* [2] (c. 977–983) and another tremendous work of the same kind the *Ts'e fu yüan kuei* [3], was completed in 1013. A marked interest in zoology and botany is also conspicuous. Needham[2]) has given the following account of these sciences:

> "The books of pharmaceutical botany reached an unprecedently high standard, and several recensions of the *Pen Tshao* or Codex were produced, notably not only in the Sung but also in the northern Chin country. Thus the illustrations in certain editions of the *Ta Kuan Ching Shih Cheng Lei Pen Tshao* of the 12th and 13th centuries were better than those of European botanical books of the 15th and 16th. Particularly characteristic of the period, however, are the numerous botanical and zoological monographs, of which Han Yen-Chih's *Chü Lu* (Orange Record) of 1178 may be considered a type specimen; it deals

[1]) Lin Yutang, *The Gay genius. The life and times of Su Tungpo.* New York 1947.

[2]) *Science and Civilization in China.* Vol. 1, p. 135.

in detail with all aspects of citrus horticulture, and was the first book on the subject in any language—but besides this there were monographs on bamboos, lichis, aromatic plants, cucurbits, and flowering trees, as well as Crustacea, birds and fishes."

The interest in the past and the collection and systematization of antiques of different kinds, especially bronzes is also a typical feature of the whole Sung dynasty, and several important catalogues on this subject were published. The oldest of them is Lü Ta-lin's *K'ao ku t'u* [4], which describes bronzes in the imperial and private collections, published in 1092. It was later followed by the continuation *Hsü k'ao ku t'u* [5].[1]) The collection of the art-loving artist-Emperor Hui-tsung was published at the beginnig of the 12th century by a group of scholars under the name of *Hsüan Ho Po Ku T'u* [6], and was later revised and new acquisitions were added.[2]) Also among private scholars the habit of collecting was steadily growing, and during the Southern Sung period we know that there was a striving antique trade in Hang-chou. Among the most personal and moving accounts found, on the pleasures and hardship of collecting, is the famous essay by Li Yi-an (1081–c. 1141) in which she tells the story of the collection assembled by her husband and herself, and how it was dispersed upon their flight from the Chin invasion and after her husband's tragic death.[3])

Painting is of course l'art de préférence of the Sung dynasty, and so many works have been written on this subject that it would be preposterous to try to add something in this connection. But a few general remarks have to be made. During previous centuries the emphasis had been on figure painting and paintings with religious subjects, and not until the 10th century did landscape painting attain the important position it was to maintain ever since. The development of landscape painting during Sung and the intimate and spiritualized approach to the subject are perhaps one of the most fascinating chapters in the art history of the world. The feeling of affinity with nature and man as just one little unimportant part in the great and ever-changing universe, was still more strengthened during the Southern Sung dynasty when the political disasters had brought about a general feeling of the futility in human endeavours. The intensified studies of taoism and the new teachings of the *Ch'an* Buddhist sect further intensified these tendencies.

A distinctive feature of Sung culture is its pronounced interest in art theory and art criticism, which found expression in several treatises on those subjects already during Northern Sung. During Southern Sung the aestheticism reached its zenith, and the elegance and refinement had come to a point where it could go no further. Among some artists this resulted in a mere performance of empty skill and formal theoretical learning without spontaneity or feeling.

---

1) For a discussion on these catalogues see: Robert Poor, *Notes on the Sung Dynasty Archaeological Catalogs. ACASA* XIX. 1965. p. 33.

2) Already the Emperor Jen-tsung (reign 1023–63) had arranged a special room in the palace for an archaeological collection of bronzes.

3) Lin Yutang, *The Importance of Understanding*. New York 1960.

Characteristic of the Sung culture is also the scholar painter, the literatus, who was not only an official well versed in literature and poetry, but also himself an artist and calligrapher. Some of the finest artists of the period are found among these *wen-jen* painters who painted for pleasure and gave their paintings away to their friends. The branch of painting especially favoured by the painters of this type was the monochrome ink-painting, especially the painting of bamboo, which was close to calligraphy and which was the ideal subject for the quick brush and the inspired moment.

Besides the types of painting already mentioned, a very important branch of Sung painting, which was especially favoured by the Emperor-painter Hui-tsung and his academy, was the realistic paintings of birds, flowers, animals and insects. It is recorded how painting competitions were held in the imperial garden and how the artists tried to give the most faithful rendering of their motif. But a mere realistic depiction of birds, flowers and trees was not enough, the painter also had to grasp the inner reality and the spirit of his subject.

It seems that the artistic tradition of Northern Sung continues unbroken into Southern Sung, and we cannot observe any strong difference or sudden change between the two parts of the dynasty, but it seems that something of the freshness in the early realism was lost in the superaesthetical dream-world of the latter period. Most of the large collection of paintings brought together by the Emperor Hui-tsung, which is said to have numbered over 6000 paintings, had been transferred to Hang-chou, and the academy continued its work in the new and beautiful surroundings. Even outside the academic circles the interest in art and culture in general was a typical feature of the time. One of the main reasons for this was the prosperity of the capital and its thriving trade which put wealth into the hands of the merchant class. Professional painters decorated the homes and the shops of wealthy merchants, and even in the tombs we have good examples of this kind of decorative paintings. Genre paintings and realistic paintings of flowers, birds and animals were the favourite subjects. The information available of life in Sung China is almost inexhaustibly rich, the literary sources preserved cover almost every aspect of daily life at the time into its most minute details.[1])

The art and culture in the northern part of the country occupied by the Chin dynasty has been neglected by most writers on the art of this time. It has generally been considered that nothing of particular interest happened during the Chin supremacy, and only the names of a few important painters have been mentioned. But in some recent articles by Susan Bush[2]) an attempt has been made to give credit to the cultural development in the Chin Empire. It seems that the Chins were already strongly influenced by Chinese culture before the capture of North China, and once they were firmly established the sinization was very rapid. As

[1]) Jacques Gernet, *Daily Life in China on the Eve of the Mongol Invasion 1250–1276.* London 1962.

[2]) *Literati Culture under the Chin. OA* Vol. XV No. 2, 1969, p. 103.

"Clearing after snow in the Min mountains" and Chin landscape painting. OA Vol. XI, 1965, p. 163.

the relations with Southern Sung were limited it was quite naturally the culture of Northern Sung which came to be one of the main sources of inspiration for the scholars and artists of the time. The just-mentioned author has also pointed out the great prestige Su Tung-p'o and his circle possessed among the Chins and the great influence of his works on their culture.[1])

The art which developed during Chin time seems to have continued the Northern Sung style, and as the interest in Chinese culture increased and deepened it also took up more of older Chinese elements. It does not seem to be a mere coincidence that several archaistic art objects have been found in Chin tombs. The richness of the Chin tombs excavated so far, with wall-paintings, stone-carvings and sculptures also testifies to a flourishing cultural life.[2])

The general tendency of Chin art seems to be a fruitful fusion of the realistic interest in Nature found in late Northern Sung with its own T'ang-Liao inspired traditional art. Unfortunately we do not know enough about the arts of the period to give a more detailed picture of their development. An interesting question is also to what extent art objects were exchanged and traded between the two Empires of Southern Sung and Chin. It is known, that at the beginning of Chin, specimens of this kind were sold to Sung China, but it seems that during the later part of the period an increasing demand for Chinese art in the North might have caused art objects to travel the other way. Collections of paintings and other art objects were also formed in the North.[3])

This short historical and cultural background to the Sung time has shown some of the main tendencies of the period under discussion and we shall try to further emphasize some trends which have been of particular importance in the forming of the ceramic art of the period. We have seen how the creative activity of the period was enormous in almost all fields; fine arts, literature, philosophy, history and science. But also how the political situation cut off the country from cultural exchange with foreign countries; this makes the Sung style more purely Chinese than that of almost any other dynasty.

Almost all writers on the art of the Sung dynasty stress the archaistic interest of the period and the important influence caused especially by the imperial collection of archaic bronzes. The most decorative branch of the applied arts found in Sung, and the most important, is undoubtedly ceramics. One would accordingly expect to find the archaistic tendencies especially strongly developed in this material. But on the contrary, we find very few designs we might call archaistic. The key-fret border and the dragons of *ch'ih* type may, of course, be regarded as designs of this type, but the way they are used and worked into purely realistic compositions clearly tells us that they were never intended as replicas of antiquities, but only as

[1]) When the Chin army sacked K'ai-feng the literary works of Ou-yang Hsiu and Su Tung-p'o were carried away.

[2]) *Cp. Kao Ku* 1959:5, p. 227; *Kao Ku* 1962:4, p. 182.

[3]) Some Chin tombs have yielded ch'ing-pai ceramics of obviously Southern Sung manufacture.

decorative designs. Bronze shapes found in ceramics have also been considered an important criterion of Sung archaism, but even here a closer examination reveals that the bronze forms are limited to very few wares. It is mainly among the undecorated wares of Ju and Kuan type and in Lung-ch'üan that we come across the bronze shapes. Many of these specimens are also extremely hard to date, and a closer and more thorough study of this material will undoubtedly give the result that the majority of bronze-shaped objects belong to Yüan and Ming and some to late Sung and Chin. The only ceramic objects we know of which are undoubtedly meant to be imitations of ancient bronzes are made of pottery and are apparently intended for tomb use; they usually date from Chin and later. A Chin tomb in *Pa-lin* yielded two very fine pottery examples of this kind,[1] one bottle-shaped vase[2] and one tripod; they are both completely covered with archaistic bronze designs, but these are executed in a much more strict and truly antiquarian style than those fantastic inlaid bronzes which are usually attributed to the Sung dynasty.[3]

If the archaic tendency is not especially apparent in ceramics it might be assumed that it was instead expressed in some other material. It has often been pointed out that the Sung period was famous for its bronze imitations of older vessels, and it would of course have been most natural to copy the old bronzes in the same material. In several exhibitions of Sung art, so-called Sung bronzes, usually with rich inlay, have been presented,[4] but the real evidence for such a dating is, as we have already stated, non-existent. We do not know of one single specimen of archaistic bronze of the type generally referred to as Sung that has actually been excavated from a Sung time tomb. It could be argued that objects of this kind were never intended as tomb gifts, but purely as decorative objects d'art for the collectors. But, as we well know, there is no strict borderline between objects made for the living and those used in the tombs, and one would have expected at least a small specimen of this kind of inlaid bronze to have been found in a Sung tomb. There has been quite a large number of Liao, Sung and Chin tombs recently excavated in China, but the bronze objects found in them have generally been of ceramic shapes and mostly completely devoid of decoration. The only exceptions are the bronze mirrors, which of course offer an excellent space for decoration. But the Sung mirrors, which have been found in many tombs, all have very realistic floral scrolls etc. of the same type as we find in ceramics (Fig. 39:a)[5], or else are completely undecorated except for inscriptions. It could hardly be taken as anything else than

1) *Wen Wu* 1959:7, p. 63, and end cover.

2) An almost identical vase from the Eumorfopoulos collection is in the British Museum (Basil Gray, *Early Chinese pottery and porcelain*. Pl. 4) and has been attributed to Han or Six Dynasties.

3) The same style is found in a square *hu* vessel of pottery decorated with dragons on a *lei-wen* ground which was discovered in an early Yüan tomb dated 1266. *Wen Wu* 1958:6, p. 57. Fig. 13. It can also bee seen on a very fine *kuei* vessel of stone found in a tomb in Kiangsi, datable to 1159. *Wen Wu* 1959:10, p. 85. Fig. p. 86.

4) *OCS Sung exhibition 1960*. Nos. 231–234, 237, 239.

5) *OCS Sung exh.* Nos. 229, 230.

an indication that the archaistic style was not particularly strong, especially not in Northern Sung. The late Sir Percival David was of the opinion that there was a shortage of bronze during Sung and accordingly no larger or more important vessels were made. Even if this point should not be stressed too hard it is a factor to be considered, and it is a fact that most bronzes recovered from tombs of Sung time are very thin and of poor quality.

A more thorough study of the archaistic bronzes on the whole would be a most interesting subject and would certainly help to date this difficult family which is now usually rather carelessly labelled Sung, Ming or Ch'ing. It is not our opinion that bronzes in archaic style were not made in Sung time, but they were probably not so common and not so richly inlaid as has been suggested. It seems to us that the archaistic interest in Sung expressed itself mainly in the collecting and catalogization of ancient bronzes, and also as we know in faking of old vessels,[1]) but that it was of little importance as a source of inspiration for other branches of art.[2]) But the main point which we should like to stress is that the archaistic trend was only one of many different features found in Sung art and, contrary to many other writers on this subject, we do not believe that it ended with the fall of the dynasty. On the contrary, it is our conviction that it did not reach any greater importance until the latter part of the dynasty and that it was then without any break carried further in Yüan and Ming. It is certainly no mere coincidence that specimens with archaistic designs have been found in Chin and Yüan tombs[3]) and that vessels of this kind are also depicted in Yüan painting.[4]) We shall see that the same preference for traditional designs can be found also in other patterns used by these foreign dynasties.

There are two main stylistic trends in Sung China which principally gave the profile to the ceramic art of the period. The first one is the international T'ang style, with its vigorous baroque scrolls and its various intricate and detailed designs which can be most clearly studied in T'ang metal ware and stone carvings. This style was a fruitful assimilation of traditional Chinese elements and foreign loans and influences especially from Iran and India, which led to many new and artistically convincing achievements. It seems that the powerful T'ang style, widely spread not only inside the vast empire but far outside its borders, never completely

---

[1]) William Watson, *Sung Bronzes. TOCS* Vol. 32, p. 34.

[2]) An interesting example of a Sung bronze copying an archaic specimen is a bronze bell in Huai-style, which has been discovered in a temple in the Hei-lung chiang province. This bell was one of a set of ten which was cast by the order of Emperor Hui-tsung around 1105. The bell, which is very close to its Huai prototype, was later on captured by the Chins and given to the temple in which it was found. Cp. *Wen Wu* 1963:5, p. 42.

[3]) Except for the pottery specimens already mentioned, silver vessels imitating bronzes have been found in a Yüan tomb. *Wen Wu* 1964:12, Pl. 6. Several bronze vessels with archaistic designs, which are datable to the Yüan dynasty, have also been excavated and clearly shows the strong interest for this kind of designs during that period. Cp. *Nei meng ku ch'u t'u wen wu hsüan chi.* Pls. 159–163.

[4]) Cp. Lee, S. — Ho, W.-K., *Chinese Art under the Mongols.* Pl. 257, 198.

died out, but can be felt as a strong undercurrent in the artistic field from the end of T'ang up to the Ming dynasty. It is particularly the foreign dynasties of nomadic origin, Liao, Chin and Yüan which never broke with the T'ang tradition and carried it forward until Ming. One important reason why the style was preserved especially among those dynasties was undoubtedly the strong impact of Buddhist elements found in the original T'ang style which appealed to the Central Asian nomads, among which the Buddhist faith still occupied an important position long after its golden age had passed in China proper. A good example of how persistent the T'ang style was in certain branches of art can be seen on steles and tombstones. During the T'ang dynasty stone-engravings and reliefs which are often dated, furnish us with a distinct picture of the continuous development of the T'ang style, and they are the main source for the dating of T'ang patterns on other materials. But after the fall of the T'ang dynasty very little development seems to have taken place in this particular field; the tombstones of Northern Sung, Chin and Yüan all have almost identical designs and they cannot in any way help us in the dating of other branches of art.[1])

The second stylistic trend found in Sung ceramic art and the one which can be recognized as new and significant of the period is the realistic interest in Nature. We have already pointed out that the fruitful intellectual climate of the period not only expressed itself in the flowering of the arts and humanities but also in natural science. Never before in the history of China had man with such an open mind and thirst for knowledge turned to Nature. The result was a score of works on animals, birds, and plants—many of them examples of scholarship of the highest class. The rapid development of printing during the period contributed, as we have also seen, to these studies being quickly spread and read by a larger number of people than ever before. The intensive, romantic interest in Nature reached its summit during the Southern Sung dynasty, but already during Northern Sung the new interest in Nature was clearly developed. We can find evidence of it in the fresh and realistic floral designs found in ceramics, in the paintings of landscapes, flowers, birds, insects and animals as well as in the works of the poets and essayists.

During the Southern Sung dynasty the political weakness and the general antediluvian feeling caused the intellectuals of the time to turn to art and philosophy as one means of avoiding the gloom of reality, but also to Nature and to all kinds of physical pleasures. The deepened feeling for Nature is most clearly expressed in the paintings of the period, and it was, as we have seen, the result of several different cooperating influences. One which was undoubtedly of great importance was the beautiful situation of the new capital, Hang-chou, with its West Lake, its bamboo forests and blue mountains in the distance, which could not fail to affect the people living there. The new interest for Nature and the world around us was not limited to the intellectuals, which can clearly be seen from the ceramics

[1]) Cp. *Ku tai chuang shih hua wen hsüan chi.* Hsian 1953. Pls. 72–73 and 59. See also the tombstone of the Prince of Wei from 1093; *Kao Ku* 1964:7, p. 351.

of a folk-art character where flowers and birds are among the most beloved motifs. The best examples of this kind of wares are, however, found in the kilns which, after the division of the country, came to belong to the Chin Empire, and here the simple and fresh approach to the motifs, found during Northern Sung, are preserved and further developed and undoubtedly became one of the main sources for the underglaze painted porcelain during the Yüan dynasty.

NORTHERN CELADON

The "*Northern celadon ware*" is undoubtedly among the finest of the Sung wares and its rich and varied decoration makes it a ware of great interest for the study of design. It has been well-known for a long time that the main kilns for the production of this particular ware were situated in the provinces of Honan and Shensi, but not until the last two decades have continuous excavations of some of the old kiln sites provided us with more detailed information about this ware.

Lin-ju hsien [7] (formerly called *Ju-chou*) in southern Honan has been known as one of the main centres of production of this ware and many modern Japanese writers have for a long time been using the term *Ju yao* as equivalent to the Western term *Northern celadon*. The term Ju yao, however, has already been adopted in the West for a special kind of ware, sometimes also called *Kuan Ju*, of lightly crackled, pale bluish green glaze and of which little more than thirty pieces survive outside China to-day. It would accordingly be most unfortunate and confusing to accept this term as a general denomination of the Northern celadon ware, still more so as a vast amount of the ware was not produced in Lin-ju hsien at all, but in *Yao-chou* [8] as we shall see below. The so-called Ju-ware, as we know it in the West, is a ware of extremely fine quality, and it is generally considered that it was only made in small quantities for the use of the Court over a very short period. Probably not longer than twenty years, between 1086 and 1106. It must be emphasized that no sherds or specimens so far collected at the Lin-ju kiln site have been of this type.

Recent excavations have shown that some of the finest wares in the Northern celadon group were produced in *Yao-chou* in Shensi province, and this place also seems to be the source of that fine and rare group of celadons usually labelled "*Tung yao*" [9] in Western and Japanese publications. The history and nature of the Northern celadon ware has been discussed in great detail by several writers, and we will here only give some references from some of the more interesting new Chinese sources which are of the utmost importance for our knowledge of this ware.

The four main investigations into the kilns in Lin-ju hsien and the facts drawn from them have been published in the *Wen Wu*[1]) and an abstract of the last and most important excavation carried out in 1964 has been published by the Oriental Ceramic Society.[2]) The three main kiln sites excavated in Lin-ju hsien are *Yen-ho*

[1]) *Wen Wu* 1951:2, 1956:12, 1958:10 and 1964:8.

[2]) *Chinese Translations* no. 3.

tien, [10] *Ya-hua kou* [11] and *Hsia-jen ts'un* [12]. The majority of the sherds and articles collected during the excavation were found in the first-mentioned site.

The district of Yao-chou in Shensi province has been known as one of the main sites of the Northern celadon ware, but its products have since a long time past been considered to be of inferior quality to those of Ju-chou. Recent excavations have, however, proved that the wares of Yao-chou often by far surpass those of Lin-ju both in the fine workmanship and great variation of the design and the inventiveness in creating new and varied shapes of great beauty. The main kilns of Yao-chou are situated in *T'ung-ch'uan hsien* [13] and the main site is called *Huang-pao chen* [14]; secondary sites have also been found at *Ch'en-lu chen* [15],[1]) *Shang-tien chen* [16] and *Li-ti po* [17]. More than 86,000 sherds have been found during the excavations and it has been established that these kilns were in operation from the T'ang dynasty until the Yüan dynasty, but their most prosperous time seems to have been during Northern Sung and Chin. The excavations have been published in the *Wen Wu* 1955:4 and 1959:8 and in the *Kao Ku* 1962:6, but the most important report is found in the *Kao Ku* 1959:8. Another interesting source for our knowledge of the Yao-chou ware is the publication *Yao tz'u t'u lu* by Ch'en Wan-li, published in 1956. This book contains two parts, the first part discusses objects of Yao-chou origin found in a place called *Pin hsien* [18] in Shensi. The attribution of these specimens has been carried out through comparison with fragments from the kiln site. The second part illustrates other Yao-chou vessels found in different places in Shensi. From the specimens excavated and collected in Shensi we are able to form quite a good picture of the manufacture of the Yao kilns, the production of which included not only celadons but also some white and some black wares. It is also obvious from the present information that the kiln was not only influenced by the Yüeh and Ju kilns but also from Lung-ch'üan.

A thorough investigation of the Northern celadon kilns and a comparison between the different wares in order to distinguish the characteristics of the different kiln sites cannot yet be made, but with the aid of the above-mentioned excavation reports we are at least able to sort out some typical exponents of the two different kilns. A selection of ceramic objects recently excavated in China, which includes wares both from Yao-chou and Lin-ju, was shown in Japan in 1965 and some of the exhibited material was published in a catalogue entitled *"China's beauty of 2000 years"*,[2]) which can also give us some clues as to the problem of the Northern celadon ware.

It seems that the old Chinese opinion that the Yao-chou ware was inferior to the Ju-chou is mainly founded on two sources. The thirteenth century writer Yeh Chih says in his *T'an chai pi heng* [19] that: "Ting ware being flawed by awns, the Court deemed it unfit for use, and ordered a green-glazed ware to be made in Ju Chou. T'ang Chou, Cheng Chou and Yao Chou also made green-glazed ware,

[1]) This place has still an active kiln for the manufacture of celadon wares.

[2]) Hereafter referred to as *"China's beauty"*.

but Ju Chou ware was the best." In the *Ching-te chen t'ao lu* [20], published in 1815 by Lan P'u it is stated that: "Yao Chou, which is in the present-day Hsi-an Fu, produced a green-glazed ware in the Sung dynasty. It does not compare with Ju ware either in glaze colour or in overall quality."

As we have already stated above the recent excavations give us a quite different picture of the quality of the Yao ware, which on the contrary seems to be both finer and more varied and creative than the Ju ware. Some of the differences between the two wares have been pointed out by Feng Hsien-ming, the author of the 1964 excavation report, and we shall return to this subject at the end of this chapter after having discussed the different motifs found on the Northern celadon ware. But it might be of interest to mention already here that Feng Hsien-ming has pointed out that the "*Sung Shih*" contains in its 87th *chüan* a reference to ceramics made in Yao-chou being sent as tribute to the Court during the reign of *Ch'ung-ning* (1102–1106) which seems to prove, contradictory to what has been said by the two above cited Chinese sources that the Yao-chou ware at this time must have been considered to be of very high quality. Feng also takes the dragon decorated objects found in the middle layer of Northern Sung at Yao-chou as evidence that the ware was made for the use of the Court even earlier. He believes that the Yao-chou ware succeeded the Ju ware at the Court.

Type: **Nc 1.**
Provenience: **Yao-chou.**
Shape: **Ewers and jars.**
Date: **Early Northern Sung.**
Design: **Bold floral scroll.**

One of the most beautiful designs occurring on Sung ceramics is found in this rare and interesting type. It is a deeply carved, extremely bold and vigorous scroll with big leaves and flowers. The flower resembles a lotus, but the main leaves are of a quite different type, large, broad and with a prominent ridge-like vein in the centre. The general appearance of the leaves are, however, those of a water-plant of some kind.

There are very few examples of this type known and we shall describe here all specimens known to us. The first example is a ewer in the Boston Museum of Fine Arts (Pl. 1:a). It has a globular body with tall neck and a vertical handle bent in a very characteristic way, it is provided with a twin spout and has a rather high, splayed foot. The bold floral scroll described above is encircling the body of the vessel and its details are finely incised. Round the shoulder part of the ewer is a collar of overlapping lotus petals.

A very similar ewer is in a Japanese collection (Pl. 1:b), it differs from the Boston pitcher only in two details, the spout is single and the decoration round the shoulder is formed by radiating incised lines. Fragments of a third ewer, almost identical to the one just mentioned, is in the ROM in Toronto (Pl. 1:c). Unfortunately the whole upper part is missing but what remains is enough to give us a clear idea of the piece. A ewer in the Mukden Museum (Pl. 1:d) also belongs to this group. It has twin spouts and is provided with a cover. The main design on the body is the same as on the earlier mentioned ewers, but round the lower part of the body is a band of carved overlapping petals similar to the band found on the neck of the Boston ewer (Pl. 1:a).

In the collection of the late Lord Cunliffe was another ewer (Pl. 1:e) which is of a somewhat different shape. The body is more pear-shaped but the main difference is the strange high neck, which has the shape of a large bud formed by carved, overlapping petals. Unfortunately the handle is missing. The bold scroll design is the same as on the other ewers in this group, with one interesting difference, on one side we can see a very characteristic, folded lotus leaf. This seems to give a clue to the possibility that the bold floral scroll is indeed meant to represent a lotus or at least some kind of water-plant and not, as is generally assumed, a peony or a hibiscus.

One more ewer of a different and much more elaborate workmanship, but clearly belonging to the group is in the Cleveland Museum (Pl. 1:f). The body of this ewer is lobed and it is divided into two parts by a projecting, horizontal ridge. The design is extremely rich; on the back of the handle there are birds and winged dragon-like animals on a ground of flowered lozenges (Pl. 1:l); the spout is in the form of a seated lion with a star-like flower under its front paws. On the upper part of the body is a carved bold floral scroll of exactly the same type as on the other ewers in this group. The lower part of the body has large rounded petals filled with overlapping smaller petals. All leaves and petals have finely incised details. The space between the large petals encircling the body has thin incised lines in a fan-shaped arrangement probably depicting stamina.

The above described six ewers from different collections undoubtedly form a very close group, and a recently discovered vessel from Pin hsien in Shensi published by Ch'en Wan-li[1]) (Pl. 1:g) seems to indicate that this entire group was a product of the Yao-chou kiln. The vessel in question is a jar of very uncommon shape (Pl. 1:g). It has an almost peach-shaped body with rounded belly and stands on three high splayed feet and is provided with a pointed hat-like cover. The quality is very fine and the main design is a carved floral scroll of exactly the same type as is found on the ewers, with finely incised details. Ch'en Wan-li also notes that this vessel is of the same type as those generally referred to as Tung yao in foreign publications.

In an excavation report from the Yao-chou kilns[2]) has been published still another specimen which seems to belong to this rare group. It is a small jar (Pl. 1:h) of depressed globular shape which is decorated round the belly with a carved design of flowers and petals which come extremely close to the arrangement on the lower part of the Cleveland ewer. The jar, which was excavated at the kiln site seems to be the final evidence that this entire group is a product of the Yao-chou kilns.

[1]) *Yao tz'u t'u lu*, Part I, Pl. 4 and Cover ill.

[2]) *Kao Ku* 1959:12, p. 671. Pl. 7:11.

A hitherto unpublished fragmentary specimen in the ROM in Toronto which has been considered to be a Chekiang celadon also seems to belong to this group (Pl. 1:i). The central flower is here of a somewhat different type, but we shall see below that this is just a stage in the development of the design into a flower which we have chosen to call "*the conventionalized flower*" and which is very frequent on Northern celadon wares.

The above described group is extremely characteristic both in shape and design, and we shall further on discuss an interesting group of Tz'u-chou yao specimens, which clearly belong to the same style and time, and where we also can follow the same development of the floral motif as we can see on the Northern celadon ware. The design found in this group is still very much in the T'ang tradition and the shapes are also of a characteristic early type which points to an early Northern Sung date for this entire group.

The sickle-leaf scroll

This is a very special kind of scroll which seems to be found only on Northern celadon wares, but here it is quite common and occurs on pieces of many different shapes and with various designs. The leaves found on this scroll are quite small, they are grouped in threes, they are thin and slightly bent and of half-moon shape (Pl. 1:j, k; Pl. 2; Fig. 1:a–b). Their general appearance recalls that of a sickle and we have therefore adopted the term "*sickle-leaf scroll*" as a working name for this particular leaf design. These leaves apparently have nothing to do with peony leaves or chrysanthemum leaves, the most common explanation of them, they look more like the leaves of some kind of water-plant. The origin of this scroll is no doubt the previously mentioned "bold floral scroll" where we can find smaller leaves of a similar kind together with the big main leaves, but in the sickle-leaf scroll they have been further simplified. Almost the same development of the leaf design is found on the Tz'u-chou group that is so closely related to the so-called Tung group (cp. Pl. 1:a–g and Pls. 40:j–k, 41:a–h) and a somewhat different dissolvement of the leaf scroll is also found in the ch'ing-pai group (Pls. 13–14).

The sickle-leaf scroll is found in connection with various other designs (see Pl. 4:a, b, c; Pl. 3:1 and Pl. 7:f) but it is most commonly associated with a highly conventionalized flower which we will discuss below.

Type: Nc 2.
Provenience: Yao-chou and Lin-ju.
Shape: Various.
Date: Northern Sung.
Design: Conventionalized flower and sickle-leaf scroll.

In connection with our discussion of the so-called Tung group above we have pointed out how the bold floral scroll found on this particular ware is also found on a group of Tz'u-chou ware. On the Tz'u-chou ware this design develops into a most characteristic pattern with highly conventionalized floral scrolls. The same development is also taking place in the Northern celadon ware, where the highly realistic looking leaves of the bold floral scroll turns into the above described sickle-leaf scroll and the flowers accompanying the scroll are also entirely transformed. The flowers are alternately seen from the side and from above. Those seen from above or from the front are almost circular and the outer part of the flower is built up of a row of thin, overlapping petals, the general appearance is close to that of a chrysanthemum flower (Fig. 1:b–c). But in the centre of the flower is a large arrangement, probably a seed-pod, which looks like a bunch of grapes (Fig. 3:10). When the flower is seen from the side this seed-pod is still more predominant and sticks out like large nuts from the semicircular row of petals (Fig. 3:4). This design is found on a large group of specimens of very different shapes, some of the most significant of which will be discussed here.

A most important key-piece to this entire group is a ewer in the Brundage collection (Pl. 1:j).[1]) It is of a shape very close to some of the so-called Tung yao ewers and on the shoulder there is an incised design of the same type as that found, for instance, on the Japanese ewer in that group (Pl. 1:b). The main design of the Brundage ewer is found in a broad panel filling up the front part of the body and consists of conventionalized flowers and the sickle-leaf scroll described above. The arrangement of the décor, which is not continued around the body of the vessel, is most unusual and seems to be an early feature. Another unique specimen is the remarkable wine-pot in the Metropolitan museum (Pl. 1:k) which is decorated round the body with phoenixes flying among scrolls and flowers of the type we are discussing. The close relationship between this group and the so-called Tung group on the one hand and the specimens from Yao-chou on the other will be discussed below.

The most frequent use of this type of design is found on bowls and basins of different shapes, some of the main types of which will be discussed below. Among the most common are small bowls of conical shape with everted lip and small low foot. The outside is generally plain and the design covers the whole of the interior except for a band just below the rim. In the centre is usually a rosette of oblique petals. There is one bowl of this kind in the Kempe collection,[2]) one was formerly in the Eumorfopoulos coll.,[3]) and one in the Alexander coll.,[4]) two bowls are in the Barlow coll. (Pl. 2:a) and one in the Honolulu Academy of Arts,[5]) and numerous other examples are found in different collections. The two bowls in the Barlow collection have the characters *Wang*, respectively *Yang*, inscribed in the centre of the rosette, probably family names.[6]) In the British Museum there is also a mould for impressing the ornament on a bowl of this kind (Pl. 2:b) and several other moulds

[1]) Formerly in the Eumorfopoulos collection. *GEc* B 178.

[2]) *CKc* No. 77.

[3]) *GEc* Vol. VI:F 301.

[4]) Hobson, *Private*, Fig. 6.

[5]) *Los Angeles exh.cat.* no. 177.

[6]) Cp. Type 36 below.

of this type are found in other museum collections, unfortunately none of them are dated. Sherds of bowls of this type were also found by Palmgren in *Ch'ing-ho hsien.* [21][1])

A second type of bowl here represented by a piece in the Victoria & Albert Museum (Pl. 2:c) has a similar conical shape with everted lip, but the dimension is larger and the outside of the bowl is decorated with vertical lines. Bowls of this type have also been found in Shensi and attributed to the Yao-chou kiln.[2])

The third type of bowl is rather high, with almost vertical sides, rounded below, and stands on a low straight foot. The decoration is here found on the outside of the bowl and consists of forcefully carved conventionalized flowers and the sickle-leaf scroll. Examples of this type are in the Seligman coll.[3]) and in the F. Vannotti collection (Pl. 2:d). It seems that bowls of this type were originally provided with covers, and several specimens with intact covers are still found. They all have the same kind of domed cover, crowned by a small stalk knob, with flat horizontal edge. Two specimens of this type are in the Barlow collection (Pl. 2:e), one is in the Seattle Art Museum[4]) and one in a Japanese collection.[5]) A lid from a bowl of this kind was discovered during excavations at the Yen-ho tien site.[6])

The fourth bowl type is rather uncommon. It is of a very elegant shape, almost hemi-spherical with gently curved sides, the foot is very low and slightly everted. One bowl of this type was formerly in the Oppenheim coll. (Pl. 2:g, Fig. 1:c) and other examples are known.

The fifth bowl type is also very rare. It is rather low and of a distinct five-lobed shape. The design is found both on the inside and on the outside and is set in the panels formed by the incisions marking the five lobes of the bowl. There is one flower in each panel and on the outside the flowers are only shown seen from the side. A bowl of this type is in the Tokyo National Museum (Pl. 2:h) and it is usually shown together with a wine ewer in the same collection and considered to be a set (Pl. 4:c and Fig. 1:e). Ewers of this type standing in a bowl are very common, especially during the early part of Sung and it is most likely that those two specimens belong to one another, though it could be noted that the design of the bowl and that of the ewer are different. In the Tientsin Museum there is a bowl of the same shape which is decorated with three-petalled flowers and sickle-leaves on the exterior.

Dishes and basins with this type of design are also found. Among the objects published in the *Yao tz'u t'u lu* is a low basin with rounded sides and a projecting, horizontal rim, the outside is undecorated. On the inside is a round, central field with conventionalized flowers seen both from the side and from above and the

---

1) *Sung Sherds*, Pl. p. 277 and 319. Drawings 65–66.
2) *Yao tz'u t'u lu*, Part 1, Pls. 13, 17.
3) Cat. no. D 152. (See note 5 p. 33).
4) *Los Angeles exh.cat.* no. 173.
5) *Sekai* 10: Pl. 31. (Our Pl. 2:f).
6) *Wen Wu* 1958:10, p. 34. Fig. 7.

sickle-leaf scroll; on the side is a sickle-leaf border of a peculiar stiff type, which looks like a plaited band (Pl. 2:i). Exactly the same motif is found on the inside of a dish with rounded sides and slightly everted mouth in the ROM at Toronto (Pl. 2:j). A dish almost identical to the Toronto one was recently published as coming from the Lin-ju kiln (Pl. 2:k).[1]) The Toronto dish is said to have come from *Lo-yang*, Honan. The close similarities of the designs on the above mentioned basin and the two dishes gives us a good example of how similar the wares of Yao-chou and Lin-ju sometimes are. It is quite often impossible to decide whether a specimen was produced at the one kiln or at the other. Sherds with almost identical designs of this type have also been found at the two kilns, and it seems that other kilns have also imitated this particular motif.

Among more unusual specimens with this type of décor is an ovoid jar in the Heeramaneck collection[2]) and a cylindrical one in a Japanese collection. The first one has the design round the middle and upper part of the belly and round the bottom part is a row of overlapping lotus petals. The second piece (Pl. 2:l) is of an almost cylindrical shape with slightly rounded flat shoulder and has the design all over the belly.

Peony flower designs

There is a very rich flora of different peony flowers found on Northern celadon wares, and to get a clearer view of the various types found we have tried to select some main groups which are listed below. There are naturally many more variations to be found than those mentioned here and there are also types which do not fit exactly into any of these groups but show intermediate forms. The shape of the peony flower, the treatment of the details and the general composition of the design are all important criteria. The rendering of the leaves is another important criterion when distinguishing the different peony designs, and usually a certain type of flower is always found in combination with a certain type of leaf.

Type: **Nc 3 A.**
Provenience: **Yao-chou.**
Shape: **Various.**
Date: **Early Northern Sung.**
Design: **A-type peony.**

This design is deeply and forcefully cut, and the instrument used leaves very characteristic crescent-shaped areas cut away on petals and leaves. The design is on the whole rather sketchy and there are no incised or combed details. The leaves are usually deeply lobated and the flowers are often seen from the side and give the impression of being three-petalled; this rendering of the peony not fully opened or seen from the side is most common in several of the peony designs, as will be shown in the following observations.

[1]) *China's beauty*, No. 53.

[2]) *Los Angeles exh.cat.* no. 179.

A very fine example of the A-type design is found on a ewer in the Baur collection (Pl. 3:a) where the motif occurs round the body of the vessel and also as a leaf band on the shoulder. This ewer is of an early type with splayed foot, trumpet-shaped mouth and applied stiff leaf-ornaments on the shoulder; all these elements are found on Liao and early Sung wares. A ewer almost identical to the one just described is in the Brundage collection (Pl. 3:b). Of the same general outline is also a chicken-spouted ewer in the British Museum (Pl. 3:c).

On a group of vases with flower-shaped mouth which will be discussed below under the "*serrated-petal design*" Type Nc 10, we find the A-type peony design round the belly (Pl. 3:d).

A sprinkler of *kundika* type in the Boston MFA (Pl. 3:e) and a similar one formerly in the Russell collection[1]) both have this type of design round the belly, they are also decorated round the foot part with thin pointed petals of the same type as those found on the two ewers mentioned above (Pl. 3:a, b.).

A cup-stand or lamp of so-called *tazza* shape in the Kempe collection with a standing lion forming the foot is decorated with the peony scroll on its umbrella-shaped brim (Pl. 3:f). A more sketchy type of the same design is found on another *tazza*-shaped specimen in the same collection.[2])

A slightly more detailed A-type peony design is found on a bowl in the ROM in Toronto. The bowl is deep, with rounded sides on an almost straight foot and the design is found on the outside of the bowl. An almost identical bowl has been found at the Yao-chou kiln site (cp. Pl. 3:g and h). The earlier mentioned *tazza*-shaped specimens as well as the group of vases with flower-shaped mouth are types that we also associate with Yao-chou, and the type of rather deeply cut designs which we are dealing with here also seem to be characteristic of that kiln.

Type:	**Nc 3 B.**	**Date:**	**Northern Sung.**
Provenience:	**Lin-ju and Yao-chou.**	**Design:**	**B-type peony.**
Shape:	**Various.**		

This pattern consists of quite realistic peony flowers and leaves of the common three-lobated form. The flower is rather stiffly drawn and gives the impression of being flattened. The leaves are rather broad and curly. Leaves and petals have combed details.

Good examples of this design are found on a bowl in the Fitzwilliam Museum (Pl. 3:i), on the side of a famous pillow in a Japanese collection (Pl. 3:j) and on a bowl in the Kempe collection;[3]) also on a bowl in a Japanese collection (Pl. 3:k).

---

[1]) *O.C.S. Celadon exh.* 1947, No. 95.

[2]) *CKc* no. 86.

[3]) *CKc* no. 79.

Type: Nc 3 C.
Provenience: Yao-chou.
Shape: Various.
Date: Northern Sung.
Design: C-type peony.

This flower is very close to type B, but the details of the petals are not finely combed, but incised with very short, sharp strokes that look like hatches. The flower is very simple and looks flattened. Very frequently only the flower seen sideways, forming the characteristic trefoil, is depicted. The C-type flower is only found together with that very characteristic leaf-scroll which we have named sickle-leaf scroll.

A good example of the C-type design showing both the fully opened flower and the trefoil flower is found on a ewer in the ROM in Toronto (Pl. 4:a),[1]) and the same design is also found on the remarkable ceremonial bowl and stand in the Boston MFA (Pl. 4:b). The combination of the trefoil flower only and the sickle-leaf scroll is found on a ewer in the Tokyo NM (Pl. 4:c), on the rim of the famous incense-burner formerly in the Sedgwick collection (Pl. 7:f), and on several trays and bowls, for instance, a small six-lobed tray in the Kempe coll. (Pl. 3:l).[2]) All the objects mentioned above belong to a group that is associated with the Yao-chou kiln, and all of them (except the Kempe tray) show both a clear relationship with each other as well as numerous features typical of the Northern Sung style. The Toronto ewer (Pl. 4:a) has the applied leaf design on the shoulder, which is an early feature and also a ring of thin, rising petals round the neck, the general shape of the ewer is also very characteristic of the Liao – N. Sung style. The ewer in the Tokyo NM (Pl. 4:c) has the same kind of rising petals around the neck and its shape with the wide-open trumpet-shaped mouth is also of an early type.

Type: Nc 3 D.
Provenience: Yao-chou and Lin-ju.
Shape: Bowl and dish.
Date: Northern Sung.
Design: D-type peony.

This type is similar to type C and it also has the hatch marks on the petals but the flower is more elaborate and more realistic, moreover, the leaves have the hatch marks. A simple type of this flower is found on a bowl published in the *Yao tz'u t'u lu* (Pl. 4:d), with an elegant winding scroll the leaves of which are more elaborate than the sickle-leaf scroll, but still keep some leaves of the sickle type. A more developed and complex design in which the leaves are of the usual three-lobated peony type is found on a dish in the Clark collection (Pl. 4:e), and another one formerly in the possession of Messrs. Barling of London (Pl. 4:f). The composition of these two pieces is very delicate with thin stems crossing each other in a most elegant way. Fragments with exactly this kind of flowers have been found

[1]) The monster mask in front is a later addition made to cover the hole of the missing spout.

[2]) A tray of this type was found in a tomb of late N. Sung date discovered in Shensi. *Wen Wu* 1956:12, Frontispiece.

in Lin-ju.[1]) It seems that the design with slight variations was made both in Yao-chou and Lin-ju.

Type: **Nc 3 E.**
Provenience: **Yao-chou.**
Shape: **Vase & box.**
Date: **Northern Sung.**
Design: **E-type peony.**

The flowers of this type are similar to type B, but they are not so stiff and flattened, and they give a more realistic impression. The leaves are usually smaller and more curled. The composition as a whole is more free and lively. Leaves and petals have combed details (Fig. 2:d).

Good examples of this type are found on a bottle-shaped vase in the Hakone Museum (Pl. 4:g), a similar vase in a private Japanese collection,[2]) and a third one in the Calmann collection (Pl. 4:h). A vase of a slightly different shape also in Japan (Pl. 4:i) has the same design; like most of these peony designs the flower is often seen from the side and reduced to a kind of trefoil. The finest example of the E-type flower is found on the lid of a box in the David Foundation (Pl. 4:j). The design is here enclosed by a winding peony leaf-scroll.

Type: **Nc 3 F.**
Provenience: **Yao-chou.**
Shape: **Dish, bowl & vase.**
Date: **Late Northern Sung.**
Design: **F-type peony.**

A more sketchy type. The flowers are usually non-symmetrical, the leaves are deeply lobated, almost tattered and curled in a lively movement (Fig. 2:e). Very often the flower is shown only from the side and not fully opened, looking like a trefoil. Leaves and petals have combed details. A dish with this type of design is found in a Japanese collection[3]) and a very similar one is in the Baur collection (Pl. 4:k). A dish in the ROM in Toronto shows six sprays of peonies of this type, one in the centre and the other five surrounding it (Pl. 4:l). A very important vase in the Seattle Art Museum has the design around the body (Pl. 5:a). The vase is of an elaborate type with trumpet-shaped neck, cup-like mouth and four short handles; there is a dragon figure in applied relief on the shoulder. A vase of the same shape also with the applied dragon encircling the neck but with a different main design showing lotus flowers and leaves has been published in the *Yao tz'u t'u lu* (Pl. 5:b). A bowl with a peony design of this type has been excavated from a Sung tomb in Shensi.[4])

---

[1]) *Wen Wu* 1964:8, Pl. 4:1 and Fig. 6, p. 17.

[2]) Koyama, *So-ji.* Pl. 18.

[3]) *Sekai* 10; Pl. 26.

[4]) *Wen Wu* 1956:8, Frontispiece.

Type: Nc 3 G.
Provenience: Yao-chou.
Shape: Bottle-vase & bowl.
Date: Northern Sung.
Design: G-type peony.

This type of flower is more detailed and more realistic and the leaves differ considerably from the types already dealt with. The lobation of the leaf is very deep, and it has several pointed tips which are spread out and recall the shape of a bird's tail. Details are combed. A fine example of the type is found on a bottle-shaped vase in a Japanese collection (Pl. 5:d). This vase is of a shape characteristic of Northern Sung. A bowl with the same floral design is in the Bristol City Art Gallery (Pl. 5:e). The G-type is very close to designs found on specimens from the Yao-chou kiln and it was most likely used mainly at this kiln.

Type: Nc 4.
Provenience: Yao-chou and Lin-ju.
Shape: Bowl.
Date: Late Northern Sung.
Design: Beehive-shaped peony.

This design is found on the inside of bowls and usually covers the entire surface except for a band below the rim. It is composed of a peony with one big flower, the flower is in the shape of a beehive and obviously depicts a special type of *Paeonia moutan*. This large flower, which is also found on other Sung wares, we have chosen to call the "*beehive-shaped peony*" to distinguish it from other types. The leaves on this type are deeply tattered and flat, of the same type as the one above called the G-type. The details are incised and combed. Examples are in the Barlow collection (Pl. 5:g) and in a Japanese coll. (Pl. 5:h). Fragments from a similarly decorated specimen were found in Yao-chou (Pl. 5:i), but it seems that the type was made in Lin-ju as well.

A twelve-lobed bowl in the Sedgwick collection is similar to the above-mentioned specimens but it is more sketchy and has less details (Pl. 4:j). The flower is not so high. A box found in Yao-chou has a more triangular flower and a different type of leaves (Pl. 5:f).

Type: Nc 5.
Provenience: Yao-chou and Lin-ju.
Shape: Dish.
Date: Late Northern Sung.
Design: Beehive-shaped peony and leaf-scroll.

This design is found on the inside of dishes with steep sides, and is composed of a peony spray with a big flower covering the centre and part of the sides of the bowl. Below the rim is an undulating peony leaf-scroll. Details are incised, combed and, on the petals, hatched. A dish of this type is seen on Pl. 5:k. The hatched technique is common on wares from Yao-chou,[1] but it is also found in Lin-ju hsien.

[1] *Yao tz'u t'u lu*, Part 1. Pl. 16.

The peony leaf-scroll is discussed below under Type Nc 7.

Type: Nc 6.
Shape: Bowl.
Date: Late Northern Sung.
Design: Beehive-shaped peony and boys.

This design is similar to the peony design of Type 4 above, and it is disposed in the same way on the bowl. Details are incised, combed and hatched. The composition shows two beehive-shaped peonies pointing in opposite directions, and alternating with them two boys climbing among peony leaves placed the same way. One bowl with this design is in the V & A (Pl. 6:a) and a similar one is in the Metropolitan Museum (Pl. 6:b). In the Barlow collection is a bowl of quite different shape from those just mentioned; it stands on a high foot, but the design is similar (Pl. 5:l). In this case the design is enclosed by a thin border with a classic scroll.

Type: Nc 7.
Provenience: Yao-chou.
Shape: Bowl, saucer & incense-burner.
Date: Late Northern Sung—Chin.
Design: Peony leaf-scroll.

The design characteristic of this group is a very elegantly carved undulating peony leaf-scroll with combed details. This design is found in a broad band encircling the inside of a conical bowl, just below the rim, in the Baur collection (Pl. 6:d). In the centre of the bowl is a three-petalled peony flower. Exactly the same composition is found on a shallow dish in the Barlow collection (Pl. 6:e). A rare piece with the peony leaf-scroll is an incense burner on three legs in the Tokyo NM (Pl. 6:f). Here the design is encircling the belly, and the neck of the vessel is decorated with rows of small, pointed overlapping petals. The general appearance of this piece, the legs with masks etc., seems to point to the Yao-chou kiln and an undecorated incense-burner of very similar shape is also published in the *Yao tz'u t'u lu* (Pl. 6:c). An incense-burner in the Brundage collection is closely akin to the one in the Tokyo NM, but the main design is here a lotus leaf-scroll (Pl. 6:i).

A bowl published in the *Yao tz'u t'u lu*[1]) has a peony leaf-scroll near the rim which is very similar to the one found on the Baur bowl (Pl. 6:d), and the rim of the excavated bowl has a very characteristic reinforcement, which is also found on the Baur bowl.

Type: Nc 8.
Provenience: Yao-chou.
Shape: Ewer.
Date: Chin.
Design: Peony leaf-scroll.

---

[1]) *Op.cit.* Part 2. Pl. 19.

This peony leaf-scroll design is quite different from Type 7 above; it has thinner and more elongated leaves and it is carved in a vigorous but more sketchy style. It has no combed details. The design is found on a ewer of depressed globular shape with low circular mouth and short, curved handle in the ROM in Toronto (Pl. 6:g). The shoulder of the ewer is decorated with a row of broad, overlapping lotus petals and the leaf-scroll is encircling the body. An almost identical ewer, partly broken, has been published in the *Yao tz'u t'u lu* (Pl. 6:h).

Type: **Nc 9.**
Provenience: **Yao-chou.**
Shape: **Bowl; bowl with flower holder.**
Date: **Northern Sung.**
Design: **Carved lotus petals.**

Carved lotus petals as the only design found on the outside of bowls is characteristic of one type of Northern celadon wares. Three main types are found. The first one consists of rather high, deep bowls with slightly everted lip and straight foot. Below the rim, on the outside, is an undecorated band, but otherwise the whole exterior of the bowl is carved with overlapping, pointed lotus petals. There is one bowl of this type in the Kempe collection[1]) and another one in the Hamburg Museum für Kunst und Gewerbe.[2]) A bowl of exactly the same type from Yao-chou has recently been published[3]) and gives us a sure identification of the provenience of this type (Pl. 6:j).

The second type of bowl is of a slightly different shape. Somewhat lower and wider at the mouth. The lotus petals carved on the outside are slightly broader. Bowls of this type are found in several collections, for instance in the Bristol City Art Gallery (Pl. 6:k) and similar bowls have been published in the *Yao tz'u t'u lu.*[4])

Related to these two groups is a third and more exclusive one, consisting of a special type of bowls used as flower holders. A fine example of this type is in the Brundage collection.[5]) It is a deep bowl, with a projecting, flattened mouth-rim, on a low, rounded foot. Inside are six groups of three-moulded tubular holders; rising from the centre is a reticulated dome with eight perforations alternately circular and leaf-shaped. A similar but not so elaborate a bowl is in the ROM in Toronto (Pl. 7:a). Both bowls are decorated on the outside with pointed, over-

---

[1]) *CKc* no. 65.

[2]) Feddersen, *Chinesisches Kunstgewerbe.* Abb. 32.

[3]) *China's beauty.* No. 37.

[4]) *Op.cit.* Part 1. Pl. 12.

[5]) *Cat.* Pl. XXX:C. Specimens in the *Brundage* collection are referred to with the Plate numbers in the catalogue by *d'Argencé* (see Bibliography). Specimens in the *Seligman* and *Baur* collections are referred to with the catalogue numbers found in the catalogues by *John Ayers*; and those in the *Barlow* collection with the Plate numbers in the catalogue by *Michael Sullivan* (see Bibliography).

lapping lotus petals,[1]) the petals are more sharply carved and simpler than those on the first two types. There is an undecorated band just below the mouth. The general appearance of these bowls seems to indicate the Yao-chou kiln, where bowls of similar shape have also been found.[2])

Type: **Nc 10.**
Provenience: **Yao-chou.**
Shape: **Vase, cup-stand etc.**
Date: **Early Northern Sung.**
Design: **Petals with serrated inside.**

This is a very characteristic and rather unusual design which can be seen on a small group of Northern celadon vessels and some specimens, earlier considered to come from *Yüeh-chou*. A beautiful and very clear example of this type of design is found on a vase in a Japanese collection (Pl. 7:b). The design covers the entire body of the vase and shows large oblong petals with rounded upper part and with rounded serration on the inside. On a cup-stand or lamp in the Heeramaneck collection we can find the same design, but turned upside down, round the belly (Pl. 7:c). This specimen has been considered to be of Yüeh ware, but is probably a Yao-chou piece. Of the same main outline is the remarkable piece, formerly in the Sedgwick collection, which has a group of gorilla-like men seated round the foot part (Pl. 7:f). This vessel also has the serrated petals pointing downwards as decoration round the body.

A slightly different and usually more rounded type of the serrated petal design is found on the upper part of a group of small vases with splayed, flower-shaped mouth. There are several specimens of this group found in different collections, most of them of the same general design and shape but with small variations (Pl. 3:d, Pl. 7:d). The main design round the body of these flower-shaped vases is a carved floral design of the type we have called A-type peony. Vases of this type are known from Yao-chou (Pl. 7:e).

Regarding the provenience of this group there are strong indications of its belonging to the Yao-chou kiln. The form of the two vessels of cup-stand shape is very much related to a specimen found at Yao-chou (Pl. 7:i), which also has the serrated petal design round the body, and the uniqueness of the Sedgwick piece also seems to point to this kiln, where apparently a large number of unusual vessels of similar types were produced. If we look again at the above-mentioned stand from Yao-chou (Pl. 7:i) with its dome-shaped, umbrella-like top and mask-headed legs we shall find close similarities to some earlier mentioned specimens (cp. Pl. 1:k, Pl. 3:f, Pl. 4:b). In this connection we must also mention a very beautiful cup-stand with openwork base and stem in the Brundage collection (Pl. 7:l). The design round the upper part of this specimen is almost identical to that found on the Yao-chou

[1]) A flower holder of this type with vertical incisions on the outside is in the Barlow collection (*Cat.* Pl. 76 a) and is said to be of Lung-ch'üan yao.

[2]) *Yao tz'u t'u lu.* Part 1. Pl. 10–11.

stand. The Kodaira vase (Pl. 7:b) also has a definite kinship with the jar from Yao-chou already referred to in connection with the so-called Tung group (Pl. 1:h).

Type: Nc 11.
Provenience: Yao-chou.
Shape: Lotus-leaf shaped bowl.
Date: Northern Sung.
Design: Tortoise in relief.

This group consists of small bowls shaped in the form of a lotus leaf, with rounded sides and turned-out foliate rim, standing on a small tapering foot. On the inside there are usually thin, incised leaf veins and in the centre a small tortoise in relief. One bowl of this kind is in the Seligman collection (Pl. 7:g), one in the Kempe coll., one in the Barlow coll., and one in the Hetherington coll.[1]) the last mentioned piece is said to have been one of six excavated on the site of the old Mongol city at Peking. A bowl of this type identified as Yao-chou ware was published in the *Yao tz'u t'u lu.*[2]) The design and shape found in this group have also been used both in Yüeh yao and in Lung-ch'üan yao.[3]) A small dish with the lotus veins and the tortoise delicately incised was excavated from a Liao tomb in *Ch'ing-ho men* in Northern China and considered to be of Ju-ware.[4])

Type: Nc 12.
Provenience: Yao-chou.
Shape: Bowl.
Date: Northern Sung.
Design: Waves.

This design is composed of overlapping, petal-like waves and usually covers the whole interior of conical bowls with contracted mouth. On the waves are small hatched dots or lines of a type very common among Yao-chou wares. The outside of the bowl has incised vertical lines. One bowl of this kind is in the Calmann collection (Pl. 7:j) and a similar one is in the Art Institute of Chicago (Pl. 7:k).

Type: Nc 13.
Provenience: Yao-chou.
Shape: Dish.
Date: Northern Sung.
Design: Combed waves.

This design is usually found on the inside of saucer dishes with rounded sides and is composed of waves only. Parts of the design are more deeply cut and the general impression of the motif is that of a star-shaped figure with combed details

---

1) *CKc* No. 112; *Barlow cat.* Pl. 93 B; *OCS Celadon exh.* 1947, cat. No. 80.

2) *Op.cit.* Part 2. Pl. 7.

3) Illustrations of Yüeh yao specimens are found in the *Yüeh ch'i t'u lu.* A Lung-ch'üan specimen of this type is in the Kempe coll. (CKc 113).

4) *Kao Ku Hsüeh Pao* 1954:8; Pl. 17:3, Fig. 24:3.

on a combed ground. A dish of this type is in the Victoria & Albert Museum[1]) and another one is in a Japanese collection (Pl. 8:a). A very similar dish was excavated at Yao-chou (Pl. 8:b).[2])

Type: **Nc 14.**
Provenience: **Yao-chou.**
Shape: **Bowl.**
Date: **Northern Sung.**
Design: **Duck among waves.**

This pattern, which is found on the inside of bowls, is composed of a wave design very close to Type 13 above, but in the centre is a round panel enclosing a sketchily drawn swimming duck. Good examples of this type are found in the Seligman collection (Pl. 8:c), in the Buffalo Museum,[3]) in the Winkworth coll.,[4]) and in the V & A (Pl. 8:f). A fragment of this type has also been excavated at Yao-chou (Pl. 8:e), and two very beautiful bowls of this type both with a duck in a round panel surrounded by a star shaped wave pattern, were found in a Sung tomb in Shensi. No closer date or information concerning the find is given in the excavation report.[5])

Type: **Nc 15.**
Provenience: **Yao-chou.**
Shape: **Bowl.**
Date: **Northern Sung.**
Design: **Fishes among waves.**

The design, which covers the whole of the inside of a bowl, except for an undecorated band near the mouth, is enclosed by a line incision. It consists of three fishes with big eyes and split tail-fins among combed waves. There is one bowl of this type in the Seligman collection (Pl. 8:d) and another one in the University of Michigan Art Museum.[6]) No identical specimen has been found in excavations so far, but the style and arrangement of the design as well as the shape of the bowls are all very closely akin to objects from Yao-chou. There are close similarities both to the "duck-and-wave design" Type 14 and the "combed-wave design" Type 13.

Type: **Nc 16.**
Shape: **Bowl.**
Date: **Late Northern Sung.**
Design: **Lotus tendril border and wave design.**

---

[1]) No. C 1388–1924.

[2]) Cp. also *China's beauty*, Sherd no. 238.

[3]) Hochstadter. *Early Chinese ceramics in the Buffalo Museum of Science.* No. 53.

[4]) *Venezia exh.cat.* No. 409.

[5]) *Wen Wu* 1956:8, Frontispiece.

[6]) *Los Angeles exh.cat.* No. 182.

This type is characterized by a special type of lotus tendril border which is enclosing the main design on the interior of the bowl. The border is rather stiff and angular. The main design in the central part of the bowl is shown on a ground of finely combed waves. A bowl of this type in the Baur collection has four swimming ducks as main design (Pl. 8:h), and another one in the F. Brodie Lodge coll.[1]) has ducks and lotus. A bowl in the British Museum is decorated with water-weeds and a fish (Pl. 8:g).[2])

Type: **Nc 17.**
Provenience: **Yao-chou.**
Shape: **Bowl.**
Date: **Chin.**
Design: **Lotus flowers and waves.**

This design is very common and is found on a series of small bowls with rounded sides, often with a slightly thickened rim. It covers the whole interior of the bowl except for a plain band near the mouth. The pattern shows a single lotus flower with scrolling tendrils in a thin and elegant composition surrounded by combed waves. There is one bowl of this kind in the MFEA (Pl. 8:l), one in the Barlow collection,[3]) one in the Kempe coll., and a pair in the Gure coll.[4]) A fragment of a bowl of this kind has also been excavated at Yao-chou[5]) and is dated Northern Sung by the excavators but the type undoubtedly continues into the Chin dynasty. The shape of the bowls in this type is very close to Types 20–22 below which also are datable to Late N. Sung and Chin.

A most interesting bowl in the Heeramaneck collection (Pl. 8:i) is closely related to the above described group. On the inside wall of this bowl is found a design of two lotus flowers floating among combed waves. The central area of the bowl, which is unglazed, has a Chin dynasty date equivalent to 1162 (the *Jen-wu* year of *Ta-ting*) written in ink. If this date is correct the wave patterns of this type must have continued well into the Chin dynasty which seems most likely.

In the catalogue of Ju ware in the Taiwan Palace Museum is one single piece of the type we call Northern celadon.[6]) This piece, which is labelled Lin-ju ware, is extremely close to the dated bowl just mentioned. The Palace Museum bowl is of the same conical shape, with rounded, contracted lip, and on the inside is, in the centre, a design of two lotus flowers and two lotus leaves on a combed wave ground with cut outlines. Below the rim is a border of stiff leaves. The design is closely akin to that of the dated bowl, especially in the way the lotus flowers are rendered with their characteristic elongated outline. The two bowls undoubtedly

[1]) *OCS Celadon Exh.* 1947, Cat.no. 96.
[2]) For a very similar design on Ting yao see Type Ti 22.
[3]) *Cat.* Pl. 66 a.
[4]) *Venezia exh.cat.* No. 410.
[5]) *China's beauty.* No. 236.
[6]) *Ju ware of the Sung dynasty.* Hong Kong 1961. Pl. 24.

come from the same kiln. The border found on the Palace collection bowl is of a type that is generally associated with the 12th century and later.

Type: **Nc 18.**
Provenience: Yao-chou.
Shape: **Bowl.**
Date: **Northern Sung.**
Design: Fishes and waves.

This design is found on a bowl in the David Foundation (Pl. 8:j) and another one in the Honolulu Academy of Arts.[1]) The design, which covers the whole interior of the bowl except for an undecorated band near the mouth, is composed of very finely moulded overlapping waves which give a most realistic impression. Among the waves are four fishes, and in the centre is a shell and a small toad. An almost identical bowl was published in the *Yao tz'u t'u lu*.[2])

Type: **Nc 19.**
Provenience: Lin-ju.
Shape: **Bowl.**
Date: **Late Northern Sung.**
Design: Waves and shells.

This design is usually found on shallow bowls with slightly thickened rim, and covers the whole inside of the bowl except for an undecorated band below the rim. The design consists of a series of circles with waves, and in the centre three large shells. Although similar to the preceding type the rendering of the waves is much more stiff and symmetrical, and the details are different. A bowl of this type said to have come from Chü-lu hsien is in the British Museum[3]) and another one is in the Neave-Hill collection (Pl. 8:k). Fragments of a bowl of this type were recently excavated at the site of the Ju kilns in Lin-ju hsien.[4])

Type: **Nc 20.**
Provenience: Yao-chou.
Shape: **Bowl & dish.**
Date: **Chin.**
Design: Lotus flower.

This design is usually found on the inside of round bowls and dishes, and covers the whole interior except for the area just under the rim. It is composed of a rather sketchy lotus flower with thin, pointed petals, a large flat lotus leaf seen from the side and a very characteristic winding scroll with rolled up ends keeping the composition together (Fig. 9:d). Typical examples of almost identical design are found

---

[1]) *Los Angeles exh.cat.* no. 181.

[2]) *Op.cit.* Part. 2. Pl. 18.

[3]) Gray, *Early Chinese pottery and porcelain.* Pl. 67.

[4]) *Wen Wu* 1964:8, p. 18, fig. 9 upper left.

in the Buffalo Museum,[1]) in the Tokyo NM,[2]) in the British Museum (Pl. 9:a) and in the former Rücker-Embden coll. (Pl. 9:b). One bowl of the same type and a fragment from another were found in Yao-chou (Pl. 9:d), which gives us a certain provenience for this type.

Two more specimens, one dish in the Cleveland Museum of Art[3]) and another one in the Tokyo NM (Pl. 9:c) also carry the same design with minor variations, the petals of the lotus are more pointed and sharp and the big lotus leaf is not so wide and a little more spread out.

A similar design is also found on an extremely fine and unusual vase in the Yamato Bunka-kan (Pl. 9:f), where it covers the whole side of the vase except for the area round the foot which is carved with a row of over-lapping lotus petals. The special technique used in this kind of carving with its peculiar scrolls with rolled up ends seems to be characteristic of the Yao-chou kiln. The same type of scroll is used also with other décor motifs the composition of which is very close to this type.

Type: **Nc 21.**
Provenience: **Yao-chou.**
Shape: **Bowl.**
Date: **Chin.**
Design: **Sea-star and floral scroll.**

This design is very close to the preceding one, with similar composition and the same characteristic scrolls. In this case, however, the design shows a big sea-star and two flowers which are not lotus flowers. The design is found on a bowl in a Japanese collection (Pl. 9:e).

Type: **Nc 22.**
Provenience: **Yao-chou.**
Shape: **Bowl.**
Date: **Chin.**
Design: **Rhinoceros viewing the moon.**

This design is most unusual and as far as we know has only been found on bowls and fragments found in Yao-chou. It is composed of a rather sketchily depicted rhinoceros viewing the moon and surrounded by scrolls of the same characteristic type that we have seen in Types 20–21 above (Pl. 9:g). It has been dated Chin by the excavators, which seems very plausible if we accept the idea that the specimens in the related groups belong to the end of Northern Sung and the earlier part of the Chin dynasty. We also know that the "rhinoceros viewing the moon" motif seems to have been most popular during the Chin and Southern Sung periods. The motif will be discussed later on.

---

[1]) Hochstadter *op. cit.* No. 54.

[2]) *Sekai* 10; Fig. 19.

[3]) Sherman Lee, *A History of far Eastern Art.* Fig. 481.

Type: Nc 23.
Provenience: Yao-chou.
Date: Chin.
Design: Boy among scrolls.

The typical scroll characteristic of the types discussed above seems to have been used also together with the well-known design of boys climbing among floral scrolls. A sherd from a specimen with this décor was found during the excavations of the Yao-chou kilns (Pl. 9:h).

Type: Nc 24.
Provenience: Yao-chou.
Shape: Vase.
Date: Chin.
Design: Lily scroll.

This design consists of lily-like flowers on a thin deeply carved scroll with rather stylized leaves. A good example of the design is found round the belly of a bottle-shaped vase in the V & A (Pl. 9:i). On the neck of the vase is a band of stiff petals enclosed by two heavy scroll borders (a similar scroll border is found on the shoulder of the lotus-decorated vase Pl. 9:f), there is a row of overlapping petals surrounding the bottom part of the vase.

Type: Nc 25.
Shape: Dish.
Date: Late Northern Sung—Chin.
Design: Lily scroll.

A lily scroll of a different and more formal type than in the preceding type is found on the inside of a dish in a Japanese collection (Pl. 9:l). The composition shows two winding scrolls, with rather realistic peony-like leaves ending in two very formal lyre-shaped flowers. The workmanship is extremely fine, and the design is rare.

Type: Nc 26.
Shape: Pillow.
Date: Late Northern Sung.
Design: Star-shaped flowers.

This design, which is very unusual shows a winding scroll with five-petalled star-like flowers. The leaf-scroll is of a type generally appearing together with peonies and some of the leaves are quite close to the so-called "sickle-leaf" type, but they are not so strongly conventionalized. A fine example of this design is found on top of a pillow in the Boston Museum (Pl. 10:a). On the front of the pillow is a peony design of the F-type and in the corners are *cash* patterns.

Type: Nc 27.
Shape: Bowl.
Date: Chin.
Design: Boys and star-shaped flowers.

A floral scroll of a similar type to the one in the preceding type with five-petalled flowers is also found together with climbing boys. A bowl with this design is in the Seligman collection (Pl. 9:j) and a similar one is in another collection (Pl. 9:k). The leaf-scroll found on both these bowls is quite near to the "sickle-leaf" type. The design is rather sketchy and not so detailed. The shape of the bowls points to a 12th century date.

Type: Nc 28.
Provenience: Yao-chou and Lin-ju.
Shape: Conical bowl.
Date: Late Northern Sung.
Design: Ducks and lotus.

The design is found on small conical bowls. It covers the inside of the vessel except for a small undecorated band near the mouth. It is composed of ducks, lotus flowers and leaves on a wave ground. The pattern is very well moulded with fine details. An example of the type is in the Kempe collection (Pl. 10:d) and another one is in the collection of H.M. the King of Sweden (Pl. 10:e). Fragments with identical design have been found in Yao-chou (Fig. 31:c), the treatment of the waves is very characteristic, but similar sherds have also been excavated in Lin-ju.[1]) Bowls of the same type, only decorated with lotus scrolls are also found.[2])

Type: Nc 29.
Shape: Dish or cup-stand.
Date: Late Northern Sung—Chin.
Design: Ducks and lotus.

A design similar to the preceding is found on a dish of shallow concave shape with rising sides in the Seligman collection (Pl. 10:f). In the centre of the dish is a round medallion with a thin lotus spray and in a surrounding band are swimming ducks, lotus flowers and sagittaria on a finely moulded wave-ground. A very similar specimen, which in the centre has a stop ridge to hold a cup, was in the Eumorfopoulos collection (Pl. 10:g).[3])

Type: Nc 30.
Shape Conical bowl.
Date: Late Northern Sung.
Design: Boys among lotus flowers.

This type is related to the design with ducks and lotus flowers described above as Type 28. The composition of the design, the fine details of the moulding as well as the conical shape of the bowls, are all very similar. The design in this case shows small boys climbing among lotus and sagittaria. The position of the boys is most characteristic with their big hands holding the floral stems in a steady grip. One bowl with this design is in the Barlow coll. (Pl. 10:h) and another one is in the Buffalo Museum.[4])

---

[1]) *Wen Wu* 1964:8, Pl. 4:2 lower right and *China's beauty.* No. 273.

[2]) *GEc* vol. II; B 194.

[3]) *GEc* vol. II; B 176.

[4]) Hochstadter *op.cit.* No. 55.

Type: Nc 31. **Date: Late Northern Sung—Chin.**
Shape: Dish. **Design: Clusters of floral sprays.**

In the David Foundation is a dish (Pl. 10:i) with rounded sides and everted lip, the design of which is close both to the boys among peonies design of Type 6 and the lotus and duck design of Type 28 but shows a unique composition. The design is composed of three clusters of lotus sprays, beehive-shaped peonies, sagittaria and other flowers bound together, and three medallions inscribed *san pa lien* [22] (three lotus bundles), supported by lotus seed-pods. On each side of the medallions is a butterfly (Fig. 10:b). The composition is unusually fine and elegant, and the piece is most likely a product of the Yao-chou kiln.

Type: Nc 32. **Date: Late Northern Sung.**
Shape: Dish. **Design: Chrysanthemum flowers.**

Realistic representations of chrysanthemums are extremely rare on Northern celadon wares but are found on a dish in the Seligman collection (Pl. 10:j). It is of shallow saucer-shape with upturned rim and rounded sides. The composition of the design, which is very delicate, shows a scroll with two big flowers and two leaves.[1])

Type: Nc 33. **Date: Northern Sung.**
Shape: Dish. **Design: Flying apsaras.**

A rare buddhist design is found on a dish of shallow shape with spreading sides in the Seligman collection (Pl. 10:k). The design which is very fine and detailed shows two *apsaras* in streaming garments among plants, one carrying a bowl the other one holding a flower spray (Fig. 41:b). The style of the composition seems quite early and is still in the T'ang–Liao tradition. No similar specimen is known.[2])

Type: Nc 34. **Date: Northern Sung—Chin.**
Shape: Various. **Design: Cash-pattern.**

The *cash* design, although very common in Sung and Chin architecture, is quite rare on ceramics. In the ROM in Toronto is an incense-burner which is decorated on the outside with a deeply cut band of *cash* motifs (Pl. 6:l), the shape of this piece is close to that of some incense-burners from Yao-chou. A deep conical bowl

[1]) A realistic chrysanthemum is also found under the lion forming the spout of the Cleveland ewer. Pl. 1:f.

[2]) In tomb stone-carvings *apsaras,* and other Buddhist motifs are, however, quite common both in Liao and N. Sung. Cp. *Kao Ku* 1962:5, Pl. 10:2, for a Liao time *apsara* very close to the one on the Seligman dish. Cp. also, *KKHP* 1962:2, Pl. 19:1.

in the Barlow collection,[1]) considered to be a problem piece, also has the *cash* design as part of the exterior decoration. The pillow with design of five-petalled flowers in the Boston Museum (Pl. 10:a) has on the two front oblique sides a deeply cut *cash*-pattern.

A purely architectural use of the *cash*-pattern is found on the ceremonial bowl and stand in Boston (Pl. 4:b), where the open-work stand is built up in *cash*-shaped circles.

Type: Nc 35.
Shape: Cup.

Date: Northern Sung.
Design: Basket work pattern.

Ceramic pieces imitating basket work of different kinds are quite common among several kinds of Sung ceramics, but they are relatively rare in Northern celadon. A small cup in the Terada collection in Tokyo (Pl. 10:b) of a shape usually called rice-measure, with rounded sides and an everted, slightly rolled lip, has this type of design. It consists of finely incised semicircular bow lines covering the whole outside of the vessel. A similar specimen but with wider and more deeply carved bands of the same appearance is published in the *Yao tz'u t'u lu* (Pl. 10:c). This cup stood on a very elegant stand with a raised lotus-soccle-shaped support in the centre.

Type: Nc 36.
Provenience: Lin-ju.
Shape: Bowl.

Date: Northern Sung.
Design: Overlapping petals and flower rosette.

Conical bowls of Northern celadon ware with moulded interior design of overlapping petals are very common. One bowl of this kind is in the Kempe coll.[2]) and another one in the Eugene Bernat coll. (Pl. 7:h). Very often there is a round floral rosette in the centre of the bowl, of the same type as we have seen already on the bowls with conventionalized flowers of Type 2 above (Pl. 2:a, b). At the excavations on the Lin-ju kilns many specimens with different kinds of petal designs of this type were found. Two bowls had the characters *T'ung* [23] and *Wu* [24], both surnames, impressed on the central flower.[3])

Type: Nc 37.
Provenience: Yao-chou.

Date: Northern Sung.
Design: Lung dragon.

Dragon designs on Northern celadon wares seem to be extremely rare and we do not known of any piece in the West. It is, however, possible that some pieces

[1]) Cat. Pl. 141 C.

[2]) *CKc* no. 80.

[3]) Cp. Type 2 (Pl. 2:a).

earlier known as Yüeh yao might on a closer study be transferred to this group.[1]) During the excavations of the Yao kilns several specimens with dragon designs were found (Pl. 10:l) and the appearance of this design, has as has already been mentioned above, been used as evidence for the official character of the Yao-chou ware. All dragon-decorated specimens so far excavated seem to have dragons of the so-called *lung* type, and no archaic or *ch'ih* dragons are known.

In the above made descriptions of some of the main designs found on the Northern celadon ware we have tried, when possible to attribute the different types to either the Yao-chou or the Lin-ju kilns. However, as we have seen, several of the designs are found on wares from both kilns—and sometimes we have no clues at all from what kiln a certain object emanates. With the aid of the excavation reports we will try to state some of the characteristics of the two wares and their differences. To give a clearer picture of the types of designs found we have arranged them according to subjects at the end of this chapter. We have not divided up the material in incised and moulded wares as we have done with some of the other wares, mainly because such a division is rather difficult to make in the Northern celadon group and many objects have designs in which both the carved, incised and moulded techniques are used simultaneously.

The body of the Yao-chou ware is usually finer, thinner and harder than that of Lin-ju; it is also more vitrified and resonant. Most Yao wares have a light crackle or an orange-peel glaze. The glaze is rather thin and not so uniform in colour. The Lin-ju glaze is thicker and more uniform but contains more bubbles.

The Yao ware is mostly moulded but there are also many carved and incised pieces found. The moulded pieces are usually of high quality and the carved ones are lively and vigorous. The Lin-ju ware is to a great extent moulded, and the carved pieces are often stiff and less vigorous.

Regarding the designs, we have already seen that several motifs are found on both wares; but it seems that the Yao ware has both a greater variety of designs and more elaborate and original compositions. Among the motifs found on fragments from the excavation of the Yao kiln are mentioned: lotus flowers, peony, grass and cranes, phoenix, lilies, three fishes in the water, ducks, geese, rhinoceros looking at the moon, dragon, water-weeds, ripples and children climbing amidst floral scrolls.

When it comes to shapes, it is obvious that there is also much more variation in the Yao group. Bowls and dishes are the most frequent shapes in Lin-ju and are also very common in Yao-chou, but in the latter kiln there is also a rich variety of other shapes many of them unique. Among the objects known can be mentioned: basins, pots, jars, cup-stands, five-feeted *lou* (tea-warmer), boxes, cups, vases, ewers and lamps, and also small figures of animals and human beings.

[1]) Cp. for instance the bowl in the Metropolitan Museum (Gompertz *op.cit.* Pl. 17) with extremely elegant dragon design, supposed to have been made in *Shang-lin hu* [25] (Fig. 11:b).

LIST OF DESIGNS FOUND ON THE NORTHERN CELADON WARE

Special floral motifs

The bold floral scroll	Type Nc 1
The sickle-leaf scroll	Page 24
The conventionalized flower	Type Nc 2

Peony

Peonies are undoubtedly the most common motif found on the Northern celadon ware, the main types are:

Peony flowers	Type Nc 3 A–G
Beehive-shaped peony	Type Nc 4
Beehive-shaped peony and leaf scroll	Type Nc 5
Beehive-shaped peony and boys	Type Nc 6
Peony leaf-scroll	Type Nc 7–8
Clusters of floral sprays	Type Nc 31

Lotus

The lotus is not quite so common as the peony but is found in many combinations.

Lotus flower	Type Nc 20
Lotus flower and waves	Type Nc 17
Ducks and lotus	Type Nc 28–29
Boys among lotus flowers	Type Nc 30
Lotus tendril border	Type Nc 16
Clusters of floral sprays	Type Nc 31

Lotus flowers are also found in other combinations; see Pl. 5:c and Pl. 6:i.

Sagittaria

Is very often found together with lotus flowers but is never found alone. Fine examples can be seen in Type Nc 29 and 31.

Chrysanthemum

Are very rare but a fine example is shown under Type Nc 32. The conventionalized flower of Type Nc 2 has often been described as a chrysanthemum but if we compare it with the just mentioned very realistic design we might be quite sure that it is not the same flower. Another realistic chrysanthemum is found under the lion spout of the ewer Pl. 1:f.

Lily

Lily-like flowers are found only in two combinations.

Lily scroll	Type Nc 24
Lily scroll with stiff flowers	Type Nc 25

Five-petalled flower

Five-petalled flower scroll	Type Nc 26
Five-petalled flower and boys	Type Nc 27

Petals

Design of lotus petals and other types of stiff petals are very common; some of the main types are:

Carved lotus petals	Type Nc 9
Serrated petals	Type Nc 10
Overlapping petals	Type Nc 36

Rows of lotus petals used as borders in combination with other designs are most common especially on Yao-chou wares.

Boys among floral scrolls

With beehive-shaped peonies	Type Nc 6
With rolled scrolls	Type Nc 23
With star-shaped flowers	Type Nc 27
With lotus flowers	Type Nc 30

Other human representations

Those are rare on Northern celadon wares. The most striking specimen in this group is the Seligman stand with its five grotesque, seated gorilla-like men round the lower part (Pl. 7:f). The Metropolitan wine-ewer (Pl. 1:k) also has a small, crouching human figure on its handle. Toys representing human figures have been found in Yao-chou.

More or less human-like masks are also found on the upper part of the feet of some specimens, the most realistic ones are on the feet of the Boston stand (Pl. 4:b). Similar masks but of a more *t'ao-t'ieh* like type are found on the tea-warmer from Yao-chou (Pl. 7:i).

A unique Buddhist design with a motif of two flying *apsaras* is found on a dish in the Seligman collection, Type Nc 33.

Dragon (*Lung*)

Dragons are found on some fragments excavated at the Yao-chou kiln but the motif seems to be rare, Type Nc 37.

Small snake-like dragons with wings are found on the handle of the ewer Pl. 1:l.

Phoenix

Two fine examples of phoenix birds are known, one is found on the Metropolitan wine-pot (Pl. 1:k), and the other one on top of the fine pillow in the Iwasaki coll. (Pl. 3:j). The motif seems to be as rare as the dragon.

Rhinoceros viewing the moon

(*Hsi niu*) [26]

This motif is only know from objects excavated and collected in Yao-chou, Type Nc 22.

Lion

Lion figures are mentioned among the objects found at Yao-chou. The spout of the ewer Pl. 1:f is made as a lion sculpture, but otherwise this motif is not found. Lion masks are sometimes found on the feet of some objects, a fine example is the incense-burner Pl. 6:f.

Tortoise

Is found in relief in Type Nc 11.

Ducks and geese

Are rather common and are mainly found in the following combinations:

With combed waves	Type Nc 14
With lotus and other water plants	Type Nc 28—29
With lotus tendril border	Type Nc 16

Other bird designs

In the Yao-chou excavation report are mentioned designs of cranes, but no piece with this design is known. Probably the bird referred to is a variety of phoenix. Other birds are rare on this ware, but on the handle of the ewer Pl. 1:l are two small birds, looking like kingfishers.

Toad

Is found in the centre of bowls of Type Nc 18.

Fishes

Several combinations are found

With combed waves	Type Nc 15
With waves and toad	Type Nc 18
With lotus tendril border	Type Nc 16

Sea-star

Is found on the design of Type Nc 21.

Shells

Are found in the design of Type Nc 19.

Waves

Waves of different types are very common. They are found as the only design in Types Nc 12–13 and in combination with other motifs in Types Nc 14–19.

Cash pattern

The so-called *cash* pattern is found together with other motifs but is comparatively rare, Type Nc 34.

Basket-work pattern

Objects with this type of design have been attributed to Yao-chou but the design is quite rare, Type Nc 35.

Inscriptions

Are sometimes found on Northern celadon wares. The following types are found:
1) Names: *T'ung*, *Wu*, *Wang* and *Yang*.
2) Dates: *Ta Kuan* (1107), *Cheng Ho* (1111), *Ta An* (1210), all on sherds from Yao-chou.
   Inscription in ink *Jen Wu* year of *Ta Ting* (1162) see Pl. 8:i.

CH'ING-PAI

The term *ch'ing pai* has now been generally accepted in the West for the other main group of Sung porcelain besides the Ting yao. As has been pointed out by Sir Percival David[1]) and John Pope[2]) the earlier used term *ying ch'ing* [27] is a twentieth-century term and the old Chinese name of the ware is ch'ing-pai. The earliest use of the term seems to be in the *Chu fan chih* [28] of Chao Ju-kua, where he lists *ch'ing pai tz'u ch'i* [29] among the commodities used by foreign merchants trading in Java.[3]) This work was probably written before the middle of the 13th century.

If we consider the extremely fine quality of some of the ch'ing-pai wares and the enormous quantity of this ware, which has been produced and exported, it receives surprisingly little notice in the commentaries of subsequent Chinese writers on ceramics. It is not until modern times that a greater interest for this ware has developed.

The ch'ing-pai ware is undoubtedly among the finest porcelain wares ever produced. Its body is fine, white and pure and of a sugary structure. The potting is surprisingly thin and the ware is highly translucent. In spite of its delicateness it is rather strong owing to its high feldspar content. The glaze varies from a strong

[1]) *Ying-ch'ing, a plea for a better term. OA*, I, 2 (Summer 1955), p. 52.

[2]) *Chinese Porcelains from the Ardebil Shrine.* Washington 1956.

[3]) Pope, *op.cit.* p. 43.

bluish-green to a pale-blue or almost white tone. The designs are either incised, carved or moulded. The incised ware is often worked with a thin pointed tool, and combed lines are also very frequent. Moulded designs are more common during the end of the Sung period and Yüan, and at that time applied ornaments of different kinds also became popular. The designs of the ch'ing-pai ware show a very pronounced relationship with those found on the Northern celadon ware and also with some of the Ting yao patterns.

It seems that the ware was in great demand abroad and great quantities have been found in South-East Asia, in India, South Arabia and East Africa. Recent excavations in the Philippines have revealed large amounts of the ware and will undoubtedly be of much help in our dating of the ware.[1]) The specimens hitherto excavated in this area seem, however, to cover only a rather short period from the end of Southern Sung to the beginning of Ming. The excavated material provides, however, evidence to show that the ch'ing-pai ware was one of the main export wares of China during the Sung and Yüan dynasties.

It has earlier been assumed that the ch'ing-pai ware was produced both in North China and in South China. Excavations carried out in China during the past twenty years has once and for all dismissed the opinion that there ever was a Northern ch'ing-pai ware. But the excavations have also shown that the ware was produced in many other places than we have known of before, and that it is, in fact, an enormous family.

The two main provinces for the production of the ch'ing-pai ware are Kiangsi and Fukien, but kiln sites have also been found in Chekiang, Anhui and even Yünnan. The great, and for a long time past, well-known centre of the ware, is of course the area in and around *Ching-te chen* in Kiangsi, but several other kilns in the same province have been found. Also in Fukien a large amount of kilns have been discovered, the main ones around the well-known *Te-hua* site [30], but smaller kilns seem to have been found all over the province.[2]) The time of production of those kilns varies, but some of them apparently go back to the T'ang dynasty and some to the Five Dynasties. Most of the production seems to have stopped at the end of the Yüan dynasty.

Ch'ing-pai specimens have been excavated from a number of Sung tombs especially in Kiangsi, and with aid of this material it has sometimes been possible to date some types more exactly than before. However, one of the main difficulties when dealing with this ware is that the usually very fine and delicate designs are difficult to reproduce, and the illustrations found in most Chinese excavation reports are of such a bad quality that a closer analysis of designs is very often impossible.

---

[1]) Leandro and Cecilia Locsin, *Oriental Ceramics discovered in the Philippines*. Tokyo 1967.

[2]) For names and location of the ch'ing-pai kilns hitherto excavated see: Feng Hsien-ming's article in *Wen Wu* 1965:9, pp. 26–56. This article called "Important Finds of Ancient Chinese Ceramics since 1949" was published in 1967, in translation by the OCS (*Chinese Translations*, No. 1).

Very few attempts have been made in this paper to attribute the ch'ing-pai specimens discussed to any specific kiln because of both the great similarity found between most of the wares and also the insufficient material available for such an attribution. Some wares might, however, for good reasons be ascribed to either Kiangsi or Fukien kilns.

The material has been divided into two main groups, the first containing the incised and carved designs, and the second the moulded patterns, but the distinction between these two groups is not always quite clear and some types could be put in either of the groups. In the second group have also been included wares with designs in thread-relief and those with different types of applied ornaments and details.

Incised designs

Type: Cp 1 A. **Date: Early Northern Sung.**
Shape: Ewer & basin, vase. **Design: Conventionalized flower Type A.**

The design which we have chosen to call "*conventionalized flower*" is one of the most popular found on ch'ing-pai. The same design has already been introduced into our discussion of the Northern celadon group, above and a more detailed investigation of the design will follow.

Several different types of this design, more or less dissolved, can be found, and we have selected here only three of the main types which we have termed A, B and C type.

The A-type is the most beautiful in the group and it is rather rare. It consists of flowers of an almost triangular shape with thick-set petals surrounding a central seed-pod of plume-like appearance. The leaves are broad and have a feathery appearance. Good examples of the type are a ewer and basin in the Boston Museum (Pl. 11) and a vase in the British Museum (Pl. 12:a). The ewer is of ovoid shape with slender, curved spout and curved handle, the cover is cylindrical and has a seated lion on its top. The basin is of almost cylindrical shape, with slightly expanding sides, and stands on a high foot. The design is most clearly seen on the outside of the basin.

A ewer of almost identical shape, also crowned by a seated lion, was excavated from a Northern Sung tomb in *Nan Ch'eng* in Kiangsi[1]) (Pl. 12:b). The ewer was accompanied by a basin of similar shape to the Boston one but with five-petalled, flower-shaped mouth. The tomb is datable to the 2nd year of *Chia-yu* (1057). This type of ewer standing in a basin is very common during the Northern Sung period and many examples are found in tomb paintings, for instance in *Pai-sha* in Honan.[2]) The above-mentioned excavated pieces are considered by the excavators to have been produced by the *Pai-che* [31] kiln in *Nan Feng* [32], Kiangsi.

[1]) *Kao Ku* 1965:11, p. 571. Pl. 9:3.

[2]) *Pai sha Sung mu*. Peking 1957. Fig. 58:1. Cp. also our Fig. 35:c.

The vase in the British Museum (Pl. 12:a), which was formerly in the Eumorfopoulos collection, is of an elegant ovoid shape with short lip. The design, which is divided by finely incised vertical lines, is of the same appearance as that on the ewer and basin. It covers about two thirds of the belly.

Type: Cp 1 B. **Date: Northern Sung.**
Shape: Bowl. **Design: Conventionalized flower Type B.**

In this type the flower has become much more sketchy and its shape is now almost completely triangular. Some flowers are frequently shown from the side showing the typical seed-pod, somewhat reminiscent of a group of acorns (Fig. 3:5). We have already seen the same development on the Northern celadon ware (Fig. 3:2). The leaves are also very much conventionalized and only a few pointed ones are found, most of them are small and rounded and look like small buds. We have chosen to call this motif *"the bud-tendril"*. Characteristic of this type is also the hatched background of the design. Good examples of the type are found on two bowls, on high foot with six-foil rim, in the Kempe coll. (Pl. 13:a, Fig. 4:b) and in the Baur coll.,[1]) and conical bowls in the British Museum,[2]) the G. Abraham and the D. Cohen collections.[3])

Type: Cp 1 C. **Date: Northern Sung.**
Shape: Bowl. **Design: Conventionalized flower Type C.**

This is the last stage of simplification of the conventionalized flower. All that remains of the flower is now a circle surrounded by radiating lines, as can be seen on a pair of conical bowls in the Kempe collection.[4]) The leaves have now disappeared completely and instead we have the above-mentioned bud-tendril. The ground is still hatched.

An interesting transitional form between Types B and C can be seen on a bowl with a six-foil rim in the Boston Museum (Pl. 13:b). Here the triangular flowers are still found, but they are extremely small and the bud-tendril is the dominating motif.

Type: Cp 2. **Date: Northern Sung.**
Shape: Vase, box & ewer. **Design: Bud-tendril.**

In this type the flowers have disappeared completely and the design consists of more or less elaborate bud-tendrils on a hatched ground. A very fine example

[1]) *Baur Cat.* No. A 121.

[2]) Gray *op.cit.* Pl. 76 B.

[3]) *OCS Sung exh.* Nos. 214, 215.

[4]) *CKc* No. 540.

of the design is found on a *mei-p'ing* vase of Northern Sung shape in the Honolulu Academy of Arts (Pl. 14) and a similar vase in the Peking Palace Museum (Pl. 12:c). Other examples of the same design are found on a round box with domed cover in the MFEA (Pl. 15:b) and on a cylindrical box in the Kempe collection. The latter box (Pl. 15:a) is of cylindrical shape with a flat outer cover and an inner cover with a small knob. The bud-tendril design is found round the belly of the box. On the top of the flat cover is still seen a very dissolved flower of the conventionalized type viewed from the side (Fig. 4:a).

The bud-tendril design is also found round the upper part of the belly of small melon-shaped ewers with short handle and spout and sunken cover. One ewer of this kind is in a Japanese collection (Pl. 29:j). The shape of this ewer is typical of Northern Sung (cp. our Type Cp 37 below).

Type: Cp 3. — **Date: Northern Sung.**
Shape: Bowl. — **Design: Waves.**

This design which is found on the interior of bowls of round or six-foil shape is composed of incised and combed waves only. The outline of the design is incised and has usually a flower-like shape, and the details are combed. A pair of round bowls in the Kempe collection have this design (Fig. 4:c) and a bowl, with deeply cut six-foil rim, of conical shape in the Seligman collection (Pl. 12:d). Two similar bowls are in the MFEA. The design is closely akin to Type Nc 13 among the Northern celadon ware.

Type: Cp 4. — **Date: Late Northern Sung.**
Shape: Bowl. — **Design: Waves and sketchy lotus flowers.**

This design is similar to the preceding but the waves are overlapping in a very characteristic way and have a cloud-like appearance; it is incised and combed. Among the waves are two very sketchy lotus flowers floating. The composition is found on a deep bowl with rounded sides in the MFEA (Pl. 16:a). The shape of the bowl as well as the design points to a late Northern Sung date.

Type: Cp 5. — **Date: Late Northern Sung—Southern Sung.**
Shape: Bowl. — **Design: Fishes among waves.**

This design is composed of a finely incised and combed pattern of two large fishes among waves, the motif is rather sketchy and no details are shown. These types of design are often very difficult to reproduce, but a bowl with rounded sides and a wide mouth formerly in the Eumorfopoulos collection is quite sharp.[1])

[1]) *GEc* Vol. II, B31, Pl. 12.

This design is, however, mostly found on shallow bowls with unglazed edge, the sides of which are divided inside into six segments by slightly raised, radial ribs. In the centre is a round panel with the fish motif. The waves are formed like long combed bands. One bowl of this kind is in a Swedish collection (Pl. 16:b) and others are found in the British Museum,[1]) the Seligman coll.,[2]) and the Hetherington collection.[3]) A bowl of this type has also been discovered during the excavation of a well in Chekiang datable on the ground of the excavated material to South Sung (Fig. 29:d:4).[4]) The shape of the waves found in this design, formed like long combed bands, is a feature which is common in Northern Sung and the relatively simple design is also of a type generally associated with that period. The design was probably used during the 12th century and hardly later.

Type: Cp 6.
Shape: Bowl.
Date: Late Northern Sung—Southern Sung.
Design: Fishes among waves.

This design which is found on the interior of a bowl with wide mouth and six-foil rim shows two small fishes swimming among waves. The waves cover almost the whole surface and are finely combed, but the two outer rows are more deeply incised with rounded tops. The two fishes are quite small and placed on opposite sides and swimming in opposite directions. The details of the fishes are very fine. A good example of this type is in the Bristol City Art Gallery (Pl. 17:a).

Type: Cp 7.
Shape: Bowl.
Date: Late Northern Sung—Southern Sung.
Design: Ch'ih dragons among waves.

This design, which is most unusual, is found on a bowl in the Bruce coll. (Pl. 12:e). It is of the same shape as the bowl described in Type 6 above, and it has a wave design which is almost identical, but instead of the fishes there are two large dragons. The dragons are of the *ch'ih* type with flat, band-like bodies, long tails split into two parts, each with rolled up ends, and they have strange, human-looking faces (Fig. 12:d). In the centre between the two dragons is a stylized cloud-like ornament, apparently meant to represent the precious pearl.

Type: Cp 8.
Shape: Dish & bowl.
Date: Late Northern Sung—Southern Sung.
Design: Revolving lotus petals.

[1]) Hobson, *Private*: Fig. 221.
[2]) *Cat.* No. D 226.
[3]) Hobson-Hetherington, *The Art of the Chinese potter*. Pl. XCV.
[4]) *Kao Ku* 1964:11, p. 559. Fig. 2:4.

This design consists of rather deeply carved revolving lotus petals and usually covers almost the whole interior of round dishes or bowls. There is often a small round panel in the centre which has a small, sketchy incised lotus. A beautiful example of this composition is found on a dish in the Hakone Art Museum (Pl. 12:f) and a very similar bowl is in the Boston Museum.[1]) In Boston is also a saucer of the same type but without central panel; the revolving petals cover the whole interior.

Type: Cp 9.
Shape: Hexagonal dish; round bowl.
Date: Late Northern Sung—Southern Sung.
Design: Skewed lotus panels.

This design is incised with combed details and is mostly found on dishes or shallow bowls with hexagonal, foliate rim, but also on some round bowls. It is composed of six skewed lotus panels, which are not thin and pointed as in the preceding type, but broad and with a straight or gently curved upper part. The combing on the panels are made in the shape of long bands.

Closest to the preceding type is a dish in the Seligman collection (Pl. 12:g) which has in the centre a round panel, with a sketchy lotus spray, from which six skewed lotus panels radiate. A similar dish, also with hexagonal foliate rim, is in the Kempe collection (Pl. 17:b). The only difference is the central panel, the motif of which is very sketchy and probably meant to represent a leaf. A slight variant of the motif is found on another hexagonal dish in the J. C. Thomson collection (Pl. 12:h), here the central panel is lacking and the lotus panels all emerge from the centre, which makes the motif look like a big, *Althaea*-like flower. A round bowl with the same lotus panel design is in the Barlow collection (Pl. 12:i) and hexagonal ones in a Japanese collection[2]) and in the Hilleström collection.[3])

Type: Cp 10.
Shape: Bowl; vase with foliate rim.
Date: Southern Sung.
Design: Sketchy lotus.

This design which shows a very sketchy and cursory incised lotus-spray, is usually found on the outside of low bowls with rounded sides, very short foot and unglazed rim. A bowl of this type is in the Kempe collection,[4]) and another one is in the Barlow collection.[5]) A more unusual piece with this design is a vase in the MFEA (Pl. 18:a) with ovoid body, cylindrical neck and six-foil everted mouth. This vase is of a shape which we associate with late Southern Sung and Yüan (Cp. Types

[1]) *Hoyt cat.* No. 358.
[2]) *To so mei do ten.* Pl. 147.
[3]) *MFEA Exh.cat. No. 8.* Cat. no. 210.
[4]) *CKc* No. 538.
[5]) *Cat.* no. 117 a.

Cp 19–20 below and Pl. 22:g–j) which gives us a clue to the dating of this particular design.

Type: Cp 11.
Shape: Bowl.
Date: Late Northern Sung—Southern Sung.
Design: Ch'ih dragon.

Dragon designs are most unusual on Sung ch'ing-pai wares, and it seems that the *lung* dragon does not appear on this ware until the Yüan dynasty or at the very end of Sung. One exception to this is when the dragons occur in relief designs as seen on a group of funerary vases (Pl. 30). But the dragon which does occasionally occur on incised wares is the lizard-like type usually referred to as the *ch'ih* dragon. In connection with the wave designs we have already mentioned a bowl in the Bruce collection with *ch'ih* dragons on a combed wave ground (Pl. 12:e). A peculiarity of these dragons is their almost human faces. The same type of dragons, but in a somewhat different composition, is found on the inside of a bowl in the Bristol City Art Gallery (Pl. 12:k, Fig. 12:e). The same type of dragons with their band-like bodies are also found on a bowl in the Clark collection.[1]) The composition of the design of this bowl is identical to that on the Bruce bowl, and the shape is of a kind very typical of ch'ing-pai, almost conical with everted rim and high small foot. The design is in this case finely incised and the details are difficult to make out.

Type: Cp 12.
Shape: Six-foil bowl.
Date: Northern Sung.
Design: Cartouches with sketchy birds.

Extremely dissolved and sketchy designs of different types are quite common among the incised ch'ing-pai ware. One design of this type, which is usually found on the inside of bowls with six-foil rim, shows three oval cartouches on the side in each of which a very dissolved bird design is incised. Of the bird only the outline of the wings is still visible. One bowl of this kind is in the Barlow collection (Pl. 12:l), and another one was recently excavated in a Northern Sung tomb in *Ma Ch'eng* in the province of Hupeh (Fig. 29:b).[2]) The tomb is datable to the year 1113 (*Ch'eng-ho* 3rd year), which gives us sufficient evidence to date this design to Northern Sung.

A bowl with similar but still more highly dissolved designs, which look more like leaves, is in the Kempe collection (Fig. 29:c).

Type: Cp 13.
Shape: Conical bowl.
Date: Northern Sung.
Design: Sketchy birds.

[1]) Gray *op.cit.* Pl. 80.

[2]) *Kao Ku* 1965:1, p. 23.

A bird design still more dissolved than the above mentioned one is usually found on small bowls of conical shape. It shows three birds in flight incised in a swift, almost calligraphic way. One bowl of this kind is in the Seligman collection,[1]) and two others are in private Swedish collections (Pl. 18:b).[2])

Realistic bird designs are surprisingly rare on incised ch'ing-pai, which is quite unexpected as they are frequent both on Northern celadon and Ting yao and also on the moulded variant of the ware.

Type: Cp 14. **Date: 12th century.**
Shape: Bowl. **Design: Boys among peonies.**

Designs showing two or three small boys climbing among flowers are constantly found on ch'ing-pai. The design is mostly found on the inside of bowls and dishes of round or six-foil shape. There are two main types which are characterized by the different types of flowers which are used in combination with the boys. Both types are found in many variants more or less sketchy and dissolved. Sometimes the motif is so dissolved that it is almost impossible to figure out without previous experience what to look for.

Our first type shows the boys among flowers of the type we have labelled "*pomegranate-peonies*" because of their characteristic, big pomegranate-shaped central part. The leaves are usually elongated, pointed and have a feathery appearance. A very fine and clear example of this type of pattern is found on a bowl with six-foil rim in the Boston Museum (Pl. 19:a). The three boys are hiding among the elaborate floral scrolls, but they are still clearly visible. A very similar bowl, with plain rim, and with two boys in the design, is in Japan,[3]) and a second one in a German collection.[4]) A third bowl of this type is in the collection of H.M. the King of Sweden (Fig. 17:a). The more dissolved type of the design is exemplified by a round bowl in the Röhsska Konstslöjdmuseet, Gothenburg (Pl. 19:b; Fig. 17:b). Here the motif is like a puzzle-picture; the feathery leaves of the peonies are still quite clear, but the flowers themselves are reduced to combed oval panels, and the boys are merely outlined; only the big heads and the contours of the bodies are recognizable.

A bowl of this type was recently excavated from a well in Chekiang,[5]) where the material found seems to indicate a Southern Sung date (Fig. 29:d:1). But the design was most probably in use already during the end of Northern Sung.

Type: Cp 15. **Date: 12th century.**
Shape: Bowl. **Design: Boys among peonies.**

[1]) Cat. No. D 225.
[2]) *MFEA Exh.cat. no. 8.* No. 22 a.
[3]) *Sekai* 10; Fig. 80.
[4]) Feddersen *op.cit.* Abb. 28.
[5]) *Kao Ku* 1964:11, p. 559.

This design is close to the preceding but the flowers and leaves found in combination with the boys are different; here they are of the more common peony type. The flower is open with spread, lobated petals; petals and leaves have combed details. A deep bowl in the Cleveland Museum (Pl. 20:a) with this design is of a very fine quality and shows quite clearly a big peony flower in the centre and the boys on the side. A far more dissolved version, but carved with great vigour, is found on a bowl in the Hellner collection (Pl. 20:b, Fig. 17:d). On both the bowls mentioned it seems that the boys are not standing, as they usually are on the preceding type, but rather crawling on all fours.

Type: Cp 16. **Date: Northern Sung.**
Shape: Round bowl; six-foil bowl. **Design: Peony spray.**

This design, which is incised with combed details, is among the most beautiful found on ch'ing-pai, and it is usually seen on bowls of thin translucent porcelain of very high quality. The pattern, which is very vigorously incised, covers the whole interior of bowls and is compared of two thin, elegant leaf sprays with a big open peony in the middle. The design is often described as being a lotus, but the lobated petals of the flower and the thin elongated leaves are characteristic of the peony of *shao-yao* type. A fine example of the motif is found on a bowl with a six-foil rim in the MFEA (Pl. 21:b), and similar bowls are also in the Bristol Museum (Pl. 21:a), the Seligman collection,[1]) the Barlow collection[2]) and the Tollner collection.[3]) Similar round bowls with a little more sketchy design are in the Kempe collection (Fig. 4:d) and in the Dreyfus collection.[4])

Type: Cp 17. **Date: Southern Sung.**
Shape: Six-lobed bowl. **Design: Peony flower.**

This peony design is more compact in the composition and not so elegant as the preceding type. It is usually found on shallow, open bowls with six-foil rim and the interior of the sides divided into six lobes by small raised bands. The quality of these bowls is variable, but they are usually made of a quite thick porcelain with an uneven glaze. The design is found on the almost flat inside centre and is composed of a big peony flower and curled cloud-like leaves, with combed details. Bowls with this design are quite common, there is one example of the type in the MFEA, and many others are known (Pl. 12:j). This peony is sometimes also found

[1]) *Cat.* No. D 220.

[2]) *Cat.* Pl. 113 c.

[3]) *OCS Sung exh.* No. 206. Other examples are in the coll. of H. M. the King of Sweden and in the Tokyo National Museum.

[4]) *OCS Sung exh.* No. 198.

together with a climbing boy[1]) and the design is related to the above mentioned Type Cp 15.

Type: Cp 18. **Date: Northern Sung.**
Shape: Vase. **Design: Carved floral scroll.**

Several different types of floral scrolls are found on ch'ing-pai, some of them more or less realistic floral scrolls, some purely ornamental. Our first type is found on vases of elongated ovoid shape with small mouth. It is composed of leaf-scrolls rather similar to the tendril-scrolls we have seen in connection with the conventionalized flower design; among the scrollwork are sketchy open flowers of peony type. Examples of this type of vases are in the Bristol City Art Gallery (Pl. 22:b) and in the Boston Museum.[2])

A somewhat similar design but more deeply carved and with more realistic flower design was recently excavated at Nanking (Pl. 22:a). This vase is almost completely ovoid with rolled mouth-rim. It came from a tomb datable to 1027 and could be recognized as an early prototype for the kind of vase which later developed into the typical *mei-p'ing* shape. The two earlier mentioned vases could not be so early, but they probably belong to the later part of Northern Sung.

Type: Cp 19. **Date: Southern Sung—Yüan.**
Shape: Mei-p'ing; vase with foliate rim. **Design: Spiral scroll.**

This design shows a more or less cursorily incised spiral scroll motif and is found mainly on two different types of objects, vases of *mei-p'ing* shape and vases with flower-shaped foliate rim. On an example of the first type in the British Museum (Pl. 22:c) the entire surface of the vase is filled with small, rolled spirals. A vase in a Japanese collection (Pl. 22:d) of a slightly more heavy type shows an almost identical design. On a third vase of the same shape, also in Japan,[3]) the design is still more dissolved and the scrolls are almost S-shaped.

The second type is represented by a vase in the Baur collection (Pl. 22:g) of the above described type with foliate rim, the scroll design of which is very close to the last-mentioned vase. Round the neck of this vase is a band of stiff petals. A recently excavated vase of exactly the same shape and with the same petal design on the neck has been attributed by the excavators to the Yüan dynasty (Pl. 22:h).[4]) The scrolls of this vase are more curled and have a cloud-like appearance. A similar vase is in the Royal Scottish Museum, Edinburgh (Pl. 22:i).

[1]) An example with this design is in the MFEA.

[2]) *Hoyt cat.* No. 367.

[3]) S. Hayashiya & G. Hasebe, *Chinese ceramics*. Tokyo 1966. Fig. 107.

[4]) Excavated in Kuang Han Hung Shui Nien, Ssuch'uan. *Ch'üan kuo chi pen* . . . Shanghai 1956. Pl. 253.

A more elaborate scrollwork is found on a vase of *mei-p'ing* shape in the Metropolitan Museum (Pl. 22:e), the scrolls are here very close to the formal classic scroll and of a type generally associated with the Yüan dynasty.

Type: Cp 20. **Date: Southern Sung—Yüan.**
Shape: Various. **Design: Composite floral scroll (sometimes with boys).**

This design has close similarities with the preceding type and seems to be almost contemporary. The design is found in different varieties but they are all of the same general composition. The floral scroll found in this pattern is usually composed of lotus flowers, a lily-like flower and peonies, sometimes just one of these flowers is used, sometimes all of them. Some specimens have boys climbing among the scrolls. The design is usually deeply carved and the ground is striated by fine combing. Several different shapes are found.

A vase in the ROM in Toronto (Pl. 22:j) is of exactly the same shape with foliate flower-shaped mouth as the previously mentioned vase in the Baur collection (Pl. 22:g) and has similar stiff petals round the neck; round the belly of the vase is a carved scroll with lily-like flowers. A vase of *mei-p'ing* form with the same design was formerly in the Eumorfopoulos collection.[1] A large *mei-p'ing* in the Chicago Art Institute (Pl. 22:k) has the same kind of flowers but also shows realistic lotus flowers and small boys climbing among the scrolls. A vase in a Japanese collection (Pl. 22:f) with more conventionalized scrolls also has the lotus flowers and the large characteristic lotus leaves together with the boy motif. Another *mei-p'ing*, also in Japan (Pl. 22:l), has peonies and lotus flowers of the same type, and an unusual gourd-shaped ewer in the Musée Guimet (Pl. 23:a) has a very realistic peony design.

Objects of other shapes with this type of design are also found; a beautiful example is a large cup with straight sides in the Mayer collection (Pl. 23:b) with lotus design and a small ewer in a Japanese collection (Pl. 23:c). The latter is of almost globular shape with short spout and handle; an identically shaped ewer but without decoration, only with a small iron spot on the belly, is in the Tokyo National Museum.[2] This large and beautiful group is representative of a style characteristic of the late Sung and early Yüan dynasty.

Type: Cp 21. **Date: Northern Sung.**
Shape: Various. **Design: Carved petals.**

Carved lotus petals used on the outside and occasionally also on the inside of vessels is a motif quite common on ch'ing-pai. There are several different types.

[1]) *GEc* Vol. II, B 34.

[2]) *Sekai* 10. Fig. 89. Excavated at Kanzeonji, Fukuoka, and datable to the Southern Sung dynasty.

Our first type is exemplified by a cylindrical pot in the Kempe coll. (Pl. 23:d), with almost straight sides slightly expanding towards the mouth and standing on a low foot, the lip and a band around it are unglazed.[1]) The exterior of this bowl is covered by rather thin, pointed, overlapping petals, deeply carved. The quality of the porcelain is thin and very fine. A piece of exactly the same appearance was recently excavated from a Sung tomb in Hupeh datable to 1113 (*Ch'eng-ho* 3rd year).[2])

The carved petal design is also very common on a group of small jars with cover. They are usually of globular shape with slightly domed cover, provided with a small tube-like knob and a broad flat edge. A jar and cover of this type is in the Kempe collection (Pl. 23:e) and an identical one is in a Japanese collection.[3]) A jar of the same type without cover is also in the Kempe coll.[4]) A similar carved petal design is also used round the bottom part of a small incense-burner with openwork cover in Japan (Pl. 23:f). Among more unusual specimens with this design is a ewer in Japan (Pl. 23:g). The upper part of the belly of this ewer is of eight-lobed melon-shape, but the lower part has rows of overlapping petals. The shape of the ewer is quite near to that of a ch'ing-pai ewer recently excavated in Kiangsi from a Sung tomb tentatively dated to around 1100.[5])

Type: Cp 22.	**Date: Northern Sung.**
Shape: Stem-cup.	**Design: Carved lotus petals.**

This design, which is quite rare, is the finest in the carved petal group. It is found on stem-cups standing on a frilled base which is pierced in a very characteristic way typical of ch'ing-pai. The upper part of the cup is shaped like a lotus chalice with large, strongly carved, overlapping petals. The area just under the lip, on the exterior is finely striated. There is one cup of this type in the Garner collection (Pl. 23:h) and another one in the Honolulu Academy of Arts (Pl. 23:i).

Type: Cp 23.	**Date: Southern Sung.**
Shape: Bowl.	**Design: Carved petals.**

Carved overlapping lotus petals of a type similar to that so commonly found among the Lung-ch'üan ware is also used on ch'ing-pai, often on the exterior of shallow bowls with everted lip. The design is usually rather mechanically executed and gives a very stiff impression. Bowls of this type are quite common in several

[1]) The shape is similar to that of the bowl Pl. 11.

[2]) *Kao Ku* 1965:1; Pl. 5:8.

[3]) *Sekai* 10: Pl. 86 upper.

[4]) *CKc* No. 526.

[5]) *Wen Wu* 1964:4, p. 63. (Fig. 5, p. 64).

collections,[1]) the majority of them seem to be of late Southern Sung date. Occasionally the lotus design is also found on the inside of bowls with a plain exterior. A bowl of this type is in the Baur collection,[2]) the shape of this bowl is conical with straight foot and it belongs to a type generally associated with the late 12th century. A bowl of this type was found in a Chin dynasty tomb dated 1184 (Fig. 35:a:3).

Moulded designs

Type: Cp 24.
Shape: Bowl.
Date: Southern Sung.
Design: Phoenixes and composite floral scroll.

The phoenix motif is hardly ever found on ch'ing-pai specimens with incised design, but it is most common on the moulded variety. Only a few of the main types where the phoenixes are the dominating motif will be mentioned here.

The first type is found on the inside of deep bowls with rounded sides which stand on a very low foot; the mouth rim is unglazed. In the centre of the bowl is usually a round panel occupied by a lotus plant with two flowers. The main band of decoration is found on the side and consists of two phoenix birds flying in the same direction, one of them has his head turned backwards as if he were looking at the other one. Between the phoenixes, which are placed opposite, to each other, is a composite floral scroll with lotus, peonies and other flowers. Immediately above the main band of décor is a formal key-fret border.

Bowls of this type are most common, there are three in the MFEA (Pl. 24), one in the Lundgren collection, and one in the Barlow collection,[3]) and examples of the type can be found in most collections. The quality of these bowls is very different; some are perfectly moulded and the porcelain is thin and translucent and the glaze light blue, others are white or yellowish in colour and the moulding is crude and the porcelain thick and coarse.

Type: Cp 25.
Shape: Box.
Date: Southern Sung.
Design: Pair of phoenixes.

This design is found on low round boxes with almost flat covers. The design occupies the whole surface of the cover, the rest of the box is undecorated. The composition shows two phoenixes flying in a gently curved movement with their heads turned and looking at each other, between them is a small chrysanthemum flower. The phoenixes are of a similar appearance to those in the preceding type with a plume-like crest on the head, characteristic neck-tuft and two scrolled

1) *Barlow cat.* Pl. 118 a; *OCS Sung exh.* No. 212.
2) *Baur* cat. A 122.
3) Cat. Pl. 113 B.

streamers at the neck; the tail is split into long thin feathers. One box of this type is in the Kempe collection (Pl. 25:a) and another in the Barlow coll.[1]) The first one has a light blue glaze, the second one is almost white. A third box with the same design is in a Japanese collection.[2]) Another box of a similar type in the Kempe collection (Pl. 25:b) has a more detailed and very finely moulded design where floral sprays have been added to the phoenix motif.

Type: Cp 26. **Date: Southern Sung—Yüan.**
Shape: Shallow bowl. **Design: Boys among floral scroll.**

This design is moulded into a kind of linear relief which is typical of this group. It is usually found on shallow bowls with unglazed rim. There is a central round panel, a main design band on the side and an outer beaded border. The central panel shows either two fishes among waves, as can be seen on a bowl formerly in the Eumorfopoulos collection,[3]) or two phoenixes as on a bowl in the Kempe collection (Pl. 26:a). The phoenixes on the latter bowl are of a type with short tail and broad flattened wings, which is very common on Yüan wares. The main décor band shows two crawling boys among flowers and two panels with what look like bunches of stamina.

Type: Cp 27. **Date: Southern Sung c. 1200.**
Shape: Conical bowl. **Design: Pair of phoenixes, lotus flowers.**

This type of design, which is moulded in a kind of linear relief, is found on conical bowls with small, straight foot and flat base. They are thinly potted and have a light blue glaze. The design is moulded in thin lines with very few details and it usually consists of two rather dissolved phoenix birds. Bowls of this kind are in the Barlow collection,[4]) the Brodie Lodge collection,[5]) the collection of H.M. the King of Sweden and in a private Swedish collection (Pl. 26:b). The design is enclosed by a rather broad key-fret border.

The same kind of design but with four lotus flowers as main motif is also found; one example is in the Baur collection.[6])

The thread relief designs of this type seems to be typical of late Sung and Yüan Fortunately enough we are able to date this particular design to around 1200 as a bowl of this type with décor of two phoenixes and small lotus flowers was recently

[1]) *Cat.* Pl. 115 b.
[2]) *Sekai* 10; Fig. 82.
[3]) *GEc* Vol. II: B 37.
[4]) *Cat.* Pl. 117 c.
[5]) *OCS Sung exh.* No. 204.
[6]) *Baur cat.* A 126.

excavated from a tomb at *Cho-tao ch'üan* in *Wu-chang*, Hupeh (Fig. 29:a). The tombstone was dated the 6th year of *Chia Ting* (1213).[1])

Type: Cp 28. **Date: Southern Sung.**
Shape: Bowl. **Design: Panels with potted plants.**

This design, which is very frequent, is mostly found on bowls with rounded sides, both shallow and deep; they all have unglazed rim and low foot. The design found on the interior is composed of a central panel, surrounded on the side by six radiating segment-shaped panels below a key-fret border. The most common central motifs found are a lotus-spray, a pair of phoenixes or a flying goose. The side panels could either show six wide tray-like pots with flowers, or alternating panels with flowers in vases and flowers in trays. A pair of bowls in the Kempe collection (Pl. 27:a; Fig. 4:e) has a lotus spray in the centre and in the panels alternating pear-shaped vases with flowers and trays with flowers. The flowers are of several different types. A bowl with similar arrangements in the panels with a pair of phoenix birds in the centre was formerly in the Eumorfopoulos collection.[2]) A bowl in the Barlow coll.[3]) also has a lotus-spray in the centre and trays with lotus flowers and pear-shaped vases with different flowers in the panels. A bowl in the MFEA, finally, has a flying goose in the centre and lotus flowers in shallow trays in all the six panels on the side (Pl. 27:b).

Type: Cp 29. **Date: Southern Sung—Yüan.**
Shape: Bowl. **Design: Panels with flowers.**

This design is mostly found on bowls of the same shapes with unglazed rim as in the preceding type. The décor is also closely akin, the only difference being that the flowers in the radiating panels are not potted. They are single sprays of different flowers usually very delicately and precisely moulded. A pair of bowls with this pattern in the Kempe collection (Fig. 4:f) has a lotus spray in the centre and sprays of lotus, peony, chrysanthemum and other flowers in the panels.

Type: Cp 30. **Date: Southern Sung—Yüan.**
Shape: Dish & bowl. **Design: Composite floral scroll (sometimes with phoenixes).**

This design is found on dishes or bowls of a shape related to Type 24 above, but the bowls are usually not so deep and have more spreading sides. The rim is unglazed and the design is arranged with a central round panel and a main band

[1]) *Kao Ku* 1964:5, p. 239.

[2]) *GEc* Vol. II: B 36.

[3]) *Cat.* Pl. 119 a.

of décor on the side enclosed by a key-fret border. However, the moulding is usually more exact and perfect than in the earlier type, and the design is more detailed and varied and often gives a crowded impression. The central panel usually shows some floral motif, lotus, chrysanthemum or prunus, and the design band has often phoenixes and flowers of different types. A saucer-dish of this type in the Baur collection[1]) has a spray of *celastrus* in the centre and round the sides two short-tailed phoenixes flying among peonies and other flowers. Another bowl in the same collection[2]) has a lotus spray in the centre, and round the sides is a composite floral scroll including peony, chrysanthemum, lotus and prunus flowers. The main difference between this type and type 24 above is the great variation of flowers found; some of them, like the chrysanthemum, prunus and celastrus are most uncommon in earlier ch'ing-pai wares and seem to be characteristic of the end of Sung and beginning of Yüan. The stiff, almost mechanical moulding and the hard and clear glaze are also significant of the type.

In the above presented survey of some of the main designs found on *ch'ing-pai* specimens the different types have mostly been classified according to the patterns found on them, but that great variety of designs sometimes found on wares which obviously belong to the same main group makes it necessary to combine them under larger groups, and within the groups to distinguish between different shapes. This arrangement will give a clearer picture of some of the large groups common during late Sung and early Yüan.

Type: Cp 31. **Date: Southern Sung—Yüan.**
Shape: Vase with scroll-handle. **Design: Prunus spray.**

This particular type is characterized by its S-shaped scroll-handles. A pear-shaped vase with tall neck and two elegant S-scroll-shaped handles in the MFEA (Pl. 23:j) is a good example of the most common type in this group. On one side of the vase is a plum spray in thread relief. An almost identical vase with the same design is in the Philadelphia Museum of Art (Pl. 23:k). A vase formerly in the Eumorfopoulos collection[3]) has the same design, but the shape is not so elegant, the body being more rounded and the neck-part taller and straighter, the S-shaped handles are not so elaborate. A pair of vases of almost the same shape, but with still more globular body, and no design, were recently excavated from a Southern Sung tomb in Nanking,[4]) and apparently show an early example of this type. From a Yüan tomb in Ssuch'uan has been excavated a vase (Pl. 23:l) which apparently shows a late development of the type; the S-shaped scroll-handles are partly free from the neck

[1]) *Cat.* No. A 124.

[2]) *Cat.* No. A 125.

[3]) *GEc* Vol. II: B 39.

[4]) *Kao Ku* 1963:6, p. 344, Fig. 1.

and are more dominant, the decoration on the body shows a prunus spray in high, moulded relief.[1])

The scroll handle is also found on other types of vases, mostly undecorated. A vase formerly in the Winkworth collection[2]) is of the spotted ch'ing-pai type and is of baluster form with simple scroll-handles shaped like two rings. A similar vase, but on an attached stand, also undecorated, is in the Locsin collection.[3]) The scroll-handles of this type are later on becoming quite common on vases and ewers during the Yüan dynasty, but the type mentioned here is interesting as an example of one of the many Sung—Yüan transition types.

Type: Cp 32. **Date: Yüan.**
Shape: Ewer, with dragon-handle and -spout.

This type consists of ewers with dragon-spouts with or without dragon-handles. The first group has a melon-shaped body on a low foot. On top of the ewer is a large reclining dragon, the head of which forms the spout and the curved body the handle. The dragon is of the *ch'ih* type with lizard-like body and split tail. The eyes of the dragon are usually glazed brown with iron oxide. One ewer of this kind is in the British Museum (Pl. 28:a) another one in the Kempe collection (Pl. 28:b) and a third one has been excavated from a Yüan tomb in Ssuch'uan (Pl. 28:c).

The second group has only the spout formed like a dragon's head. A globular miniature ewer in the Kempe collection (Pl. 28:d) is a good example of the type. A small ewer in a Japanese collection (Pl. 28:e) has the same kind of spout, but the body is melon-shaped with ribbed sides and a horizontal relief band round the belly, a shape well-known among Sung—Yüan wares, for instance, of celadon.[4]) Both ch'ing-pai ewers mentioned have the dragon's eyes glazed in iron oxide.

Type: Cp 33. **Date: Southern Sung.**
Shape: Cup with dragon-handles.

This group consists of cups of round shape, with almost straight sides, on a high foot with everted foot-rim. The handles of the cup are formed by two dragons confronting one another and placed on the side of the vessel biting over the mouth rim. The dragons are of the *ch'ih* type and have band-like bodies and the tails split

[1]) A still later version of this type of pear-shaped vase can be seen in another Yüan example (Cp. Kao Ku 1960:4, Pl. 12). In this case the handles are angular, and round the neck is a scroll of the beaded type, so characteristic of Yüan. On the body is the usual prunus spray. A tripod of bronze-shape also with the prunus design is published in the same article.

[2]) *TOCS* 1924–25, p. 9, Fig. 1.

[3]) J. M. Addis, *Some ch'ing pai and white wares found in the Philippines.* (Manila Trade Pottery Seminar introductory notes.) No. 23.

[4]) Locsin, *Oriental ceramics.* Pl. 58.

into two parts, each ending in a small spiral movement. The porcelain is thin and translucent and the glaze has a delicate bluish-green tint; the mouth is unglazed, and sometimes also the upper part of the dragon's heads. Cups of this kind with slight differences are in the Kempe collection (Pl. 28:f), the Fitzwilliam Museum (Pl. 28:g), the Honolulu Academy of Arts (Pl. 28:h), the Peter Harris collection,[1]) the Mount Trust and the Barlow collection (Pl. 28:i).

Type: Cp 34. **Date: Southern Sung—Yüan.**
Shape: Ewer or vase, with ribbed sides.

This type has the exterior of the vessel ribbed by thin relief lines. A ewer of this kind in the Honolulu Academy of Arts (Pl. 28:j) is of gourd-shape with pointed lid. It has two small scroll-handles on the sides, just at the waist, which are of a type clearly related to those found in Type 31 above. A miniature ewer of barrel-shape in the Kempe collection (Pl. 28:k) is also of this type; it has a *ju-i* shaped handle.

Type: Cp 35. **Date: Northern Sung.**
Shape: Incense-burner & vase with fluting.

Fluting of different types is a technique very often used among ch'ing-pai wares. A particularly fine group with this kind of décor is a group of cup-shaped incense-burners or lamps, which can be found in several collections. The shape is very characteristic with a high stem with two fluted flanges, cup-shaped upper part and projecting horizontal rim. Examples of this type are in the Kempe collection (Pl. 29:a), the Boston Museum,[2]) the Barlow collection (Pl.29:b), the McHugh collection[3]) and the Dreyfus coll. (Pl. 29:c). The last-mentioned piece has a more elaborate foot in six-foil shape. Incense-burners of the same type as those just mentioned are also found in Ting yao.[4])

Another type of incense-burner of a more elegant form is found in the Brundage collection (Pl. 28:l). Its upper part is almost completely spherical, half of the sphere forms the cup and the upper reticulated part the cover. The base of the high foot is splayed and fluted. An incense-burner of similar shape but with a pierced foot is in the Boston Museum.[5])

Fluting is also found on the everted foot of a group of vases with melon-shaped body often found in ch'ing-pai. Vases of this kind are found in many different collections (Pl. 29:d, e).

[1]) *TOCS* Vol. 21; Pl. 21 a.

[2]) *Hoyt cat.* No. 360.

[3]) *Chinese Ceramics, 10th–17th centuries.* Municipal Gallery of Modern Art. Parnell Square, Dublin. 1967. No. 21.

[4]) *CKc* No. 491.

[5]) *Hoyt cat.* No. 378.

Type: Cp 36. **Date: Five Dynasties—Early Northern Sung.**
Shape: Ewer with phoenix-head.

A rare and interesting type of ch'ing-pai specimens is formed by a small group of phoenix-headed ewers. The prototype of these ewers seems to be the famous ewer in the British Museum (Pl. 29:g), with carved floral patterns, supposed to have come from *Chi-chou* and generally dated T'ang. The ewer is much more elaborate than most T'ang specimens and its date is more likely to be in the Five Dynasties period.[1]) A ch'ing-pai ewer in the Brooklyn Museum (Pl. 29:h), is of the same general appearance as the British Museum ewer, but it is completely undecorated like all other specimens in this group. Around the neck are two projecting flanges of the same type as the five flanges on the BM ewer. Of related shape is also a ewer in the Honolulu Academy of Arts,[2]) with a more whitish glaze, and a very beautiful one with melon-shaped body in the Cleveland Museum (Pl. 29:i).

A very interesting specimen clearly related to this group but of a later and more typical ch'ing-pai type is a miniature ewer in the Kempe coll. (Pl. 29:f). It has an elongated melon-shaped body, spreading foot, and neck with horizontal ribs. It is crowned by a simple but finely moulded phoenix-head.

Type: Cp 37. **Date: Early Northern Sung.**
Shape: Ewer with applied leaf.

Applied leaf ornaments found on the shoulder of vases and ewers are a feature which is typical of the T'ang–Sung transition period and which is frequently found among Yüeh yao, Northern celadon and Liao wares. In the ch'ing-pai group this design is very rare. A ewer with melon-shaped body, small handle and spout, and a sunken cover in the ROM in Toronto (Pl. 29:l), has a formal leaf of this type on each shoulder. A small ewer of similar shape in the Kempe collection (Pl. 29:k) has a more realistic leaf on the shoulder, and its form is of a type well-known in Northern Sung. A similar ewer in a Japanese collection without the leaf has an incised scroll design of our Type Cp 2 on the upper part of the body (Pl. 29:j).

The Toronto ewer which still keeps much of the T'ang tradition is the earlier of the two types.

Type: Cp 38. **Date: Southern Sung—Yüan.**
Shape: Funerary vase. **Design: Applied figures and animals.**

A special group of usually rather thick and coarse ch'ing-pai type porcelain is formed by large vases often found in pairs in tombs. These vases are mostly very

[1]) The development of the phoenix-headed ewers has been dealt with in an earlier article where the British Museum ewer has been compared with a similar ewer found on a Northern Sung album leaf in the MFEA (J. Wirgin, *The Phoenix motif on Sung ceramics.* Stockholm 1964).

[2]) *ACASA* Vol. XVII:1963, Fig. 24, p. 49.

elaborately decorated with applied figures of dragons, tigers and other animals as well as rows of standing human figures, clouds and sun ornaments etc. Vases of this type are most common and can be found in many collections; the MFEA has several of the type (Pl. 30:a, b) and many more are in different Swedish collections. These vases have before been considered mostly to be T'ang or Early Sung, but stilistic evidence as well as actually excavated objects have proved that the type was most popular during the late Sung dynasty. Several very important datable finds of vases of this kind have been made lately, especially in the Kiangsi province. It seems that the type was already in use during the Northern Sung dynasty, but the more elaborate types with very tall necks full of different applied figures and ornaments seem to belong to the late Southern Sung and the Yüan dynasty.[1])

A closer study of the designs of these vases and their symbolic significance would be most interesting but is outside the scope of this paper. It should, however, be pointed out that these vases are generally referred to as mortuary urns or ash urns; this term is most misleading as the vases apparently were not used for cremation burials. They were mostly found in pairs in ordinary burials and have apparently been containers for wine or other offerings for the dead.

Type: Cp 39. **Date: Southern Sung—Yüan.**
Shape: Granary.

Small models of granaries are a type of coarse ch'ing-pai objects which are quite common as tomb objects. Because of their rather crude appearance they have often been labelled T'ang[2]) or Five Dynasties but it is quite obvious that their roughness is only due to their being intended to be used as funeral objects, and it is not significant for their dating. Most objects of this type seem to belong to late Southern Sung or Yüan. There is one piece of this type in the MFEA and one in the Kempe collection (Pl. 35:a), the latter is almost identical to a piece excavated from a Southern Sung tomb in Kiangsi dated 1260.[3]) A similar granary but of slightly different proportions was unearthed from a Yüan tomb in the same province.[4])

Type: Cp 40. **Date: Southern Sung.**
Shape: Box. **Design: Floral spray.**

Small boxes with moulded floral designs on the cover are very common in ch'ing-pai and many different types are found; one of them is dealt with under Type 41 below. The type we are dealing with here is usually quite deeply moulded and shows the flower with fine and delicate details. A good example is a box in the MFEA

[1]) See: *Kao Ku* 1965:11, p. 571 and *Kao Ku* 1963:10, p. 576.

[2]) See: *CKc* No. 514.

[3]) *Kao Ku* 1965:11, p. 571. Pl. 9:8.

[4]) *Kao Ku* 1963:10, p. 576. Fig. 2.

(Pl. 31:a). It is of octagonal shape with ribbed sides and has a single spray of peony impressed on the lid. Inside the box is a small detachable dish. An almost identical box was excavated from a Sung tomb in Kiangsi, tentatively dated to the period 1131–1162.[1]) A closely akin box but without the inside dish is in the Kempe collection, this box has a mallow flower on the cover (Pl. 31:b). A round box with ribbed sides in the Boston Museum[2]) has a peony spray on the lid and inside are three small attached dishes. This type of box is quite common in Sung ceramics and is also found in Korea.[3])

A box in the Kempe collection with an olive coloured glaze, probably a misfired ch'ing-pai glaze, has a design of lotus flowers (Pl. 31:c).

Type: Cp 41. **Date: Southern Sung—Yüan.**
Shape: Various. **Design: Flowers in thread relief.**

Among the Sung—Yüan transition wares designs made in a kind of thin thread relief are very common. Some specimens of this type have very clear and distinct patterns others are extremely thin and sketchy. The latter type is particularly common on small boxes. Many different shapes are found in this group.

Boxes are very common; they are usually round with ribbed sides. The type with very sketchy thin thread relief is found on a box in the MFEA (Pl. 32:a) and on two boxes in the Kempe collection (Pl. 32:b). A third box, also in the same collection, has a more distinct design of a floral spray with two big flowers (Pl. 32:c). Octagonal boxes are also found. they are mostly impressed in a heavier type of relief as can be seen on a box with a chrysanthemum in the MFEA (Pl. 32:d) and a similar box with prunus in the Barlow collection.[4])

Vases with thread relief designs also are found, usually the pattern is combined with deeper moulded motifs and beaded borders, as can be seen on a vase in the MFEA (Pl. 33:a). Here the main band on the body shows prunus flowers between beaded borders, but above this design is a chrysanthemum in thread relief.

Ewers are also found, often hemi-spherical in shape and with straight flat bottom. A ewer of this kind in the Honolulu Academy of Arts (Pl. 33:b) is decorated with floral sprays in panels made of raised lines. Ewers of this type are common both among ch'ing-pai specimens and white glazed wares of the Sung—Yüan transition time.[5])

As design on bowls the thread relief patterns are usually found as small flowers or borders such as can be seen on a six-foil bowl in the MFEA,[6]) decorated in the centre with a small prunus flower.

[1]) *Wen Wu* 1964:4, p. 63.

[2]) *Hoyt cat.* No. 376.

[3]) See: *Barlow cat.* Pl. 113 a.

[4]) *Cat.* Pl. 117 b.

[5]) *To-so no hakuji.* Pl. 51, lower.

[6]) *MFEA Exh.cat. no. 3.* No. 19.

Type; Cp 42. **Date: Southern Sung—Yüan.**
Shape: Vase. **Design: Flowers on beaded ground**

This type is related to the preceding. The designs found mostly on vases consist of different types of geometric patterns, stiff petal designs and borders of flowers on a beaded ground. The quality of the ware is rough and non-translucent, the body is usually made in sections luted together. The most usual shape is a kind of bottle-form with more or less depressed belly and long neck with a very characteristic square-cut rim which is found on most pieces in this group. A vase of this type with main décor band of lotus flowers and leaf band on beaded ground surrounded by stiff borders with lotus petals is in the Barlow collection.[1]) A similar vase is in the Kempe collection (Pl. 34) but it has not got the two lion masks found on the neck of the Barlow vase. A second vase in the Barlow collection[2]) has a more depressed shape and is decorated with geometrical designs and on the shoulder a lotus border on beaded ground. Many specimens belonging to this group are found in different collections; they have earlier—because of their coarse appearance—been considered pre-Sung, but as has already been pointed out in an earlier paper, they are, on the contrary, from the end of the dynasty.[3])

Type: Cp 43. **Date: Southern Sung.**
Shape: Figurines, pillows etc.

Ceramic sculptures in ch'ing-pai are very rare, and they mostly belong to the Yüan dynasty. The most important specimens of this type are a group of buddhist figures, some of them dated, which have been presented by John Ayers in a recent lecture.[4]) A few other specimens with sculptural décor of possible late Sung origin will be presented here. In the Kempe collection (Pl. 36:b) is a stand in the shape of two ferocious-looking dragons biting over each other. The stand has been attributed to the T'ang dynasty,[5]) but a recently excavated specimen now in the Peking Palace Museum (Pl. 36:a) proves that it is much later. The piece, which is a pillow, has a base of exactly the same type as the Kempe stand, formed by two interlaced dragons. It was excavated from a Sung tomb in Hupeh. The Kempe stand is obviously a base for a similar pillow. Related to these two specimens is a small sculpture in Toronto (Pl. 36:c) published by Trubner and accurately dated to the end of Sung or the beginning of Yüan.[6]) This sculpture shows a crouching lion with open mouth with big teeth, big eyes and a thick mane. An interesting feature is the thick locks of the mane which have deeply cut holes; the same technique is used on the two pieces just mentioned. The eyes of the lion are indicated by dabs of brownish glaze, a technique which we have already seen on many specimens of Sung—Yüan time.

[1]) *Cat.* Pl. 106 b.
[2]) *Cat.* Pl. 105 b.
[3]) J. Wirgin, *Some ceramic wares from Chi-chou. BMFEA* 34:1962, p. 66.
[4]) At the Brundage symposium in San Francisco 1966.
[5]) *CKc* No. 516. [6]) *ACASA* Vol. XVII, 1963, p. 38.

A pillow in the Boston Museum (Pl. 36:d) of oval shape is supported by a lion of somewhat similar type with a very heavy head with broad jaws. A very similar pillow was excavated from a Sung tomb near *Wu-han* in Hupeh, together with the above-mentioned dragon pillow and a third one with striated sides. No information is given about the tomb.[1])

Small toys of different types are quite common in ch'ing-pai. In the Kempe collection is a sheep with brownglazed eyes and also a miniature flower pot.[2]) In the Locsin collection[3]) is a seated figure with a lotus flower.

Apart from the different types of ch'ing-pai wares we have discussed above there are several other groups from late Sung and Yüan, but as their designs are not very significant of the Sung dynasty but have more in common with the later underglaze blue ware and other wares of Yüan and early Ming, they will not be discussed in detail here.

Among the most important of these types are three main groups all of which have been found in great quantities in the Philippines, Indonesia, Malaysia and other places in South-East Asia. The first group, which has been discussed in a paper by J. M. Addis,[4]) consists of a large amount of ewers, vases, jars, bowls etc. of many different and new shapes, related specimens have already been dealt with above. As an example of the group we show a small ewer in the Kempe collection (Pl. 35:b).

The second group is the spotted ch'ing-pai ware which has been unearthed in great quantities in the Philippines,[5]) but which must be considered a ware very significant of the Yüan dynasty. Almost all specimens with this kind of spotted design are of clear Yüan shapes.

The third group consists of a ch'ing-pai-like ware, which can have both a bluish and a white glaze, and is characterized by its chalky white body. The ware has mostly been produced in the Fukien province, as recent excavations have proved. Among the most interesting specimens of this type are those with a spiral scroll decoration similar to *guru*-lacquer.[6]) Carved petal designs of different types are also very popular in this group.[7])

The ceramic export must have had a great boom at the end of Sung and during the Yüan dynasty because the vast majority of ceramic objects found on sites in S. E. Asia seem to belong to this period, and the ch'ing-pai ware is no exception.

[1]) *Wen Wu* 1956:7, p. 19. The dragon pillow was also first published in this report and later in *Kao Ku* 1959:11, Pl. 6:6, and in the catalogue of the porcelain in the Peking Palace Museum (No. 35).

[2]) *CKc* Nos. 562 and 560.

[3]) *Op.cit.* Pl. 73.

[4]) *Op.cit.*

[5]) Locsin, *op.cit.* p. 94.

[6]) A typical circular box with domed cover with this design is in the Kempe collection (*CKc.* no. 567).

[7]) This group is discussed by Cecilia Y. Locsin in, *A group of white wares from Te-hua* (Manilla Trade Pottery Seminar, Introductory notes).

It is also obvious that the export trade favoured certain types of vessels and certain wares, but completely neglected others. The ch'ing-pai wares found in S. E. Asia are mostly of the three groups listed above and of the kinds we have described in our types Cp 40–42. Especially common are small jars and the boxes with ribbed sides and floral designs, an almost incredible amount of wares of this kind have been excavated from different sites outside China.

LIST OF DESIGNS FOUND ON THE CH'ING-PAI WARE

Special floral motifs		
Conventionalized flower	Incised	Type Cp 1 A–C
Bud-tendril	Incised	Type Cp 2
Carved floral scroll	Incised	Type Cp 18
Composite floral scroll	Incised	Type Cp 20
Peony		
Peony spray	Incised	Type Cp 16
Peony flower	Incised	Type Cp 17
Boys among peonies	Incised	Type Cp 14–15
Floral spray	Moulded	Type Cp 40
Panels with flowers	Moulded	Type Cp 29
Composite flower scroll	Moulded	Type Cp 30
Lotus		
Sketchy lotus	Incised	Type Cp 10
Waves and lotus	Incised	Type Cp 4
Composite floral scroll	Incised	Type Cp 20
Pair of lotus	Moulded	Type Cp 27
Potted plants	Moulded	Type Cp 28
Panels with flower	Moulded	Type Cp 29
Composite floral scroll	Moulded	Type Cp 30
Floral design on beaded ground	Moulded	Type Cp 42
Chrysanthemum		
Composite floral scroll	Moulded	Type Cp 30
Panels with flower	Moulded	Type Cp 29
Flowers in thread relief	Moulded	Type Cp 41
Mallow		
Floral spray	Moulded	Type Cp 40
Thread relief	Moulded	Type Cp 41

Potted plants	Moulded	Type Cp 28
Panels with flowers	Moulded	Type Cp 29

Prunus

Thread relief	Moulded	Type Cp 41
Scroll-handle	Moulded	Type Cp 31
Composite flower scroll	Moulded	Type Cp 30

Petals

Revolving lotus petals	Incised	Type Cp 8
Skewed lotus panels	Incised	Type Cp 9
Carved petals	Incised	Type Cp 21–23

Boys among flower scrolls

With peonies	Incised	Type Cp 14–15, 17
With composite scroll	Incised	Type Cp 20
With floral scroll	Moulded	Type Cp 26

Human representations

Are very scarce on ch'ing-pai and only found in applied relief on funerary vases of the kind discussed under Type Cp 38 and as small figures used as toys etc., Type Cp 43. During the Yüan dynasty some fine buddhistic sculptures were made in this ware.

Dragon

Ch'ih dragons among waves	Incised	Type Cp 7
Ch'ih dragons	Incised	Type Cp 11
Dragon handles and spouts etc.	Moulded	Type Cp 32–33
Applied figures	Moulded	Type Cp 38
Figurines	Moulded	Type Cp 43

(A ch'ing-pai pillow in the V & A has a large dragon head on the front.)

Phoenix

Phoenixes and composite floral scroll	Moulded	Type Cp 24, 30
Pair of phoenixes	Moulded	Type Cp 25, 26, 27
Phoenix-head	Moulded	Type Cp 36
Applied figures	Moulded	Type Cp 38

Lion

Lions are only found as small sculptures and as supports for pillows. Type Cp 43.

Birds

Birds are, except for the phoenixes, very rare as design on ch'ing-pai; on the incised type they are mostly extremely sketchy and dissolved. In the moulded type the birds are still more rare, but occasionally a duck or goose can be seen as central motif on bowls (Type Cp 28).

Sketchy birds	Incised	Type Cp 12–13

Fishes

Fishes among waves	Incised	Type Cp 5–6
	Moulded	Type Cp 26

Waves

As sole motif	Incised	Type Cp 3
With other motifs	Incised	Type Cp 4–7

Cash

The *cash* design is rare and found only on pieces of very late Sung or Yüan date, a border of this type is found on the ewer Pl. 35:b. A pillow in V & A has on the top children on a *cash*-patterned ground.

Inscriptions

Are very rare on Sung ch'ing-pai specimens but are sometimes found on small boxes. Usually only names are inscribed, a box in the Kempe coll. (CKc 552) has the inscription "*Ts'ai chia ho tzu* [33]". (Box belonging to the Ts'ai family.)

LUNG-CH'ÜAN YAO

The *Lung-ch'üan yao*, which in the West is usually known under the name *celadon* ware, is one of the largest families of Chinese ceramics and was produced and exported in almost incredible amounts during the Sung, Yüan and Ming dynasties. The ware is so well-known and thoroughly described by so many scholars that no closer description of it or account of its history is necessary in this context.[1])

In spite of the large amount of kilns in the *Lung-ch'üan hsien*, many of them having been well-known for a long time past and some newly discovered, very few have been scientifically excavated. Only two reports have been published in recent Chinese archaeological publications.[2]) Several other kilns in Chekiang, some of them producing the same type of wares as the Lung-ch'üan kilns, have, however,

[1]) See for instance: *Gompertz*, G.St.G.M., *Chinese Celadon Wares*, London 1958.

[2]) *Kao Ku* 1962 no. 10 and *Wen Wu* 1963:1. The latter report, which is the most important one, has been published as an abstract in the OCS translation series (*Chinese Translations*, No. 2).

been published in the archaeological journals mentioned. But unfortunately the illustrations accompanying the articles are mostly so poor in quality that very little use could be made of them. Excellent illustrations of many of the characteristic types of Chekiang wares are, however, published in Nils Palmgren's "*Sung sherds*",[1]) and this publication gives an interesting picture of both the varied production of the single kilns and the great similarities found between wares of different kilns. Palmgren's sherd material was unfortunately not dug out under a controlled excavation; it was, on the contrary, a rapid collection of sherds and wasters carried out within a very limited time. Accordingly, the material does not give us any definite clues as to the dating of different types. All datings must be tentative, and they are only based on the author's personal opinions.

The typical Lung-ch'üan celadon ware of the Sung dynasty is rather uninteresting if we consider the designs only. There is a very limited number of designs, and it is quite obvious that the most important development of Lung-ch'üan patterns does not fall within the Sung dynasty at all but starts in the Yüan dynasty. This is not only true regarding the applied décor left in biscuit, the high relief designs of peony scrolls, and the well-known spotted celadon, but also regarding many other types of designs both moulded and incised. The most typical Sung patterns found seem to be the carved lotus petals so frequently found on the outside of bowls and the relief designs of fishes and, of course, the large group of vases and jars with applied ornaments.

Even if the characteristic Lung-ch'üan yao is mostly devoid of decoration there is a group of early Sung celadons from Chekiang which are more richly decorated and form a link between the Yüeh yao, the Northern celadon, and the later development of the celadon wares. This group has sometimes been called *Li-shui* ware, as some Chinese sources state that the ware was not made in Lung-ch'üan hsien itself but in the neighbouring *Li-shui hsien* [34]. The excavations hitherto carried out in the Li-shui area have also brought to light objects of this particular ware, but the majority of objects of this ware, so far found, have been discovered just in the Lung-ch'üan district. It would accordingly be more correct to call this group '*Early Chekiang celadon*' which is the name we have given it in the following survey of some of the designs found on Lung-ch'üan wares.

The ware in question has much in common both with Yüeh yao and Northern celadon, and it has frequently been confused with one or the other of those wares. The characteristics of this group has been pointed out by Sir Herbert Ingram,[2]) John Ayers[3]) and Gompertz.[4])

The potting of specimens in this group is heavy and there is a preference for certain jar shapes (Pl. 37:a–e). The glaze colour is widely varying between olive

---

1) N. Palmgren, *Sung sherds*. Stockholm 1963.

2) In *Ethnos* 1946:4, p. 162.

3) In the *Seligman cat.* p. 79.

4) *Op.cit.* p. 23.

and pale green but the predominant colour has a yellowish cast. A characteristic feature of the ware is also that the glaze has been wiped or roughly scraped from the base before the firing took place. The designs found on this group are mostly incised with much use of combed details and also of hatching. The variety of patterns is not very large and they mostly look primitive in comparison with the Northern celadon and the later Yüeh ware. As we have already pointed out there is also a preference for only a small number of shapes. It would accordingly be a clearer arrangement to group this ware according to shape and not according to design. It should be remarked already here that there are still many unsolved problems concerning this group, and it is difficult to be certain of the attribution of some specimens mentioned.

In the above-mentioned excavation report (*Wen Wu* 1963:1) is published an early group of celadons which seems to be identical with the above-described type. The group consists of bowls, basins, jars, ewers and "five-tube jars" with designs that are combed and incised. Among the decorative motifs mentioned are ripples, boys among flowers, chrysanthemums and leaf scrolls. Ten kilns of this type were discovered, the majority of them in Lung-ch'üan hsien and a few in Li-shui hsien. The group is dated by the excavator to the Five Dynasties period (it should be noted that this period continued into the Sung dynasty and came to an end first in 978), and it is noted that the Lung-ch'üan ware was apparently a successor to the Yüeh yao and further developed that ware. The author of the report, Chu Po-ch'ien, also cites the *Chi le p'ien* [35] by the Sung writer Chuang Chi-yü, which states that Lung-ch'üan hsien "also made a celadon, called *pi se* [36], the ware which the princes of the *Wu-Yüeh* sent as tribute to the Court". The cited passage indicates that not only the *Shang-lin hu* kiln made the famous *pi-se* (secret colour) ware but also other kilns in Chekiang. As the amount of porcelain sent by the princes of Wu-Yüeh as tribute to the Sung Court was extremely large in quantity, it seems quite reasonable to assume that other kilns also took part in the production of the ceramic.

The later material found in the excavation is divided in the report into four groups, North Sung, South Sung, Yüan and Ming. In our discussion we will only consider the first two groups. Characteristic of the Northern Sung group is the appearance of many new shapes like vases, incense-burners, saucers, boxes etc., and much more variation in already existing types. The designs found are conspicuously less, among patterns mentioned are cloud scrolls, banana leaves, fish and lotus plants.

The South Sung group shows a considerable increase in the manufacture which was a quite natural consequence of the moving of the capital to the south and the loss of all the prominent kilns in the north. Many new forms are found among which can be mentioned incense-burners of *li*-shape, peach-shaped brush-washers, brush-rests, lamps etc. Many impressed designs and relief designs occur. A few typical groups of decorated Lung-ch'üan wares of North and South Sung will be presented in our second main group below which has simply been called "*Lung-ch'üan celadon*".

Early Chekiang celadon

Type: Lc 1.
Shape: Jars with attached tubes on the shoulder.

Date: Five Dynasties—Early Northern Sung.

This particular jar type is the most characteristic of the group. There are several different variations found. On one of the most common types the belly is built up of what looks like a series of fat rolls, and on the shoulder are five attached tubular holders. The cover is usually domed and provided with a large knob. A jar of this shape is in the Seligman collection (Pl. 37:a). The décor shows bands of overlapping combed petals, oblique line incisions and *ju-i* shaped panels on a hatched ground. The use of the attached tubes has been much discussed, and they have often been labelled flower holders. But as has been pointed out by Ayers[1]) and others their significance is still obscure.[2]) On an especially elaborate specimen in the British Museum (Pl. 37:c) the tubes are replaced by solid posts terminating in monster heads below and with small animal figures on the shoulder between them. On a piece in the Hollis collection[3]) and a similar one in the Oxford Museum of Eastern Art,[4]) the tubes have turned into flat leaf-shaped appliques. A jar in the Honolulu Academy of Arts has turned into a kind of shrine (Pl. 37:d). It has an unusually large cover with a hollow niche containing a kneeling figure in full round. On the shoulder are applied plaques with impressed décor of seated Buddha-like figures. The vase has apparently had some religious function in this case. The designs found on the jars mentioned include overlapping petals with combed details, oblique line-incisions and, in some cases, sketchy lotus leaves.

A jar excavated at Lung-ch'üan (Pl. 37:b) is of a simpler and more common type than those just mentioned. The belly is decorated with a sketchy peony scroll and there is a row of overlapping petals round the base. The shoulder part has two rows of fat rolls and five attached tubular holders. On neck and cover are incised oblique lines. The cover is shaped like a coolie-hat and has a reclining animal

---

1) *Seligman cat.* p. 79.

2) It is, however, quite clear that jars of this type, like those found in later Lung-ch'üan celadon with animals around the neck, were intended for wine. A jar in the Warren E. Cox collection (Cox, W. E., *The book of Pottery and Porcelain.* Vol. I, New York 1945, Pl. 41) of the five-tube type has the inscription "Chu the 18th thousand-year wine store made", and a vase in the David Foundation dated 1080, which has usually been attributed to the Yüeh kiln has the following inscription: "On the 15th day of the intercalary 9th month of the 3rd year of the Yüan Feng period (1080), I have baked this first class urn in the hope that it may hold fragrant wine for thousands and myriads of years; that after a hundred years, it may be handed down to my descendants; that I may have thousand sons and ten thousand grandsons; that they may have wealth and occupy high positions in the government continually; that they may live long and enjoy good fortune and unlimited happiness; and that the world may be at peace".

3) *Los Angeles exh. cat.* No. 106.

4) M. Tregear, *Early Chinese green wares. OA* Vol. XIII:1, 1967. No. 33.

on top. The animal placed on the cover is a feature very characteristic of the Chekiang kilns which is met with frequently in this ware and becomes extremely common in later Lung-ch'üan wares. The excavation report of the Lung-ch'üan kiln illustrates one more vase of the five-tube type which is rather simple and with very little decoration. It has a pie-crust-like band on the shoulder, and the five tubular holders are slightly bent and have irregular mouths—they look like cut-off floral stems. The cover is also of a type different from that of the other vase; its lower part is in the shape of a cup turned up-side-down and the upper part looks like a flower corona.

Type: Lc 2. **Date: Early Northern Sung.**
Shape: Ovoid vase with cup-shaped mouth.

Another type of vase also extremely common in this ware has an ovoid body, spreading cylindrical neck and cup-shaped mouth. The vases very often lack cover but were no doubt originally provided with domed covers of a type similar to those found in the preceding group. A vase in the Seligman collection[1]) of this type is decorated round the belly with a sketchy peony leaf design and overlapping petals on base and neck, all with combed details. A very common design on wares of this kind is large peony leaves hanging down on the body in six vertical panels. This design is found on a vase in the Seligman coll.,[2]) one in the Buffalo Museum[3]) and one in the Glasgow City Art Gallery (Pl. 37:e). On a similar vase with cover in the Tokyo National Museum[4]) the whole body is covered with overlapping petals. In the Clark collection (Pl. 37:f) is a beautiful vase of this shape with a finely carved peony scroll pattern on a hatched ground. There is a row of overlapping petals below the main design, and the lid is of the characteristic type with a high knob.

Type: Lc 3. **Date: Early Northern Sung.**
Shape: Mei-p'ing.

A more unusual shape in this group is the so-called *mei-p'ing* vase, a beautiful example of this form is in the Oxford Museum of Eastern Art (Pl. 37:g). It is decorated on the belly with sketchy lotus scrolls with combed details and on the shoulder part leaves on a hatched ground. Round the base is an overlapping petals

---

1) *Cat.* No. D 157.

2) *Cat.* No. D 158.

3) Hochstadter *op.cit.* No. 57.

4) *Old Oriental Ceramics donated by Mr. Yokogawa.* Tokyo National Museum, 1953. No. 102 (*Yokogawa cat.*).

design of the type generally found in this ware.[1]) A similar specimen in the ROM in Toronto has an elegant peony scroll, very similar to the one found on the Clark vase (Pl. 37:h), on the belly, enclosed by petal borders.

Type: Lc 4. **Date: Five Dynasties—Early Northern Sung.**
Shape: Ewer with applied leaf.

A rare type also belonging to this ware is a small group of ewers of very characteristic form. They are of squat shape with wide neck and slightly spreading mouth and have an applied leaf on each side of the shoulder. There is one ewer of this type in the Seligman collection (Pl. 37:j) with a carved design of sketchy peony scrolls round the belly and a band of lotus petals round the base, on the shoulder is a sketchy leaf design, in each case with combed details. On the shoulder are two small flat applied leaves. An almost identical ewer has been excavated at Lung-ch'üan hsien from the layer dated Five Dynasties (Fig. 43:a:5). A ewer in the Barlow collection (Pl. 37:l) is of a somewhat different shape with a more squat body and wide cylindrical neck with spreading mouth. It has the applied leaves on the shoulder and on the body a sketchy peony design. A ewer in the Honolulu Academy of Arts of more cylindrical shape also has the applied leaves on the shoulder and on the body are two rows of broad petals with combed details (Pl. 37:k). This ewer is of the more typical Lung-ch'üan ware with a pale green glaze, but its shape indicates a Northern Sung date and a close relationship with the earlier mentioned ewers.

Type: Lc 5. **Date: Northern Sung.**
Shape: Jar & cover.

An unusual specimen which probably belongs to this group is a small jar and cover in the Seligman collection (Pl. 37:i). It is of oviform shape with brief, wide neck and has a flat cover with a folded tendril knob.[2]) The belly is decorated with a sketchy design of flowers of the type we have met with before under the term "conventionalized flower" and which is most common both on Northern celadon and ch'ing-pai wares. Judging from the way the design is treated here it is very close to those found on ch'ing-pai.

The designs found on the small group of Chekiang celadon wares described above are not very rich or varied but they form an interesting link between the Yüeh

[1]) A very similar vase reported to have been found in the Visayan Islands, is now in the Museum of the University of the Philippines, Manila. (Sullivan, M., *Notes on Chinese export wares in Southeast Asia. TOCS* 1960–62. Pl. 53:a).

[2]) The shape is rather unusual but is found in a pair of small covered jars in the Barlow collection (*Cat.* Pl. 90 c) with knobs in the shape of standing elephants.

yao and Northern celadon wares on the one hand and the ch'ing-pai on the other. It is also important to notice that the designs popular during the Northern Sung period does not seem to be so provincial as usually assumed before but, on the contrary, they were apparently wide-spread.

The following types of designs are the most common on this Early Chekiang celadon group:

Incised

Peony scroll
Sketchy peony scroll
Peony leaf border
Hanging peony leaves
Carved overlapping petals
Oblique and crossed lines

Applied

Leaf on shoulder
Leaf and figure plaques
Monster masks
Animals

Among the designs found on this ware the excavation report also mentions "boys among flowers" but no illustration of this type of design is given. Among the material collected by Palmgren in *Ta-yao* [37] is a sherd from a bowl with a sketchy leaf scroll on the side and a floral rosette in the centre (Fig. 43:b) which seems to be of the same type as some of the specimens dated Five Dynasties by the Chinese excavators.

Lung-ch'üan celadon

Type: Lc 6. **Date: Northern Sung.**
Shape: Bowl. **Design: Incised lotus.**

Incised designs are rather scarce among Lung-ch'üan wares datable within the Sung dynasty but a few types are found. Among them is a sketchy lotus design which can be seen on the interior of a bowl in the Kempe collection (Pl. 38:a). The design which is incised in a sketchy but vigorous way shows lotus flowers and leaves with partly combed details. Several bowls of this type were excavated from the Northern Sung layers at *Chin Ts'un* [38] in Lung-ch'üan hsien. A similar design is found on a bowl of conical shape in the Boston Museum.[1]) This type of carved lotus designs continued into the Yüan dynasty which can be exemplified by a dish of typical Yüan shape, with horizontal brim, in the Kempe collection.[2])

[1]) *Hoyt cat.* No. 219.
[2]) *CKc* No. 146.

The difference between the Sung and Yüan designs of this type seems to be that the latter no longer have the combed details and that the design is usually more rich and provided with borders of different types. The Sung version is much more simple and in some cases the flower is merely indicated with a few swift strokes. The similarities with the ch'ing-pai group are obvious.

Type: Lc 7. **Date: Northern Sung—Southern Sung.**
Shape: Box and dish. **Design: Incised fish.**

Incised fish designs are as scarce as those with applied fish designs are common on Lung-ch'üan ware. Among the objects excavated from the Northern Sung layers in Chin Ts'un was, however, a dish with an inside design of a single fish with forked tail. A very similar design with a pair of fishes with the same kind of forked tails is found on a box with flat cover in the Seligman collection (Pl. 39:a). This box has been attributed to the so-called Li-shui group, and its general characteristics are the same as those found in the previously described Early Chekiang celadon group.

A design somewhat related to those just described but of a later date is found on a dish in the Bristol City Art Gallery (Pl. 39:b). It is a dish with horizontal, flattened rim which in the centre has a finely incised pike-like fish surrounded by combed waves, the forked tail is of the same kind as on the earlier mentioned specimens.

Type: Lc 8. **Date: Northern Sung.**
Shape: Bowl with six-foil rim. **Design: Tortoise in relief.**

Bowls with rounded sides and six-foil crinkled lip with a small tortoise inside in the centre is a type which we have already met with in the Yao-chou ware (Type Nc 11) and bowls of this kind were also made in Chekiang. An example of a bowl of this type with a bluish-green glaze is in the Kempe collection.[1])

Type: Lc 9. **Date: Southern Sung—Yüan.**
Shape: Bowl & dish. **Design: Carved lotus petals.**

Carved lotus petals on the outside of bowls and dishes is a design extremely common in the Lung-ch'üan ware. It seems to have been most popular during the Southern Sung period but continued during Yüan and Early Ming. There are four main types during Sung. The first is an open, deep bowl with rounded sides on a small, low foot (Fig. 42:c:2), good examples are in the Kempe coll. and the Seligman coll.[2]) The second type is a deep bowl on small foot with sometimes bulging, sometimes almost straight sides, examples are also in the two just mentioned

[1]) *CKc* No. 113.

[2]) *CKc* No. 120; *Seligman cat.* No. D 169 and D 177.

collections.[1]) This type is sometimes also provided with a round cover with flattened edge, also carved with petals as can be seen on a bowl in the British Museum.[2]) The third type is a shallow dish, with the outside decorated with the same type of carved lotus petals (Fig. 42:c:6); a fine example is in the Bristol City Art Gallery,[3]) and others are in the Kempe coll.[4]) The fourth type is a bowl of depressed semi-spherical shape with a contracted rim (Fig. 43:a:7). Several other variants such as bowls with slightly everted lip (Fig. 42:c:4) and with horizontal rim are found and the carved petal design seems to have been in constant use in the Lung-ch'üan kilns. Sherds with this type of design were found in many different kilns excavated by Palmgren.

Type: Lc 10.
Shape: Conical bowl.
Date: Southern Sung.
Design: Incised plum twig.

This design is found on small conical bowls of a type frequently used during the end of the Sung dynasty. One bowl of this type is in the Eugene Bernat collection (Pl. 38:b); it has on the inside a design of a prunus twig and a crescent moon incised in a free and elegant style. A similar bowl is in the Rijksmuseum, Amsterdam (Pl. 39:c); the only difference in the design is that a border with sketchy scrolls has been added. Again the freshness and simplicity of this type seems to be more typical of the South Sung than the Yüan style.

Type: Lc 11.
Shape: Box.
Date: Southern Sung.
Design: Incised peony.

Incised peony designs are sometimes found on Lung-ch'üan yao especially on round boxes. One box of this kind was formerly in the Eumorfopoulos coll. (Pl. 39:d), the design which is deeply incised shows a large spray of peony. Inside the box are three small attached dishes of the type we have already seen among ch'ing-pai. Another flat box with a finely incised flower on the cover was formerly in the Oppenheim collection.[5])

Type: Lc 12.
Shape: Bowl.
Date: Southern Sung—Yüan.
Design: Stamped.

Deeply stamped designs of leaves, inscriptions and other types of ornaments covered with glaze are sometimes found on celadon wares, the majority of them

[1]) *CKc* No. 121, 122; *Seligman cat.* No. D 173.

[2]) Gray *op.cit.* Pl. 89.

[3]) Gompertz *op.cit.* Pl. 74 b.

[4]) *CKc* No. 127, 128.

[5]) Hobson, *Private*, Fig. 111.

belonging to Yüan and Ming times. An interesting example of this kind, probably of late Sung origin is found on a shallow bowl in the Kempe collection (Pl 39:e). The design shows a boy with a lotus spray in his hand. Fragments of a similar piece were found by Palmgren at Ta-yao.[1])

Type: Lc 13. **Date: Southern Sung—Yüan.**
Shape: Various. **Design: Thread relief.**

Designs made in thread relief, of the same type as we have seen in the ch'ing-pai group, are also found in Lung-ch'üan yao. They seem mostly to belong to the Yüan dynasty and very late Sung. A box in the Kempe collection (Pl. 39:f) has on its lid a peony flower in this technique. The box is round with a slightly convex cover and is of a type still very much in the Sung tradition. A similar box in Toronto has a stiff lotus spray with two flowers in a style that is more characteristic of Yüan.[2]) A small baluster-shaped vase in the Barlow coll. (Pl. 39:g) is also of clear Yüan shape, it has stiff lotus petals around the base and a thread relief design of lotus flowers and chrysanthemums on the shoulder, its similarities with some ch'ing-pai types are obvious. The most common type of objects with this kind of design are, however, a group of small jars of depressed globular shape which seem to have been one of the main export wares to Southeast Asia during this period. Enormous quantities of similar jars have been found during recent excavations, especially in the Philippines.[3]) Jars of this type have also been excavated from the Yüan layers of the Lung-ch'üan kilns (Fig. 30:b:4).[4])

Type: Lc 14. **Date: Southern Sung—Yüan.**
Shape: Dish. **Design: Pair of fishes.**

One of the most popular of the standard designs of the Lung-ch'üan kilns seems to have been that which shows two small fishes in relief. It is usually found on shallow bowls or dishes, often with a horizontal rim, and it must have been produced in enormous quantities at many different kilns (Pl. 39:h, i). Dishes of this type are found in most collections[5]) and recent excavations both in China and in S.E. Asia have brought to light large quantities of dishes with this particular design.[6]) There

[1]) Palmgren *op.cit.* Fig. 28, No. 27.

[2]) Sherman E. Lee, *Chinese Art under the Mongols.* No. 65.

[3]) Locsin, *op.cit.* Pl. 59.

[4]) *Kao Ku* 1962:10, Fig. 4:4.

[5]) *CKc* No. 125, 126; *Barlow cat.* Pl. 84 b; *OCS Sung exh.* Nos. 175, 176.

[6]) Locsin, *op.cit.* Pls. 53, 93 and 96. Some dishes of this type found in tombs in the Philippines have been associated with Northern Sung coins. This is, however, not significant as we know that older coins are extremely common in tombs, one of the most common coins found in Sung tombs is *K'ai Yüan* of T'ang, which shows that old coins were especially treasured. One of the dishes in Locsin (Pl. 96) which was found with a coin from the *Ch'ung-ning* period (1102–1106) is of a type with a carved leaf-scroll in the cavetto, which is typical of the Yüan dynasty.

seems to be very little difference between those made in South Sung and those made in Yüan but we can be sure that they must have been produced during a lengthy period from approximately the 12th to the 14th century. Excavations at Lung-ch'üan have shown that they were definitely made already during Sung, even if many of them may be dated later.[1]) The technique of leaving the fishes unglazed so that after the firing they appear in red biscuit against the green celadon glaze, is a method which was apparently discovered during the Yüan period when a great variety of designs were treated in the same way.[2]) The fish design, however, also appears on blue-and-white dishes of a kind which is not particularly early in type, which shows that this type of design must have been popular, at least into the middle of the Ming dynasty.[3]) A dating of the fish design on a stylistic basis is not possible; only a detailed examination of the ceramic ware can give a clue to which pieces are Sung and which are later.

Type: Lc 15. **Date: Southern Sung.**
Shape: Vase with animal handles.

Handles in animal shape are a very common feature in Lung-ch'üan yao and are mostly found on vases of a so-called mallet-shape, or *kinuta* type. There are two main types of handles. The first is made of two fishes, looking like dolphins, which are graciously bent in an S-curve. Examples of vases of this type are in the Kempe coll.,[4]) the Iwasaki coll. (Pl. 39:j), The Freer Gallery[5]) and of course in the Palace collection. A more unusual specimen with this kind of handles is a vase in a Japanese collection in the shape of a *Ku* bronze beaker (Pl. 39:k).

The second type has handles in the shape of highly stylized phoenix birds. Examples of this type are found in the Fitzwilliam Museum,[6]) the Goto Art Museum and in a Japanese temple (Pl. 39:l). Vases with this kind of handles have also been excavated in Lung-ch'üan (Fig. 30:c:16).[7])

Type: Lc 16. **Date: Southern Sung.**
Shape: Covered jar with applied animals.

This type of wine-jars or covered vases is strongly related to the types Lc 1–2 described above, and they may be regarded as a Southern Sung development of

[1]) *Kao Ku* 1962:10, Fig. 3:7.

[2]) See: *Chinese Art under the Mongols*, nos. 74–83. The earlier mentioned design of a prunus twig and crescent moon is also found in this group and is represented by a dish in the David Foundation (*Op.cit.* Pl. 79); a similar dish was also formerly in the Eumorfopoulos coll. (*GEc* Vol. II, B 137).

[3]) Cp. Locsin, *op.cit.* Pl. 88.

[4]) *CKc* Nos. 98, 99.

[5]) Mayuyama, J., *Chinese ceramics in the West.* Pl. 56.

[6]) Gray, *op.cit.*, Pl. 90.

[7]) *Kao Ku* 1962:10, p. 537, Fig. 3:16.

the same type. Many vases in this group still have the characteristic fat rolls on the shoulder part. The most outstanding feature of those vases is the often very realistically rendered animals found around the neck and on the lid. Many different types are found, more or less elaborate.

A rather simple example of the type is a vase in the Clark coll. (Pl.-40:a) of barrel-shape with plain body. Around the neck is a coiled dragon of *ch'ih* type of strange appearance; it is extremely thin and bony and lacks horns, and looks more like an undernourished dog. On top of the cover is a realistically rendered seated dog. Of similar shape is a jar in the Brundage collection, but here the lower part of the body has an incised row of lotus petals (Pl. 40:b). Around the neck is a horned dragon of the usual *lung* type, and on the cover a reclining dog. There are two vases of this type in the Barlow collection, they are both of barrel-shape with raised rolls on the shoulder and have *lung* dragons chasing the pearl in relief around the neck. One of them has a bird (Pl. 40:c) on the cover the other one a crouching dog.[1]) A jar in the Tokyo National Museum has carved lotus petals around the lower part of the belly and raised rolls on the upper part (Pl. 40:d). Around the neck is a ferocious-looking *lung* dragon with wide-open mouth chasing the pearl. On the cover is a cock. Several similar pieces are known.

A very strange kind of animal is found on a jar in a Japanese collection (Pl. 40:e). It has a spotted body, four-clawed paws, large quills on the back and a very strange snout that looks like a duck's bill. A similar animal is found on a jar in the Kempe collection (Pl. 40:f) but here the paws look more like those of a dog and the face is also quite different. It seems that in the shaping of those animals the artists of Lung-ch'üan made use of a very creative imagination. It is quite obvious that those jars with their elaborate designs were intended as grave gifts, and they undoubtedly belong to the same type as those found in the above-mentioned early Chekiang group and the funerary vases of ch'ing-pai ware. Funerary vases of exactly the same type as those found in ch'ing-pai ware were also made at Lung-ch'üan during the Yüan dynasty.[2])

LIST OF DESIGNS FOUND ON THE LUNG-CH'ÜAN CELADON

Peony	Type Lc 11, 13
Lotus	Type Lc 6, 12, 13
Chrysanthemum	Type Lc 13
Prunus	Type Lc 10 (See also Type Lc 14 note 2, for this design found in biscuit)

[1]) *Cat.* Pl. 87.

[2]) *Chinese Art under the Mongols*, No. 66.

Petals Type Lc 9
Boys among flowers Type Lc 12

Dragon Type Lc 16
In Sung time the dragon only seems to occur in applied functions on Lung-ch'üan yao. The dragon seated on its hind legs (Fig. 12:a), so typical of celadon ware does not occur until Yüan, when we find it also in biscuit; in the same technique we also find the characteristic *ch'ih* dragon.

Phoenix Type Lc 15
The phoenix is mostly found used as handles on vases and very seldom occurs as a separate design before Yüan when it becomes quite popular and can also be seen in biscuit.

Birds
are found in Type Lc 16 with dogs and other animals on the cover of vases.

Tortoise Type Lc 8

Fish Type Lc 7, 14, 15

Cloud scrolls
are among the designs mentioned from the Lung-ch'üan excavation report and examples of this type are illustrated (Fig. 43:a:6). The design is dated Northern Sung.

Inscriptions
Among the material excavated from the Northern Sung layers at Lung-ch'üan are bowls with inscriptions of auspicious sayings as "*chin yü man t'ang*" [39]. And also one sherd with an impressed inscription giving the name of a kiln, "*Yung ch'ing yao chi*" [41]; and one with the inscription "*ho pin i fan*" [40].

TZ'U-CHOU YAO

Tz'u-chou yao is a term used in a generic sense applying to a widely distributed group of similar stonewares produced in North China. The Tz'u-chou district, which has given its name to this group, is situated in the southwest part of Hopei near the border of Honan. The main production centres of Tz'u-chou type wares seem to have been in Honan and Hopei, though similar wares were also made in Shansi and Shensi. Several kiln sites that produced wares of this kind have been known for a long time, but the extensive excavations which have been carried out in China during the last twenty years have given us a much more varied picture of the production of stoneware of Tz'u-chou type.

In Hopei new kiln sites have been excavated at *Kuan-t'ai chen* [42], *Tung-ai-k'ou ts'un* [43] and *Yeh-tzu ts'un* [44] all in *Han-tan shih* [45].[1])

A number of kiln sites have been investigated in Honan. The kilns in *Hsiu-wu hsien* [46] (the wares of which are known under the names *Tang-yang yü* [47] and *Chiao-tso*) [48] have been well known for a long time,[2]) but important new sites have been excavated in *Teng-feng hsien* [49] (*Ch'ü-ho*) [50] and *Mi hsien* [51] (*Yao-kou*) [52].[3]) Other important sites have been revealed in *T'ang yin hsien* [53] (*Hao-pi chi*) [54][4]) and in *Yü hsien* [55],[5]) where the main kiln was discovered in *P'a-ts'un* [56].[6])

In Shensi wares of Tz'u-chou type were also produced at *Huang-pao chen* in *T'ung-ch'uan shih*[7]) at the kiln site, the main production of which was the Yao-chou celadon ware.

In Shansi kilns of this type were found in *T'ai-yüan shih* [58] (*Meng-chia ching*) [59] and *Chieh-hsiu hsien* [60] (*Hung-shan chen*) [61], but they have so far been very poorly published.[8])

Several minor kilns have been found in other provinces, for example Shantung, Kiangsu, Kuangtung, Ssuch'uan and Anhui, but there seems to be little doubt that the main production centre of this ware was in the Hopei–Honan area.

Several kilns seem to have had a very long time of active production, some from T'ang right down to Ming, but other kilns seem to have had their most prosperous years during the Northern Sung period. A great many kilns have apparently still been very active during the Yüan dynasty.

The types of decoration found on the Tz'u-chou ware are most varied. Among the most common is the so-called *sgraffito* ware provided with one dark coloured slip with superimposed light-colour slip (or vice versa), through which the design is carved so that the darker (or lighter) body is revealed. This technique is used in a number of variations often with finely incised details.

Another very important group is the painted wares with their variety of freely painted designs, sometimes very simple and almost crude but often executed with great skill and force and a charming spontaneity. This type is of great significance as being the first real attempt to free painting under the glaze—a technique which

[1]) *Wen Wu* 1942:1, p. 56; *Wen Wu* 1959:6, p. 59; *Wen Wu* 1964:8, p. 37 (the last mentioned report is the most important and it will be cited continuously in the following discussion).

[2]) O. Karlbeck, "*Notes on the wares from the Chiao Tso potteries*". *Ethnos*. Vol. 8, No. 3, 1943. *Wen Wu* 1952:1, p. 56; *Wen Wu* 1954:4, p. 44; *Wen Wu* 1959:10, p. 44.

[3]) *Wen Wu* 1964:2, p. 54; *Wen Wu* 1964:3, p. 47.

[4]) *Wen Wu* 1956:7, p. 36; *Wen Wu* 1957:10, p. 57; *Wen Wu* 1964:8, p. 1.

[5]) One kiln in *Pa-kua-tung* [57] has not yet been published.

[6]) *Wen Wu* 1951:2, p. 53; *Wen Wu* 1964:8, p. 27.

[7]) *Kao Ku* 1962:6, p. 312.

[8]) *Wen Wu* 1964:9, p. 46; *Wen Wu* 1958:10, p. 36.

later on was developed during the Yüan dynasty and became one of the two most important methods used in the later ceramic industry.

Of no less importance is the small group of Tz'u-chou ware painted with enamel colours on the glaze to which we have devoted a special section below (p. 118). This technique was later on developed into the second main type of decoration found on later porcelain wares.

The ware decorated with coloured glazes in the same tradition as the T'ang and Liao *san ts'ai* ware was also very popular and the technique was especially used frequently for the decoration of pillows.

Monochrome glazes, especially black, brown and white, were made at several kilns. Among the most common types are the so-called *Honan temmoku* and the *Chü-lu hsien* [62] ware.[1]) As these wares are mostly completely undecorated they are of minor interest to us in connection with a study of design, but sometimes the shapes used on wares of this type afford us good help in our attempt to date a certain specimen.

The designs found on wares of Tz'u-chou type provide an abundantly rich flora. There is hardly any type of design missing, and the main difficulty is to decide what types to include in a survey such as this. Apart from the more usual designs of flowers, scrollwork, petals etc., which are extremely rich and varied, it is striking how often we come across pictorial designs on this ware. On other Sung wares representations of human beings are very scarce, and also those of animals with the exception of a few standard designs such as "*boys among flowers*", "*ducks among lotus*" etc. But in the Tz'u-chou ware they are extremely common, especially on the pillows the often flat surfaces of which formed an ideal setting for this kind of pictures. Some of the motifs of this kind seem to give evidence of influence derived from contemporary paintings, but often their style is quite different, more free and spontaneous. It is, however, obvious that the great interest for flowers, birds and animals which is such an important feature in the history of Sung culture, was not merely limited to the court circles or the intellectuals but was a general trend in Sung life and also found expression in the folk art of the time.

It has already been pointed out by several authors that Chinese scholars and collectors have never appreciated the Tz'u-chou ware but considered it a cheap popular ware far from the refined products of the official kilns. Not until the last decades have the Chinese themselves started to appreciate this ware apparently because of its folk-art character and because it was once used in the daily life of the common people. It is not very surprising on the other hand that this ware has for a long time been highly treasured by the Japanese with their special taste for the simple and rustique which has found some of its finest expressions in the tea-

[1]) The ware has got its name from the site of Chü-lu hsien where it has been found in large quantities (it has also been found in the neighbouring *Ch'ing-ho hsien*) but there is no evidence at all that there ever was a kiln at this place.

ceremony and the philosophy connected with it. Some of the finest Tz'u-chou specimens preserved to day are kept in Japanese collections.

In the present survey over some of the main types of designs found on Tz'u-chou ware we have tried to select out of the abundant material available those patterns which are either very common and typical or else important for the understanding of the development of certain decorative motifs. A ware has been assigned to a certain kiln when it has been possible to do so by comparison with excavated material or when there is strong stylistic evidence for such an attribution.

Type: Tc 1.
Provenience: Teng-feng hsien, Honan.
Shape: Ewer, jar & pillow.
Date: Early Northern Sung.
Design: Bold floral scroll.

This is a most interesting group of Tz'u-chou ware of early Sung date which is closely connected in design as well as in shape with the earlier described Type Nc 1 of Northern celadon ware from Yao-chou, which has usually been named Tung yao.

This type is made of a grey stoneware covered with a brown or dark grey slip and a superimposed white slip through which the design is carved and incised revealing the darker bottom colour; it is finally glazed all over with a transparent glaze.

A ewer of this type is in the Museum Yamato Bunkakan (Pl. 41:d) and another in the British Museum (Pl. 41:c). They are both of globular shape and decorated round the neck with a collar of overlapping petals, and on the body is the design which we have called "*bold floral scroll*" with a big flower and the characteristic curled stem with, at the top, two small, and one very large leaf, the latter with a strong vein in the middle. Both the shape of the ewers and the design are almost exactly the same as were found in the so-called Tung group (cp. Pl. 1:a–e). We have already shown how this design in the Northern celadon ware develops into what we have called the "*conventionalized flower*", which is characterized especially by the strange shape of the flower when seen from the side. We shall find exactly the same flower also on specimens in this group. There is one ewer in the Tokyo National Museum (Pl. 41:a) and one in the Cleveland Museum (Pl. 41:b) both of the same slightly depressed globular shape as we have seen in the Northern celadon group (Pl. 1:a–b); a third ewer in the ROM in Toronto (Pl. 41:e) is of a slightly different type with trumpet-shaped mouth. All three ewers have the bold scroll with its characteristic large leaf, but the stem ends in a conventionalized flower; the bottom part of the flower is semi-spherical and built up by overlapping petals and sticking out of it are three rounded ball-like forms, the general appearance of which is close to that of an acorn (Fig. 3:1).

The bold flower of more realistic type which we have already seen on some of the above-mentioned ewers is also found on a jar in the Freer Gallery (Pl. 41:f; for similar jars in the celadon group see Pl. 1:h–i) and on two pillows of five-lobed cloud-shape one in the Yamato Bunkakan (Pl. 41:j) and the other in the Chicago Art Institute (Pl. 41:g, h, k). On the latter pillow we can clearly see the bold flower on one side and the conventionalized flower on the other (Pl. 41:g, h). Both pillows have incised peony sprays on the top and on the Chicago pillow it is surrounded by finely incised white clouds against the dark background (Pl. 41:k).

Obviously belonging to this group is a ewer in a Japanese collection of the same shape as found in two ewers of this group and several in the celadon group (Pl. 41:i). The decoration on this ewer is much simpler than on other specimens in the group and of a different kind. Round the neck is a row of radial overlapping petals and on the belly are two layers of large overlapping petals, the upper one containing leaves with combed details. The design is very similar to those found on the Cleveland ewer and a jar in the celadon group (Pl. 1:f, h).

The quality of this entire group with its very vigorously carved designs is extremely fine, and it is undoubtedly one of the finest among the Tz'u-chou wares. The very close likeness between the objects found in this group and their characteristic Northern Sung shapes seems to indicate that this particular type was only made during a short period at the beginning of the dynasty. This ware has usually been called Hsiu-wu yao, but fragments recently found in the Teng-feng district in Honan seem to indicate that the ware was made here.[1]) The fragment found shows very clearly the characteristic conventionalized flower and also the leaves. There is also a small fragment from Hsiu-wu[2]) which seems to be of the same type and it is possible that the ware was made at both kilns.

Type: Tc 2.
Provenience: Teng-feng hsien.
Shape: Vase.
Date: Early Northern Sung.
Design: Finely incised scrolls etc.

This is a small group closely related to the preceding one. We mentioned above that on the Chicago pillow is a design of cloud scrolls in white on a dark ground (Pl. 41:k). The same type of design is also found on a few other pieces which are partly covered with a brown slip over the white bottom slip; the design is incised in very fine lines through the dark slip revealing the white one. The general appearance is very close to inlaid work. A vase in the Buffalo Museum (Pl. 41:l), of almost cylindrical shape with slightly rounded sides and angular shoulder, has a design of this type incised round belly and shoulder. The design consists of scroll work and sketchy flowers. Another vase, which is in the Cleveland Museum (Pl. 40:l), is of a similar shape in the lower part but is provided with a very tall neck and a large saucer-shaped mouth. The design is found in three belts on the shoulder and body. In the first band are feathery leaves, in the central main band dissolved peony flowers, and in the lower band a formal palmette scroll. The shape of this

1) *Wen Wu* 1964:3, p. 53. Fig. 4.

2) *Chinese Translations* No. 1, Pl. II:11.

vase is most characteristic of Liao and early Sung (cp. Pl. 40:g, h) and we shall find it again in the next type.

Type: **Tc 3.**
Provenience: **Teng-feng hsien.**
Shape: **Vase.**
Date: **Early Northern Sung.**
Design: **Bold floral scroll.**

This type belongs to the same group as the two preceding ones, and the decorative motifs used are the same as in the first type. All specimens in this type are of the same form as the above-mentioned vase (Pl. 40:l), with baluster-shaped body, tall neck and large saucer-shaped mouth. A vase in the Minneapolis Institute of Arts (Pl. 40:k) is decorated round the shoulder with a row of overlapping petals with incised details, on the body is a vigorously carved, bold floral scroll, and under it a sketchy scroll-border similar to the formal palmette scroll on the vase in Cleveland (Pl. 40:l). Round the base are overlapping lotus petals. An almost identical vase is illustrated in the *Sung tai pei fang*[1]) on which the conventionalized flower is clearly shown. It is interesting to note that this vase is labelled Teng-feng ware.

Another vase of this type is in the Freer Gallery; it is of a more swelling baluster-shape. The main design band on the body shows a very forceful and deeply carved, bold floral scroll with typical conventionalized flowers. The central design is enclosed by a finely incised leaf border on the shoulder and a more formal palmette scroll round the lower part of the belly (Pl. 40:j). Round the base are broad overlapping lotus petals with incised details. A vase of similar shape is also in the Museum of Fine Arts, Boston (Pl. 40:i), this vase comes close to Type 1 in general appearance. Round the shoulder are cloud-scrolls and on the belly the bold floral scroll, but the flower is here more elaborate than usual with many petals and gives a very realistic impression. Round the base are overlapping lotus petals.

Type: **Tc 4.**
Provenience: **Hsiu-wu, Honan.**
Date: **Northern Sung.**
Design: **Conventionalized flower.**

Under this type we have illustrated only one specimen which seems to be a very interesting key-piece showing the development of the conventionalized flower design (Pl. 48:l). It is a jar of ovoid shape with wide mouth and rolled lip. It is decorated under the rim with a row of petals with incised details. The main band of decoration is found round the belly enclosed by two bands with depressed key-fret, and shows a big chrysanthemum-like flower, the centre of which still keeps the strange seed-pod we have called conventionalized flower. This décor has some resemblance to the floral designs found on the front of pillows in Type 6, and on other specimens

[1]) By Ch'en Wan-li, Peking 1955, Illustrated on p. 19.

in Type 7 below. The key-fret borders and the petal design also connect it with other groups attributed to the Hsiu-wu kiln like Type 24 below.

Type:	**Tc 5.**	**Date:**	**Northern Sung, 11th century.**
Provenience:	**Teng-feng hsien, Mi hsien.**	**Design:**	**On a ground of small circles.**
Shape:	**Pillow.**		

This type includes pillows of flattened kidney-shape. Top and front are slightly concave. The ware is a buff-white stoneware with transparent glaze covering a cream slip, on which a dark design is produced by incising and stamping through to the body.

The main design, on a ground of small stamped circles, is found on the top of the pillow, in a panel of the same shape as the pillow and enclosed by one or two lines. Round the sides is a band of feathery scroll-work, which is characteristic of this type.

Recent excavations have proved that this ware was produced in Mi hsien and Teng-feng hsien in Honan. A pillow reported to have come from Teng-feng hsien with floral scrolls on the top is shown in Pl. 42:a.[1]) A similar pillow with a little more formal arrangement of a stiff floral spray is in the Hilleström coll. (Pl. 42:b).[2]) In the Royal Ontario Museum is a third pillow of the same type decorated with a large chrysanthemum spray (Pl. 42:c, Fig. 7:e).

In the Seligman collection is a very fine example with a design of a quail between two plants (Pl. 42:d). A sherd from an identical pillow was found in Mi hsien.[3]) A pillow in the Wellesley College Art Museum (Pl. 42:e), which is decorated with a flying parrot among clouds, also belongs to this type. A parrot of a very similar type among formal scrolls is found on a pillow which comes from Mi hsien (Pl. 42:f). This pillow differs from all the others previously mentioned in this group in that it does not have the feathery scroll-work on the side but instead small stamped circles alternating with star-like crosses. Fragments with this kind of stamping were found in Mi hsien.[4])

Two other pillows which also seem to belong to the same group are shown in Pl. 42:g and h. The first one has a very fine design of a drake among lotus flowers and leaves on the top and has a deeply cut *cash*-pattern on the front; the second one has a very realistic and finely drawn lotus plant as main design (Fig. 10:c).

The style of this group as well as archaeological evidence and comparisons with related pillow types point to an early Northern Sung date.

[1]) Publ. in "*China's beauty of 2000 years*", Tokyo 1965, Pl. 76. The flowers on the top, however, match completely with a fragment from Mi hsien (*Wen Wu* 1964:3, p. 50 Fig. 8:4) but the two kilns seem to have produced almost identical wares.

[2]) This design comes close to another fragment from Teng-feng (*Wen Wu* 1964:3, p. 53, Fig. 1 left and 3).

[3]) *Wen Wu* 1964:3, p. 50, Fig. 7.

[4]) *Wen Wu* 1964:3, Fig. 8:2.

Type: Tc 6.
Provenience: Teng-feng hsien, Mi hsien.
Shape: Pillow.
Date: Northern Sung, 11th century.
Design: On a ground of small circles.

This type includes pillows of kidney-shape, square and oval shape, and oval shape with lobed ends. The ware and the technique of the designs are the same as in the preceding group.

The main designs found in this group are more varied. Characteristic of the group is the design band round the side which is composed of stiff chrysanthemum flowers surrounded by leaves, or leaves only, (sometimes the flowers are more like peonies). The design of the front and those on the sides are sometimes enclosed in separate panels.

Deer are a very popular design on pillows of this type. There is one in the Boston Museum with a running deer among plants of the same type as those found on the quail pillow in the preceding group (Pl. 43:b) and one with a reclining deer between the same type of plants in the Seligman coll. (Pl. 43:a). A pillow with a running deer among plants and a garden rock is in the Lord Cunliffe collection (Pl. 43:c) and a most elaborate one in the V & A (Pl. 42:k) shows two large confronted stags among rocks and plants. All these pillows have the same front design with a big chrysanthemum surrounded by stiff leaves (with the exception of the Cunliffe pillow which has a leaf band) and this pattern is also found on an important square pillow, with a design of four characters on top, which is in the British Museum.[1]) This pillow (Pl. 42:j) has an inscription on the sides of the top dated the 4th year of *Hsi-ning*, which is equivalent to the year 1071.

To this group also belongs a pillow in the ROM in Toronto with a most elaborate design of a creeping child with flowers and scrolls (Pl. 42:l). The design at the first glance seems surprisingly realistic to be of an early Sung date, but a closer examination of its details, the scrolls, the flowers etc. shows a very close and definite resemblance to other specimens in this and the preceding group. An interesting detail is the small ingots found just below the boy's body which further stresses the auspicious character of the design, and which can also be seen on the deer pillow, Pl. 42:k. Representations of ingots are not uncommon in Sung paintings and are found e.g. in Northern Sung tomb decorations.[2])

A more simple pillow which also belongs to this type is in the Vassar college, it has a large peony spray on the top, and the stiff flower on the front is also, in this case, more like a peony (Pl. 42:i).

Type: Tc 7.
Provenience: Teng-feng hsien, Mi hsien.
Shape: Mei-p'ing and ewer.
Date: Northern Sung, 11th century.
Design: On a ground of small circles.

[1]) The inscription says: "*Chia kuo yung an*" [63] (family, country, lasting peace).

[2]) Cp. *Pai sha Sung mu.* Fig. 27. Sung dynasty silver ingots have also been excavated in several places, (cp. Kao Ku 1965:12, p. 643).

Belonging to the same group as the above-mentioned two types of pillows are also some objects of other shapes. A *mei-p'ing* vase in the Seligman coll. (Pl. 43:d) is decorated round the body with a broad band divided into three panels containing the characters *ch'ing ch'ing jen* [64] (purity, clarity, endurance) on a ground of stamped circles; the relationship with the British Museum pillow (Pl. 42:j) is obvious. Round the base are tall sketchy spirals resembling a petal design. A very similar vase in the V & A (Pl. 43:e) has a floral scroll of the type so common in this group as the main design, and the same design is also found on a vase of a more ovoid shape formerly in the Alexander coll. (Pl. 43:g) and one in the Warren E. Cox collection (Pl. 43:f). All these vases have the same sketchy spiral design round the base.[1])

In this group we also find some ewers, one formerly in the Harris collection (Pl. 43:h) is decorated with stiff leaves in quadrangular panels very similar to those we have seen on the front of pillows and another has a floral scroll (Pl. 43:i). The latter ewer is of an early Sung shape that we have already seen used in other ewers from Teng-feng hsien (Pl. 41:e).

A very interesting *mei-p'ing* vase of ovoid outline which also belongs to this group is in the Boston Museum.[2]) It is decorated with three men surrounded by clouds in the main field and has a scroll border. The men are dressed in long gowns, which are open at the front and leave the big belly bare, they all carry gourd bottles and sticks; the design is probably meant to represent taoist immortals. A vase of the same shape, also with a rare and finely executed design, is in the Peking Palace Museum.[3]) The main décor in this case shows two large ferocious-looking tigers walking on their hind legs among plants. The designs found on these two vases, which, like all the others discussed in connection with this type, are set against a ground of small circles, show the same elaborate and surprisingly realistic style of which we have already seen examples in the decoration of some of the pillows mentioned above.

Type: **Tc 8.**
Provenience: **Kuan-t'ai, Han-tan shih, Hopei.**
Shape: **Vase & jar.**
Date: **Northern Sung, 11th century.**
Design: **On a ground of small circles.**

Tz'u-chou type wares with designs on a stamped circle ground were not only produced in the above-mentioned kilns in Honan, but also in other kilns in both Honan and Hopei. Owing to the close similarities found among the patterns and techniques used in these kilns it is very difficult to make a certain attribution founded on the scarce material hitherto revealed by excavations. However, some of the main kilns of Tz'u-chou ware have been found to be in Han-tan shih in Hopei.

---

[1]) Cp. sherds with this design from Teng-feng hsien. *Wen Wu* 1964:2, Pl. 6:3.

[2]) *Hoyt cat.* No. 284.

[3]) *Ku kung po wu yüan ts'ang tz'u hsüan chi.* Peking 1962. Pl. 36.

Some characteristic fragments found at the Kuan-t'ai kiln there help us with the attribution of another group of stamped wares.

A *mei-p'ing* vase in the City Art Museum of St. Louis (Pl. 43:j) is decorated in three broad bands, the upper one containing a very characteristic leaf scroll and the middle one a *cash*-pattern, both on ring-stamped ground. Round the lower part is a sketchy petal design. A globular jar in the Boston Museum (Pl. 43:k) is likewise decorated in three bands, and here the two upper bands have the same type of leaf scroll, though still more conventionalized. Scrolls of exactly this type have been found on fragments from Kuan-t'ai (Fig. 31:a).[1])

Another group which we would also attribute to the same kiln is of a slightly different type, but here too the design is shown on a ring-stamped ground. These pieces are usually covered with a white slip through which the design is carved and stamped, revealing a body of bluish-grey or light greyish-red colour. At the Kuan-t'ai kiln site was excavated a jar with six cylindrical tubes attached to the shoulder, which had a carved design of this type round the body.[2]) A very similar jar was found by Palmgren in Ch'ing-ho hsien (Pl. 44:a). The design on the jar is divided in three horizontal bands; the upper band with stylized clouds, the middle one with a leaf scroll, both on stamped ground, and the third one round the base with a kind of skewed lotus panels with wavy upper part. The same kind of lotus panels are found on two *mei-p'ing* vases, one in the Bristol Art Gallery (Pl. 44:b) and the other one in the Malcolm collection (Pl. 43:l). Both have the main décor arranged in three horizontal bands; the first one has stylized clouds and leaves, and the second one *cash*-pattern.

Type:	**Tc 9.**	**Date:**	**Northern Sung, 11th—early 12th century.**
Provenience:	**Kuan-t'ai.**		
Shape:	**Leaf-shaped pillow.**	**Design:**	**On striated ground.**

This type includes a group of pillows with leaf-shaped or *ju-i* shaped head-rest. They are made of a fine grey clay covered with a white slip; the designs are incised through the slip to the grey body and then covered with a transparent glaze. Pillows of this type are known to have been found in Chü-lu hsien, and in the ROM in Toronto are eleven of these pillows, all reported to have come from the "new cemetery near *Shun-te fu*" (identified as Chü-lu hsien).[3]) Paine[4]) mentions two pillows of the same type figured in the *Chü-lu Sung ch'i ts'ung lu*, one of them dated 1103.

[1]) *Wen Wu* 1964:8, Pl. 6:2.

[2]) *Wen Wu* 1959:6 p. 58 Fig. 3.

[3]) Fernald, H., *Chinese Mortuary Pillows in the Royal Ontario Museum. FECB* Vol. IV, No. 1, 1952, p. 8.

[4]) Paine, R. T., *Chinese Ceramic Pillows. FECB* Vol. VII, No. 3, 1955, p. 29.

The designs on these pillows are found in a leaf-shaped panel enclosed by a thin line incision; two more line incisions are found near the edge. One of the pillows in the ROM shows the character *jen* (to be patient, to endure) against a ground striated by finely incised lines; the background is characteristic of this type (Pl. 44:d). Another pillow from the same collection shows a peony spray with a large triangular flower and pointed leaves (Pl. 44:e). A similar pillow in the Boston Museum has an almost identical design (Pl. 44:f).

At the excavations of the Kuan-t'ai kiln site were found fragments of a pillow of this type (Pl. 44:c) with the design of a figure holding what looks like a cage. The shape, the enclosing lines and the background striations are all identical to what is found on the above-mentioned pillows. We have already seen in the preceding type that specimens discovered in Chü-lu hsien are proved to have been produced in Kuan-t'ai, and the same seems to be the case with this type, which is very natural as the two places are not very far from each other and Chü-lu apparently did not have any ceramic production. The striated ground seems to be a feature characteristic of the Kuan-t'ai kiln and we shall see also other examples of this technique.

Type: **Tc 10.**
Provenience: **Kuan-t'ai.**
Shape: **Various.**
Date: **Northern Sung, 11th—early 12th century.**
Design: **On striated ground.**

We have already pointed out above that the striated ground is significant of the Kuan-t'ai kiln and during the excavations at the kiln site there was also found a round dish with an incised lotus design on this kind of ground.[1]) An almost identical dish is in the Barlow collection (Pl. 44:g).[2]) Large basins, with a horizontal projecting edge with peony designs of the same type as those found on the pillows from Kuan-t'ai, are also found. There is one in the de Menasce coll.[3]) and another one in the collection of H.M. the King of Sweden (Pl. 44:h). The latter piece has a typical Ch'ü-lu hsien water patina.

In the Clark collection is a globular cup with an incised sketchy leaf design on striated ground, which obviously also belongs to this group (Pl. 44:i). A cup-stand in the Warren E. Cox collection, of a type that is very common among the undecorated so-called Chü-lu hsien yao,[4]) has a design of stylized clouds on a striated ground (Fig. 28:c). A pillow with exactly the same design, belonging to our preceding group 9, was formerly in a private Swedish collection and considered by Karlbeck to come from Chiao-tso.[5])

[1]) *Wen Wu* 1959:6, p. 58, Fig. 1.

[2]) A bowl of similar type with peony design is in the Boston Museum (*Hoyt.cat.* No. 269).

[3]) *OCS Sung exh. Cat.* no. 105.

[4]) Cp. *Hoyt cat.* No. 277.

[5]) *FECB.* Vol. IV, No. 4, p. 13, Fig. 8.

Type: Tc 11.
Provenience: Kuan-t'ai.
Shape: Vase & jar.
Date: Northern Sung, 11th—early 12th century.
Design: Incised and painted flowers, insects, etc.

Among the objects excavated from the Kuan-t'ai kiln are also specimens of a light greyish-white stoneware covered with a creamy white slip, and with a superimposed black slip through which a design is cut, the whole is covered with a transparent glaze. In some cases the design is only painted. Several different shapes are found.

Among the material published from the Kuan-t'ai excavations is a bottle-shaped jar of the type called "*tou lou p'ing*" decorated with a finely drawn leaf spray of a type close to ink-painting.[1]) An almost identical jar from Ch'ing-ho hsien has been published by Palmgren (Pl. 44:j). A number of jars of this shape with the same kind of simple, but vigorously drawn designs are known (Pl. 44:k, l).

Another shape common among this type is a globular, cup-shaped jar on a high foot. One piece of this kind from Ch'ing-ho hsien is decorated with a peony spray and small insects (Pl. 45:a). Sherds with exactly the same kind of insects have been found in Kuan-t'ai.[2]) Several similar jars with décor of leaf sprays, peonies and insects are known (Pl. 45:b).

Other shapes known are; *mei-p'ing* vases, as can be seen from an example in the Barlow collection with painted design,[3]) and baluster-shaped vases with everted foot and foliate flower-shaped mouth. A vase of the latter shape was found in Ch'ing-ho hsien (Pl. 45:d). A covered jar in the Seligman collection[4]) with vertical side and close-fitting cover resembling an inverted saucer, has a design of feather-like leaf sprays of the same type as on the above-mentioned vase in the Barlow collection and a jar in the same collection (Pl. 45:c). A jar almost identical to the Seligman one and with the same décor was found in Kuan-t'ai,[5]) which gives us a certain provenience of the feathery leaf design.

Type: Tc 12.
Provenience: Kuan-t'ai.
Shape: Leaf-shaped pillow.
Date: Late Northern Sung—Chin.
Design: Various.

The same technique of incised designs on a black slip superimposed over a white one is also found on a group of pillows of the leaf-shape we have already seen in Type 9 above. The criteria formed by the shape of these pillows and their design make an attribution to the Kuan-t'ai kiln most possible.

---

1) *Wen Wu* 1959:6, p. 58, Fig. 2.
2) *Wen Wu* 1964:8, p. 42, Fig. 10.
3) *Cat.* Pl. 56 b.
4) *Cat.* No. D 113.
5) *Wen Wu* 1964:8, p. 41, Fig. 8:4.

Designs very close to the preceding group are found on two pillows in Japanese collections (Pl. 45:e, f). Both with peony designs on top. A pillow in the Iwasaki collection is decorated with a beautiful peony of the large beehive-shaped type (Pl. 45:g). A peony spray in white against a black background is found on a pillow in the Tokyo National Museum (Pl. 45:h), and the same technique is used on a very fine pillow in the Boston Museum with a bird on a large floral spray (Pl. 45:i).

Many unusual designs are found on pillows of this type. There is one in the British Museum which shows a dancing bear (Pl. 45:j), one in a private collection with a cat (Pl. 45:k), one in the Brundage collection with a deer among clouds (Pl. 45:l) and one in the Museum Yamato Bunkakan with a pair of fishes (Pl. 46:a).

Two pillows of this type are decorated with typical sgraffito designs of peony scrolls of a kind which is well-known from fragments excavated at Kuan-t'ai[1]) (Pl. 46:b, c).

Type: **Tc 13.**
Provenience: **Tung-ai k'ou, Han-tan shih, Hopei.**
Shape: **Oval pillow.**
Date: **Late Northern Sung—Chin.**
Design: **Different, painted.**

There are several large groups of pillows with inscriptions stating that they have been made by the *Chang* family, which have been discussed by different authors.[2]) According to their shape and decoration they apparently belong not only to different times but also to different kilns. Some of the finest and most elaborate seem to belong to the Yüan dynasty, but other groups are definitely much earlier. Recent excavations in China have revealed some pillows of these types from Sung and Yüan tombs, but the most important discoveries made are from the two sites of Tung-ai k'ou and Yeh-tzu ts'un in Han-tan shih, Hopei. At those two kiln sites there have been found many fragments from pillows with Chang family inscriptions and a large material of sherds with designs typical of the Chang types. Some of the types clearly associated with the Han-tan kilns will be discussed below.

Characteristic of pillows of this type is usually a light buff ware covered with white slip and painted and incised in black. On the front and sides of the pillows is very often a conventionalized leaf-scroll of very distinctive appearance.

The first main type is of oval shape with a slightly depressed top and projecting rim. A good example of this type is in the Boston Museum (Pl. 46:d). It is decorated on the top with a long-tailed bird on a flowering branch within an ogee-shaped

[1]) *China's beauty*, Nos. 434, 436, 439.

[2]) John Ayers mentions the most important articles written on this group of pillows in his Seligman catalogue (p. 67). The most elaborate of the pillows in the Chang group are those of long rectangular shape which are very richly decorated with animals, flowers and different scenes from tales and mythology (Cp. Paine Pl. 27–30). The designs found on this group are more related to painting, and they are also probably later than the other Chang pillows; for this reason they will not be discussed in this paper. A special study on these pillows is under preparation by an English scholar.

panel framed by line borders. The sides have a continuous band of simplified leaf-scrolls of the type we know from Tung-ai k'ou[1]) (Fig. 42:d). On the base is an impressed mark in a lotus frame with the inscription *"Chang chia tsao"* [65] in raised characters. The frame and writing are identical to those on sherds found at Tung-ai k'ou (Fig. 40:a). A pillow closely akin to the Boston one has been excavated in Honan and attributed to the Sung dynasty (Pl. 46:e). This pillow also has the design of a bird on a bough, and interesting small features found on both pillows are the short scroll ornaments found between the outer border and the frame enclosing the main motif. A third pillow with a very similar bird-motif is in the City Art Museum of St. Louis.[2]) This pillow has no leaf design round the sides. It has the Chang family mark on the base.

A pillow in a Japanese collection of the same oval type shows a partly incised design of a floral spray on a combed background (Pl. 46:f); on the sides is the usual continuous leaf-scroll. An unusual pillow in the Heeramaneck coll. has a very charming design of a child riding on a bamboo hobby-horse[3]) (Fig. 17:g). Painted in the same spirit is a pillow in the Hopei Provincial Museum which shows a fishing boy; the motif that is given in a few simple lines is extremely skilful and lively (Fig. 17:e). The pillow has the usual leaf-scroll on the side and has the Chang family mark, it was excavated in Hopei.

In a recently excavated tomb near Hsi-an in Shensi was also discovered a pillow belonging to this group with a design of a crane and flowers on the top and the usual stylized leaf-scroll on the sides.[4]) The tomb is datable by the stone tablet to the 2nd year of *Chih-yüan* of the Yüan dynasty equivalent to 1266 A.D. This date is still within the official Sung dynasty, which seems to indicate that this type of pillows must have been in use already during Chin.

Type: **Tc 14.**
Provenience: **Tung-ai k'ou.**
Shape: **Octagonal pillow.**
Date: **Late Northern Sung—Chin.**
Design: **Different, painted.**

This group is very close to the preceding one, but the shape of the pillows is mostly octagonal. The top is slightly concave with projecting edge. Most pillows in this group also have the same stylized leaf-border around the sides, but some are plain, just as in the type described above.

A pillow with undecorated sides in a Japanese collection has on the top a running hare in a free and simple style (Pl. 46:g) very similar to designs found on sherds from Tung-ai k'ou. Many of the sherds found at the kiln site were decorated with cranes among reeds, and ducks and bamboo (Fig. 31:b) and pillows with this kind of designs are found in different collections and also cocks and small birds on bamboo

[1]) *Wen Wu* 1964:8, p. 45, Fig. 19.
[2]) *Los Angeles exh.cat.* No. 214.
[3]) Cox, W. E., *The book of pottery and porcelain.* Vol. I. Fig. 389.
[4]) *Wen Wu* 1958:6, p. 59, Fig. 15.

twigs (Fig. 26:d-e). One pillow of this type was excavated from a tomb in Hopei, it is decorated on the top with a standing deer with stiff flowers on each side (Fig. 31:e).[1]) On the back is stamped "*Chang chia tsao*". The tomb is dated by the excavators as probably middle Northern Sung, which seems very early, but might be an indication that this type of design was already in use at least around the end of the Northern Sung dynasty, and was probably used continuously until the end of Chin.

Several pillows with inscriptions of poems etc. as main décor are found in this group and fragments of this kind were also found at the kiln site. One pillow of this kind in a Japanese collection (Pl. 46:i) has an inscription of 28 characters, and another one, also in a private collection in Japan, has four;[2]) both have the leaf scroll on the sides. Another pillow in Japan has a finely drawn floral spray on the top (Pl. 46:h), and a pillow in the Honolulu Academy of Arts (Pl. 46:j) is decorated with a swimming swan. The main motif on all pillows mentioned in this type is enclosed by one thin and one broad line border.

Very similar in type to the Honolulu pillow is one decorated with a large fish in the Art Institute of Chicago (Pl. 46:k), but it is of cloud-shape and is a kind of transitional type between this type and the following one.

Type: **Tc 15.**
Provenience: **Tung-ai k'ou.**
Shape: **Cloud-shaped pillow.**
Date: **Late Northern Sung—Chin.**
Design: **Different, painted.**

Of the same type as the preceding one, also with mostly painted, but sometimes incised, designs and with the stylized leaf-border on the sides, is this type which is cloud-shaped or of *ju-i* like form. The design on the top is enclosed by one thin and one broad ogee-shaped line border. The designs found in this group are most variating and executed with great skill, it is perhaps the finest and best painted type among the Chang pillows. The similarity of some of the designs to those found in the leaf-shaped pillows of Type 12 from the Kuan-t'ai kiln is obvious.

A characteristic feature of all pillows of this type is the thin leaf-border found on the edge of the pillow, the leaves of which look like ink bamboo painting. A pillow in the ROM in Toronto (Pl. 47:a) shows a child with a big lotus leaf driving a duck. The similarities of the dress of the child with that found on an earlier mentioned fragment of a leaf-shaped pillow from Kuan-t'ai is striking (Pl. 44:c).

[1]) *Kao Ku* 1959:7, p. 369. Fig. 1.

[2]) The four characters are *feng* (wind), *hua* (flower), *hsüeh* (snow) and *yüeh* (moon). This is a most common phrase in Chinese poetry with several different meanings. It could mean "the four seasons", but could also allude to a general poetic feeling (as these are some of the standard things used by poets), or hint at a gay life with women. In Sung time the phrase is known from a famous poem by Su T'ung-po. Two more pillows with the same characters are found in Type 26 below.

On the base of the Toronto pillow are the three characters "*Chang chia tsao*" stamped within a double-line rectangle.

A pillow in the Cleveland Museum shows a landscape with a running stag (Pl. 47:b) and one in a Japanese collection shows a bird sitting on a bamboo branch (Pl. 47:d). A pillow in the MFEA has a painting of unusually high quality showing a shore-landscape with reeds and two geese, the composition is very close to Sung paintings (Pl. 47:c). In the Plumer collection is a pillow with a most amusing painting of a crouching tiger, the landscape is indicated with three small tufts of grass in the same way as on the stag pillow (Pl. 47:e).

In a Japanese collection is a pillow which shows, on a partly combed ground, a spray of peony of a type very similar to a pillow in the oval group (Pl. 46:l; cp. 46:f).

The general characteristics of this group, its high quality and its similarities with the above-mentioned groups from Kuan-t'ai of Northern Sung date, all indicate that this type is among the earliest of the Chang pillows and probably dates from the end of Northern Sung and the beginning of Chin.

Type: Tc 16.
Provenience: Han-tan shih, Hopei?
Shape: Octagonal pillow.
Date: Late Northern Sung—Chin.
Design: Different, painted and incised.

Besides the above-mentioned different types of pillows from kilns in Hopei there are also some closely akin types, the origin of which is not certain, but they may be attributed to the kilns in Han-tan shih.

An octagonal pillow of this kind is in the ROM in Toronto, it is decorated on the top with a peony spray within a broad border of thick and thin lines (Pl. 47:f). On the sides are sprays with freely painted peony leaves. Of similar type is the design on the side of a pillow in Boston[1]) which has on the top an incised and painted design of a bird on a bough watching a butterfly. The main design is enclosed by a partly combed line border. Of similar type is another pillow in the Boston Museum (Pl. 47:i) decorated with a long poem incised in white through the black slip. On the sides of the pillow are peony scrolls of the standard sgraffito type. A pillow in a Japanese collection has a very similar décor of an incised poem.[1])

Type: Tc 17.
Provenience: Hopei.
Shape: Four-lobed, oval and rectangular pillows.
Date: Late Northern Sung.
Design: Incised and stamped.

---

[1]) Paine, *op.cit.* no. 20.

[1]) *Toji zenshu*, Vol. 13, *So-no jishu yo*. Pl. 59.

This is a small group of pillows, some of them found in Hopei and apparently produced in one of the Tz'u-chou ware kilns. They are made of a greyish-buff stoneware with incised and stamped designs filled-in with brown slip and glazed with a transparent glaze. One pillow of this kind is in a Japanese collection (Pl. 48:a). It is of four-lobed shape and has on the top a panel of the same shape with a deer carrying a flower spray in its mouth, wandering in a landscape. The central motif is surrounded by a border with small stamped flowers made of circles. The same flower motif is also stamped on the side of the pillow; below the edge is a border with circles. A pillow of exactly the same shape and execution but with a reclining deer as main motif was earlier in the Ryojun Government Museum.[1])

A pillow almost identical to the first mentioned one (Pl. 48:a), but of oval shape, was recently found in a tomb at *Shih Chuang* in *Ching Hsing hsien*, Hopei. This pillow has the same kind of deer with a spray in its mouth in a four-lobed panel on the top surrounded by a border with small stamped flowers; the side is undecorated.[2]) In another tomb at the same place was excavated a pillow of four-lobed shape with a panel containing two confronted deer in a landscape with clouds and triangular, stiff leaf-sprays (Pl. 47:1); the design was enclosed by a leaf-scroll border.[3]) Two other tombs at this site yielded rectangular pillows with concave top, one of them decorated with three bands of stiff leaf-sprays on the top, and the other with stiff leaf-sprays enclosed by a scroll similar to that on the four-lobed pillow.[4]) All tombs were datable to the beginnig of the 12th century.

A pillow said to have come from Ch'ü-lu hsien in the Heeramaneck collection (Pl. 48:b) seems to belong to the same group. It is of oval shape and decorated on the top with a baby and a duckling, in a panel enclosed by stamped stiff flowers. On the side are stamped small star-like flowers.

This type forms a characteristic and easily recognizable group of pillows which on good grounds can be attributed to Hopei and the early 12th century.

Type: **Tc 18.**
Provenience: **Hopei.**
Shape: **Rectangular pillow.**
Date: **Northern Sung, 11th—early 12th century.**
Design: **Chrysanthemum.**

This is a much debated group of pillows with the Chang family stamp.[5]) They are of rectangular shape with four concave sides and are found either with a creamy white or a dark brown glaze. On two sides is a moulded lattice design with quatrefoil medallions enclosing a chrysanthemum flower with stiff leaves. On the other

[1]) *Selected specimens of Archaeological Collections in the Ryojun Government collection.* Port Arthur 1935. Pl. LIX.

[2]) *K'ao ku hsüeh pao* 1962:2, Pl. 25:6.

[3]) *Op.cit.* Pl. 25:3.

[4]) *Op.cit.* Pl. 26:1 and 5.

[5]) For a discussion of this type see S. Shirae-W. E. Cox, "*A group of Sung Tz'u-chou pillows*". *OA* Vol. II, Autumn 1949, p. 69.

two sides are three chrysanthemums also with stiff leaves, sometimes on a plain, sometimes on a beaded ground (Pl. 48:c). There are a number of these pillows, all with the mark "*Chang chia tsao*" and some marked with the date "*Chih-ho san nien*" (1056 A.D.), some dated "*Hsüan-ho yüan nien*" (1119 A.D.). The marks are stamped within a double-line frame on the two ends of the pillow. The inscriptions are of a different type to those found on the earlier discussed Chang groups and look more stiff and mechanical. The design with the sketchy chrysanthemum with stiff leaves pointing out from it harmonizes very well stylistically with the earlier described Type 6 above.

Some of these pillows are said to have been found at Chü-lu hsien, but no pieces of this kind are known from scientifically controlled excavations. The authenticity of this group is still questionable, and they have a cold and stiff perfection which is disturbing, but it may only be a sign of mass production. Two pillows of this kind —one with white glaze in the MFEA and one with brown glaze from the Boston Museum—are reproduced here (Pl. 48:c, f).[1]

Type: Tc 19.
Shape: Eight-sided pillow.
Date: Northern Sung.
Design: Different.

This type includes pillows of a most characteristic wide, eight-sided shape with incurved edge. The design is carved through a white slip against a brown ground and covered with a transparent glaze. Pillows of this type have been attributed to Fen-chou in Shansi, but they seem to have close similarities with some of the pillows from Hopei.

One pillow of this type is in the Rübel collection, it has an eight-sided panel on the top separated into three by uprights (Pl. 48:d). In the centre is a stylized leaf-spray and on the sides are peony leaf-sprays with entwined stems. A pillow in the Bristol City Art Gallery has the same design in the side panels but a stiff peony-spray in the central field. A pillow in the Cleveland Museum of Art has a small bird on an branch in the central field and stylized leaf-sprays in the side panels (Pl. 48:e). In a Japanese collection is a pillow with a variation of the same design (Pl. 48:h), and here the side panels have entwined peony leaves. Pillows of this type with the motif in one big panel on the top have also been found. There is one in the Brundage collection[2]) with a peony spray and two in Japanese collections, both with peony sprays with entwined stems and big flowers (Pl. 48:g).

Type: Tc 20.
Provenience: Hsiu-wu, Honan or Tz'u-chou, Hopei.
Shape: Deep globular bowl.
Date: Late Northern Sung—Chin.
Design: Flowers and lozenge pattern.

---

[1]) For further examples see Shirae-Cox, *op.cit.*

[2]) *Avery Brundage Collection Chinese Ceramics.* Pl. XL:B.

This is a small but very distinct group of greyish white stoneware covered with white slip and with a superimposed black slip on the upper half, through which a design is cut. The whole is covered with a transparent glaze. The prevailing shape is a deep bowl of globular shape, with sides curving inwards at the mouth, standing on a small, high ring-foot which is slightly everted. The most common designs found are lozenge patterns and flowers.

A bowl of this type in the Seligman collection (Pl. 47:g) is decorated in a broad band with lozenge patterns which have incised details looking like small flowers in the centre. A similar bowl reproduced in the *Sung tai pei fang* (Pl. 47:h) shows a design in three bands. The upper one is a slanting key-fret, the lower one consists of wave-like petals, and the middle band has small flowered lozenges of the same type as on the above-mentioned bowl. A third bowl very close to the foregoing is in the Metropolitan Museum (Pl. 47:k). It has two main bands of décor, the upper one is a slanting key-fret and the lower one consists of large stiff leaves; placed between those are small wheel-like flowers which obviously are remains of the earlier lozenges with flowers. A fourth bowl, which belongs to the same type, is in a Japanese collection (Pl. 47:j) and is called Hsiu-wu yao. The design is here quite different, with just one band strongly carved with large *cash*-patterns separated by small flower-like circles.

The exact provenience of this group is not known, but it is very close to some of the designs and shapes found in the Han-tan kilns; however, there are also strong similarities with several groups from Hsiu-wu, and the type was most likely produced in one of these two areas.

Type: **Tc 21.**
Provenience: **Hsiu-wu, Honan?**
Shape: **Vases & jar.**
Date: **Northern Sung—Chin.**
Design: **Sgraffito décor of peonies etc.**

Some of the finest sgraffito decorated wares are usually attributed to the Hsiu-wu kiln in Honan, but the similarities between this kiln and the Tz'u-chou kilns of Hopei are so close that a more definite attribution is impossible until further excavations of the kiln sites have been carried out. Some of the main types of designs will be described below and mostly arranged under the different shapes predominating.

The peony scroll is one of the most frequent designs found in the early Tz'u-chou ware, together with sprays of peony. Both designs are frequently found on *mei-p'ing* vases.[1]) The design is on this type usually found in a broad central band around the belly enclosed by overlapping petals round the neck and base. A

[1]) An unusual specimen with this kind of sgraffito design of peonies is the body of a drum, in hour-glass form, in the ROM in Toronto (Trubner, H. *ROM. The Far Eastern collection.* 1968). A specimen of the same shape but with a simple petal design is in the Tokyo National Museum (*Sekai* 10, Pl. 116). A drum of Ting type is in the David Foundation (*David Ting cat.* no. 167).

mei-p'ing in the Brundage collection (Pl. 49:a) of tall slender form has a design of peony scrolls with small leaves and almost triangular flowers. A vase of a slightly heavier shape with similar design is in the Metropolitan Museum (Pl. 49:b), and another one in the Kyoto National Museum.[1]) Vases of this type with green glaze over black slip are also known; a fine example is in the British Museum (Pl. 49:c). Of the same shape and composition as the two first-mentioned vases, and also like those decorated in black against a light background, is a vase in Japan, decorated with stiff sprays of peonies (Pl. 49:d). A rare vase belonging to this group is the famous one in the Hakutsuru Art Museum which is decorated with a large three-clawed dragon (Pl. 49:e Fig. 12:b).

Another shape common with this type of design is a vase of ovoid shape with a high, spreading foot and a trumpet-shaped neck with turned-over lip. Vases of this type are also found with green glaze, an example with the peony scroll design is in the collection of H.M. the King of Sweden, and another one with the usual black design on a white ground is in the Bristol City Art Gallery.[2]) A vase with the stiff peony spray is in a private French collection (Pl. 49:g). Another vase with green glaze with a design almost identical to that found on the British Museum *mei-p'ing* (Pl. 49:c) is in Japan (Pl. 49:f). The equivalent of the dragon *mei-p'ing* in this shape is found on a vase in the Nelson Gallery of Art (Pl. 49:h).

The bottle-shaped vases of a form called *tou lou p'ing* are also found with this type of design, as can be seen from two vases of this shape with black designs of peony scrolls (Pl. 49:j, k) and a rare white one with stiff peony sprays (Pl. 49:l), all in Japanese collections.

Jars of *kuan* type are rare in this ware, but a fine example with a design which fits into this group is in a Japanese collection. It has peony scroll designs on the shoulder and on the body panels with floral motifs alternating with peony sprays of the same type (Pl. 49:i). The designs found in the panels of this jar are very close to those found on sherds from Hsiu-wu, note especially the way the branches with thin leaves are rendered compared with a sherd with a bird from the kiln site (Fig. 25:b).[3])

Type:	**Tc 22.**	**Date:**	**Late Northern Sung—Chin.**
Shape:	**Vases.**	**Design:**	**Lotus plant.**

This group is decorated in the same kind of sgraffito design as the preceding one and has the same composition, but the motif is different. It shows a lotus plant with characteristic leaves and large almost triangular flowers together with sagittaria. A fine example of this design is found on a *mei-p'ing* vase in the City Art Museum of St. Louis (Pl. 50:a). A vase with trumpet-shaped mouth and turned-

[1]) *Sekai* Vol. 10, Pl. 94.

[2]) *Venezia exh.cat.*, No. 512.

[3]) *Sekai* Vol. 10, Fig. 105.

over lip with the same design is in the Freer Gallery (Pl. 50:b). In comparison with the peony design the lotus is very rare.

Type: Tc 23. **Date: Late Northern Sung—Chin.**
Shape: Mei-p'ing. **Design: Peony scrolls.**

This group is quite similar to Type 21 above and has also the sgraffito design with a similar composition, but there are some differences in the rendering of the motifs. The predominant shape in this group is the *mei-p'ing*. Around the base of these vases is the design of overlapping sketchy petals, but round the neck is a collar of broad, quite realistic lotus petals; this motif is characteristic of the type. The flowers found on this type are of several kinds and they differ from those in the group described above. One type of flower which is very common has an almost triangular shape; it is often hanging down and looks like a bunch of grapes. One vase with this design is in the Fitzwilliam Museum (Pl. 50:c), another with decoration in white against a darker ground was in the possession of C. T. Loo (Pl. 50:d), and a third one with a more lively scroll design is in the Metropolitan Museum[1]) and a fourth one in the Cleveland Museum.[2]) A *mei-p'ing* vase in a Japanese collection has a different kind of flower, very large and with serrated petals (Pl. 50:e). A very strange and unusual flower occurs on a vase formerly in the Loo collection (Pl. 50:f); it is very big with striated petals and looks like a large butterfly.

The majority of specimens belonging to this type probably still belong to the Northern Sung period, but it seems somewhat later than the preceding two groups, and it is most likely that this type continued well into the Chin dynasty. There are specimens of very late Chin and Yüan date which obviously are influenced by this type, which seems to indicate that it was in use over a long period.

Type: Tc 24. **Date: Northern Sung.**
Provenience: Hsiu-wu, Honan. **Design: Chequer pattern.**
Shape: Vase & jar.

This is a small group of sgraffito decorated wares with a very characteristic chequer pattern. A *mei-p'ing* vase (Pl. 50:g) of this type is of a globular shape and has a décor arranged in three bands round the belly. The central belt has peony leaves and the two others a chequer pattern built up of white and dark squares; round the shoulder is a formal scroll design. Both the above described chequer pattern and the scroll work tally exactly with sherds found at the Hsiu-wu kiln site.[3]) In the Warren E. Cox collection[4]) is a jar of *kuan* type surrounded by a kind

[1]) Cox, *op.cit.* Fig. 365.

[2]) *Los Angeles exh.cat.* No. 236.

[3]) *Toji zenshu.* Vol. 13. *So-no jishu yo*, p. 10, Fig. 12.

[4]) Cox, *op.cit.* Fig. 376.

of depressed key-fret borders of a type which we have seen on other wares of Tz'u-chou type. A third specimen belonging to the same group is a jar of ovoid shape with wide mouth (Pl. 50:h); it has a band with the same kind of key-fret below the rim and on the belly a scroll border enclosed by two chequer bands. In a Japanese collection is a cylindrical jar with straight sides and with a similar chequer pattern enclosing a leaf-scroll;[1]) and another jar of this kind is in the Boston Museum; the pattern on the latter includes the key-fret band.[2]) An interesting piece belonging to this type is a bowl formerly in the Eumorfopoulos collection.[3]) It is a deep bowl with rounded sides and has on the exterior the chequer pattern round the rim and a band of peony-leaf sprays on the body. The shape of this bowl is the same as that in Pl. 45:a–c and Pl. 47:g, h. j, k.

The general appearance of this group is rather rough and "rustique", and it is quite different from specimens generally associated with the Hsiu-wu kiln, but the origin of the ware is quite clear and the designs found on it match very well with other patterns from the same kiln.

Type:	**Tc 25.**	**Date:**	**Late Northern Sung.**
Provenience:	**Hsiu-wu.**	**Design:**	**Formal leaf-scroll.**
Shape:	**Pillow & brush-bath.**		

The formal leaf-scroll which we have seen in the preceding type has been found on many sherds from Hsiu-wu, and is also found on several other sgraffito decorated wares from the same kiln. A pillow in a Japanese collection (Pl. 50:j) of rectangular shape with slightly concave sides is decorated on the front in a sgraffito design with a leaf-scroll of this type, which is almost identical with some of the above-mentioned sherds; on the sides are peony sprays. In the Buffalo Museum is a pillow of exactly the same shape with a similar peony design on the front;[4]) this pillow is said to have come from Tangyangyu (the kiln site in Tang-yang yü in Hsiu-wu hsien was formerly used to name this ware). A pillow in the Malcolm collection of kidney-shape has round the sides a peony scroll of similar type and, on the top, a design which includes the formal leaf-scroll significant of this group (Pl. 50:k). A similar pillow in a Japanese collection has an incised design on the top, but the same peony border round the side as the Malcolm pillow (Pl. 50:l).

A pillow of the three-colour glaze type in a Japanese collection has also strong similarities with the two pillows just mentioned. It has the same peony scroll round the side, and on the top is a peony spray with pointed leaves enclosed in a panel surrounded by formal leaf scrolls (Pl. 51:a).

---

[1]) *Sekai* Vol. 10, Pl. 112.

[2]) *Hoyt cat.* No. 282.

[3]) *GEc.* Vol. III, C 394.

[4]) Hochstadter, *op.cit.* Pl. 98.

Clearly related to the above described group of pillows is a brush-bath in the Mayer collection (Pl. 50:i). It is of circular shape and decorated on the shoulder with a formal leaf-scroll, and round the side with the same kind of scroll with round strawberry-like peony flowers. A brush-bath of the same form, also with a leaf-scroll design on the side, is in the Calmann collection.[1])

Type: **Tc 26.**
Provenience: **Hsiu-wu.**
Shape: **Kidney-shaped pillow.**
Date: **Late Northern Sung—Chin.**
Design: **Different.**

With a starting-point from the last described pillow in the preceding type (Pl. 51:a) we will describe a large group of pillows of a similar type which, for good reasons, may also be attributed to the Hsiu-wu kilns. They are all of kidney-shape and have carved designs of different types covered with coloured glazes of the *san ts'ai* type. The main motif on the top of these pillows is always enclosed by a frame made of several thin lines. We have attributed those pillows to the Hsiu-wu kiln mainly on stylistic grounds, but it is interesting to note that both Fernald[2]) and Hochstadter[3]) mention that this type is considered to come from Tang-yang yü. One pillow of this type was found in a tomb, from the end of Northern Sung, in Lo-yang, Honan.[4]) Fragments of pillows of this type have also been found in Ch'ing-ho hsien.

A pillow in the Buffalo Museum (Pl. 51:b) is decorated on the top with a lotus plant with big leaves on a ground of formal leaf-scrolls of the same type as we have seen in the preceding type. Near the edge are four freely incised wavy scrolls, a feature which is seen on several pillows in this type and which is also found on a pillow fragment found by Palmgren in Ch'ing-ho hsien.[5]) In the Baur collection (Pl. 51:c) is a pillow with a melon vine on a ground of formal leaf-scrolls. This pillow has a peony scroll border, of the same type as that found on the preceding type, round the side. This pillow also has the freely incised scrolls in the outer border on top. A pillow in a Japanese collection has in the main field a round panel, with the character "*fu*" on a ground of formal leaf-scrolls, surrounded by two lotus sprays; round the edge is a band of large, rounded leaves (Pl. 51:d). All pillows hitherto mentioned have had the formal leaf-scrolls, but several pillows which obviously belong to this group have not got this design.

In the ROM in Toronto is a pillow with a peony spray on a plain background in the main field (Pl. 51:e), and a similar one in the Tokyo National Museum[6])

---

[1]) *Venezia exh.cat.* No. 520.
[2]) *Op.cit.*, p. 10.
[3]) *Op.cit.*, p. 32.
[4]) Kao Ku 1960:10, p. 12. Fig. 4.
[5]) Palmgren, *Sung sherds*, p. 319.
[6]) *Yokogawa cat.* No. 120.

has a very elegant spray of mallow, both pillows have the wavy scrolls in the outer border. A simpler type of pillows without the outer borders, and sometimes with rather stiff designs, are found in many collections. There is one in the ROM in Toronto with a peony spray as main design (Pl. 51:f) and a very similar one in the Tokyo National Museum.[1]) A pillow in the Brundage[2]) collection has a stiff lotus design and a similar one, also with a lotus motif, is in a Japanese collection (Pl. 51:g); the latter has lotus leaves in the outer border. A pillow in a Swedish collection has a peony spray with two flowers (Pl. 51:j), and one in a Japanese collection has a spray of chrysanthemum (Pl. 51:h).

A more unusual design also on a pillow in Japan shows a peacock standing in front of a bamboo (Pl. 51:i), and another pillow has cross-shaped bamboo leaves surrounded by lotus leaves (Pl. 51:k). Pillows with inscriptions of poems and other characters are also met with in this group; one pillow of this kind, in the Rübel collection (Pl. 51:l), has a poem in the centre and surrounding it are the characters for "wind, flower, snow and moon". The same characters are also found on another pillow in this group, which is in Japan, and we have seen them used before on pillows in Type Tc 14.[3])

This is a large and interesting group which is very well kept together by several characteristic features and it is undoubtedly closely related to the three-colour wares of T'ang and Liao, especially the latter. The type was probably used during the later part of Northern Sung and continued into Chin.

Type: Tc 27. **Date: Late Northern Sung—Chin.**
Shape: Rectangular pillow. **Design: Different.**

This is another group of pillows with coloured glazes of *san ts'ai* type, which has often been attributed to the Shansi province, but no archaeological evidence for this provenience has so far been found. Pillows in this group are usually made of a reddish stoneware and are of rectangular shape with incurved front. The main design is incised on the top of the pillow within a double line frame, the design is frequently divided into three panels. On the side is often found a border made of stiff bamboo leaves of the same type as we have seen on a pillow in the preceding group (Pl. 51:k).

A pillow of this type in the Freer Gallery has on the top a central panel with two children playing in a garden, enclosed by two smaller panels with chrysanthemum flowers (Pl. 52:a). On the side is the earlier described stiff leaf-border, which looks like a kind of cut-off *cash*-design. A similar one in the British Museum has a flying pheasant among chrysanthemum sprays in the central panel (Pl. 52:b),

---

[1]) *Yokogawa cat.* No. 119.

[2]) *Cat.* Pl. XXXVII:A.

[3]) See note 2 page 100 above.

and another one in the Tokyo National Museum[1]) has a large fish. On both pillows is the central panel flanked by panels with floral sprays. A pillow in the Rübel collection (Pl. 52:c) has an amusing design of a boy in a landscape. He is either flying a lotus-leaf-shaped kite or holding a lotus stem while the leaf is flying away with the wind. On the sides of the main panel are panels with floral sprays. A very elaborate pillow of this type was formerly in the possession of Messrs. C. T. Loo of New York,[2]) the main panel shows the drunken poet Li Po and two attendants in a garden scene, the side panels have lotus plants. On the side is the stiff leaf design so common in this type. In the Boston Museum is a pillow which has a peony scroll in the main field and the stiff leaves in the side panels (Pl. 52:d). Some pillows in this group have only one large rectangular panel on the top. One pillow of this kind in the Buffalo Museum (Pl. 52:f) shows a boy climbing in a lotus plant with large flowers, and another one in the Malcolm collection (Pl. 52:e) has two swans swimming in a lotus pond; on the side is the stiff leaf-border.

Some of the designs found on wares of this type, for instance that on the last mentioned pillow, have close similarities with Liao *san ts'ai* wares both in the subject of the pattern and in the execution. A dated *san ts'ai* dish in the collection of M. Calmann with the design of a duck among aquatic plants is also closely connected with the group.[3]) The dish carries the inscription "Made by *Ch'en* in the second year of *Cheng-ho*", the date is equivalent to 1112.

Type: Tc 28. **Date: Late Northern Sung—Chin.**
Shape: Six-sided pillow. **Design: Different.**

This is a group of pillows of red clay similar to the preceding ones and with incised and carved designs. The pillows in this group are mostly of six-sided shape and favour a green colour in combination with other colours of *san ts'ai* type. Characteristic of the type is a geometric fleur-de-lis pattern found on the sides. One pillow of this type in the Boston Museum (Pl. 52:h) has a design with a large round peony flower on the top (Fig. 7:c) and fleur-de-lis patterns on all sides except on the back panel, which is decorated with a peacock at a garden rock. A pillow with an identical top design is in the MFEA; it has the same fleur-de-lis pattern on the sides, and in the back panel is a *t'ao-t'ieh*-like monster.

A pillow of the same shape in the collection of H.M. the King of Sweden shows a design of two ducks at the waterfront in yellow and white against a green background (Colour plate). The sides have a fleur-de-lis pattern (Pl. 52:g).[4]) A pillow in the Honolulu Academy of Arts has the same design on the side, but is of less angular shape. On the top of the pillow is a deer with a large floral spray in its

[1]) *Yokogawa cat.* No. 118.

[2]) *Los Angeles exh. cat.* No. 252.

[3]) *Venezia exh. cat.* No. 528.

[4]) For an identical pillow in the Brooklyn Museum. See: Cox, *op.cit.*, Pl. 28.

mouth (Pl. 52:i). Pillows of this type have also tentatively been attributed to Shansi, but there is no evidence of an archaeological nature in support of this theory.

Type: **Tc 29.**
Provenience: **Hao-pi chi, Honan.**
Shape: **Tiger-shaped pillow.**
Date: **Late Northern Sung—Chin.**
Design: **Different.**

Among recently excavated kilns with Tz'u-chou type wares the kiln at Hao-pi chi in T'ang-yin hsien, Honan is among the most interesting and has yielded a large amount of different wares from T'ang to Yüan. A considerable amount of the excavated material is datable to the Northern Sung dynasty. Among this material was found a fragment of a pillow in the shape of a tiger[1]) (Fig. 31:d). A pillow of exactly the same shape is in the Art Institute of Chicago and was recently included in the Yüan exhibition in Cleveland (Pl. 52:j). On the flat and slightly concave head-rest on the tiger's back is a painted design of a floral spray. One very similar tiger pillow in the Brundage collection (Pl. 52:k) is decorated on the top, with a bird on a bough, and another one in the Tokyo National Museum, has a flying crane among reeds (Pl. 52:l). The designs found on these pillows are of the same type as those on some of the Hopei pillows, and a late Northern Sung date is most likely.

Type: **Tc 30.**
Provenience: **P'a-ts'un, Yü hsien, Honan.**
Shape: **Vase, stand.**
Date: **Yüan.**
Design: **Sketchy leaf spray.**

A quite common group of Tz'u-chou type with a decoration painted in dark brown or black on a white ground is now, due to recent excavations, possible to attribute to the P'a-ts'un kiln in Honan. The decoration found on this type consists mostly of a kind of sketchy leaf sprays of a characteristic shape. The material found at the site is datable to the Yüan dynasty, and the shapes found among the objects of this ware support this dating.

Among the objects recovered from the kiln site is a vase of bottle shape with tall neck and turn-over lip, decorated with a sketchy spray on the belly (Pl. 53:a). In the collection of H.M. the King of Sweden is a vase with almost straight, slightly rounded body, tall neck and turn-over lip which comes very close in style (Pl. 53:b). The decoration on this vase shows a rather rich leaf-design which tallies very well with another specimen from the same kiln, a vase with flower-shaped foliate mouth (Pl. 53:c). Both vases have the same border of stiff leaves. Vases of *mei-p'ing* shape and other forms are also found in this group (Pl. 53:d), and a small stand in the collection of H.M. the King of Sweden also seems to belong to the group (Pl. 53:e).

[1]) *Wen Wu* 1964:8, Pl. 2:14.

A style of decoration similar to that of the specimens in this group has a pillow in the Rübel collection (Pl. 53:f). It is in the shape of a flat wine-jar and is painted with chrysanthemum flowers and leaves in brownish black. On the shoulder is an inscription reading: *Shih-yüan erh nien ssu yüeh erh shih ssu jih Li Ming-chi chin* ("The second year of *Shih-yüan* [1336], the fourth month, the twenty-fourth day, the jar pillow of *Li Ming-chi*").

Type: **Tc 31.**
Provenience: **Yü hsien, Honan; or Shensi?**
Shape: **Wine-jar.**
Date: **Chin—Yüan.**
Design: **Sketchy leaves etc.**

This group is close to the preceding one; it contains wine-jars of ovoid shape with small, splayed mouth surrounded by four loop-handles. They are made of stoneware with a white slip and transparent glaze and often have designs painted in brown. Sometimes the bottom part of vessels are glazed brown. The most usual patterns are different sketchy bird-and-flower designs and inscriptions.

In the British Museum is a jar (Pl. 53:g) of this type inscribed in *P'ags-pa* script "good wine". *P'ags-pa* (*Bashba*) is the alphabet of Chinese sounds in Tibetan writing invented by Lama P'ags-pa in the 13th century. In the Cleveland Museum[1]) is a similar jar with four Chinese characters (meaning "enough to spare year after year") as the only décor. A vase of similar type decorated with a sketchy leaf design (Pl. 53:h) between broad bands was found in a tomb attributed to the Chin dynasty in *Liao-yang*, Manchuria. Four more vases of the same type were found in tombs in the Hei-lung chiang province attributed to the Chin dynasty.[2]) Two of them are illustrated in the excavation report. One is decorated with four characters saying "purified wine and fat sheep", the other has sketchy designs of flying birds between broad bands.

A jar in the Seligman collection (Pl. 53:i) is decorated with three freely drawn feathery motifs which are explained by Ayers as possibly representing phoenixes. A jar in the Hallwyl collection[3]) indeed shows bird designs which are very close to the pattern on the Seligman jar, and has also different calligraphic designs, among them four characters saying "keep the heart patient and lenient".

Many more examples belonging to this type are known, but the examples cited may be enough to gain a clear picture of this specific group. We do not know where these jars were made but, as we have already pointed out, they are quite near to some of the objects from Yü hsien both in the way they are painted and in the potting, especially the way the mouth is executed. The group seems to be clearly datable to the end of Chin and the beginning of Yüan.

---

[1]) *Chinese Art under the Mongols*, No. 44.

[2]) *Kao Ku* 1962:1, p. 31.

[3]) No. V:F d 1.

Type: Tc 32.
Provenience: Honan and Hopei.
Shape: Various.
Date: Northern Sung.
Design: Applied ribs.

This type is made of greyish-white stoneware covered with a lustrous black or dark-brown glaze, and adorned with ribs made by applied threads of clay which show through the glaze. The ware is usually called *Honan temmoku*. Sherds and wasters of this type have been found during recent excavations at several sites, the most important of which are P'a-ts'un,[1]) Hao-pi chi[2]) and Tuan-tien in Honan and Tz'u-chou in Hopei.[3]) It should also be noted that many specimens of this type have been found in Ch'ing-ho hsien. On the basis of the material so far excavated it is not possible to attribute specimens to any particular kiln, but it seems that the main part of this ware comes from kilns in Honan. Most objects of this type are of shapes very characteristic of the Northern Sung style and the ware seems only to have been in use during that period.

Several different shapes are found, one of the most common being a small globular jar of melon-shape. There is one jar of this type in the Seligman collection (Pl. 53:j) and one in the Buffalo Museum,[4]) said to have come from Ch'ing-ho hsien. Palmgren also illustrates a jar from the same site (Pl. 54:a, left). A jar of this type with green glaze was excavated from a Northern Sung tomb in Hopei. In the same tomb was also found a black glazed jar with two loop handles of the type we shall describe below.[5])

Another type of jar which is very common is of ovoid shape with short, straight neck and two loop-handles on the side. Jars of this type are in the Malcolm collection (Pl. 53:k), the Brundage collection,[6]) the Buffalo Museum[7]) and the Sherman E. Lee collection.[8])

Vases with ovoid body, spreading foot and foliate flower-shaped mouth are also found with this décor. There is one in the Boston Museum[9]) and another one in the Tokyo National Museum (Pl. 53:l).

Bottle-shaped vases with this decoration are not very common, but there is one example in a Japanese collection[10]) and one with large trumpet-shaped mouth was found in Ch'ing-ho hsien (Pl. 54:a, right).

A ewer of this type in typical early Northern Sung shape is in the Hellner collection (Pl. 54:b) and another one, with cover, is in a Japanese collection (Pl. 54:c),

---

1) *Wen Wu* 1964:8, p. 34 Fig. 17.
2) *Wen Wu* 1964:8, p. 1.
3) *China's beauty*, Nos, 488 and 490, cp. also 486, 487 and 489.
4) Hochstadter, *op.cit.* No. 76.
5) *Kao Ku* 1959:7, p. 351, Pl. 2: Fig. 11 left and 10 left.
6) *Catalogue* Pl. XXXVIII:B.
7) Hochstadter, *op.cit.* No. 75.
8) *Los Angeles exh.cat.* No. 250.
9) *Hoyt cat.* No. 317.
10) Exh. *To-so mei do ten.* Tokyo. No. 201.

a third one, also with cover but of a more sturdy shape, is in the Museum Yamato Bunkakan.[1]) A miniature jar of ovoid shape is in the Kempe coll.[2]) and a *mei-p'ing* vase in the Clark collection.[3])

Type: **Tc 33.**
Provenience: **Teng-feng hsien, Honan.**
Shape: **Cup.**
Date: **Northern Sung.**
Design: **Basket pattern.**

Among the objects excavated from the Teng-feng kilns[4]) was a cup of hemispherical shape covered with white glaze and with a design of carved, curved lines filled-in with a dark glaze in imitation of basket-work (Pl. 48:j), the cup is called *Ch'ü-ho yao*. A very similar cup is in the Boston Museum.[5]) In the same collection is also another cup[6]) of similar type but here the carved lines are vertical around the body.

Type: **Tc 34.**
Provenience: **Hopei.**
Shape: **Jar & cover.**
Date: **Northern Sung.**
Design: **Basket pattern.**

Another type of basket pattern is usually found on jars with cover and loop-handles. A jar of this type is in the Kempe collection. It is of a flattened oval form with flat base trimmed at the edge, and has a rounded cap-cover with two loops on the rim, corresponding to two others on the shoulder of the jar. The surface is moulded in basket pattern (Pl. 48:i). It is made of a grey stoneware covered with a light-brown glaze. These jars are of two different types, the first one has the just described dark glaze, the second has a creamy buff glaze. Examples of the second type are in the Boston Museum[7]) and in the former Eumorfopoulos coll.[8]) The ware and provenience of both types are undoubtedly the same, and they clearly belong to the same family as the pillows in our Type 18 above, which has also been observed by earlier writers.

Type: **Tc 35.**
Shape: **Jar with curled leaves.**
Date: **Northern Sung.**

---

1) Exhibition of Chinese ceramics. 1961. No. 40.
2) *CKc* No. 267.
3) *OCS Sung exh.* No. 80.
4) *Wen Wu* 1964:2, Pl. 6:4.
5) *Hoyt cat.* No. 280.
6) *Ibid.* No. 281.
7) *Hoyt cat.* No. 353.
8) *GEc.* Vol. III, C 206.

This group is formed by a group of small jars with the outside ornamented with five rows of looped petals (Pl. 48:k), the general appearance is very similar to that of a pineapple. These jars are made of a buff-white stoneware covered with a white slip and glazed with a transparent glaze. There are many similar pieces in different collections.[1]) One is in the MFEA and one in the Kempe coll. (Pl. 48:k). Pieces of this kind are reported to have been found in Ch'ing-ho hsien and many of them have the brownish stained water-patina typical of wares inundated at Ch'ing-ho and Chü-lu.[2]) Sullivan suggests that those jars might have been used in Buddhist funeral ceremonies and they do have similarities with other types of so-called funeral vases.

Type: Tc 36.
Provenience: Shansi?
Shape: Mei-p'ing, foliate vase.
Date: Chin.
Design: Painted floral sprays.

This is a group of vases painted in black, dark brown or dark grey on a white slip and covered with a transparent glaze. The painting on this group is very characteristic and favours lofty sprays of peonies, irises and other flowers. Wares of this type have been attributed to Shansi,[3]) but the excavation reports so far published from this province have not revealed any examples of the type.

The most common form found is a tall heavy vase of *mei-p'ing* shape. The design is very finely drawn and shows light and elegant flower-sprays, as can be seen on a vase in a Japanese collection (Pl. 54:d); many vases of the same kind are found in different collections.[4]) A vase of the same shape in the Guimet Museum shows a slightly more compact design of peony sprays (Pl. 54:f).

In the British Museum is a vase of ovoid shape with foliate flower-shaped mouth and with the same type of elegant floral sprays (Pl. 54:e).

The treatment of the design on this type is very special, and the group is not clearly related to any other known type of Tz'u-chou ware. The shapes prevailing in this group clearly indicate a very late Northern Sung or Chin date.

Type: Tc 37.
Provenience: Shansi?
Shape: Mei-p'ing.
Date: Chin.
Design: Carved flowers etc. under yellow glaze.

This is a small group of Tz'u-chou type wares clearly related to the preceding group, which has also been attributed to Shansi. Specimens in this group are dec-

[1]) *Barlow cat.* Pl. 58 b; *Los Angeles exh. cat.* No. 247 (a pair in the Sickman coll.).

[2]) In the MacDonald collection, Singapore is an oviform vase which has exactly the same kind of looped petals arranged around the neck as four handles (*A loan exhibition of Chinese Art.* Singapore Art Society, 1952. No. 19).

[3]) Two vases of this type are illustrated in the *Sung tai pei fang*, and are labelled Shansi (p. 24–25).

[4]) *OCS Sung exh.* 1949, no. 103. A similar vase is in the V & A and another one in the Art Inst. of Chicago.

orated with carved and incised floral designs under a brownish-yellow glaze. There is in a Japanese collection (Pl. 54:g) a *mei-p'ing* vase of a very fine quality which is characteristic of this type. The decoration is arranged in three horizontal bands on the body of the vase. The upper band has open flower sprays, of a type similar to those found in the preceding type, the middle band has a large *cash*-pattern and the bottom band has leaves and flowers like those on the upper band. All the designs are on a striated ground. A similar vase is illustrated in the *Sung tai pei fang*; it has two bands with peony sprays on a striated ground.[1]) A vase in the Fitzwilliam Museum[2]) which also apparently belongs to the same type has a design of overlapping petals in several rows, covering almost the whole body.

Type: **Tc 38.**
Provenience: **Yao-chou, Shensi.**
Shape: **Bowl.**
Date: **Chin.**
Design: **Lotus flower under yellow glaze.**

Related in style and appearance to the preceding type is a bowl in a Japanese collection (Pl. 54:h). It is carved and incised under a yellow glaze. On the interior is a lotus flower with combed details, and on the exterior a scroll band, and under the rim a border of small crescent-shaped strokes deeply carved. An almost identical bowl, with the same kind of exterior border, has been identified as Yao-chou ware[3]) (Pl. 54:i).

Type: **Tc 39.**
Provenience: **Shansi.**
Shape: **Vase & jar.**
Date: **Yüan.**
Design: **Flowers on wavy ground.**

One of the Tz'u-chou types which seem to be typical of the early Yüan period is a buff stoneware with black glaze and carved sgraffito design of a very characteristic appearance. The main design, usually a flower spray, is placed in a shaped panel, and the surrounding dark glaze area is incised with fine striations of curved lines forming a wavy pattern. One vase of this kind, of typical almost cylindrical shape with angular shoulders, is in the Chicago Art Institute (Pl. 54:j); it is decorated with a chrysanthemum spray in a panel surrounded by the just described wavy pattern. Two similar jars, one almost identical to the one just mentioned, were discovered from a Yüan-time find in Inner Mongolia.[4]) The type is very common and found in many collections. Globular jars of a type usual during Yüan are also found with this kind of design (Pl. 54:k). Chinese scholars usually attribute this ware to the Shansi province.[5])

[1]) *Op.cit.* Pl. 22.
[2]) Gray, *op.cit.* Pl. 51.
[3]) Published in *China's beauty*, no. 51.
[4]) *Wen Wu* 1958:5, p. 72.
[5]) See: *Sung tai pei fang* . . . p. 29–30.

Type: **Tc 40.**
Provenience: **Shansi.**
Shape: **Vases & jars.**
Date: **Yüan.**
Design: **Carved through black slip.**

This group is very large and seems to have been one of the most popular during the Yüan dynasty. It is characterized by a greyish stoneware with decoration cut through a thick, treacly black glaze to reveal a body which is burnt buff. This ware is also generally attributed to Shansi. Several different types and shapes have been found; some of the main ones will be presented here.

The first kind includes a group of *mei-p'ing* vases of characteristic slender form with rather straight sides and a tall tapering mouth-section. The design is arranged in horizontal bands around the body and includes rounded leaf scrolls, peonies and stiff lotus petals (Pl. 54:l); very often the design is shown against a striated ground (Pl. 55:a). Besides the examples illustrated, vases of this kind are in the Tokyo National Museum[1]) and the Buffalo Museum.[2])

The second group favours jars of ovoid shape with short cylindrical neck and two loop-handles on the shoulder. Here also the design is found in horizontal bands and is often composed of characteristically rounded leaf forms of different types and scale patterns (Pl. 55:b). Animal designs are also found and can be seen on a vase in the Tokyo National Museum (Pl. 55:c) with a design of hares and flowers.

The third kind is of a very characteristic Yüan shape, a bottle-vase with pear-shaped body and trumpet-shaped mouth. The décor usually consists of bands of the same type of rounded leaf scrolls as we have seen before. A fine example of this type is in the Honolulu Academy of Arts (Pl. 55:d) and many similar ones are known.[3])

The fourth type includes jars with wide mouth and short lip. These jars are found in many sizes from small miniature ones to very large ones. The design is usually bands with leaf-scrolls of the common, rounded type (Pl. 55:e, f).[4]) Some show more realistic flower scrolls of different types (Pl. 55:g).

The fifth type has jars of globular or ovoid shape with very short neck. Among the designs found are most of the types we have seen above, rounded leaf bands,[5]) designs on striated ground (Pl. 55:h), panels with peonies[6]) etc. A very interesting specimen in this group is the jar in the British Museum (Pl. 55:i) with the design of a boy among foliage which is inscribed "eighth year of *Ta-te*, seventh month" (1305), which gives us an approximate date of this entire group.

---

1) *Yokogawa cat.* No. 68.
2) Hochstadter, *op.cit.* No. 80.
3) *Sung tai pei fang* . . . p. 33; *Yokogawa cat.* No. 147; *Hoyt cat.* No. 306.
4) *Barlow cat.* Pl. 61 a.
5) *Sung tai pei fang* . . . , p. 32.
6) Cox, *op.cit.* Fig. 634; *Chinese Art under the Mongols,* No. 57.

The enamelled group

The earliest enamelled wares of China are found in the Tz'u-chou group. They are usually made of a reddish or buff stone-ware coated with a milk-white slip, then covered with a transparent glaze and fired. Subsequently they are painted on the glaze with designs chiefly in red and green and sometimes also yellow enamel, and finally fired again, this time at a lower temperature. The colours were badly controlled and are frequently degraded in surviving specimens, but they show great freshness and boldness in the painting.

A few specimens in this group are dated with 13th-century dates of the Chin dynasty. A bowl in the Buffalo Museum of Science[1]) is said to have come from Shansi and a recently excavated tomb in that province datable to around 1212 has also yielded a specimen of this type.[2]) Fragments have also been found in Yüan dynasty sites in Mongolia.

Recent discoveries of ancient kiln sites in China have revealed several sources for this type of ware. One kiln was found in Yü hsien in Honan,[3]) and another in *Pa-i* [66] in Shansi; the latter has unfortunately not been published so far. A third kiln has been discovered in *Han-tan shih* in Hopei.[4])

Several different types of designs are found on this ware.

Type:	**Tc 41.**	**Date:**	**Chin, c. 1200.**
Shape:	**Bowl.**	**Design:**	**Different.**

In this type the main design is found in a central round or six-lobed panel. Characteristic is the border, enclosing the central panel, which is built up by several line borders, the main one divided five times by an hour-glass-shaped figure.

Only three specimens of this particular type are known to us. One is the well-known bowl in the Tokyo National Museum[5]) (Almost identical to the one illustrated in our Pl. 55:j.) with an inscription on the base of the first year of *T'ai-ho* of Chin (equivalent to A.D. 1201). These bowls are decorated with a very beautiful peony design. The third specimen is also in a Japanese collection, and here the central panel is decorated with a duck flying over a lotus pond (Pl. 55:k).

Type:	**Tc 42.**	**Date:**	**Chin.**
Shape:	**Bowl.**	**Design:**	**Peony.**

The main motif in this group consists of different types of peonies and sprays of mallow flowers which are found in the centre of the bowls. The central design

[1]) Hochstadter, *op.cit.* No. 96.

[2]) *Kao Ku* 1961:12, p. 681. Fig. 1:3 (p. 682).

[3]) *Wen Wu* 1964:8, p. 27.

[4]) *Wen Wu* 1964:8, p. 37.

[5]) *Yokogawa cat.* No. 93.

is surrounded by line borders containing from two to four lines. There are four main variants.

The first kind has as main design an open sketchy peony flower. Examples of this type are found in the MFEA (Pl. 55:l), the Barlow collection,[1]) and in a Japanese collection.[2])

In the second type the main design consists of two open peonies placed close together, they are of the same sketchy type as the preceding kind. There are two bowls of this type in Japan[3]) (Pl. 56:a).

In the third kind the central design shows a large peony of the type we have called beehive-shaped. There is one bowl of this type in a private collection in London,[4]) one in Japan (Pl. 56:b) and a third one in the Baur collection (Pl. 56:c). The last one is slightly different from the others; the usual line border is here of a special type, where the lines are at intervals interrupted by short wavy sections.

In the fourth kind the main design is also a peony of the beehive-shaped type, but it is accompanied by a mallow spray. A fine example is in Japan,[5]) and two more bowls are in the Fitzwilliam Museum (Pl. 56:d) and in the British Museum (Pl. 56:e); on the latter bowl the flowers are placed in a pot; both examples only show the mallow from the side and the main motif is the peony. Another example shows only a very elegantly drawn spray of mallow flowers.[6]) Characteristic of this whole group is the enclosing border which consists of two thin lines with a broader one in between.

Type: Tc 43.
Shape: Bowl.
Date: Chin, c. 1200.
Design: Different.

This is a large group with many different designs, usually found inside bowls. Characteristic of the type is the border encircling the main motif, which is composed of different combinations of thinner and broader bands, but they are all decorated with groups of round dots applied on the border. Sometimes they are well fitted into the border, sometimes they are very casually applied. There are several variants.

One type has as main design a finely drawn lotus flower and a large lotus leaf. Examples are in the Buffalo Museum,[7]) said to have come from Shansi, and in the Art Institute of Chicago (Pl. 56:f).

On a bowl in the Seligman collection[8]) and one in the Eugene Bernat coll. (Pl. 56:g) the main design shows a big fish. On the last mentioned piece there is a lotus

[1]) *Cat.* Pl. 64 c.

[2]) *Sekai* 10; Pl. 124 lower.

[3]) *Sekai* 10; Fig. 141.

[4]) *Venezia exh.cat.* No. 515.

[5]) *Sekai* 10; Fig. 140.

[6]) *Sekai* 10; Fig. 137.

[7]) Hochstadter, *op.cit.* No. 96.

[8]) *Cat.* No. D 116.

plant beside the fish. A third bowl with the same motif is in a Japanese collection.[1])

The central design sometimes consists of characters. Two bowls in Japan both show four characters, but in one of them each character is set in a square (Pl. 56:h).[2]) A bowl in the Tokyo National Museum (Pl. 56:i) is decorated with one single character within a shaped cartouche. A very similar bowl, with the character *"ch'ing"* [67] on the inside within a frame, was excavated from a Chin tomb in Shansi datable around 1212 as we have already mentioned above.[3])

Designs of mallow sprays and beehive-shaped peonies very similar to type 42 are also found with the dotted border. The peony design can be seen on a bowl in the Metropolitan Museum[4]) and the mallow spray on one in the Honolulu Academy of Arts (Pl. 56:j), and a similar one in the Tokyo National Museum.[5]) The latter bowl has an inscription dating it to the 7th year of *Cheng-tai* of Chin (1230).

Type: Tc 44. **Date: Chin—Yüan.**
Shape: Saucer dish. **Design: Bird and flowers.**

This type of design is found on the inside of small saucer dishes. The main central motif is in a shaped panel surrounded by several line borders. A dish of this type with the design of a mandarin duck and a lotus plant was in the Seligman collection (Pl. 56:k), and a similar one with a phoenix-like bird among mallow sprays is in the Freer Gallery.[6]) The latter is very much worn and the design is partly illegible.

Type: Tc 45. **Date: Chin—Yüan.**
Shape: Bowl. **Design: Birds and flowers.**

In this type the main design is usually found inside the bowl, and on the exterior are formal lotus petals encircling the side.

One bowl of this type with the design of a lotus flower with a leaf and a three-petalled flower is in the Baur collection.[7]) A similar bowl with a flying bird and a lotus plant is in the Seattle Art Museum (Pl. 56:l). Other bowls of the same kind are in the collection of H.M. the King of Sweden and in the Brundage coll.[8]) The last-mentioned bowl shows a crane with raised wings in a standing position. With the exception of the Seattle bowl, all the examples mentioned above have the main motif enclosed in a shaped panel which is encircled by line borders, the main one with dots. The Seattle bowl has only simple line borders.

[1]) *Chinese Arts of the Sung and Yüan periods.* Tokyo National Museum 1961. No. 278.

[2]) Cp. *Sekai* 10; Fig. 139.

[3]) *Kao Ku* 1961:12, p. 682. Fig. 1:3

[4]) *So-no jishu yo.* Pl. 49.

[5]) *Sekai* 10; Fig. 142.

[6]) Sirén, *Kinas konst.* Vol. II, Fig. 358.

[7]) *Cat.* no. A 84.

[8]) *Cat.* Pl. XXXVII:D.

Some variants of this type are also found. In the Cleveland Museum (Pl. 57:a) is a bowl of a different shape, a rather high cup form, with rounded sides and low everted foot, which on the outside has a design almost identical with that on the Seattle bowl. A bowl in the Detroit Institute of Arts[1]) is decorated on the inside with a duck swimming in a lotus pond in a very similar style. The design is enclosed by a simple line border; there is no décor on the exterior.

In the MFEA is a covered bowl with almost straight, high sides of a shape similar to that of the Cleveland bowl. On the exterior are formal lotus petals, and on top of the domed cover is a lotus spray (Pl. 57:d).

Type: Tc 46. **Date: Chin—Yüan.**
Shape: Vase & bowl. **Design: Cartouches and scroll-work.**

Besides the above-mentioned designs there are also more geometrical types of designs and scroll-work sometimes found in combination with more realistic patterns. A bottle-shaped vase formerly in the Eumorfopoulos coll. (Pl. 57:b) is decorated with several borders on the neck, and on the body are cartouches separated by scroll-work. In the cartouches are the four characters "*fu kuei ch'ang sheng*". A bowl in the British Museum with almost straight walls is decorated with *cash*-shaped cartouches with leaves on the sides.

In the MFEA is a pear-shaped vase similar to the one just mentioned, a form very typical of Yüan as we have seen earlier, which has quadrangular cartouches in which are beehive-shaped peonies. Between the panels are dotted scrolls (Pl. 57:c).

Type: Tc 47. **Date: Chin—Yüan.**
Shape: Figurines.

Figurines of different types and sizes, often in the form of small toys, are very common in the enamelled Tz'u-chou ware. Fragments of figurines have been found in P'a-ts'un in Yü hsien, Honan. Figurines are also found in great numbers in different collections, many of them are obviously Yüan and Ming but some are undoubtedly Chin. Many pieces were in the Eumorfopoulos collection, and there are several specimens in the MFEA; some of them show children on horses and others depict women. In the Cleveland Museum is the figure of a lady holding a vase (Pl. 57:e) and in the Brundage collection is a small baby figure,[2]) whose face is almost identical to a face excavated at the earlier mentioned P'a-ts'un kiln.[3]) A figure of a child in a long robe in Yüan style is in the Baur collection.[4]) A closer

[1]) *Chinese Art under the Mongols.* No. 53.
[2]) *Cat.* Pl. XXXVII:B.
[3]) *Wen Wu* 1964:8, p. 33 Fig. 14.
[4]) *Cat.* No. A 83.

study of all these different types of figures would no doubt be most interesting but is beyond the scope of this paper.

In connection with the figurines must also be mentioned a fine and rare bowl with a figure design in the Kempe collection (Pl. 57:f). The design, which is painted in red and green enamels, shows a standing man dressed in a long robe, on which is seen a number of dots of the same type as we have seen on the borders in Type 43 above. The style is simple but the drawing very skilful and refined.

The variety of patterns found on the Tz'u-chou yao is very great and it is not possible to give a comprehensive list of all the different designs found on the ware, but some of the main ones will be listed below.

LIST OF DESIGNS FOUND ON THE TZ'U-CHOU WARE

Special floral motifs

The bold floral scroll	Type Tc 1, 3
The conventionalized flower	Type Tc 1, 3, 4
Finely incised scroll	Type Tc 2
Formal leaf scroll	Type Tc 25

Peony

Is extremely frequent and found in most types; some of the main ones are Type Tc 6, 9, 10, 12, 15, 16, 19, 21, 23, 25, 26, 36, 37, 41, 42, 43, 46

The beehive-shaped type is found in	Type Tc 12, 42, 46
Lotus	Type Tc 5, 10, 22, 26, 27, 38, 45
Sagittaria found with lotus e.g. in	Type Tc 22
Chrysanthemum	Type Tc 5, 7, 18, 26, 39
Lily	Type Tc 7, 36
Mallow	Type Tc 26, 42, 43

Other plants

Iris is found in	Type Tc 36
Melon-vine is found in	Type Tc 26

Bamboo is often found together with birds

Boys

Are found in many different combinations

with flowers	Type Tc 6, 27
with ducks	Type Tc 15, 17
playing in a garden	Type Tc 27
with hobby-horse	Type Tc 13
with kite	Type Tc 27
fishing	Type Tc 13
and also as figurines	Type Tc 47

Other human representations

Are not so common, but we have mentioned taoist immortals in Type Tc 7 and a drinking scene with Li Po in Type Tc 27; figurines are also found in the enamelled group Tc 47, and in the same group is illustrated a bowl with a man. A very interesting specimen is the dated pillow (Fig. 28:d), which is discussed on p. 185 below.

Dragon

Is extremely rare, which is not surprising since this ware was a typical people's ware An exception is found in Type Tc 21, where we have two dragon-decorated specimens, both dragons are of *lung* type. The *ch'ih* dragon is not found.

Phoenix

It is not found in Sung wares, but sometimes met with in Yüan.

Lion

Is not very common, but examples of a lion with embroidered bowl are known from pillows.

Tiger	Type Tc 7, 15, 29

Deer

Are very common and many different types are found

Type Tc 6, 12, 14, 15, 17, 28

Other animals

Among other animals found are

Bear	Type Tc 12
Cat	Type Tc 12
Hare	Type Tc 14, 40

Ducks and geese	Type Tc 5, 14, 15, 28, 41, 44, 45
Swan	Type Tc 14, 27

Other birds

Small birds on a bough are very common and found in many types.

	Type Tc 12, 13, 14, 15, 16, 19, 29
Cock	Type Tc 14
Crane	Type Tc 13, 14, 29, 45
Parrot	Type Tc 5
Quail	Type Tc 5
Peacock	Type Tc 26, 28
Pheasant	Type Tc 27

Insects

Are often found with the birds	Type Tc 11

Fish	Type Tc 12, 14, 27, 43
Cash pattern	Type Tc 5, 8, 20, 37
Chequer pattern	Type Tc 24
Fleur-de-lis	Type Tc 28
Basket pattern	Type Tc 33, 34

Inscriptions

Are quite common on this ware and several different types are found

a) Poems and lucky characters etc.	Type Tc 7, 9, 14, 16, 26, 31, 43, 46
b) Potter's name	Type Tc 13, 14, 15, 18
c) Dates, the following are found	

Chih-ho san nien	1056	Type Tc 18
Hsi-ning ssu nien	1071	Type Tc 6
Cheng-ho erh nien	1112	Type Tc 27
Hsüan-ho yüan nien	1119	Type Tc 18
Ta-ting shih pa nien	1179	(Fig. 28:d)
T'ai-ho yüan nien	1201	Type Tc 41
Cheng-tai ch'i nien	1230	Type Tc 43
Ta-te pa nien	1305	Type Tc 40
Shih-yüan erh nien	1336	Type Tc 30

TING YAO

Ting yao is undoubtedly the least mysterious of the classical Sung wares; it corresponds so closely with the literary descriptions given of it that there has never been any difficulty in identifying it. The localization of the actual kiln site in the province of Hopei was, however, a problem for quite a long time because of alterations in the administrative units in China after the Sung period. The kiln which during the Sung dynasty was situated in the prefecture of *Ting Chou* is to-day under the administration of the neighbouring *Ch'ü-yang hsien* [68]. The first modern scholar who was able to locate the actual kiln site was Fujio Koyama, who after studies of Chinese source material came to the conclusion that the kiln was to be found in *Chien-tz'u ts'un* [69] in Ch'ü-yang hsien. His visit to the kiln site in 1941 and his report on the finds are well-known, and we will not go into details about his discoveries but merely point out a few important facts.[1])

Koyamas exploration of the Ting kilns was extremely short; he only visited the kiln for about one hour, but he was nevertheless able to collect more than a 1000 sherds and wasters. Since Koyama published his report the kiln has been visited by Ch'en Wan-li, and studies by him and Feng Hsien-ming[2]) have appeared in Chinese periodicals, which have further established that the primary site of the ware is Chien-tz'u ts'un and that some smaller kilns have been found in neighbouring villages. The first excavation on a larger scale of the kiln site was, however, carried out in 1961–62, and the report was published in 1965.[3])

The material collected during the recent excavation of the Ting kiln at Chien-tz'u ts'un clearly proves that the kiln was already in operation at the end of the T'ang dynasty and that it probably already had a kind of official status during the Five Dynasties period. The evidence found at the kiln site is further strengthened by literary sources cited by Feng Hsien-ming and Ch'en Wan-li.[4]) According to the majority of Chinese writings on the subject the best period in the production of Ting yao was during *Cheng-ho* (1111–1117) and *Hsüan-ho* (1119–1125). This statement seems to emanate from the *Ko ku yao lun* [70] (this work is said to have been completed in 1387) and it is impossible to verify its correctness. What is more interesting to find out is when the operation of the Ting kiln actually came to an end. Most earlier writers seem to be of the opinion that the ware ceased to be made after the Chin tartars had conquered North China in 1127, and they usually cite a traditional quotation stating that when the Court fled south the potters from Ting chou emigrated too and established new kilns in the district of Chi-chou in Kiangsi province, where they produced a ware almost identical with the one they had made in the north. The *Ko ku yao lun* has been cited as the source of this information, but, as has already been pointed out by previous writers on the subject, this is due to a misreading, and the source does not actually say so.[5])

---

[1]) Koyama, "*On the discovery of the ruins of Ting yao*". Bulletin of Eastern Art, Tokyo Nos. 23–24, 1941. English reprint in the *ACASA* Vol. III, 1948–49 p. 61.

The best general discussion so far written about the products of the Ting kiln and its history is Mrs. Hin-Cheung Lovell's excellent catalogue of the Ting wares in the David Foundation (hereafter referred to as *David Ting cat.*).

[2]) *Wen Wu* 1953:9 pp. 91–106; *Wen Wu* 1959:7 pp. 67–71.

[3]) *Kao Ku* 1965:8 pp. 394–412. An abstract of this article was published in 1968 in the OCS Translation series (*Chinese Translations* No. 4).

[4]) *Op.cit.* See also, *David Ting cat.* p. xix.

[5]) N. Ozaki, "*Chinese Literature on Ceramics*". *OA* III:1 (Spring 1957) p. 25.

The opinion that the kiln ceased to operate at the end of Northern Sung is also held by Koyama, who stated in his excavation report: "On the top of the heap of relics of Ting yao in Chien-tz'u-ts'un there were numerous fragments of late Northern Sung dynasty ware, and not a piece of later age was found. Was it not because, as the tradition says, the kiln fell into disuse when the potters fled to the south from the attacking forces of the Chin tribe"[1])

Koyama's statement is somewhat astonishing. How can he be so sure that none of the fragments he found were not later than Northern Sung? It is still very difficult to determine what is the exact date of a Ting specimen, and it seems quite clear that Koyama's opinion is coloured by a previous conviction that the kiln stopped in 1127. A similar opinion is held by Feng Hsien-ming, who declares that everything was burnt and destroyed by the Chin tartars when they invaded the province. As has already been remarked by Hin-Cheung Lovell, this statement seems highly exaggerated. It is hardly possible, and not very sensible, to devastate a conquered land to such an extent, and it is not in accordance with what we know of the later rapid development of the Chin Empire into a prosperous land with a great and pronounced interest in Chinese culture and art. Moreover, the authors of the latest excavation report are of the opinion that the decline of the Ting kiln was a result of the disturbances caused by the Chin invasion, and they hold the view that no quality pieces were made after this event, even if the kiln continued to work until at least the end of the Yüan dynasty. Only a few specimens of bad quality found during the excavation are attributed to Chin and Yüan, and those pieces were collected rather than actually excavated. It should, however, be pointed out that the excavations so far carried out are very preliminary, and the dating of the different layers given in the excavation report is in the present author's opinion, very questionable; we will return to this matter later on. Even in this case it seems likely that the excavators have been misled by preconceived opinions.

The evidence on which we support our view that the Ting kiln continued to work even after the Chin takeover is of two kinds; one is founded on purely stylistic reasons, the other is a small but very important group of dated specimens. There is quite a large group of Ting yao pieces, especially with moulded designs, which, to judge both from their shape and their designs, must obviously be considered later than Northern Sung, and we shall present them in the following survey of the designs. The dated group is not large but contains some moulds used for impressing designs on Ting yao, which give us very good help in dating some significant designs. The moulds bear the dates 1184, 1189 and 1203, and they are all dated with reign marks of the *Chin* dynasty. There is also a Ting dish in the British Museum which is inscribed with a date corresponding to 1271 and a covered bowl dated 1162. These specimens clearly indicate that the Ting kiln continued to work for a long time, probably until the end of the Yüan dynasty. It is also significant that many

[1]) Koyama, *op.cit. ACASA* Vol. III 1948–49.

tombs clearly datable to Chin have yielded characteristic Ting specimens which would hardly have been the case if the kiln had not been still active.

The question of a Southern Ting ware and how to distinguish it from the Northern variant has been a major problem for most scholars dealing with Ting yao. Some of the finest wares have been attributed to the Chi-chou kiln, and in the old Palace Museum all significant pieces were labelled "Southern Ting", and this extreme view is still held by the museum authorities in Taiwan. Some writers have, for no particular reason considered the moulded ware to be of southern origin.[1])

The recent excavations carried out at the Ting kiln site in Hopei have, however, proved once and for all that all the well-known types of Ting wares were actually made at this kiln. And furthermore the extensive excavations which have recently been carried out at the Chi-chou kilns in *Yung-ho* [71] have not revealed any trace whatsoever of a ware of Ting type comparable in quality to that made in the north.[2])

A puzzling specimen is still the famous dish in the David Foundation on the base of which is inscribed "*Shao-hsing nien Yung-ho Shu chia tsao*" (made by the Shu family of Yung-ho in the Shao-hsing [1131–62] period). The *Yung-ho* referred to is presumably the place in Kiangsi where the Chi-chou kilns are situated. It seems, however, almost too good to be true that a dish inscribed with the potter's name, which is extremely rare during Sung, should have been preserved and that the name on this piece furthermore is that of a family actually mentioned in the *Ko ku yao lun*. According to Lovell,[3]) "The inscription has been scientifically examined in the British Museum laboratory, and its contemporaneity with the dish is above suspicion". If this is really the case we are still faced with something of a mystery, but we still think that the genuineness of the inscription is open to debate.[4]) Anyhow, the recent excavations of the Ting kilns have clearly proved that wares of exactly this type and with an identical design were made here.

The status of the Ting ware has been discussed in detail by Lovell[5]) and has been summed up by her in the following way: "We may conclude that Ting ware was never an imperial ware in the sense that the *pi-se* variety of Yüeh ware or Ju ware was. Although it found favour at court and was used in the palace, it remained

[1]) Gray, *op.cit.* mentions in connection with the covered bowl in the British Museum carrying the date 1162, "Probably this is a southern Sung piece and much of the moulded Ting yao is likely to be so too". This is all the more astonishing as the piece referred to bears the *nien hao* of the Chin dynasty and accordingly could hardly have been produced in the south. A similar bowl has recently been excavated at the Ting kiln site.

[2]) *Chi chou yao.* Peking 1958.

[3]) *Op.cit.* p. xxii.

[4]) Some other potters' names are found on Ting yao specimens but they are either rather casually inscribed in the bottom of the piece before firing or added after the firing. A Ting bowl in the Baur coll. has a name which could be a potter's name incorporated in the interior border design (cp. Type Ti 46 below).

[5]) *Op.cit.*, p. xxiii.

first and foremost a popular ware. And the switch of royal attention to another ware did not have any appreciable, let alone, disastrous, effect on the industry."

This statement probably gives us a very accurate description of the status of the ware, and it is obvious that earlier writers have put too much emphasis on its being an imperial ware. It seems now quite clear that Ting yao was already used by the court from the very beginning of the Sung dynasty and probably up to the end of Northern Sung, though not exclusively but together with products from other kilns. The idea that Ting yao was replaced by Ju yao in imperial favour is a later invention, and it does not correspond with the earlier mentioned opinion that the best Ting yao was made during the end of the Northern Sung period. The most substantial fact, however, is proved by the remains of the Ting kilns themselves, which are spread over an extremely large area and give evidence of an enormous output. A kiln of this gigantic scale could never have been intended for official use only, nor could the workmen of an industry of this size have been removed to the south in a hurry—which did not give even the Emperor and the court time enough to escape.

Some inscriptions found on Ting pieces show that they were intended for official use. The inscription *Shang shih chü* [72] incised in a vertical line is found on the base of some specimens collected at the Ting kiln site. This is the name of the office in charge of the supply of food to the imperial household in the Northern Sung dynasty. In the Kempe collection is a deep cup of thick porcelain which carries the inscription *Shang yüeh chü* [73] (Office in charge of Imperial medicine) in one horizontal line incised on the front of the bowl under the glaze.[1]) There are also in the Palace collection, and in other collections, specimens which bear inscribed names of different palaces etc., but these inscriptions are done after the firing and merely show that the object had at some time belonged to the palace.[2])

The recent excavations of the Ting kiln mentioned above have clearly shown that the Ting yao is a mere continuation and evolution of the white T'ang ware often referred to with the somewhat inadequate term *Hsing yao*. The main difference between the Ting yao and the earlier white wares is the colour of the glaze. Whereas the T'ang white wares (and most other Sung white wares as well) usually have a cold bluish glaze and usually are provided with a slip under the glaze, the Ting glaze is of a characteristic warm ivory colour. The Ting glaze is relatively thick and contains small air bubbles which give it a very delicate, almost moistened look. Its smooth, slightly fat, surface is also pleasant to touch, which was undoubtedly one of the reasons for its becoming so popular. The ware is generally uncrackled, but where the glaze is thick it has often assembled into small gum-like drops which have been given the name "tear-drops" and have come to be regarded as a sign of genuineness of the ware. The body is fine and close-grained of a light greyish-white colour and clearly translucent, the transmitted light having an orange tint.

---

[1]) *CKc* 398.

[2]) See note 1, p. 140 below.

Except for white wares the Ting kilns also produced other types of porcelain. The *Black Ting* and *Purple Ting* have already been famous for a long time in the literature, but the excavations have now proved that wares of this kind were indeed made at the Ting kiln. Both variants have the fine porcelain body of the white ware, but the glaze is, in the first case, a lacquer-black glaze of very high quality, and in the second case an almost soya-sauce coloured glaze of reddish tint. Fragments of other types have also been found in the kiln, among which could be mentioned specimens with designs in iron oxide.

The white Ting ware is found either plain or decorated. In this paper we are only concerned with the decorated variant, although some of the finest examples of the ware are found in the undecorated group. We have divided the decorated ware into two main groups, the Incised and the Moulded. The first group covers objects which have incised or carved designs, as these two techniques are often used simultaneously, and it is also almost impossible to make a distinction between the two types. The designs selected are meant to give a general survey of some of the most common and significant designs found on the ware, but several rare and uncommon designs are also presented, especially when they can give us a clue as to the dating of a special group or if they could in any other way be of interest to our study.

It should be mentioned here that white wares of Ting type were of course produced in many other kilns during the Sung dynasty, for instance in Chi-chou, but as they are of very little significance in connection with our study of designs we have decided to concentrate here on the Ting ware. Some comparative reference to wares of other types is, however, given especially towards the end of this chapter.

Carved and incised.

Type: Ti 1. **Date: Early Northern Sung.**
Shape: Jar; mortar. **Design: Overlapping petals.**

This particular design, which is deeply and forcefully carved, is found on a small group of objects usually with a greenish-white glaze. In a Japanese collection is a jar (Pl. 57:g) with cylindrical body, sloping shoulder and low circular foot; the jar is decorated round the body with a design of overlapping petals. The petals are pointed and have lobed sides and deeply incised details, they are placed on larger rounded petals (this arrangement we have also seen in the early Northern celadon group Type Nc 1 above). Round the shoulder of the jar is a row of radiating, overlapping petals.

The same type of design is found on a covered jar in the David Foundation (Pl. 57:h). This jar is of ovoid shape with marked shoulder, has four angular loop-handles on the shoulder and is provided with a flat cover with stalk-knob. The overlapping petal design is found in two rows round the body, and on the shoulder is a collar of petals.

A more unusual specimen belonging to this group is a mortar in the David Foundation.[1]) It is made of two vessels, one a round dish with a flat rim and the other a cylindrical basin, joined together at the lip. The general shape is that of a drum, and around the exterior just below the lip is a row of twenty appliqué bosses. The design on the exterior shows two rows of overlapping petals. A white glazed piece of exactly the same shape but with different décor has been found in a Liao tomb (Fig. 37:o).[2])

A very rare specimen which also seems to belong to this type is an incense burner, or lamp in so-called *tazza* shape in the Kempe collection (Pl. 58:a). Outside the bowl of this piece is a deeply carved design of overlapping petals with finely incised details. Coiled around the stem is a ferocious-looking dragon of *lung* type in relief, which seems to carry the bowl. The arrangement is very similar to what we have seen on the famous Northern celadon piece formerly in the Sedgwick collection (Pl. 7:f). On the foot are finely incised clouds. The flat horizontal brim has a deeply carved, fine and detailed peony design (Fig. 8:a).

Type: Ti 2.
Shape: Vase; ewer.
Date: Early Northern Sung.
Design: Carved peony scroll.

This type is related to the preceding one but features a realistic peony design. In combination with the main design, specimens in this group have round the neck a band of radiating, overlapping petals. A good example of the type in question is a small vase of ovoid shape in the Bristol City Art Gallery (Pl. 58:b). It has a large realistic peony design, with finely incised details, deeply carved round the body and the overlapping petal band round the shoulder.

In the Clark collection[3]) is a similar but more rounded vase which has lost its neck. It is decorated round the belly with a similar peony design with finely incised details. Round the base are two rows of large, pointed, overlapping petals, and round the shoulder is the radiating petal band.

A ewer in the Calmann collection (Pl. 57:i) of a shape generally associated with Northern Sung has a similar peony design round the shoulder and overlapping, pointed petals round the lower part of the body. Just below the neck is an arrangement of radiating petals exactly corresponding to that seen on the Clark vase. A ewer formerly in the Rücker-Embden collection (Pl. 57:j) of related shape has the peony design carved all round the globular body and the overlapping, radiating petals on the shoulder.

---

[1]) *David Ting cat.* No. 182.

[2]) Tomb No. 3 in *Ta Yin Tzu* (Jehol), *K K H P* 1956:3, Pl. 7:4. This specimen is decorated with a typical Liao design, a flower with two stiff leaves. Similar specimens with three-colour glazes have also been excavated from Liao tombs (See: *Liao tz'u hsüan chi.* Peking 1961. Pl. 11.).

[3]) Gray, *op.cit.* Pl. 40.

Type: Ti 3. **Date: Early 12th century.**
Shape: Eight-lobed bowl. **Design: Peony and lotus in panels.**

In the Clark collection[1]) is a big bowl of a shape quite unusual in Ting yao. It has a flat bottom and straight, high, eight-lobed sides. The interior is decorated on the flat bottom with a peony spray with a large flower and leaves in a round panel (Fig. 5:b) and on the side are eight panels, each enclosing a lotus plant; combed details. The shape as well as the combination of the very finely carved peony and the sketchy lotus plants on the side are unusual. A bowl of the same shape is in the David Foundation;[2]) it is only decorated with a rather mechanically incised flower in the centre.

Type: Ti 4. **Date: Early 12th century.**
Shape: Six-lobed bowl. **Design: Peonies in panels.**

This design is found on six-lobed bowls with rounded sides and foliate rim. Moulded ribs divide the interior into six panels radiating from the flat centre. Inside each panel and in the central medallion is a finely incised single spray of peony. There is one bowl of this type in the David Foundation[3]) and another one in the Baur collection.[4])

Type: Ti 5. **Date: Early 12th century.**
Shape: Six-lobed bowl. **Design: Sketchy lotus in panel.**

This design is found on the interior of six-lobed bowls with foliate rim. Moulded ribs divide the interior into six panels radiating from the flat centre. The design is found in the round central panel (the others are undecorated) and consists of a sketchy lotus spray with flowers seen from the side, a large lotus leaf and feather-like reeds. A fine example of this type is a bowl in the Heeramaneck collection (Pl. 58:c), and similar bowls with a smaller central panel are found in the Seligman collection[5]) and in the Victoria & Albert Museum.[6]) Two bowls of this type were excavated from a tomb in Manchuria datable, on the basis of comparison of the material excavated with that from other tombs in the same region, to the end of Liao or beginnig of Chin.[7]) Also during the excavations of the Ting kiln site specimens of this type were discovered and dated very early to T'ang – Five Dynasties. This date seems highly improbable (Cp. Fig. 33:20).

---

[1]) Gray, *op.cit.* Pl. 39.
[2]) *David Ting cat.* No. 104.
[3]) *David Ting cat.* No. 106.
[4]) *Baur cat.* No. A 12.
[5]) *Seligman cat.* No. D 79.
[6]) Formerly in the Eumorfopoulos coll. *GEc* III: C 131.
[7]) *Kao Ku* 1964:2, p. 82 Fig. 3:1, 3.

Type: Ti 6. **Date: Late Northern Sung.**
Shape: Six-lobed bowl. **Design: Two fishes among waves.**

This design, which is very common, is found on six-lobed bowls with rounded sides and foliate rim. Moulded ribs divide the interior into six panels radiating from the flat centre. In the round central panel are two fishes swimming one over the other on a combed wave ground. The waves are made of rows of incised rounded lines getting larger and larger. A good example of this type is in the Seligman collection[1]) and several examples have been found at the Ting kiln site[2]) (Fig. 32:20). The type is almost identical to Type Cp 5 found among the ch'ing-pai ware. In ch'ing-pai this type is usually considered to be of Southern Sung date, but the Ting variant seems to have been slightly earlier.

Type: Ti 7. **Date: Northern Sung.**
Shape: Dish; six-foil bowl. **Design: Lotus spray.**

This design is found on shallow dishes and bowls with six-foil rim, and it generally covers the whole of the inside. The design consists of a spray with rolled, feather-like leaves, a large open lotus flower with thin, pointed petals with combed details, a sagittaria also with combed details and a large lotus leaf seen from the side with combed details and serrated side (Fig. 9:b). The design is enclosed by a thin incised line. This pattern is found on a dish in the Lundgren collection (Pl. 59:a) and on a deep bowl in a Japanese collection.[3])

Type: Ti 8. **Date: Northern Sung.**
Shape: Bowls and dishes, often with six-foil rim. **Design: Lotus spray.**

This design, which is similar to the preceding one, is one of the most common patterns found on Ting yao. It is usually covering the whole interior of bowls or dishes of round or six-foil shape. The design shows a lotus flower, rather sketchily depicted with thin, pointed petals, a sagittaria of similar type, and scrolls with small, curled feather-like leaves and a thin elongated lotus leaf seen from the side, with serrated side. No combed details are found in this type. There are a great many specimens with this design in various collections, all of them with the same general outline but with minor variations in the composition. Some typical specimens are illustrated (Pls. 59:b, 60), and references can be given to several other examples.[4]) Fragments with this design were also found during the excavations of the Ting kiln (Fig. 33:16).

[1]) *Seligman cat.* No. D 77.

[2]) *Kao Ku* 1965:8, p. 407. Fig. 10:2, 6.

[3]) Koyama, *Chinese ceramics.* Pl. 48.

[4]) *Venezia exh. cat.* No. 530 (Clark coll.); and 538 (Ex. Traugott); *Baur Cat.* No. A 11; *Seligman Cat.* No. D 78; Gray, *op.cit.* Pl. 42 (Seligman).

Type: Ti 9. **Date: Late Northern Sung—Chin.**
Shape: Different. **Design: Lotus flower and sketchy leaves.**

This type is very close to the preceding one and to Type 5, the main difference being that the lotus leaf has disappeared and that the whole design generally is of a more sketchy type. The feather-like leaves are still more stylized and look like thin plumes. The design can be more or less sketchy, and sometimes it is just indicated by a few swiftly incised strokes. In Chinese publications this design is often referred to as *Hsüan Ts'ao* [74], a day-lily (*Hemerocallis Flava*), but, as we have already shown, it is in fact a mere conventionalization of a lotus motif. Specimens of many different shapes are found with this design, shallow dishes, deep bowls, bowls with six-foil rim etc.

The most well-known piece with this design is no doubt the famous dish in the David Foundation[1]) with the inscription "*Shao-hsing nien Yung-ho Shu chia tsao*", which has already been discussed above (p. 127). The design is quite sketchy and dissolved (Fig. 9:a). Other examples with this design are in the Kempe collection (Fig. 8:c) and in Cologne.[2]) Specimens of this type have also been excavated at the Ting kiln (Fig. 33:18). It is interesting to note that several specimens with this type of design have been excavated from sites datable to Chin and Southern Sung.[3]) An interesting piece in this connection is a jar in the Clark collection (Pl. 57:k). It has fluted sides and a domed cover with small stalk knob. On the lid is an incised spray of the feather-like type. This jar is of the same type as the one in the British Museum with a Chin date equivalent to 1162 (cp. Pl. 84:f).

Type: Ti 10. **Date: Late Northern Sung—Chin.**
Shape: Dish; bowl. **Design: Lotus spray.**

This design, which is mainly found on round bowls and dishes, is of the same general appearance as Type 8 above, but there are some small differences in details. In this type we have the same feather-like leaves, the sagittaria and the lotus flower with the lotus leaf seen from the side, but the execution is not quite the same. The details are finer, the lotus flower is not so sketchy and it has combing on the petals. One bowl of this type is in the British Museum, and it is said to have been excavated from a Manchurian tomb datable to the 12th century.[4]) On this dish the seed-vessel of the lotus is visible, a feature which is rather uncommon in this group. A typical example of this type is a bowl formerly in the Rücker-Embden collection (Pl. 57:l). An interesting specimen which also belongs to this group is

[1]) *David Ting cat.* No. 184.

[2]) Feddersen, *op.cit.* Abb. 33.

[3]) *Kao Ku* 1962:4 p. 185 Fig. 8:2 (Our Fig. 35:a). *Kao Ku* 1964:11 p. 559 Fig. 2:2, 3. (cp. also our Fig. 35:b).

[4]) Hobson, *Handbook*, Fig. 49.

a large bowl in the Victoria & Albert Museum.[1]) It is of rounded shape with rather straight, high walls, and the outside has carved overlapping lotus petals. The lotus design covers the inside of the bowl. This bowl is of exactly the same type as Type 21 below, with fish design.

Type: Ti 11.	**Date: Late Northern Sung.**
Shape: Basin; vase.	**Design: Sketchy lotus.**

This design is of a more sketchy type and has similarities with the peony design of Type 13. It shows a lotus flower with broad rounded petals and leaf-scrolls of the feather-like type with rather broad, curled leaves. The design is found on a vase with barrel-shaped body and tall cylindrical neck in the David Foundation (Pl. 61:a) and also on a basin with almost straight sides in the Kempe collection (Pl. 62:a). A basin with eight-lobed side and foliate rim in a Japanese collection[2]) also has the same design.

Type: Ti 12.	**Date: Late Northern Sung.**
Shape: Dish; bowl.	**Design: Sketchy lotus.**

This is a sketchy lotus design of a type similar to the preceding one, the main difference being that the lotus leaf is always shown. A fine example is a dish with vertical sides in the Kempe collection (Pl. 62:b), which in the flat bottom has a lotus flower, a sagittaria and a large lotus leaf, all with combed details (Fig. 8:d). A little more sketchy type of the same design is found on a six-lobed bowl with foliate rim in the same collection (Pl. 63:a). It shows several lotus flowers and leaves in a freer arrangement on the sides and bottom of the bowl.

Type: Ti 13.	**Date: Late Northern Sung.**
Shape: Mei-p'ing: bottle-shaped vase.	**Design: Sketchy peony.**

This design is composed of scrolls of peony with rather sketchily depicted open flowers and short broad leaves. Petals and leaves have incised details. A very fine example of this design is found on a *mei-p'ing* vase in the David Foundation (Pl. 61:b). It has radiating overlapping petals round the neck, a main band with the peony design round the belly and a row of large overlapping petals with combed details round the base. The arrangement of the design is very similar to what is found on Northern Sung vases of Tz'u-chou type.

Another example of this design is found on a bottle-shaped vase in the Barlow collection (Pl. 61:c). It is of globular shape with long neck and flanged lip and has

[1]) Fry-Binyon, *Chinesische Kunst*, Tafel 32:C. Another bowl of this kind is in the Brundage coll. (*Cat.* Pl. 33.)

[2]) *Sekai* 10, Pl. 79.

a splayed base. The shape is rare in Ting yao and is of a type that we associate with the Imperial wares of Ju and Kuan type. This is probably an example of the official Ting ware. The design is found round the body and is freely incised.

This type is very close to the lotus type 11 above.

Type: Ti 14. **Date: Late Northern Sung.**
Shape: Basin. **Design: Peony scroll.**

This design comes close to the preceding one and is found on a round basin with flat bottom and straight sides in the David Foundation (Pl. 61:d). The design is found both on the exterior and the interior and consists of very elegant peony scrolls with small pointed leaves and large open flowers with combed details on the petals. This shape is also rare in Ting yao and very closely related to Ju and Kuan. The quality is extremely fine.

Type: Ti 15. **Date: Late Northern Sung.**
Shape: Conical bowl. **Design: Pomegranates.**

This design, which is very rare, is found on a bowl of conical shape in the Boston Museum (Pl. 63:b). It is finely incised and shows a pomegranate branch with thin elongated leaves and two fruits. The design covers the whole interior of the bowl and is enclosed by a thin incised line.

Type: Ti 16. **Date: Northern Sung.**
Shape: Six-lobed bowl. **Design: Panels with ducks and lotus.**

Swimming ducks or geese is a most common design on the incised Ting yao, and several different types are found which are all closely related to each other. Some of the main types will be listed here (Types nos. 16–20).

Our first type is found on six-lobed bowls with rounded sides and foliate rim. Moulded ribs divide the interior into six panels radiating from the centre. Inside the round central panel is a lotus spray and the side panels have alternating lotus plants and swimming ducks, both on combed waves. A bowl of this kind is in the Kempe collection (Pl. 64:a, Fig. 8:e).

Type: Ti 17. **Date: Northern Sung.**
Shape: Six-foil bowl; dish. **Design: Ducks and sagittaria.**

This design is composed of, in the centre, a sagittaria leaf surrounded on the side with alternating stands of sagittaria and swimming ducks placed opposite to each other on a ground of combed waves. A bowl with a six-foil rim of this type was formerly in the Holmes collection (Pl. 64:b) and a dish with slightly everted, sloping sides with the same design, is in the Barlow collection.[1]) The waves are made in the form of long combed bands, as is usual in this group.

Type: Ti 18.
Shape: Conical bowl.
Date: Northern Sung.
Design: Ducks and reeds.

This design is found on bowls of conical shape with rounded sides. The design covers the whole of the interior and is enclosed by a thin incised line. It shows two large ducks swimming side by side, and in front of them a stand with reeds, on a ground of waves made in the shape of long combed bands. Good examples of the type are found in the David Foundation[2]) and in the Museum of Fine Arts in Boston (Pl. 65).

Type: Ti 19.
Shape: Dish with flaring sides.
Date: Northern Sung.
Design: Ducks, reeds and sagittaria.

This design is found on dishes with slightly everted, sloping sides and is very similar to the preceding one. It shows in the centre two ducks swimming side by side, to the left is a stand with sagittaria and to the right reeds; combed waves of the usual type. Examples are in the Kempe collection (Pl. 66:a, Fig. 8:f) and in the David Foundation.[3])

Type: Ti 20.
Shape: Shallow bowl.
Date: Northern Sung.
Design: Ducks, reeds and lotus.

This design is very similar to the two preceding ones, but in front of the two swimming ducks is a large lotus plant with flower and bud and a large leaf; to the right are reeds. Combed waves of the usual type. A bowl of this type is in the Hellner collection (Pl. 66:b).

Type: Ti 21.
Shape: Deep basin.
Date: Late Northern Sung.
Design: Fish among water-weeds.

This design is found on big, deep basins with curved sides and slightly thickened lip. On the inside is a big fish among water-weeds. Two thin creepers of water-weed are coming in from the left side and enclose the large fish, which is placed in the centre of the bowl (Fig. 8:g). The fish has deeply cut crossed lines on the body and is surrounded by waves made by long combed bands. There is one bowl of

[1]) *Barlow cat.* Pl. 42 a.

[2]) *David Ting cat.* No. 100.

[3]) *David Ting cat.* No. 160.

this type in the Kempe collection (Pl. 67); the outside of this latter bowl is plain, except for a deeply incised line below the rim. Two other bowls with the same design, one in the David Foundation[1]) and the other one in the MFEA both have carved overlapping petals on the outside.[2])

Type: Ti 22. **Date: Late Northern Sung.**
Shape: Bowl. **Design: Two fishes among water-weeds.**

This design is found on the interior of round bowls and is similar to the preceding one in its composition. One bowl of this kind in a Japanese collection[3]) shows three long, thin creepers of water-weed coming in from the left and enclosing two small fishes swimming among combed wave-bands. The fishes are in this type much smaller and of a different kind. Another bowl (Fig. 27:a) shows a variation of the motif. Here the water-weeds are growing from the lower part of the design and the fishes are placed in opposite directions, one on the left and the other one on the right side. A design almost identical to this one is found on Northern celadon (cp. our Type Nc 16, and Fig. 27:a and b).

Type: Ti 23. **Date: Chin.**
Shape: Dish. **Design: Two fishes among waves.**

This design is found on dishes with vertical, slightly rounded sides. It shows two fishes, one over the other, swimming in opposite directions among waves. The waves are here of a different type from those found in previous wave designs, they are built up by rows of incised rounded lines getting larger and larger, and on top of these roll-like waves there are hooked crests. A very fine example of this type is in the Fitzwilliam Museum (Pl. 61:e); this latter dish has a small horizontal edge. A similar dish, but smaller, is in the David Foundation.[4])

Type: Ti 24. **Date: Chin.**
Shape: Dish with horizontal rim. **Design: Two fishes among waves.**

This design is found on a dish with low, rounded sides and horizontal flattened rim, with slightly thickened edge; it is in the David Foundation.[5]) The design is found on the flat interior and shows a net-like arrangement with wave-pattern of a similar type to that found in the preceding type. Inside the net there are two

---

1) *David Ting cat.* No. 154.

2) Bowls of the same type with lotus designs are also found (see our Type 10).

3) *To-so no hakuji*, Pl. 43 upper.

4) *David Ting cat.* No. 191.

5) *David Ting cat.* No. 176.

small fishes swimming. The fishes are very hard to see, and the composition looks like a kind of puzzle-picture. No similar piece is known.

Type: Ti 25. **Date: 1271.**
Shape: Dish with horizontal rim. **Design: Fish and floral spray.**

This design is found on a dish in the British Museum; it has a rounded side and a horizontal flat rim, slightly thickened at the edge. On the inside is a round panel showing a large fish and a floral spray with mallow-like flowers. Under the glaze in the bottom is an incised inscription reading: "*Chih yüan pa nien tsao kung yung*" (made in the eighth year of Chih-yüan, [1271] for official use). Chih-yüan is the *nien hao* of Kublai Khan, who was master only of Northern China at that time. This dish seems to prove that Ting wares were still produced during the beginning of the Yüan dynasty. It is also interesting to note that this dish is of a shape very common during late Sung and Yüan, and at the same time it follows up a Liao tradition (Pl. 61:f; Fig. 27:c).

Type: Ti 26. **Date: Northern Sung.**
Shape: Saucer-shaped dish. **Design: Lung dragon.**

Dragons of the more "naturalistic" *lung* type are comparatively rare on incised Ting yao but are found on the inside of some dishes of saucer-shape with a slightly thickened rim.[1]) A very fine dish of this type is in the Kempe collection (Pl. 68). The dragon is seen side-face from the left in the traditional composition pursuing the pearl, which is placed just above the right front claw. The head is particularly well rendered with its open jaws, long whiskers and big horns. The dragon is three-clawed. A characteristic feature which becomes very common later on is the loop formed by the tail and one of the hind legs. The scaly body is indicated by deeply carved semi-circular incisions and the tufts of hair on face and legs by long combed bands. A very similar decoration is found on a dish in the David Foundation.[2]) The main difference between the two are the tufts of hair which here are not combed but incised with deeper lines. Both dragons are very vigorously carved.

Type: Ti 27. **Date: Late Northern Sung—Chin.**
Shape: Bowl; dish. **Design: Ch'ih dragon.**

The dragon of archaic type often called *ch'ih* is more common than the *lung* dragon on Ting yao, and it is found in several different combinations. There are

---

[1]) Feng Hsien-ming mentions, however, in his article on Ting yao in *Wen Wu* (1959:7 p. 67, *Tz'u ch'i ch'ien shuo*) that several sherds with this motif have been found on the Ting kiln site.

[2]) *David Ting cat.* No. 159.

two main types, and we shall first describe a variant which is probably the earlier of the two.

Characteristic of this type is that the dragon is seen from the side. The body is band-like and bent into a C-curved shape, the hind leg and the tail forming a loop. The head of the dragon is seen sideways from the left, and has two curved horns; it is still quite near to the more "naturalistic" *lung* type, but the lizard-like body is characteristic of the *ch'ih* type. Dragons of this type are found on specimens of different shape and in combination with other motifs, some examples will be given below.

a) In the Kempe collection is a deep bowl with rounded sides and the exterior decorated with carved overlapping petals. On the interior is a dragon of this type as the only design; it is rather sketchily depicted (Fig. 13:f).

b) In the British Museum[1]) is a dish with flat bottom and rather tall flaring sides. The interior is decorated in the centre with a dragon of this type surrounded by realistically rendered lotus flowers and leaves similar to those found in the lotus design of Type 10 (Fig. 13:c). An almost identical dish is in the David Foundation.[2])

c) In the Kempe collection there is a shallow bowl with rounded sides and a six-foil rim (Pl. 69:a). The interior is decorated on the side with a very finely carved realistic peony scroll with two large flowers, and in the small round central panel is a dragon of *ch'ih* type (Fig. 21:e). The leaves are fine, thin and elongated, and the petals have combed details. A very similar bowl with a larger central panel is in the Hellner collection (Pl. 69:b); otherwise the designs are almost identical.

Type: Ti 28. — **Date: Chin.**
Shape: Dish; incense-burner? — **Design: Ch'ih dragon.**

The second type of *ch'ih* dragon is quite different from the first one. The body is of the band-like lizard type, but it is often much more richly ornamented, especially on the body and tail, and cloud-scrolls have been added which are so closely connected with the dragon bodies that it is almost impossible to distinguish the two elements. The faces of the dragons have also changed; they have now a three-lobed shape and are often seen from above with both eyes visible. It also seems that the dragons mostly have just one horn. Several different variations are in existence.

a) This is a very simple type found on a dish with flat bottom and flaring side in the E. Bernat collection.[3]) The dish has no decoration except for the dragon found in the round panel formed by the flat interior. The body forms a C-curve,

---

[1]) Hobson, *Private*, Fig. 222.

[2]) *David Ting cat.* No. 114.

[3]) *Chinese ceramics of the Sung dynasty.* The Currier Gallery of Art. Manschester, New Hampshire 1959. Cat. No. 11.

the head is seen from above and is *ju-i* shaped with two large ears and an S-shaped horn; nose and eyes are merely indicated.

b) This design is found on a dish with rounded sides. In the small, round central panel is a *ch'ih* dragon with the head seen from above. On the side are two large *ch'ih* dragons with thin elongated bodies among scrolls; one of the dragons is seen from the side and the other one from above. Just below the rim is a thin somewhat dissolved classic scroll border (Pl. 70:a Fig. 13:b).

c) This design is found on a dish with flat bottom and horizontal, flattened rim with a slightly thickened edge. The arrangement of the design is very similar to the **a**-type above with a single dragon in a round panel (Pl. 70:b). But the dragon is more elaborate with more details, on the dragon's body are small incised scrolls which give the impression of being dots (Fig. 13:e). On the flat rim is an incised angular key-fret border.

d) This design is found on a well-known dish in the David Foundation with flat bottom and horizontal flattened rim with a slightly thickened edge (Pl. 61:g). In the centre are two curling dragons very similar to type **b** above, but both dragons's heads are seen from above (Fig. 13:a). On the flat rim is a thin, somewhat dissolved, classic scroll border.[1])

e) In the Kempe collection is an unusual Ting yao specimen, it is a large cylinder, probably an incense-burner, with double relief bands at top and bottom. Round the belly is an incised design of two dragons (Fig. 8:b) of this type, and between the relief bands are angular key-fret borders.[2])

Apart from the dragon design this type has several other characteristic features *inter alia* the angular key-fret, the classic scroll and the dish shape with flat rim, which bounds them together as a group.

Type: Ti 29. **Date: Chin.**
Shape: Dish; bowl; cup-stand. **Design: Lotus scroll.**

---

[1]) The two characters "*Feng hua*" [75] are carved on the base after the firing. In the catalogue over the David Collection written by Hobson it is remarked that the Feng-hua hall was the residence of Liu Kuei Fei, concubine of the Emperor Kao-tsung, who died in 1187, and it has therefore been suggested that the dish was made before that date. This statement does not seem to be able to be verifiable and it is most likely that there have been many palaces with this name. There are several other Ting specimens in the Palace Museum in Peking with this inscription and also the inscriptions *feng hua* [76] *tz'u fu* [77], *chü hsiu* [78] and *chin yüan* [79]. These inscriptions are mentioned by Feng Hsien-ming in an article in the *Wen Wu* (1959:7 p. 67, *Tz'u ch'i ch'ien shuo*) and illustrated by him (Fig. 35: d). A bowl with lotus design with the inscription "*hua yüan*" is in the David Foundation (Cat. no. 177). Specimens of Ju yao with the "*feng hua*" inscription have also been found.

All these different names are probably names of palaces and wings of palaces. It should, however, be observed that all these inscriptions were made after the firing, and they do not give us much aid in the dating of specimens, as they could have been put on very much later.

[2]) The shape of this piece is similar to the mortar in the David Foundation (see Type Ti 1 above) made by two vessels put together.

This is a group of Ting yao (Types 29–31) which has many common characteristics in shape and design, and it could be arranged in different ways, but we have chosen to do it after designs, but references will be made continuously to similar specimens with different designs.

The main design in this Type is found on the inside of dishes with flat interior and consists of a lotus scroll. The scroll is quite realistic with two large lotus flowers and two leaves, and in the centre a characteristic lotus seed-pod. The design is deeply cut with much force and some tendrils have a peculiar wavy, almost serrated side. The design is found in an almost identical execution on three different types of dishes.

a) Dish with flat bottom and horizontal flattened rim with a slightly thickened edge shaped in eight foliations. The main design is found on the flat inside, and on the rim are eight groups of scroll ornaments matching the foliations of the edge. A dish of this type is in the Freer Gallery (Pl. 71).

b) Dish with flat bottom and horizontal flattened rim with thickened edge. The central design is the same, but the flat rim has an angular key-fret band. A dish of this type is in the Tokyo National Museum. (Pl. 61:h; Fig. 9:c).[1])

c) This dish, which is in the Boston Museum, is of the same shape as **b** above and has the same central design, but the flat rim has a finely incised formal palmette scroll of characteristic appearance (Pl. 72:a).

d) The design of this type differs from the above-mentioned ones, but the execution is the same. It is found on a small dish in the Kempe collection (Pl. 72:b) of octagonal shape with flat horizontal rim slightly thickened at the edge. The interior of the dish is round. In the centre is a carved design of a lotus plant with a flower, a big leaf and a sagittaria. On the broad, flat rim are dissolved spiral scrolls. This type of lotus scroll design is also occasionally found on specimens of other shapes than dishes, and we will give two such examples.

e) A bowl from the Ting kiln site (Pl. 61:i) is of conical shape and has the design covering the whole of the inside of the bowl.

f) A very rare specimen in the Hellner collection (Pl. 73:a) is a cup-stand in the shape of a low rounded bowl standing on a saucer with slightly rounded side and low spreading foot. There is no bottom to the bowl, which shows that the piece has been used as a stand for a larger cup. Both the exterior of the cup and the inside of the dish are decorated with the lotus scroll design, finely carved. On the exterior and interior of the bowl and on the saucer just below the rim are dissolved classic scroll bands. The general appearance of this cup-stand is closely akin to those found later on in carved lacquer.

Type: Ti 30.
Shape: Dish.

Date: Chin.
Design: Peony spray.

---

[1]) *Sekai* 10; Pl. 76.

This design shows a very realistic peony spray with a large flower, a bud and elongated pointed leaves. It is found on the interior of dishes of two types.

a) A dish in the Nelson Gallery (Pl. 74) is of the type with flat bottom and horizontal, flattened rim with a slightly thickened edge. The peony design, which is strongly carved, has finely incised details, and the petals are combed. The design covers the whole of the flat inside. On the flat rim is a formal palmette scroll of exactly the same type as was found on the dish of identical shape in the Boston Museum and belonging to our Type 29 c above.

b) The same central design is found on a dish with flat bottom and slightly flaring sides in the David Foundation.[1]) This dish has an angular key-fret border just under the rim. (Fig. 5:a).

Type: Ti 31. **Date: Chin.**
Shape: Dish; bowl. **Design: Peony scroll.**

This design shows a peony scroll with two flowers and feather-like leaves. The execution of the design is very similar on all specimens in the group, but there are slight variations in the way the flowers are rendered.

a) Dish with wavy edge shaped in eight foliations. The bottom is flat and the rim is horizontal and flattened with thickened edge. In the round panel formed by the flat inside of the dish is a scroll with two peony flowers with pomegranate-shaped centres. The leaf scrolls are thin with feather-like curly leaves. On the flat rim is a dissolved scroll border. The dish is very similar to Type 29 a above, it is in a private collection in Holland (Pl. 73:b).

b) Dish with flat bottom and horizontal flattened rim with thickened edge. The inside has a peony scroll of a type closely akin to the above-mentioned dish. On the flat rim is a thin classic scroll border. This dish (Pl. 75:a) is in the Kempe collection (Fig. 21:b).

c) This dish, which is in the Hellner collection, is of the same shape as **b** above (Pl. 75:b). The interior peony scroll is somewhat different, the flowers are almost triangular with tightly overlapping petals and small centre. The leaf scroll is of the usual type. On the flat rim is a finely incised formal palmette scroll and on the cavetto are sketchy clouds.

d) This dish, which is in the British Museum (Pl. 76), is of similar shape and almost identical to Type 29 c and Type 30 a above. The peony scroll has large flowers with peculiar hooked petals. On the flat rim is the formal palmette scroll.

e) This is the only specimen in this group which is not a dish but a bowl of conical shape. But it is obvious that the design is the same. The bowl, which is in the Baur collection (Pl. 61:j), has a small rosette of overlapping petals in the centre, and surrounding it is a scroll of the curled feather-like type with four large flowers.

---

[1]) *David Ting cat.* No. 175.

The flowers have the same pomegranate-like centre as types **a** and **b** but the petals are hooked like in type **d**. There is no border.

The three types just described (Nos. 29–31) obviously belong to the same group; we have many small characteristics which turn up in all three types regarding both shape and design. The dissolved scroll border, the formal palmette scroll, the angular key-fret, the horizontal rim with thickened edge on the dishes etc., all these are features which keep the group together and also show their close connection with the archaic dragon group Type 28 above. The scroll on the flat rim of the Kempe dish (Pl. 75:a) is the same as that on the David dragon dish (Pl. 61:g). The shapes, as well as the border designs found in this entire group, point towards a rather late Chin date.

Type: Ti 32. **Date: Northern Sung.**
Shape: Flower-shaped dish. **Design: Mallow.**

Dishes in the shape of a mallow-like flower are found in Ting yao as well as in ch'ing-pai (Type Cp 9). One dish of this type of five-petalled shape is in the Kempe collection (Fig. 28:e); it has a star-like flower in the centre and finely incised leaf-veins. Sherds of identical specimens were found at the Ting kiln site (Fig. 32:25). A dish in the David Foundation (Pl. 61:k) is of eight-petalled shape and also has a star-shaped flower in the centre, surrounded by a mallow-like flower with combed petals. Another dish of this type is in the collection of H. M. the King of Sweden.[1])

Moulded designs

Type: Ti 33. **Date: Late Northern Sung.**
Shape: Shallow dish. **Design: Dragon among clouds.**

Dragons of the *lung* type are rare among the moulded Ting ware although some examples are found. In the Eugene Bernat collection is a shallow dish with rounded sides with this design on the interior. It shows a big dragon seen side-face from the right surrounded by a broad band of cloud-volutes (Pl. 77). A single-line border encloses the design. The dragon is vigorously executed and forms a C-shaped figure; the neck is S-shaped and the head slightly lifted and looking upwards, the tail and hind-leg form a characteristic loop. The dragon is four-cleft, the left claw is lifted and just above it is the flaming pearl. A dish almost identical in every detail is in the collection of the Shanghai Museum.

Type: Ti 34. **Date: Chin.**
Shape: Large dish. **Design: Different.**

[1]) *MFEA Exh.cat.* No. 7, No. 160.

This is a large group of dishes with various designs but forming a very definite type with the same shape and composition. The dishes are large and of saucer-shape, with rounded sides and low foot. The rim is unglazed. There are several variations found in the motifs of the patterns, but the arrangement of the design is always the following: In the centre a round panel surrounded by a key-fret border (sometimes another type of border) and on the sides a broad décor band enclosed by double (sometimes triple) thin relief lines just below the rim. The exterior is undecorated.

a) Lotus and peony design. A dish with this design is in the David Foundation (Pl. 78:a). It is decorated in the central panel with lotus and small three-petalled flowers. There are several lotus flowers in the composition, many of them depicted as buds and arranged two and two together. The décor band on the side shows a very detailed and realistically rendered peony scroll with large flowers. This design is enclosed by a triple-line border. A dish with similar design but with double-line border is in the Barlow collection[1]) and another one in the Lindberg collection.[2])

b) Lotus, sagittaria, mallow and peony. This design is very similar to the preceding one but the composition in the central panel is more rich and includes lotus leaves, sagittaria, mallow and a sedge-like plant with corncob-like spike-rushes. The décor band shows a peony scroll, but the flowers are a little more open and lily-like than those found in the **a**-type. Double-line border. Examples of this type are in the Victoria & Albert Museum,[3]) the Cleveland Museum (Pl. 78:b) and the Peking Palace Museum.[4]) A similar specimen with minor differences is in the Glasgow Art Gallery.[5])

c) Ducks and lotus. This design is found on a dish in the Kempe collection.[6]) In the centre is a lotus pond with two big ducks swimming among lotus flowers and reeds. The décor band on the side shows lotus flowers and leaves together with small four-petalled flowers. The lotus flowers are of the bud-like type, looking like artichokes and placed two and two with the bottoms together. Double-line border.

d) Phoenixes, peacocks and flowers. This type shows in the centre part a pair of phoenixes with short tails flying among scrolling tendrils with lotus flowers of the "artichoke" type and small three-petalled flowers. The side décor band shows four realistic peacocks with long tails flying among peony scrolls. Double-line border. There is one example of this type in the Freer Gallery (Pl. 79:a) and another one is in the Baur collection.[7])

---

[1]) *Barlow cat.* Pl. 45 A.

[2]) *BMFEA* Vol. 25, Pl. 79 (Gustaf Lindberg: *Hsing-yao and Ting-yao*).

[3]) V & A No. C 361–1921.

[4]) *Ku kung po wu yüan* . . . Pl. 16.

[5]) Burrell coll. No. 38/269.

[6]) *CKc* No. 459.

[7]) *Baur cat.* No. A 17.

e) Fishes and lotus. This design, which is somewhat different from the other four types just described, is found on a dish in the Freer Gallery (Pl. 79:b). The design on this dish is considerably larger than on the other one but otherwise is of the same general appearance. In the central panel are two large fishes, with their heads pointing towards the right-hand side of the dish, swimming among lotus flowers and leaves, sagittaria, small three-petalled flowers and water-chestnuts. The central panel is enclosed by a plaited band; this is very rare; all other specimens in this group have the key-fret. The décor band on the side has big lotus flowers of the "artichoke" type often placed two and two together, lotus leaves, two and three-petalled small flowers, sagittaria etc.; double-line border.

Type: Ti 35. **Date: Chin.**
Shape: Conical bowl. **Design: Palmette-like peony.**

The design is found on the interior of conical bowls with undecorated exterior. In the centre of these bowls is usually a small five-petalled mallow-like flower, and the main décor band on the side is enclosed by an angular key-fret band below the rim. A bowl in the Victoria & Albert Museum (Pl. 80:a) is a good example of the type. The design in the main band is built up by a scroll with three almost triangular palmette-like peonies. The leaf-stems are crossed in a very characteristic way and the large top leaves sometimes take the shape of cloud-volutes. Similar specimens are in the Honolulu Academy of Arts (Pl. 81), the MFEA, the ROM in Toronto[1]) and in a Chinese collection (Fig. 1:d). They all have minor variations in the shape of the flowers and in the details of the design but they all have the same general characteristics. A fine example of the type was earlier in the possession of Messrs. C. T. Loo (Pl. 80:b) and it shows that the central part of the palmette-like peony could be differently executed even on the same scroll. Several sherds with this type of design have been found on the Ting kiln site.[2]) A dated mould with this kind of palmette-like flowers is in the British Museum and will be discussed below.

Type: Ti 36. **Date: Chin.**
Shape: Conical bowl. **Design: Pomegranate-like peony.**

This design has many features in common with the preceding type. It is found on bowls of the same conical shape which in the centre have a rosette-like flower with radiating overlapping petals; in the centre of this flower is sometimes a group of small dots indicating the seed-vessel. The main décor band on the side is enclosed by an angular key-fret band under the rim. The design shows a peony scroll

---

[1]) ROM 922.20.104.

[2]) *Kao Ku* 1965:8 p. 397 Fig. 2:15; p. 407, Fig. 10:3. (Our Figs. 32:15, 34:3).

with large flowers which have a characteristic pomegranate-like centre. The leaves are of the same elongated type with crossed stems and long wavy ends sometimes taking the shape of cloud-volutes. A fine example of the type is in the Victoria & Albert Museum and almost identical ones are in the Cleveland Museum of Art[1]) and the Oxford Museum of Eastern Art (Pl. 82). The moulding on all these specimens is very clear and sharp and of high quality. Sherds with this type of design have been found on the Ting kiln site[2]) (Fig. 32:7).

Type: Ti 37. **Date: Chin.**
Shape: Conical bowl. **Design: Boys among fruit scrolls.**

The design of small boys climbing among scrolls is also found in the conical bowl group. A specimen of this type is in the MFEA (Pl. 83). It has the three-petalled flower in the centre and the usual angular key-fret below the rim. The main design on the side shows a very detailed and finely moulded composition of three boys climbing among realistic scrolls with fruits of pomegranate, apricot and melon.

A similar bowl in the British Museum (Pl. 84:a, Fig. 19:f). has a more elaborate star-like flower in the centre, and on the side are three boys climbing among lotus scrolls, melon-vine with fruit and other plants. Below the rim is a classic scroll border.

Type: Ti 38. **Date: Chin.**
Shape: Conical bowl. **Design: Phoenixes and composite floral scroll.**

This type is the most interesting in the group of conical bowls with related designs. The bowls in this case have the same angular key-fret below the rim as the other types, but the central flower is here usually three-petalled. The main design is very finely moulded with delicate details and shows two phoenixes flying among elegant composite floral scrolls. The phoenixes are of a slender type with long, straight or very lightly bent beak. On the head of the bird is a thick plume curving backwards. The neck is long and thin and gracefully S-curved. The wing feathers are carefully drawn. The tail is long and thin and split into two parts, each ending in a spiral, like those found among the *ch'ih* dragons. The floral scroll, which is very light and elegant, shows realistic flowers of camellia and mallow type (Fig. 22:b). There is one bowl of this type in the British Museum[3]) (Pl. 84:b), one in the David Foundation[4]) (Pl. 84:c), one in the Boston Museum[5]) and one in the

---

1) No. 56.699.
2) *Kao Ku* 1965:8, p. 397, Fig. 2:7.
3) Gray, *op.cit.* Pl. 43.
4) *David Ting cat.* No. 108.
5) *Hoyt cat.* no. 256.

Bristol City Art Gallery.[1]) They are all closely akin, and probably made from the same mould.

A most important aid to the dating of this particular design is a mould in the David Foundation (Fig. 22:a). This mould has obviously been used for a Ting yao bowl of a similar type. The main difference with our bowls is that the central small flower here is exchanged for a larger round panel showing that the mould was made for a specimen of somewhat different shape. The central panel of the mould is decorated with an elegant floral scroll with small star-like five-petalled flowers and a melon-vine with two fruits; the rendering of the motif is very similar to the floral scrolls on the phoenix bowls. The main décor band shows two phoenixes of exactly the same type as described above, among floral scrolls. The scroll and the flowers are, however, not of the same type as on the phoenix bowl, but they are of the palmette-like type which we have already seen in our Type 35 above. In this way the mould just described ties together still more the different types within this group,[2]) and we shall see later on that they in their turn are only one link in a long chain of specimens with different designs, all of which have a close stylistic connection.

What makes the David mould so important is its inscription found on the back, reading; "*Ta-ting erh shih ssu nien ssu yüeh nien lu jih Wang Sheng Chi tsao*" (made by *Wang Sheng Chi* on the twenty-sixth day of the fourth month in the twenty-fourth year of *Ta-ting*). This inscription not only gives us the exact date, 1184 A.D., of this mould and with that, the design as such, but as Ta-ting is the *nien-hao* of an Emperor of the *Chin* dynasty it also proves that the Ting kiln was in fact still working during that dynasty and able to produce specimens of excellent quality. Moreover, this mould is not an isolated specimen; we know of at least two other moulds of related designs with Chin dates. Those moulds are both in the British Museum, and one of them we have already mentioned above in connection with our discussion of the palmette-like flower. This mould (Fig. 23:b) is for a bowl which has in the centre a round panel decorated with a realistic peony with leaves, and on the side is a scroll with palmette-like peonies of the kind we have seen under Type 35 above. Below the rim is a classic scroll border. The inscription on the mould reads: "*T'ai-ho san nien p'en*" (the third year of *T'ai-ho*), which is equivalent to the year 1203 of the Chin reign. These two moulds are very important evidence of the Chin date of this group.

Among the specimens excavated at the Ting kiln site was also a mould for a dish with design of a phoenix and a scroll with five-petalled flowers. The mould is apparently for a dish with a flattened, horizontal rim of a type of which we know many examples[3]) and it is closely related not only to our phoenix bowl but also to Type 54 below. On the side of the bowl is an elegant lotus border of a type which

[1]) *Venezia exh. cat.* No. 546.

[2]) See also Type 39 below, which features the phoenixes and the palmette-like flowers together.

[3]) *Kao Ku* 1965:8, p. 407, Fig. 10:12.

we will see on several specimens later on, a characteristic feature of this border is the artichoke-like lotus buds placed with their bottoms against each other.[1]) The mould is dated Northern Sung by the excavators like the main part of the excavated material, but, as we shall show later on, the dating of this site seems most unreliable.

Type: Ti 39.
Shape: Dish.
Date: Chin.
Design: Phoenixes and palmette-like peonies.

We have already pointed out above how the David mould links the palmette-like flower with the phoenix design, and further evidence of their contemporaneousness is a dish in the Museum of Eastern Art in Oxford (Pl. 85:a). This dish has a central round panel with palmette-like peonies and large curled leaves, and on the sides two phoenixes of the long-tailed type among palmette-like peonies of different types. The leaf-scrolls have partly taken the shape of cloud-volutes. There is a key-fret border below the rim.

Type: Ti 40.
Shape: Dish with steep sides.
Date: Chin.
Design: Different.

This is a group of dishes with the same shape and the same arrangement of the patterns, but with different design motifs. Dishes of this type are round with flat bottom and steep, slightly rounded sides. The main design covers the whole of the flat inside and is generally surrounded by a band of angular key-fret. On the side is a décor band, and below the rim a key-fret band. In this group we find several unusual designs.

a) Ch'i-lin and palmette-like peony. A dish in the Neave-Hill collection (Pl. 85:b) is decorated in the central field with a mythical creature with horns, a flame-like tail and a lion's body; it is probably representing a *ch'i-lin*, which has a floral spray in its mouth. The animal is surrounded by scrolls with palmette-like peonies of the kind we have seen under Type 35 above. Both flowers and leaf-stems are identical to that type. On the side is a thin elegant scroll of five-petalled flowers, leaves and buds of a realistic type.

b) Lion (and ball) among pomegranate scrolls. A dish of this type in the David Foundation (Pl. 86:a) is decorated in the centre with a lion sporting with the embroidered ball. The ball is of round "*cash*"-shape and has a four-petalled flower in the centre, it has long ribbons attached to it, tied into rosettes. The main motif

[1]) The border is not shown in the drawing in the just mentioned report in the *Kao Ku*, but can be seen upon a close study of the Plate 10:11.

is surrounded by leaf-scrolls of the cloud-volute type, one of them ending in a pomegranate. The main panel is enclosed by a key-fret band. On the side are two elongated dragons of the *ch'ih* type among cloud-volutes. A dish with similar design is in the Seattle Art Museum.[1]) The design on this dish is rather worn and very difficult to distinguish, but the central motif is apparently a large ferocious-looking lion surrounded by pomegranate scrolls. The design on the side band also shows pomegranate scrolls.

c) Ch'ih dragons and pomegranate scrolls. A dish in the Museum of Eastern Art in Oxford is decorated in the central panel with a pair of *ch'ih* dragons of the same type as those found on the David dish. The side band shows forceful pomegranate scrolls which have taken the shape of cloud-volutes (Pl. 86:b).

d) Winged dragons among scrolls. A dish in the Malcolm collection (Pl. 87:a) has in the central panel a most unusual dragon design. The composition shows two dragons with fish bodies, large wings and ferocious-looking heads with open jaws and long beards. The dragons are depicted as if they were chasing each other and around their bodies are elaborate formal scrolls probably meant to represent flames. On the side is a pomegranate scroll of the cloud-volute-like type.

e) Ch'ih dragons and lotus border. Slightly different in shape from the other specimens in this type is a dish in the Seligman collection (Pl. 87:b), which has rounded sides and a slightly everted rim. The round central panel is decorated with a pair of *ch'ih* dragons closely akin to those found on the Oxford dish (Type **c**). The central design is enclosed by an angular key-fret band. On the side is an elegant lotus border composed of lotus flowers, leaves and seed-pods, sagittaria etc. Below the rim is another key-fret band (Fig. 41:a).

Type: Ti 41. **Date: Chin.**
Shape: Dish with steep sides. **Design: Boy among lotus scrolls.**

This type is closely related to the preceding one but has minor differences. The shape of the dish and the arrangement of the design are, however, identical. A dish in the Kempe collection (Pl. 88:a) has in the central panel a boy wearing a loose open jacket, tied with a ribbon at the neck and adorned with groups of small dots. The boy is climbing in a realistic floral scroll with lotus flowers and leaves and sagittaria. The main panel is enclosed by a classic scroll-band on a dotted, granulation-like ground. The design on the side is an elaborate classic scroll, and below the rim is a key-fret border. The moulding of this dish is extremely fine and distinct and every detail, for instance in the boy's face, is clearly visible (Fig. 21:d).

Type: Ti 42. **Date: Chin.**
Shape: Dish with steep sides. **Design: Phoenix among peony scrolls.**

[1]) No. 7.581.

This type is more elaborate than the two preceding ones and more closely related to Types 54 and 55 below. In the central panel is a large flying phoenix with flame-like tail, spread wings and gently curved long neck (Pl. 88:b). The bird has in its beak a winding peony scroll which is encircling it; in the scroll are also small insects (cp. Type 55 below). The central panel is enclosed by an eight-lobed frame built up by one beaded border and two thin and one broad line-border. In the incurving sections of the lobed exterior border are groups of small dots. On the side is a composite floral scroll with lotus flowers and leaves, five-petalled flowers, sagittaria etc. Below the rim is a key-fret border. The dish is in the British Museum.

Type: Ti 43. **Date: 12th century.**
Shape: Dish or bowl with six-foil rim. **Design: Different.**

This is a group of saucer-shaped dishes or shallow bowls, with six-foil rim. The interior décor is found in a round central panel and on a broad band on the side, but the pattern is continuous and no frame or border encloses the central part. There is an angular key-fret band just below the rim. Specimens of this type have a wave-design covering the whole decorated part. The waves are of a very characteristic type formed like large spirals. Several different types of designs are found.

a) Fishes, ducks, cranes and lotus. A bowl in the Victoria & Albert Museum (Pl. 89:a) is decorated in the centre with two large fishes swimming one over the other with their heads pointing to the right side. On the side is a very elaborate design showing realistic lotus plants, pairs of swimming ducks and standing and flying cranes or egrets, all on the spiral wave ground. The motifs are repeated twice but are differently rendered. Sherds of a similar type have been found at the Ting kiln site. Some of the waves are adorned with the characteristic crests that were later on so common in Yüan and Ming ceramics.

b) Ducks, lotus and fish. In the Freer Gallery (Pl. 89:b) is a dish decorated in the central panel with two ducks and a lotus plant. The ducks are placed one on each side of the lotus facing each other, a composition common in early blue-and-white.[1]) The décor band on the side has two groups with three ducks and one with two ducks among lotus flowers, sagittaria and other water plants, all on the spiral wave ground. Under one of the lotus plants is a single, small fish. The irregular placement of the fish is most unusual.

c) Lotus and four fishes. In this type the central panel is occupied by a large lotus plant, and the décor on the side shows four large fishes alternating with lotus plants and reeds. This design is found on a dish in the Sedgwick collection[2]) and one in the Fitzwilliam Museum (Pl. 84:d). In the Kempe collection is a bowl (Pl. 90:a)

---

[1]) Cp. Pope, *Ardebil collection* Pl. 7; Pope, *Topkapu*, Pl. 20.

[2]) *O.C.S. Sung exh.* No. 25.

with similar design showing two fishes on the side. This bowl is covered with a brown glaze and has sometimes been called purple Ting. The piece is rather course and is probably a waster of some kind or an experimental piece. The waves in this composition have crests.

d) Fishes among lotus. In this type we find two large fishes in the central panel, and on the side are eight more fishes swimming among lotus and other water plants. The waves are partly of the crested type. A good example of this design is in the Brundage collection.[1])

Type: Ti 44.
Shape: Bowl with six-foil rim.
Date: 12th century.
Design: Ducks and lotus.

This type is very close to the preceding one but there are some minor differences. The shape of the bowl is deeper and the central panel is smaller. The spiral wave design does not cover the central panel but only the main décor band. The key-fret below the rim is of a more rectangular type. An example of this type is a bowl in the Honolulu Academy of Arts. It is decorated in the centre with a lotus plant and on the side with three groups of ducks in pairs, alternating with lotus plants, among different water-plants all on a spiral wave ground (Pl. 90:b).

Type: Ti 45.
Shape: Dish or shallow bowl (sometimes with six-foil rim).
Date: Chin.
Design: Central pair of fishes.

The shape of the specimens in this group and the arrangement of the design are similar to Type 43 above. The main difference is that the spiral wave design is found only in the small central panel and not as ground to the décor on the side. The spiral waves in this group are all of the crested type. There is a key-fret band below the rim.

a) A dish of this type in the Malcolm collection (Pl. 91:a) has in the central panel two fishes swimming with their heads pointing to the right side. On the side is a band with lotus flowers, sagittaria and other water-plants. The lotus flowers are rather stiff, and one of the leaves is in the centre shaped like a cloud volute.

b) A bowl in the Baur collection[2]) is decorated in the central panel with two fishes swimming with their heads pointing to the right side. On the side is a very elaborate and detailed design showing three short-tailed phoenixes among lotus flowers and several other kinds of plants.

---

[1]) No. B 60 P 1406, not illustrated in the catalogue.

[2]) *Cat.* no. A 18.

c) Similar to the above-mentioned bowl is one in the Cleveland Museum (Pl. 91:b). In the central panel are as usual, two fishes, but they are here swimming in different directions. The décor band on the side has two ducks flying among lotus flowers and other kinds of water plants, very fine and detailed in the moulding. The two ducks are both shown in a flying position but they are quite different in appearance. One has the characteristic neck-tuft of the mandarin duck and the other one looks more like a goose. It is possible that the artist has meant to depict a drake and a duck.

Type: Ti 46. **Date: Chin.**
Shape: Deep bowl. **Design: Pair of fishes and lotus.**

Related to types **b** and **c** above is a bowl in the Baur collection.[1]) It is of deep conical shape with rounded sides. In the central panel is the usual design of two fishes on a ground of spiral waves. On the deep sides is a fine and elaborate design of lotus plants, water-chestnuts, duckweed, sedge with large spike-rushes, and other water-plants. Below the rim is an angular key-fret band of the usual type, but within this border is a panel containing the inscription "*Li weng*" (Old Li), presumably the name either of the potter or of the owner. Such inscriptions are rare on Ting yao but are found on a pair of bowls in the David Foundation.[2])

Type: Ti 47. **Date: Chin.**
Shape: Bowl. **Design: Ch'ih dragon and peony scroll.**

This design is found on bowls with rounded sides. On the interior is a round central panel, a main décor band on the side and an angular key-fret border below the rim. In the small central panel is a *ch'ih* dragon seen from above with a characteristic band-like body with scrolled tail and triangular head. On the side is a realistic peony scroll with large flowers. The moulding is clear and sharp with fine details on flowers and leaves. There is one bowl of this type in the Seattle Art Museum (Pl. 92:a) and another one in the Museum Yamato Bunkakan.[3])

Type: Ti 48. **Date: Chin (— Yüan).**
Shape: Bowl. **Design: Rhinoceros viewing the moon, and boys among peonies.**

[1]) *Baur cat.* no. A 19.

[2]) *David Ting cat.* no. 137–138. The name found on these bowls is *Wu Ming-chih.* The bowls have a carved fluting on the exterior, and the interior design shows a detailed floral pattern. The bowls are labelled "Ting-type ware" in the catalogue and are dated Yüan.

[3]) Museum Yamato Bunkakan. *Exhibition of Chinese Ceramics* 1961, Cat. no. 29.

This design is found on a bowl of the same shape as in the preceding type in the Kempe collection (Pl. 92:b, Fig. 21:a). In the central panel is a detailed design of a reclining rhinoceros, on a tongue of land surrounded by crested waves, looking at a crescent moon and stars in the sky. On the side are three boys climbing among realistic scrolls of peony with large flowers. The boys are all in different, more or less acrobatic, positions and they are wearing loose jackets similar to that found on the boy in Type 41 above. There is a band of angular key-fret below the rim. Fragments with exactly this design have been found during the excavations of the Ting kilns (Fig. 32:8). The motif with the *hsi-niu*, usually referred to as a rhinoceros, viewing the moon is comparatively rare in early Chinese ceramics. We know it from Northern celadon pieces of Chin date[1]) and we find it on Yüan and Ming wares, and it seems that this design was mostly in favour during Chin and Yüan.[2]) In the Freer Gallery (Pl. 93) is a mould, probably for a Ting piece, with this design. It is found in the central panel of the mould and shows the rhinoceros reclining on a land-tongue with water and reeds with spike-rushes surrounding it. In the sky is the crescent moon and a heavy cloud-band. On the side is a vigorous formal scroll on a granulated ground enclosed on both sides by bands of key-fret. Below the rim is a thin classic scroll-border. The general stylistic character points to a late Chin or Yüan date. We also meet with the design on a dish formerly in the Oppenheim collection (Pl. 84:e). This dish has a flat horizontal rim of ogee-shape with thickened edge. In the flat central part is a design finely incised showing a triangular tongue of land with tufts of grass on which the rhinoceros is reclining watching the crescent moon and a constellation of stars in the sky. The lower part of the panel is decorated with large, crested waves. On the side is a sketchy leaf design of a type very common in Yüan and early Ming celadons.

Type: Ti 49. — **Date: Chin.**
Shape: Dish with six-foil rim. — **Design: Boys among peony scrolls.**

This design is found on a dish of saucer-shape with six-foil rim. The dish has a round central panel but the design continues all over the inside without interruption. It shows a realistic peony scroll of a light and elegant type with four climbing boys. One boy is placed in the centre of the dish and the three others on the side; they are all in more or less acrobatic positions and are of a type almost identical to those found on the Kempe bowl in the preceding type. The design is enclosed by a single-line border. The dish was formerly in the Peters collection.[3])

Type: Ti 50. — **Date: Chin.**
Shape: Shallow bowl. — **Design: Phoenixes and cloud scrolls.**

[1]) See page 39 above.

[2]) For a further discussion of this motif see p. 196 below.

[3]) Hobson: *Chinese, Corean and Japanese potteries.* New York 1941. No. 348.

This design is found on a shallow bowl with rounded sides in the Lundgren collection (Pl. 94:a), of the same shape as Type 48 above. In the round central panel are two peonies of the palmette-like type with long pointed leaves. On the side are two phoenixes among scrolls which have taken the shape of elaborate cloud-volutes. The birds are of a peculiar type, with their tall wings laid together backwards instead of being expanded, and a very short flame-like tail which is almost hidden among the cloud scrolls. The head has a mushroom-shaped crest which is not placed, as is usual, at the back of the head but very far forward at the beginning of the beak. The neck-tufts are thin and long, and the top one is very elaborate with a scroll ending (Fig. 14:e). The phoenixes are flying in the same direction and one of them turns his head backwards as if he were looking for the other one. The style and décor of this piece is obviously related to Types 35–39. A very similar dish, with the same kind of phoenixes, is in the collection of H.M. the King of Sweden, the main difference being that this dish has a spray of mallows in the centre. The phoenixes are both looking in the same direction and none of them has the head turned.

Type: Ti 51. **Date: Chin.**
Shape: Shallow bowl. **Design: Peony scroll.**

This design is found on a shallow dish in the Victoria & Albert Museum (Pl. 94:b). It has a round central panel and a key-fret band around the rim. The design is covering the whole of the interior and shows a peony scroll with large flowers, one of which covers the central panel. The peony flowers are of a type with features both from the palmette-like type and the pomegranate type. The leaves are of the elongated type with crossed stems.

Type: Ti 52. **Date: Chin.**
Shape: Deep bowl. **Design: Peony scroll.**

This design is found on a deep bowl with rounded sides in the Cleveland Museum (Pl. 95:a). It has a small central panel decorated with finely incised pomegranate—peonies. On the side is a design of peony scrolls. The peonies are of an open lily-like type with curved tendrils emerging from the centre. The leaves are of the common elongated type with crossed leaf-stems. The composition is very elegant and elaborate with finely worked details.

Type: Ti 53. **Date: Chin.**
Shape: Bowl and cover. **Design: Fluted sides.**

Among the few Ting specimens which are dated is a covered bowl in the British Museum. It is of a quite common type, with an almost cylindrical body and low foot, and provided with a domed cover with a short stalk-knob on the top and flat, horizontal, projecting edge. The sides are moulded in a kind of chrysanthemum fluting. The specimen in the British Museum (Pl. 84:f) carries a long inscription in ink reading: "*Shih liang shih tung shih ta ting erh nien erh yüeh shih ssu jih sheng wang chi* (recorded as memorial of Shih Liang-shih neé Tung, on the 14th day of the second month of the second year of *Ta Ting* [1162 in the Chin era]). A bowl of the same kind but lacking the cover was unearthed at the Ting kiln excavation and dated by the excavators as Chin. An interesting specimen in this group is a bowl of this kind in the Clark collection (Pl. 57:k). It is identical to the two bowls just mentioned but the lid of this bowl has a finely incised design of a sketchy lotus of the feather-like type which we have seen above under Type Ti 9.

Type: Ti 54. **Date: Chin.**
Shape: Dish. **Design: Different.**

This is a group of Ting yao dishes with extremely fine and detailed designs featuring different motifs. The dishes are mostly of the type with flat bottom and horizontal flattened rim with thickened edge, but some other types are found.

a) Deer and pomegranate scrolls. A dish of this shape in the Victoria & Albert Museum (Pl. 96:a, Fig. 20:a) is decorated on the flat interior with a very fine and detailed design of two deer with big antlers and spotted bodies (the spots made by small groups of four dots) among forceful scrolls of the pomegranate type with volute-shaped leaves. In the cavetto is an elegant lotus scroll with flowers, leaves and seed-pods on a granulated ground.[1])

b) Peacocks and clouds. In the Kempe collection is a dish with flat bottom and steep side with cut mouth-rim (Pl. 96:b). In the flat interior is a very fine and detailed design of two large peacocks with long magnificent tails. In their beaks they hold a long ribbon tied into a rosette and they are surrounded by clouds. On the side is an elegant lotus border of the same type as found on the deer dish with flowers, leaves, seed-pods and sagittaria (Fig. 21:c).

c) Pomegranate scrolls. A dish in the Nydell collection (Pl. 95:b) with flattened horizontal rim is decorated on the flat interior with pomegranate scrolls with cloud-volute-like leaves. In the cavetto is a formal palmette scroll.

d) Phoenixes among lotus scrolls. A dish in the Kempe collection (Pl. 97:a) is of a similar shape to the preceding one. It is decorated on the flat interior with two short-tailed phoenixes flying among a composite floral scroll with lotus and many other plants. On the cavetto is an elegant lotus border of a type similar to

[1]) There are two more identical dishes one in the Eugene Bernat collection (*Chinese Ceramics of the Sung dynasty*, The Currier Gallery of Art. No. 17) and one in the Metropolitan Museum (Cox, *op.cit.* Pl. 55). All three dishes seem to have been made by the same mould.

that found on types **a** and **b** above (Fig. 21:f). On the flat rim is a triangular key-fret band.

e) Mandarin ducks in lotus pond. A dish of the same shape as the one just mentioned but with a little broader rim in the E. Chow collection (Pl. 97:b) is decorated on the flat interior with a lotus pond with lotus, sagittaria, water-chestnuts and other water-plants. On a small tongue of land is a standing mandarin duck and another one is swimming in the pond; a dragon-fly is flying over the lotus plant. In the cavetto is a band of cloud-volutes.

f) Mandarin ducks and goose in landscape. A dish in the David Foundation (Pl. 98) has a flat bottom and slightly curved sides with the interior moulded in a chrysanthemum-like fluting. On the flat inside is a shore-landscape with a willow-tree, lotus flowers and sagittaria, water-chestnuts, water-fern etc. in the surrounding water. To the left is a large goose standing with his head turned to the right, to the right at the foot of the willow is a standing mandarin duck and another one is seen coming down from the sky to the left of the willow in a steep dive. The character *Chao* (a surname) is incised in the centre and three more characters are incised on the base reading: "*T'ien shui Chün*" (a place name). Both inscriptions are made after the firing and need not be contemporary with the dish. The execution of the design is very similar to that on the preceding dish.

g) Mandarin ducks in lotus pond. In the Brundage collection[1]) is a dish of the same shape as the preceding one with fluted sides. The design on the flat inside is very similar to that found on Type **e** above. It shows a lotus pond with lotus flowers, sagittaria, water-chestnuts etc. and two mandarin ducks placed opposite each other, one standing on a tongue of land the other one swimming in the pond.

Type: Ti 55. — **Date: Chin—Yüan.**
Shape: Dish with flat or scalloped rim. — **Design: Different.**

This is a group of dishes of somewhat different shapes but all of which have in common a flat bottom and the cavetto divided into segments.

a) Phoenixes and lotus flowers. A dish in a Japanese collection (Pl. 84:g) has a scalloped, pointed flat rim and the side lobed into sixteen segments. On the flat interior is a cloud collar panel formed by three bands, the inner one with beads, enclosing two short-tailed phoenixes flying among lotus flowers and other plants. The design and composition is closely akin to our Type 42 above. The cavetto is divided into sixteen segments with alternating flowers and insects. On the flat rim are spiral scrolls.

---

[1]) No.B 60 P 1394.

b) Boys and ducks in garden. In the David Foundation is a dish with flat bottom and horizontal flattened rim (Pl. 99). The flat interior is decorated with a garden scene showing in the foreground two small boys chasing a pair of ducks and in the background an elaborate garden fence with a rock behind it with flowering camellias. In the garden are reeds, flowers and insects. The fence is decorated with a fine classic scroll-work. The cavetto is divided into ten segments with flowers and insects in each one.

c) Peacocks in garden. In the David Foundation is also an eight-lobed dish with flattened horizontal rim[1]) (Pl. 84:h). The flat interior is decorated with a garden scene with a large rock and a tree-peony in the centre, a large peacock is perched on the rock and another one is sitting to the left of it. Around the garden rock are flowers and reeds. In the cavetto are eight segments with floral sprays. On the flat rim is a triangular key-fret (Fig. 25:a).

Type: Ti 56. **Date: Yüan.**
Shape: Dish with scalloped rim. **Design: Peony scroll.**

This is another type of dish with scalloped rim which seems to be still later in time than the preceding one and of a shape generally associated with Yüan and early Ming blue-and-white. The dish has a flattened horizontal rim with scalloped, thickened edge. The interior is not flat but slightly convex and the cavetto is fluted in lotus-panel-shaped segments. An example of the type is in the Museum of Eastern Art in Oxford (Pl. 100:a). The interior is decorated with a rather heavy peony scroll with large leaves and rounded flowers. On the flat rim are scroll ornaments.

Type: Ti 57. **Date: Chin—Yüan.**
Shape: Dish with flattened rim. **Design: Peacock and flowers.**

In this group we find again the dish with flat bottom and horizontal flattened rim with thickened edge which we have seen in several other types from Chin and Early Yüan. This type shows a most elaborate design with close similarities to the blue-and-white group. A dish of this type (Pl. 100:b) has in the centre a large peacock with expanded wings and long heavy tail, the bird is surrounded by an elegant floral scroll with five-petalled flowers. This design is enclosed by a thin line border in an eight-lobed panel. Outside this border is another floral scroll which in its turn is enclosed by a raised eight-lobed band decorated with dissolved scrolls. In the cavetto is again a floral scroll enclosed by a double-line border.

A still more elaborate design with border after border is found on a dish of the same shape in the Brundage collection.[2]) The central panel here also shows a peacock

[1]) *David Ting cat.* no. 161.

[2]) *Brundage cat.* Pl. XXXIV:C.

with heavy tail, but now standing on a garden rock and surrounded by flowers. This motif is enclosed in a five-lobed raised frame decorated with a continuous leaf-scroll. Outside this frame is another broader leaf-scroll of the feather-like type and then a key-fret band. On the cavetto is a *cash*-pattern band and on the flat rim a sketchy classic scroll. This dish is interesting since the designs found in the different borders show the relation of this type to several other types which all belong to the later part of the Chin dynasty and the beginning of Yüan.

Type: Ti 58. **Date: Chin—Yüan.**
Shape: Dish with fluted sides. **Design: Rhinoceros viewing the moon.**

This group consists of small dishes with slightly rounded sides which on the interior are fluted like chrysanthemum petals. There is one dish of this type in the Royal Scottish Museum (Pl. 101:a). It is decorated on the inside with a reclining *hsi-niu* among waves looking at the sky where a crescent moon can be seen among cloud-volutes. The waves are of the spiral type with crested tops. The design is similar to the rhinoceros and moon design we have seen before (Type 48) but the animal is a little different and looks more like a donkey.[1])

A similar dish is in the Oxford Museum of Eastern Art (Pl. 101:b) and here the central design shows a one-horned animal, which is more like a stag, reclining among *ling-chih*-shaped waves and looking at the sky. The crescent moon and stars are seen among cloud-volutes and in the centre is a moulded character, *Ch'u* (a name).

Type: Ti 59. **Date: Chin.**
Shape: Dish with fluted sides. **Design: Garden with fence.**

The dish with sides in chrysanthemum fluting, of the shape described above, is common with various designs and among the most frequent ones are garden scenes. One example of this type is seen in Pl. 102:a. In the foreground is an elaborate fence with lotus-shaped pillar-heads and on the other side of the fence is a large garden rock and plantains. The plantains seem to be a very popular design on this type and are frequently seen.

Type: Ti 60. **Date: Chin.**
Shape: Dish with scalloped rim. **Design: Stag among peonies.**

A still more elaborate shape than in the preceding types is found in this group. It is a dish with flat bottom and chrysanthemum-fluted side which has a flattened

[1]) This dish seems to be the same one which was sold at the Burchard sale in 1928, and which is described in the catalogue as decorated with "Wellenornamente mit springendem Fabeltier". (*Die Sammlung des Herrn Dr. Otto Burchard.* Berlin 1928. Pl. IV, nr. 83.)

horizontal rim, scalloped corresponding to the interior fluting. A dish of this type is in the Neave-Hill collection (Pl. 102:b). The flat interior is decorated with a stag with big antlers standing among realistic peonies. The stag is standing in a rather stiff position and it seems that he wears a halter. The fluted panels on the side are each decorated with a scroll ornament. On the flat rim are dissolved scroll ornaments similar to overlapping petals.

Type: Ti 61. **Date: Chin.**
Shape: Eight-lobed fluted dish. **Design: Peony scroll.**

A shape very rare in Ting yao is found on a dish in the Brundage collection.[1]) It is of an eight-lobed shape with fluted sides and flat bottom. This shape is found in late Sung celadon and also in the early blue-and-white. The design on the Brundage dish is found only on the flat interior and is composed of luxuriant peony scrolls of a type very similar to those found on a mould in the British Museum dated the *Chi-ya* year of *Ta Ting* which is equivalent to the year 1189 of the Chin dynasty (Fig. 23:a). A dish of the same shape as the Brundage dish, with the date 1210 is in the David Foundation and is discussed on page 165 below.

Type: Ti 62. **Date: Chin - Yüan.**
Shape: Shallow dish; bowl. **Design: Overlapping petals.**

This design which consists of pointed overlapping petals with marked leaf-veins is usually found on small dishes with different motifs. A dish of this kind is in the Kempe collection (Pl. 103:a). In the centre is a flower-shaped medallion with a fruit spray. On the side are overlapping petals with finely moulded details. A dish of similar shape in the Victoria & Albert Museum (Pl. 103:b) has a lotus spray in the central field and fluted sides with overlapping petals. In the Honolulu Academy of Arts there is a dish of the same kind with two fishes in the central panel and two rows of overlapping petals on the side (Pl. 104:a).

Bowls with this design also are found. One example is in the Seattle Art Museum (Pl. 104:b). It has a four-petalled flower in the centre inside and three rows of overlapping petals on the side. Below the rim is a key-fret border from which triangular key-fret ornaments are coming down between the top leaves.

Type: Ti 63. **Date: Sung—Ming.**
Shape: Various. **Design: Basket pattern.**

Basket patterns are quite commonly found on Ting yao and wares of Ting type but the majority of those seem to be made later than Sung. Among the earlier

[1]) *Brundage cat.* Pl. XXXIV:B.

types can be mentioned a small box and cover of circular shape and a hemi-spherical cup both in the Kempe collection.[1]) Both have a rather coarse type of basket work on the exterior which is very near to what we have seen in the Tz'u-chou type (cp. Pl. 48:i), and they may very well have been made at one of the Tz'u-chou kilns. There are two more small hemi-spherical cups in the same collection[2]) which have basket pattern, but here the basket work is a little bit different and looks like small grains put together. Also these pieces have a glaze and body which is not of typical Ting character and they probably belong to some other kiln.

Most famous of the Ting pieces with basket work design are small bag-shaped jars usually called *yü-lou p'ing* and considered to be imitations of plaited willow fish-baskets. The basket-pattern is made in the way of long, vertical, rounded strings in relief, with lightly incised horizontal double-lines at intervals, probably meant to represent willow twigs bound together with strings. Round the neck of the jar is a cord ending in two knots at the sides. There is one piece of this kind in the old Palace collection (Fig. 28:a),[3]) two in the David Foundation[4]) and one in the Kempe collection.[5]) Glaze and potting are in all these vases not typical of Sung Ting yao and they are likely to be considerably later. There is one more piece in the Palace collection (Fig. 28:b),[6]) which is of a little more heavy shape and has no cord round the neck, but is provided with a flat cover also with basket work. A similar piece without cover is in the David Foundation.[7])

Apart from the Ting yao designs discussed above there are of course a great many more, especially among the late Chin and Yüan wares. These late designs, and perhaps the moulded variant in general, are more difficult to find in the available literature because specimens of this kind have never attracted the eye of the collector in the same way as the early incised wares. It is understandable because the later moulded wares have a tendency to become a little crude but their designs are nevertheless extremely interesting because of their influence on the early blue-and-white and they help us to understand the later development of decorative designs on Chinese porcelain.

It should also be remarked in this connection that small sculptures of different kinds, toys, figurines etc. were also made at the Ting kilns and objects of this kind have been found at the excavations in Chien-tz'u ts'un. Many of these specimens are quite crude but some of them are rather fine sculptures in small size. Among the favourite subjects are small animals of different kinds, dogs, lions, rabbits,

---

1) *CKc* No. 353, 354.

2) *CKc* No. 351, 352.

3) *Illustrated catalogue of the Chinese Government Exhibits* . . . Vol. II. *Porcelain.* Nanking 1936. No. 3.

4) *David Ting cat.* No. 125, 126.

5) *CKc* No. 438.

6) *Op.cit.* No. 1.

7) *David Ting cat.* No. 127.

horses (sometimes with rider), chickens etc. Small children is a very popular theme as always and fine examples can be seen for instance in the Kempe collection where we have one child holding a bunch of lotus flowers, one with a dog in its lap and one with a doll.[1]) Small statues of monks and persons in worshipping attitude are also quite frequently found.[2]) A very fine and realistic monk's or *lohan's* head was found at the Ting kiln excavation, it is of a type generally associated with the Liao dynasty, although it is dated T'ang by the excavators.[3]) In the Kempe collection is also a 19 cm. high statue of a Buddha seated on the lotus throne which is of unusually fine quality and showing all signs of being a Sung piece.[4])

Pillows of Ting yao and Ting type are also found occasionally, many of them rather crude and some obviously later than Sung. Among the finest examples is a pillow in the Brundage collection (Pl. 84:1) which shows a small child reclining on a rectangular couch on the sides of which are incised grooves suggesting tapestry folds. The child is holding an enormous fungus which serves as the head-rest of the pillow. The top of the fungus is decorated with a carved floral pattern.

There are undoubtedly many different wares of Ting type made at other kilns both in the North and in the South but it is not possible to discuss them at any length in this context. One of the places where such Ting type wares were produced was *Chi-chou*, we know that both from earlier excavations and from the recent ones carried out by the Chinese. What has been published so far from excavations at Chi-chou seems to indicate that the white ware produced here was mainly influenced in its designs from the ch'ing-pai ware, which of course seems most natural. No specimens which in glaze, shape or design could be said to be close copies of Ting yao have so far been found.

It seems that the majority of the better Ting imitations were made during the very end of Sung and during Yüan and most specimens we know of this type have designs very characteristic of the Sung—Yüan transition style. The body, glaze and general appearance of these wares are quite different from the true Ting yao. As examples of this type we shall show a few specimens.

A bowl in the Eugene Bernat collection (Pl. 84:i) is of a shape well-known in late Sung—early Yüan celadon and has a design showing a blossoming plum branch and a crescent moon which also tallies with designs found on celadon (Pl. 38:b). Another bowl in a private collection (Pl. 84:j) has the interior covered with a dense *cash*-pattern on which are three shaped, window-like panels. The panels show plum, bamboo and pine. A third bowl (Pl. 84:k) has on the interior side a broad belt with big fishes among lotus flowers, and in the centre a round panel showing a blossoming plum branch and a crescent moon reflected in the water. The bowls are all very different in design, but it is interesting to note that they all feature the plum blossoms

[1]) *CKc* Nos. 464, 465, 469.

[2]) *CKc* Nos. 470, 471.

[3]) *Chinese Translations* No. 4. Pl. I:7.

[4]) *CKc* No. 407.

and the moon, which seems to have been one of the favourite motifs of the Sung-—Yüan transition time.

LIST OF DESIGNS FOUND ON THE TING WARE

Special floral motifs		
Composite scroll	Moulded	Type Ti 34, 38
Palmette-like peony	Moulded	Type Ti 35, 39, 40, 50
Pomegranate-like peony	Moulded	Type Ti 36, 40, 54

Peony

Peony scroll	Incised	Type Ti 2, 14, 31, 30
Peony scroll	Moulded	Type Ti 51, 52, 56, 61
Sketchy; with lotus; in panels	Incised	Type Ti 13, 3, 4

The above listed designs are only some of the most typical ones. Peonies are found in many other combinations for instance in composite scrolls.

Lotus

Lotus are extremely common on Ting yao and found in an endless number of combinations.

Lotus sprays and plants	Incised	Type Ti 7–12
Lotus scroll	Carved	Type Ti 29
With peony; in panels	Incised	Type Ti 3, 5
With ducks	Incised	Type Ti 16, 20
With fish, duck etc.	Moulded	Type Ti 43–46, 54, 55

Sagittaria

Is very common in combination with lotus and other water-plants, cp. Ti 34.

Chrysanthemum

Realistic representations of this flower are not found.

Mallow Incised Type Ti 32, 35

Mallow-like flowers are also common in the composite scrolls in different combinations.

Prunus

Are very rare, see p. 161 above.

Willow

Are rare but occasionally found among late examples. Type Ti 54.

Pomegranates

Are found in one more realistic design,	Incised	Type Ti 15
and with boys	Moulded	Type Ti 37

in combination with peonies they form the characteristic pomegranate-like peonies, see above.

Melon

Is found with boys in Type Ti 37, and also on the mould discussed under Type Ti 38. Other fruits are found together with the melon in the boy design and alone in Ti 62.

Petals

Overlapping petals	Incised	Type Ti 1
	Moulded	Type Ti 37
Rosette of petals	Moulded	Ti 31, 37

Boys

With fruits	Moulded	Type Ti 37
With lotus scroll	Moulded	Type Ti 41
With peonies	Moulded	Type Ti 48, 49
With ducks	Moulded	Type Ti 55

Other human representations

Are discussed at the end of the chapter p. 160 above.

Dragon

Lung type	Incised	Type Ti 26
	Moulded	Type Ti 33
	Relief	Type Ti 1
Ch'ih type	Incised	Type Ti 27, 28
	Moulded	Type Ti 40, 47
Winged-dragon	Moulded	Type Ti 40

Phoenix

Is only found in the moulded variant.	Moulded	Type Ti 34, 38, 39, 42, 45 50, 54, 55

Lion	Moulded	Type Ti 40
Rhinoceros and moon	Moulded	Type Ti 48, 58
Ch'i-lin	Moulded	Type Ti 40
Deer	Moulded	Type Ti 54, 60

Ducks and geese

Ducks and water-plants	Incised	Type Ti 16–19
	Moulded	Type Ti 34, 43, 44, 45, 54
With boys	Moulded	Type Ti 55

Other birds

Crane (with ducks)	Moulded	Type Ti 43
Peacock	Moulded	Type Ti 34, 54, 55, 57

Insects

Are often found in the moulded type cp. Ti 54–55.

Fish	Incised	Type Ti 6, 21, 22, 23, 24, 25
	Moulded	Type Ti 34, 43, 45, 46, 62

Waves

In combination with fish, ducks etc.	Incised	Type Ti 6, 21–24
	Moulded	Type Ti 43–46
Basket-work	Moulded	Type Ti 63
Palmette scroll	Carved	Type Ti 29–31
Classical scroll	Moulded	Type Ti 41, 55
Dissolved scroll band	Incised	Type Ti 29, 31

Inscriptions

Several different kinds are found on Ting yao and most of them have been discussed above. There are four main types.

a) Potter's names and names of owners etc. Mostly applied after the firing but some made before.

Li Weng (Type Ti 46); *Chao* (Ti 54); *Ch'u* (Ti 58); *Liu Wan-li* [80] (found at the kiln site, dated Five Dynasties by the excavators).

b) Inscriptions indicating official use.

Kuan and *Hsi Kuan* are common in Liao tombs but has also been found at the Ting kiln site.

Shang shih chü and *Shang yüeh chü;* these inscriptions have been discussed above p. 128. *Wu-wang Fu* [81] (on sherd from the kiln site). "Residence of Wu Wang". Wu Wang was the ruler of the principality of *Tung-p'ing Chün* [82], he was enfeoffed in 1044 A.D., and died two years later. The sherd with this inscription can accordingly be dated to the years 1044–1046 A.D.

Inscriptions indicating general use.
Ting chou kung yung (David no. 172). Stamped.
Kung yung (dish, date 1271. Ti 25).

c) Names of palaces and places.
Feng hua, feng hua, tz'u fu, chü hsiu, chin yüan, hua yüan (Fig. 35:d). These inscriptions have been discussed above p. 140. *T'ien shui chün* (Ti 54).

d) Dates:
Yüan-yu ssu nien (1089). On an undecorated box in the Kempe coll. (No. 403).
Shao-hsing (1131–62) David no. 184.
Ta-ting erh nien (1162) British Museum (Pl. 57:k).
Ta-ting erh shih ssu nien (1184) Mould (Ti 38).
Ta-ting chi ya (1189) Mould (Fig. 23:a).
T'ai-ho san nien (1203) Mould (Fig. 23:b).
Chih-yüan pa nien (1271) British Museum (Ti 25).

In the David Foundation (No. 194) is a saucer dish of a shape similar to our type Ti 61, which has an inscription on the base reading *Chia-ting pao yung* in two lines at the centre, *keng wu nien tsao* in one line at the lower left, and *san hao* obliquely at the lower right. Lovell (*David Ting cat.*, p. 18) gives the following explanation of the inscription:

"It would appear that the inscription dates the piece to the keng wu year of the Chia-ting period, namely 1210, and that the piece was third in a series. The meaning of the phrase pao yung is not very clear. It might indicate the potter's wish that the piece might be treasured."

The inscription is inscribed on the dish after the firing and there is no indication that it has been done immediately after its manufacture. It is very strange that the piece carries a Southern Sung *nien hao*. It is provided with a barely visible moulded floral design, and has all the characteristics of a northern piece. It is possible that it is a piece which has come to the Southern Sung Empire through commerce with the Chins, and that the inscription has been added at that time. The rather crude scraping away of the glaze on the base in order to be able to inscribe the dish seems to indicate this procedure. However, the dish is certainly not sufficient evidence for a Southern Sung Ting manufacture.

SOME PRINCIPAL MOTIFS

One of the most significant features of Sung art is, as we have seen, the increased and deepened interest in nature. Motifs from nature and the animal world are the principal subjects of the ceramic of the period. But even if the Sung style often seems very realistic and its motifs are taken directly from nature, we must not forget that the subjects depicted were preferably chosen not merely as beautiful pictures, but primarily because of their symbolic significance. In the animal world some of the favourite motifs are obviously mythical beasts like the dragon and the phoenix, but even those animal patterns which are more or less realistic representations of deer, ducks, fish etc., were mainly selected because of the message of an auspicious character which they carried and which was easily understood by those initiated. Also flowers and trees were singled out owing to their symbolic meaning which could generally be understood by anyone; but many motifs also had literary associations which could be interpreted only by the educated.[1])

Among the most common messages that these symbols convey are wishes for a *long life*, *happiness*, *fertility*, a *happy marriage*, *wealth* and *rank*. Several different types of symbols are found, many of them built on puns and plays with words which have a similar pronunciation, and they are sometimes very difficult to decipher.[2]) The intriguing and extremely complicated world of Chinese symbolism has been dealt with by many authors,[3]) and in this connection we have only tried to give a few more general hints as to the possible meaning of some of the patterns found in this summary of the principal motifs, mostly taken from the animal and floral world, which we find used on Sung ceramics.

PEONY

The peony flower was exceedingly popular during the Sung dynasty. As decoration on ceramics it is the most frequent of all flowers; it even outnumbers the lotus.

The peony (especially the *mou-tan* variety) is considered by the Chinese to be the King of Flowers (*Hua Wang*) and it is rich in symbolic value. It symbolizes wealth and honour and happiness in general. But it is also an emblem of love and affection

[1]) Osvald Sirén (*Chinese Painting*, Vol. II. p. 61) quotes a passage from the catalogue over the painting collection owned by the Emperor Hui-tsung, *Hsüan ho hua p'u*, which shows how important this intellectual symbolism was to the painters and art lovers of Sung China.

[2]) S. Cammann, *Types of symbols in Chinese art.* Chicago 1953.

[3]) See especially several works by S. Cammann listed in the bibliography, and C. A. S. Williams, *Outlines of Chinese Symbolism.* Peiping 1931.

and a symbol of feminine beauty. It also takes its place as one of the flowers representing the Four Seasons, where the tree-peony is the sign of Spring.

There are several different species of peony in China, but the two main ones that are usually favoured by artists are *mou-tan* and *shao-yao*. Mou-tan (*Paeonia moutan, paeonia suffruticosa*) is known as the tree-peony and is also called *Pai Liang Chin* (A hundred ounces of gold) and *Fu Kuei Hua* (Flower of wealth and rank). Shao-yao (*Paeonia albiflora*) is the herbaceous peony; it is found in several different species and occurs as a wild plant native to various parts of China. Shao-yao has been cultivated in China since a very long time back; it is already mentioned in the Book of Odes. The history of mou-tan is much shorter and it did not come into cultivation until the T'ang dynasty, but it very rapidly became one of the most popular flowers in China.

During the Northern Sung dynasty the mou-tan peony had become the favourite flower and its centre of cultivation was Loyang. There was a saying that "The Moutan of Loyang ranks first in the whole world".[1]) Many different colours of mou-tan were found, the most popular being red and yellow. One of the most exclusive colours was the so-called Yao's yellow and a single graft of this variety was paid with five-thousand pieces of cash. This can be read in an essay entitled "On the Customs of Loyang" [83], which is part of the work "A Treatise of the Mou-tan peony of Loyang" by the famous scholar Ou-yang Hsiu (1007–1072). From this book we can also learn that more than 90 varieties of mou-tan were known to be in cultivation at this time, which gives us some idea about the fantastic popularity of the flower. Among other contemporary writings about the flower can be mentioned "Account of the Mou-tan peony of Loyang" (*Lo yang mou tan chi*) [84] by Chou Hsü (second half of 11th c.); "Treatise on the Mou-tan peony of T'ien-peng [in Ssuch'uan]" (*T'ien peng mou tan p'u*) [85] by Lu Yu (1178); "Treatise on the Mou-tan peony of Ch'en Chou" (*Ch'en chou mou tan chi*) [86] by Chang Puang-chi (c. 1111–1117); "Classified arrangements of the varieties of the Mou-tan peony" (*Mou tan jung ju chih*) [87] by Ch'iu Chün (13th c.).

During the Sung dynasty the shao-yao peony was almost as popular as a garden flower as the tree-peony. One of the most famous centres for the cultivation of this flower was Yangchou, then called Kuanglin. From this time comes the old saying "Mou-tan in Loyang, shao-yao in Kuanglin". More than thirty varieties of the flower were cultivated at this time, among them were red, purple and white blossoms, but the most valuable and rarest was the yellow one. Many different monographs on shao-yao were published in the Sung dynasty, but the most complete work is the "Treatise on the Shao-yao peony of Yangchou" by Wang Kuan (1075).

Used as decoration on ceramics we find many different kinds of peonies, more or less conventionalized. Some designs are quite realistic and both flowers and

[1]) An excellent survey of the history of Chinese plants is given in H. L. Li, *The Garden Flowers of China*. New York 1959, from which much information about the history of the flowers in this chapter has been obtained.

leaves are easily recognized, others are so highly conventionalized that we can only guess what the original has been like. In between these two kinds there are many transitional forms, where we could either recognize leaves or flowers although they are stylized. A major difficulty met with in most Chinese floral designs, and which is not especially typical of the Sung dynasty, is a tendency to mix flowers of different types and combine them with leaves and scrolls that belong to other plants. This sometimes makes it impossible to identify a certain floral design; this is one of the reasons why we have chosen to use such terms as *"conventionalized flower"*, *"sickle-leaf scroll"* and *"pomegranate-peony"*.

As an ornamental flower the peony comes in rather late in Chinese art-history, and it seems that it did not become popular until the introduction of the mou-tan variety in the T'ang dynasty. In T'ang applied arts the realistic peony designs are still rare and they do not seem to appear more frequently until the Five Dynasties. The first ceramic ware where we can find realistic peony designs seems to be *Yüeh yao* and, as we have seen, the motif is soon adopted also by other kilns in the Chekiang province. It seems that at the beginnig of the Sung dynasty the motif was already firmly established and used on most ceramic wares produced at this time. A short recapitulation of the design as found in the different main types of wares discussed might be useful in this connection.

We have seen that on the *Northern celadon* ware the peony designs were extremely common already during Northern Sung, and many different varieties are found. The majority of the designs seem to depict the mou-tan, and especially fine examples of this flower are found in the type we have chosen to call beehive-shaped peony because of the shape of its extremely large flowers (Fig. 7:a, Pl. 5:f–k); this flower is also frequently found together with climbing boys (Pl. 5:l, Pl. 6:a–b). In the latter combination the auspicious meaning of the design is quite obvious and may be seen as a wish for wealth, high rank and numerous offspring, but the popular boy motif will be dealt with separately further on.

It is interesting to note that the types of peony flowers used on the Northern celadon ware are already very varied and both leaves and flowers can be handled in many different ways. It is also interesting to note that very similar flowers can be found in combination with different types of leaves (Pl. 4:b, e), but as a rule one type of flower is always seen with a certain kind of leaf, which seems to indicate that the designs were to a great extent based on realistic observations of nature.

In the *ch'ing-pai* ware the peony is also a popular motif, but not to the same extent as in Northern celadon. The finest examples found of the motif are probably the early incised peony designs (Pl. 21), which are fine and elegant and seem to depict the shao-yao peony with its thinner and more elongated leaves. These designs are clearly influenced by the early Chekiang celadon wares. Among the later ch'ing-pai ware the peony design is especially common in the moulded patterns where it is found both as single sprays (Pl. 31:a) and in combination with other flowers in composite floral scrolls. The so-called pomegranate-peony is also found in ch'ing-pai, mainly in combination with the boy motif, but both these patterns will be discussed later on under pomegranate and boy respectively.

We have already pointed out above that the Yüeh yao was the first of the ceramic wares which took up the realistic peony design and that the design was very soon adopted by other celadon kilns in Chekiang. We have seen that among the Northern Sung wares from *Lung-ch'üan* and its surroundings peony designs are among the most frequent patterns; some of them are quite realistic (Pl. 37:g, h), others are more sketchy (Pl. 37:b, j, l). Peony leaves are also a common pattern on this ware (Pl. 37:e). In the true Lung-ch'üan ware the peony design is rather rare during Sung but incised examples are sometimes found (Pl. 39:d). It is not until the end of Sung and the beginning of Yüan that peony designs are becoming more popular again both in the carved and the moulded type and also in the thread relief technique.

When we come to the *Tz'u-chou* ware the peony designs are abundant, and they seem to have been one of the most popular designs from the very beginning of the period right down to the end. The nature of the Tz'u-chou ware and its many different techniques of decoration are of course ideal for realistic designs in general, so it is not surprising that this is the case. As this ware, however, is not one of the official wares but, on the contrary a typical ware for everyday use it is interesting to note that peony designs at this time must have been already extremely popular not only among the intellectuals and the ruling class but to an equal extent among the common people. The dynastic change does not seem to have affected the popularity of the flower and, like most other motifs from nature, it was further developed during Chin, and some of the finest peony designs found on Tz'u-chou apparently belong to this time.

On some of the early sgraffito wares the peony designs are rather stiff and formal (Fig. 5:c, d. Pl. 49), but they soon became more and more free and true to nature (Fig. 6, Fig. 7:b–d, Pl. 44:e–f) and some of them are amazingly accurate in detail (Pl. 48:g), and others have rendered the essential characteristics of the flower in a few swift strokes, which are undoubtedly inspired by contemporary brush painting (Pl. 45:a). The huge beehive-shaped mou-tan is one of the favourite motifs and its most excellent representation is perhaps the one found on the beautiful pillow in a Japanese collection (Pl. 45:g, Fig. 7:b). In the enamelled Tz'u-chou group both the beehive-shaped flower (Pl. 56:b, c, Fig. 7:f) and more simple types (Pl. 55:l) are frequently found.

In *Ting yao* peony designs are again abundant. We find realistic designs already developed in early Sung both in the deeply carved variant (Pl. 57:j, Pl. 58:b) and among the more finely incised type (Fig. 5:b). The close relationship of those designs to the early celadons both of the Northern ware and from Chekiang is obvious (Fig. 8:a). Even if the peony is found among the finely incised ware in very beautiful examples (Pl. 61:b–d), more or less sketchy, it is not at all so common as the lotus. But during the Chin dynasty we find extremely fine carved peony designs which are very realistic (Pl. 74; Fig. 5:a) and we also have examples of palmette-like and pomegranate-type peonies (Pl. 73:b, 75:a–b). In the moulded variant of Ting the peony is very common, but the more realistic types are usually found in combination with other motifs (Pl. 92) or in composite scrolls, sometimes the designs are extremely detailed and fine (Pl. 78).

The above-mentioned examples of peony designs found in Sung ceramics clearly show that the flower during this time was one of the main motifs of decoration and that it must have been the favourite flower of the people of this time. The use of the peony was in no way limited to ceramics, the design most often found on Sung bronze mirrors is peony scrolls (Fig. 39:a)[1]) and we find it on gold and silver as well.[2]) In Sung painting peonies is a favourite motif and we also find them used in tomb murals; a very fine example has recently been unearthed in *Pai-sha*, which shows realistic peony scrolls.[3]) Peonies are also very commonly found in stone carvings from tombs (Fig. 39:b:2).[4])

LOTUS

The sacred or Indian lotus, *Nelumbo nucifera*, is the second most popular flower used in Sung ceramic designs, it is only outnumbered by the peony. The lotus is indigenous to China but the introduction of Buddhism attached new significance to the flower, and it has ever since been closely connected with the Buddhist faith. In Buddhism the flower became a symbol of purity because it rises clean and stainless out of the muddy water in which it grows. During the Sung dynasty the flower already seems to have lost most of its specific Buddhist significance, but its symbolic meaning had been adopted among the secular symbols and it had also developed new and typical Chinese conceptions. A famous essay by the Confucian scholar Chou Tun-i (1017–73), in which he praises the lotus as "the flower of purity and integrity"[5]) became very popular and was learned by heart by every schoolboy during former times. Since this period in accordance with Confucian ethics the lotus flower has been a symbol of the perfect or princely man, and the honesty of an uncorrupt official was symbolized by lotus flowers and egrets (the bird was added because it also kept clean in the same muddy water).[6])

But the lotus flower also had several other symbolic meanings. It was the emblem of Summer among the flowers of the Four Seasons, conveying the idea of happiness in maturity.

---

[1]) Cp. also *OCS Sung exh.* Cat.nos. 229, 230.

[2]) *Chinese Gold and Silver in the Carl Kempe coll.* Pl. 53 b.

[3]) *Pai sha Sung mu.* Pl. 47. For other fine examples see also a Chin dynasty tomb in Honan. *Kao Ku* 1965:7, p. 352. Pl. 7:1–2.

[4]) *KKHP* 1962:2, Pl. 7:4, 7; Pl. 19:3, Pl. 23:5–6.

[5]) See Li, *op.cit.* p. 65.

[6]) See Cammann, *Substance and Symbol in Chinese Toggles*, p. 110. From this work we have also in the following received valuable information about different symbols.

The two most common names for lotus in Chinese are *ho* and *lien* [89], the first is the usual name of the flower while the second often refers to the fruit only. As has been pointed out by Cammann and others, puns built upon the similarity in pronunciation of words with different meanings is one of the most common types of Chinese symbols. The name for lotus, *ho*, is pronounced the same way as the word for "unity" or "harmony" and the word *lien* forms a pun on the word "successively", which makes both words very useful in rebuse pictures with wishes for repeated luck, wealth etc. The lotus seed-pod is very often depicted and it obviously expressed a wish for fertility,[1]) which is also obviously the case when the lotus is found together with children.

Even if the lotus motif was full of symbolic meanings it was undoubtedly the splendour and beauty of the flower itself which mainly created its enormous popularity in Chinese art. The large showy flowers, usually of pink, red or white colour, and the large decorative leaves form a most impressive sight. It would be difficult to find a motif more suitable for an artist.

Already during the T'ang dynasty the lotus flower was a most popular motif in decorative arts and is constantly met with on the stone carvings of the period and also in precious metal, as has been shown by Gyllensvärd, and it is at this time clearly dependent on Indian influences. The similarities of the lotus designs found in the cave paintings of Ajanta with those of T'ang art is striking,[2]) and it seems quite clear that the more realistic rendering of the lotus in Chinese art is due to Indian influence. If we turn to the field of ceramics we will find that the lotus designs of T'ang and Liao are still rather stiff and ornamental and even in the Yüeh yao, where more realistic lotus designs are found, the main feature of the design is usually not the flower itself but its ornamental leaves.[3]) It is not until the beginning of the Sung dynasty that a more realistic rendering of the motif is found. Unlike the peony the lotus is usually not so often conventionalized, and it is mostly quite easy to identify.

The *Northern celadon* ware is quite rich in lotus designs, some featuring the lotus alone, but more often it is found in combination with other motifs. In the first category we find a very elegant design which seems to originate from the 12th century (Pl. 9:a–c, Fig. 9:d), but which in its winding movement is still very closely akin to the Ajanta scrolls. Another free and elegant lotus design is the lotus and wave pattern (Pl. 8:i, l), which is unusually simple to be a Northern celadon pattern. Among the combined designs, lotus and ducks and lotus and boys are the most common (Pl. 10:e, f, h); the lotus plants in these designs are usually quite realistic (cp. also Pl. 6:i). An unusual design is that found on the dish in the David Foundation (Pl. 10:i), which shows three bundles of lotus and other flowers (Fig. 10:b).

[1]) For further details about this use, see Cammann, *op.cit.* p. 111.

[2]) Gyllensvärd, *op.cit.* Fig. 83–87.

[3]) Gray, *op.cit.* Pl. 16. Palmgren, *Selected antiquities . . .*, Fig. 268 b. See also *Yüeh ch'i t'u lu.*

In *ch'ing-pai* lotus designs are mostly found during Southern Sung and they are especially common in the moulded variety. Among the earlier designs may be mentioned the incised design of sketchy lotus flowers and waves (Pl. 16:a), which is obviously related to the above-mentioned design on Northern celadon. A sketchy lotus design is also found during the end of Southern Sung (Pl. 18:a), but more typical for this time is a deeply carved composite floral scroll, which frequently features lotus flowers often in combination with boys (Pl. 22:k, l). In the thread relief designs datable to around 1200 and later, the lotus motif is also found (Type Cp 27) as well as in the Sung—Yüan transitional designs on beaded ground (Pl. 34). In the moulded variety the lotus flower is very common. Fine and detailed examples are found both in the designs with flowers in panels (Fig. 4:f) and with potted plants (Pl. 27:a, Fig. 4:e) and in composite floral scrolls, sometimes in combination with phoenixes (Type Cp 30); in all these variants the central panel is also often occupied by a lotus plant.

In *Lung-ch'üan yao* lotus petals are frequently found on the outside of bowls, but this motif is found in most wares and will not be discussed here. Otherwise lotus flowers are not so common in Sung celadons; there is, however, one type of rather sketchy incised lotus which seems to be datable to Northern Sung (Pl. 38:a). The majority of lotus designs found in this ware, however, seem to belong to the end of the dynasty and the beginning of Yüan (Pl. 39:g) and are found among the thread relief designs. A stamped design with a boy and a lotus flower possibly belongs to the same time (Pl. 39:e).

The *Tz'u-chou* ware with its more pictorial designs is well fitted for lotus patterns and some very fine examples are found especially on the pillows. For instance, a very fine and realistic example of this kind is found on a pillow with ring-matted ground (Pl. 42:h, Fig. 10:c), and other examples occur in the *san ts'ai* variety (Pl. 51:b, g), in this type we also find the boy and lotus design (Pl. 52:c, f). Realistic lotus designs are also found in bowls with a design on striated ground and in bowls with yellow glaze (Pl. 44:g, 54:h). In the typical sgraffito decorated ware the design is not so common, and when it is found it is generally rendered in a rather stiff way (Pl. 50:a–b). Also in the enamelled group we find realistic lotus plants (Pl. 56:f) often in combination with ducks (Pl. 56:k, l). Many more types are found, but compared to the peony the lotus is not so dominant in Tz'u-chou, and on some varieties it is very rarely seen.

Ting yao is that Sung ware in which the lotus motif is most frequently found, and it occurs in an almost endless number of variations and combinations. Only a few of the main types can be pointed out in this context. Among the incised wares some of the finest lotus patterns are found; they are often very simple and sketchy and the artist has succeeded in capturing the spirit and grace of the flower in a few swiftly incised strokes (Pl. 59:a–b, Pl:60, Fig. 9:a–b). This style seems to have originated already during the middle part of Northern Sung but must have continued well into Chin. Some designs are very sketchy (Pl. 62:b, 63. Fig.8:d), others are more detailed (Pl. 57:1). Some of the most satisfying designs in this group are those with a combination of ducks and lotus flowers (Pl. 64:a, 66:b, Fig. 8:e, 24:a). Among the more deeply carved specimens from Chin there are some very forceful lotus designs (Pl. 71–73:a, Fig. 9:c). Among the moulded Ting yao patterns lotus flowers and scrolls and lotus borders are extremely common, they are often very fine and minute in details (Pl. 78:b, 91:b). A curious feature found in this group of designs is lotus flowers or buds which look like artichokes,[1]) and are often placed two and two together (Pl. 78:a, 79:b); this motif is also found in borders (Pl. 97:a), and it seems to be characteristic of Ting yao and is not found in other ceramic wares. Some of the lotus borders found in the moulded group are extremely fine and detailed (Pl. 96) and bear witness to close studies of nature. A fine design of this type is found in combination with the boy motif (Pl. 88:a, Fig. 21:d). In combination with fishes and ducks on wave ground the lotus motif is recurrently found, but is usually rather stiff and ornamental (Pl. 89, 91:a); some of these designs are very close to Northern celadon. One specimen in this group (Pl. 89:a) is decorated with ducks and birds which could be egrets, and the design might have the symbolic meaning which we have indicated above. At the end of Chin we find some more free landscape compositions very close to contemporary paintings, which also feature lotus plants (Pl. 98).

Like the peony, the lotus motif during Sung seems to have penetrated into all kinds of art and is constantly met with. Lotus painting was a very important branch of Sung painting,[2]) and lotus flowers are often found as decoration in tomb architecture, both carved (Fig. 39:b:3)[3]) and painted.[4])

CHRYSANTHEMUM

In Chinese symbolics the chrysanthemum was the emblem of Autumn among the flowers of the Four Seasons and it symbolized a radiant middle age. The flower has a long history and is already mentioned in the Ancient Chinese texts, but it was the poet T'ao Yüan-ming (372–427) who first made the flower popular in wider circles because of his pronounced love for this flower which he expressed in his poetry. These poems have been considered among the finest ever written in China and have had a constant popularity ever since. The poet resigned from his official position and retired to his country home, where he occupied himself with writing and the cultivation of chrysanthemums. The chrysanthemum thus became the symbol of a recluse who has hidden away from the bustling life and enjoys his old

---

[1]) A similar rendering of the lotus bud is found in a Chin tomb mural in Shansi. *Kao Ku* 1965:7, p. 352, Pl. 7:6.

[2]) *Chinese art of the Sung and Yüan periods.* Tokyo National Museum 1961. Nos. 43–44. Cp. also Benjamin Rowland Jr., *Early Chinese Paintings in Japan: the problem of Hsü Hsi. A. A.* XV. 1952.

[3]) Cp. *KKHP* 1962:2, Pl. 7:5, 24:3–4 (Tomb from the beginning of the 12th c.).

[4]) For a very fine example in a Chin tomb in Shansi see *Kao Ku* 1965:7, p. 352, Pl. 7:6.

age in quietness. The symbol is all the more appropriate as the flower itself blooms in the Autumn when it does not have to compete with all the flowers of Spring and Summer.

During the Sung dynasty several monographs dealing with different garden forms of the flower appear, and it seems to have been among the most popular garden flowers of the time. Soochou was one of the places famous for chrysanthemum cultivation during this period.

Chrysanthemum representations are found in Chinese art from most periods, but in the applied arts it does not seem to have become a more popular motif until the later part of T'ang. In late T'ang and Liao *san ts'ai* wares chrysanthemum designs are sometimes found, most of them rather stiff and formal (Fig. 37:h), but in the more free and realistic designs found on Yüeh yao, flowers which could with confidence be identified as chrysanthemums are rare. As a rule the chrysanthemum designs found in Sung time are rather formal, and realistic flowers are quite rare, especially if we compare them with the lotus and peony, which show a prominent domination. It seems that the motif became more popular towards the end of the dynasty and the beginning of Yüan.

In the *Northern celadon* ware the chrysanthemum design is extremely rare and only one really realistic design of this type is known to us, but this is a splendid example closely studied after nature (Pl. 10:j). The design we have called "conventionalized flower" and, which we have seen in several different wares, have sometimes been mistaken for a chrysanthemum, but, as we have seen, it has nothing to do with that flower.

In *ch'ing-pai* we find the chrysanthemum only in the moulded variety, but here it is quite common. We have it in the pattern with flowers in panels (Fig. 4:f) and also in the composite floral scroll, sometimes with phoenixes (Type Cp 30). In the thread relief designs from the end of the Sung dynasty the motif is often seen and the flowers are now usually very realistic, as can be seen on a vase of this type (Pl. 33:a) and a very fine small box (Pl. 32:d).

In the sparsely decorated celadons of *Lung-ch'üan* the chrysanthemum is a rare design, and it only becomes more usual at the end of Sung, when it is often found in the same kind of thread relief as we have seen in ch'ing-pai (Pl. 39:g).

In *Tz'u-chou* ware we can see how the formal chrysanthemum designs of T'ang—Liao are adopted at the beginning of Sung. A fine example is the ewer in Pl. 43:h, which can be compared with similar designs from Liao wares (Fig. 37:h). The same stiff chrysanthemum design is also found on a group of pillows (Pl. 42:j, l) where they usually decorate the front. One pillow of similar type has a chrysanthemum spray as main design on the top panel (Pl. 42:c, Fig. 7:e). The stiff chrysanthemum design is also found on a small group of white or brown glazed pillows dated in the 11th and early 12th centuries (Pl. 48:c, f). In the rich flora of designs found on Tz'u-chou pillows of later date the chrysanthemum is surprisingly seldom found; examples are occasionally met with (Pl. 51:h) but they are not so frequent as might be expected.

In the typical sgraffito ware the design is mostly found towards the end of Sung (Pl. 54: j) but rarely earlier.

In Sung *Ting yao* realistic chrysanthemum designs seem to be totally lacking. Even in the different composite floral scrolls from Chin time no flowers that can be identified as chrysanthemums are found. In this connection it should be mentioned that the shape of the chrysanthemum flower has constantly been borrowed for ceramic forms, and most of the dishes with fluted sides seem to go back to this motif. Chrysanthemum-shaped specimens are found in almost all wares.

If we sum up what we have said above about the chrysanthemum design on different Sung ceramic wares we shall find that the design is surprisingly rare, especially if we consider that the flower apparently was exceedingly common as garden flower and that it at the same time was one of the favourite subjects of the Sung poets. In Sung tomb paintings and stone carvings realistic chrysanthemums are quite common[1]), but in the applied arts the flower is rare (Fig. 39:b:4).

PRUNUS

The favourite flower of the Chinese in the prunus family is the *mei hua* or Japanese apricot (*Prunus mume*), very often referred to as a plum flower.[2]) The flower is already mentioned in the earliest existing literature in China.

Because of its early blooming the *mei hua* was considered the herald of Spring and also a symbol of Spring itself.[3]) As five is a lucky number the five-petalled flowers became a very popular design, and because Spring is in general a happy time of the year the flower became a symbol of happiness and cheerfulness. By extension of this meaning the flower came to stand for eternal Springtime and rejuvenation, and thus combined two of the main wishes in Chinese symbolism: happiness and longevity.

Already the T'ang poets praised the beauty of the flower, and during the Sung dynasty many poets were inspired by it. The most famous of all poems written about it at this time is composed by Lin Ho-ching (967–1028) who lived as a recluse at the West Lake of Hang-chou. Special treatises on *mei* also appeared for the first time during Sung. An interesting work which was published around 1238 is the *Mei hua hsi shen p'u* [90] (Portraits of mei flowers) by Sung Po-jen. This work depicts in one hundred simple brush sketches the development of the flowers from bud to fading, and each sketch is accompanied by a short poem.

In Sung painting the flower is one of the favourite motifs, but in ceramics the *mei hua* does not seem to have been popular until the end of the period.

In *Northern celadon* the prunus is not found at all. In *ch'ing-pai* we find it very definitely limited to wares from the end of Sung and early Yüan. The finest examples

[1]) *KKHP* 1962:2, Pl. 23:7,3,4.

[2]) See Li, *op.cit.*, p. 48.

[3]) Together with the bamboo and the pine, the *mei hua* forms the "Three Friends in Winter", a popular motif symbolizing faithful companions.

of the design are found on a series of vases on which a blossoming *mei hua* twig in relief is the main pattern (Pl. 23:j, k, l). In the thread relief type the flower is also found (Type Cp 41) both as a spray and with the flowers alone used as a design (Pl. 33:a). In the composite moulded floral scrolls the prunus is also seen (Type Cp 30), but mainly in very late examples.

The prunus twig is often combined with a crescent moon, and this design is almost the only prunus pattern found in *Lung-ch'üan yao*. It is mostly found on small conical bowls of characteristic shape (Pl. 38:b, 39:c), and is also later on used in the biscuit-type designs usual during Yüan. In the actual *Ting yao* the design is not found, but wares of Ting type from the end of Sung sometimes have the prunus and moon. We have illustrated a bowl (Pl. 84:i) of a type almost identical with the just-mentioned Lung-ch'üan bowls, and the design is also found in the centre of specimens with moulded patterns (Pl. 84:k). Even in the *Tz'u-chou* ware the flower is hardly ever found.

Among the wares from *Chi-chou*, both those of temmoku type and those with different painted and carved designs, the prunus twig with or without the crescent moon is one of the favourite motifs, as we have shown in an earlier paper.[1]) These wares also mostly belong to the Sung—Yüan transition period. Among the very early blue-and-white the motif is also frequently found, as we have shown in the just-mentioned article. All these different records seem to indicate that for some reason the *mei hua* design was not adopted by the Chinese potters until the end of Sung.

OTHER FLOWERS

Apart from the main floral motifs discussed above, many more flowers are found on Sung ceramic wares, but they are mainly depicted in combination with other flowers and they probably do not have any specific symbolic meaning, but are just further evidence of the strong interest in nature so characteristic of the Sung dynasty.

Together with the lotus we very often find the sagittaria (*Sagittaria sagittifolia*) with its characteristic three-pronged spear-shaped leaves. In Ting yao it is constantly depicted together with the lotus (Pl. 59:a, 66:a), but is also found alone (Pl. 64:b), both in the incised and in the moulded variety (Pl. 79:b, 88:a, 89, 91); a very fine example is seen in Pl. 98. Characteristic examples are also found in the Northern celadon (Pl. 10:f-i) and in Tz'u-chou (Pl. 50:a–b). Other types of aquatic plants, water-weeds, duck-weed, water-chestnuts etc. are often found especially in Ting yao.

Flowers belonging to the mallow family are frequently found in composite floral scrolls in ch'ing-pai (Type Cp 28–29) and Ting yao, and in Tz'u-chou they are found in the enamelled type (Pl. 56:d, j). Dishes in the shape of mallow flowers are often found in Ting yao (Fig. 28:e) and in the same ware small mallows are placed in the

---

[1]) *Some ceramic wares from Chi-chou. BMFEA* 34. 1962.

centre of bowls (Pl. 81). A ch'ing-pai box also shows a beautiful design of a flower of this type (Pl. 31:b).

Lily-like flowers of different types are also quite common. In Northern celadon they can be seen in Pl. 9:i,1. The flower found in Tz'u-chou ware in Pl. 43:g is usually described by Chinese authors as a day-lily (*Hemerocallis*). In combination with birds several different kinds of flowers are also seen.

BAMBOO

Bamboo has since Sung time been one of the favourite motifs of the Chinese artists, and no other plant is so characteristic of Chinese culture as the bamboo. In art it is often considered a symbol of long life and of courage in adversity because it bends but does not break, even in a strong wind. Together with the pine and the prunus it also forms the group known as the "Three Friends in Winter". A bowl of Ting type with this design is shown in Pl. 84:j.

During the Sung dynasty bamboo painting became a special branch of painting notably practised by the scholar painters, and the bamboo came to represent the gentleman-scholar. In applied arts the bamboo motif is not often found, and in Sung ceramics the motif is rare. We find in the Tz'u-chou group birds on bamboo twigs (Pl. 47:d, 52:k) and garden scenes with bamboo (Pl. 51:i), and sometimes the leaves are used to form borders or decorative patterns (Pl. 51:k) but the design is quite uncommon. On temmoku bowls from Chi-chou we sometimes find panels with bamboo design (Fig. 36:a), but it is not until Yüan and Ming that the bamboo becomes one of the standard motifs on ceramics.

POMEGRANATE

The pomegranate (*Punica granatum*) is not indigenous to China but was probably introduced from the Near East towards the end of the Han dynasty, and it has since then been valued in the Chinese garden both for its flower and its fruit. The fruit is especially often depicted in art, and because of its many seeds it is an obvious symbol of prolific progeny. As Cammann has so strikingly put it: "the Chinese were obsessed with the idea of fertility"[1]) and this fruit soon became a favourite motif very often used on wedding presents. In Chinese art the pomegranate fruit is usually conventionalized in a special way, with the three sepals at the top greatly exaggerated and with a hole cut through the rind to disclose the seeds.

In T'ang applied arts the pomegranate is already common and it is often seen in silver specimens both as part of more decorative patterns and in more realistic designs.[2]) One of the designs typical of T'ang art is luxuriant floral scrolls to which Gyllensvärd has given the name "composite scrolls". In this kind of scrolls flowers of the lotus and the peony are mixed with pomegranates and luxuriant leaves in

[1]) *Op.cit.*, p. 114.

[2]) Gyllensvärd, *op.cit.*, Fig. 76, 97.

a rich and swirling composition.[1]) This kind of scroll is often further embellished by adding auspicious animals or Buddhist motifs to the composition, and it seems that it became so popular that it continued for more than fivehundred years in tomb stone carvings and other traditional monuments. In our study of the designs on Sung ceramics we have called this design the pomegranate-peony because when we meet it in Sung art it is generally composed of the flowers and leaves of the peony with the fruit of the pomegranate added to the centre of the flower or placed among the curling leaves. In stone carvings we can see typical designs of this type used both during Chin and during Yüan,[2]) and the general appearance of the design is very close to the monuments from T'ang of similar type.[3])

In ceramics from the period we are dealing with the design is mainly found in moulded *Ting yao*, where it is very common in a number of different combinations. We have already dated these designs to the Chin dynasty and stated that they seem to be a traditional type of pattern which was from T'ang taken up by the Liao people and from them transmitted to the Chins.

A simple type of the design can be seen in Pl. 82; here the composition is built up only of the large flowers with their promegranate-shaped seed-vessels and the winding luxuriant leaves. In the dish Pl. 86:a we find the same kind of scrolls, but a lion is added to the composition making it almost identical with the earlier-mentioned stone carving from a Chin stele. In another dish (Pl. 86:b) we find the pomegranate-scroll on the side, and here the leaves have become much more conventionalized and have taken the shape of cloud-scrolls; another not less stylized type is seen in Pl. 95:b. In the beautiful dish in Pl. 96:a (Fig. 20:a) we find the pomegranate scroll combined with deer. It also seems quite obvious that our "palmette-like peony" is clearly related to the pomegranate one, and they probably both derive from the same T'ang prototype.

Another moulded Ting yao specimen has the pomegranate-peonies as central design (Pl. 95:a) and we also find a quite realistic pomegranate together with boys on a bowl (Pl. 83), but this design will be discussed later on in connection with other patterns featuring children.

A very unusual specimen is the incised Ting yao dish (Pl. 63:b) which gives an unusually realistic rendering of a pomegranate plant. The design is represented with the same realism and artistic abbreviation as the lotus designs so common in the same ware, and the fruit is not open to disclose the seeds as in the more ornamental designs in the T'ang tradition.

In *ch'ing-pai* the pomegranate-peony is found chiefly in combination with boys usually in extremely dissolved designs (Pl. 19:a–b, Fig. 17:a–b).

---

[1]) Gyllensvärd, *op.cit.* Fig. 95.

[2]) *Ku tai chuang shih hua wen hsüan chi.* Pls. 72–73.

[3]) The lotus flowers so often found in combination with this kind of scrolls in T'ang does not seem to occur in these later versions of the motif.

In Sung gold and silver works we also find the pomegranate-peony used; a particularly fine example can be seen on a beaten gold dish in the Kempe collection.[1]) The design is also found in tomb paintings from Late Northern Sung and Chin.[2])

MELON

The melon is a fruit which seems to have been introduced rather late into China, probably not until the 10th century. In art it makes its appearance during the Sung dynasty, and like all other fruits with many seeds it becomes a symbol of fertility. The vine of the melon is usually also depicted with the fruit and Cammann[3]) has pointed out that this is not merely because of its decorative value but it served as a pun symbol. The Chinese word for the vine is *wan*, and the word for the stem is *tai*, and together they make the phrase *wan tai*, which could also have the meaning "ten thousand generations". It is accordingly very natural that we often find the melon in combination with boys, which further emphasizes the symbolic wish for numerous children and continuous generations of descendants. A very fine design with this motif is found on a Ting yao dish (Pl. 83). The fruits, the flowers and the vine are very realistically rendered and undoubtedly depict the ordinary melon, *Cucumis melo*. A similar design where the lotus flower is added to it is in the British Museum (Pl. 84:a). On the dated mould for impressing ornaments on a Ting yao specimen, which we have discussed earlier, there is in the centre another realistic melon design; in this case the shape of leaves and fruits seems to indicate the water melon, *Citrullus vulgaris* (Fig. 22:a). In Tz'u-chou yao we have a fine detailed design of the ordinary melon on a pillow (Pl. 51:c); again the motif is very realistic.

The shape of the melon has obviously inspired the forms of many ceramic pieces, examples of which are found already at the beginning of Sung (Pl. 53:j) but are especially common at the end of the period, when such shapes are found in celadon, ch'ing-pai and Chi-chou wares.[4])

The examples quoted of melons found on Sung ceramics are not many, but they are interesting as they show us that the motif was fully accepted at this time and that it is always realistically rendered. The last feature shows that there is a clear tendency in Sung art for a realistic interpretation of nature, especially when a motif is recent and has not already obtained a traditionally established form.

BOYS AMONG FLORAL SCROLLS

A motif most common during Sung and later but appearing already in late T'ang is children among floral scrolls. The explanation of the motif as a symbol of fertility and numerous progeny is generally accepted, but when the design first

---

1) *Chinese Gold and Silver*. No. 52.

2) *Pai sha Sung mu*. Fig. 63.

3) *Substance and Symbol . . .*, p. 115.

4) Cp. *CKc* no. 94. Locsin, *op.cit.* Pl. 71. Wirgin, *Some ceramic wares from Chi-chou*, Pl. 11:a.

occurs in art it seems to be the result of a combination of different motifs, the sources of which we shall try to explain.

It seems to be quite clear that the child motif is of Indian origin. Even if the small fat children look very Chinese, there are some features that show an Indian influence, for instance the footrings round the ankles and the marks on the forehead so often found on many of them. Several authors have suggested the paintings in the caves of Ajanta, where naked figures are seen among lotus scrolls, as the source of the motif. Coomaraswamy[1]) has explained the Indian motif as being the lotus born of a *yaksa* when the scrolls come out of the navel of the figure. But there are other paintings with naked boys which seem to be more closely related to those found in Sung decorative art. Among Chinese Buddhist paintings from the T'ang dynasty we quite often find small boy figures, frequently, though not always, sitting on lotus flowers. These children are supposed to represent reborn souls which in the shape of infants are carried on lotus flowers. Paintings of this type are found in Tun-huang and Chotscho (Fig. 16:b). Another motif also found in Tun-huang consists of a demon bearing on his hand a boy which is standing against a foliage background. This boy has a red trefoil mark on his forehead (Fig. 16:a). A boy on the demon's hand is also found on a prayer-sheet from Ch'ien-fo-tung dated A.D. 947 (Fig. 16:c).

It is not until late T'ang and early Sung that the "boys among floral scrolls" motif becomes more frequent. On the bottom of two silver bowls of late T'ang date in the Art Institute of Chicago there is a design of naked boys among lotus scrolls (Fig. 17:h). A gold hairpin in the Minneapolis Institute of Arts, also of late T'ang date, consists of a boy holding a lotus stalk.[2]) At the beginning of Sung the motif becomes very popular. It is found in various materials such as silver,[3]) bronze, textile and jade, but above all in ceramics. Why is it that this motif suddenly becomes so popular? In our examination of the origin of the motif we have found that it is of Indian type and was more or less a Buddhist design when first adopted by the Chinese. But the power of Buddhism had already declined at this time as a result of the persecutions in the ninth century, and it is not very probable that the design is an expression of Buddhist faith even if it still maintained some of its power, especially among the Liao people and other nomadic tribes on the outskirts of China.[4])

A small jar found in the Liao city of Tung-ching in Liao-yang, Manchuria, gives us a hint to one possible solution of the problem. This jar is decorated with wrestling

[1]) *Yaksas*, I–II. Smithsonian Miscellaneous Collections. Vol. 80, No. 6, 1928–31.

[2]) Gyllensvärd *op.cit.* Fig. 82:e.

[3]) A comb in beaten silver in the Kempe coll. (*Chinese Gold & Silver* Pl. 143) is probably an early Sung piece. It is decorated with an openwork representation of children among floral scrolls.

[4]) That the motif was, however, still found in a Buddhist context at the end of Northern Sung can be seen from stone carvings in temples. A fine example is to be found at the Shao-lin ssu in Teng-feng, Honan; it shows boys among floral scrolls and apsaras, heavenly musicians and other Buddhist figures. Cp. Tokiwa—Sekino, *Buddhist monuments in China*. Vol. II, Pl. 128:2.

boys and boys carrying lotus flowers. Wrestling or *chio-ti* was very popular among the Khitan people. Ryuzo Torii[1]) gives us the following description of this practice:

"The practice of Chio-ti or 'wrestling' prevailing among the Khitan people is recorded in the Liao-shih and other sources. — — — During the flourishing days of the Khitans, the children's chio-ti existed in the city of K'ai-feng-fu, the then capital city of Northern Sung in the southern part of the territory under its rule. In the section 'ching-wa-chi' in book 5 of the Tung-ching-meng-hua-lu, a work which appeared in the latter part of the Northern Sung dynasty, the matter is recorded. — — — In the time of the Khitans, that is the Liao dynasty, the practice of chio-ti was mainly sponsored by the Imperial courts as a part of their ceremonies. The art of chio-ti was originally practised by the Khitans, but sometimes the Han people living in the Khitan's country also did it, especially in the capital city of Shang-ching, where, like in the capital city of K'ai-feng-fu of Northern Sung, it was practised almost every day and almost exclusively by the Hans. — — —"

It is interesting to find that on the earlier mentioned Liao jar (Fig. 18:c) we have a decoration which consists of wrestling scenes and boys with lotus flowers. It seems as if the Liao artisans had adopted the old "boys among floral scrolls" pattern and combined it with one of their favourite motifs, that of wrestling scenes.[2]) The relationship between the boy motif and another subject related to the wrestling scenes has been pointed out by Sherman E. Lee[3]) in an article in which he compares on stylistic grounds an ivory statue of two acrobats, probably from early Sung, with the boy motif.

However, the interest in wrestling and acrobatics is certainly not the main reason for the adoption of the boy motif, even if it has contributed to the popularity of the design. The principal reason is undoubtedly the symbolic significance of the design which, as we have already stated, mostly explains why a certain motif is favoured in Chinese art.

In an article by Schuyler Cammann[4]) the design is explainded, as it is found on a Sung bronze mirror, in the following way:

"However, since lotus flowers, familiar emblems of fertility, are shown along with the more characteristic, auspicious peonies, the pattern as a whole would seem to be just another expression of good fortune and fertility, probably a rebus akin to the later *lien sheng kuei-tzu* [91] motifs which also featured children and lotuses. Good fortune and fertility: these two themes were very dominant in the decorative arts of later China. In Chinese folk art in general, pictures of small children, as well as many seeded melons and pomegranates and fish, almost always refer to hopes for numerous progeny—although they can also suggest other forms of abundance—and this mirror pattern would seem to fit into that category."

Cammann's explanation of the motif no doubt gives us the main reason why the boys among floral scrolls became such a popular design during Sung and the later dynasties.

---

[1]) *Chio-ti of the Khitans. Yen Ching Hsüeh Pao*, 29. 1941.

[2]) The habit of wrestling is still very much alive among the Mongols and the children usually start with it already at the age of four or five. Cp. *China Pictorial*, 1957:10, p. 12.

[3]) *Two early Chinese ivories. Artibus Asiae*, Vol. XVI, 1953.

[4]) *Significant patterns on Chinese bronze mirrors. ACASA*. IX, 1955.

We have already mentioned that the boy motif is found in various materials during Sung. We can see it on the bronze mirror described by Cammann (Fig. 18:a), the design of which comes very close to what we find in the contemporary ceramic art. Apparently the motif was constantly used on mirrors, as well as on ceramics, even in Ming time and later. A mirror in the MFEA with a decoration of boys among flowers with heart-shaped leaves is probably not earlier than the beginning of Ming (Fig. 18:b).

Textiles that can be dated Sung are indeed very scarce, but a piece of silk in the Seattle Art Museum with a décor of boys climbing among large peonies is most likely of Sung origin (Fig. 16:e).

The boy motif is no doubt most common on ceramics, being frequently used on all the main types of decorated Sung wares.

In *Northern celadon* the boys are usually seen in combination with flowers. Most common are the peonies, usually large luxuriant examples of the beehive-shaped type which, in combination with the boys, form an emblem of happiness and numerous progeny (Pl. 6:a–b, 5:l; Fig. 16:d). A sherd from a large dish with this design was found outside Khara-khoto (Fig. 18:g).[1] A more unusual design which seems to occur only in this ware, are boys among scrolls with star-like, five-petalled flowers (Pl. 9:j, k). With lotus flowers, forming a pun on the phrase *lien tzu* "successive sons", the boys are often seen; usually the plants are very large and the boys hold on to them and try to climb them in acrobatic positions (Pl. 10:h).

In the incised version of the *ch'ing-pai* ware the boys are found both with peonies of the pomegranate type (Pl. 19:a–b, Fig. 17:a–b) and more realistic peonies (Pl. 20:a–b; Fig. 17:d), the patterns of these types are generally very much dissolved. In the more deeply carved variety of the same ware, found at the end of Sung, boys are often seen among scrolls of lotus and other flowers (Pl. 22:f, k). In the moulded ware the motif is quite rare but is seen, for instance, in the peculiar thread relief pattern illustrated in Pl. 26:a. A ch'ing-pai pillow in the Victoria & Albert Museum, probably a little later than Sung, is decorated on the top with three children at play (Fig. 18:d).

In Sung *Lung-ch'üan* ware the motif is rare, but we have mentioned one example with a boy holding a lotus spray which might date from the end of the dynasty (Pl. 39:e).

In *Tz'u-chou* ware boy designs of different types are extremely common, and it seems that the artists working with this more popular ware have taken a special pleasure in humoristic representation of these jolly, plump children occupied with different games. The designs are preferably found on the top of pillows which are ideally suited for more pictorial designs. The popular boy with lotus motif is found on a pillow of rectangular shape (Pl. 52:f), the boy is only wearing an embroidered bib and usually in this type of designs, which are obviously fertility symbols, they

[1]) B. Sommarström, *Archaeological researches in the Edsen-Gol region. Inner Mongolia.* Part I. Pl. 24:12.

are clad in this way or in short open jackets which leave the lower part of the body unprotected. A pillow in the Boston Museum shows on the sides boys among lotus scrolls, but here the boys have the upper part of their body bare, and they look like wrestlers (Fig. 19:a). An interesting point about this pillow is that on the top it is decorated with a man reading a book with Uighur or Mongol text.[1]) This suggests that the pillow was made for one of the barbarian tribes on the outskirts of China other than Liao, and it seems to support our opinion about the relationship between the boy motif and the wrestling scenes.

A most interesting Tz'u-chou pillow is the one found in Pl. 42:l (Fig. 19:e). The boy is clad in a finely embroidered bib and has an elaborate cloud-collar round his neck. He has a mark on his forehead and bracelets round wrists and ankles. He is holding a flower in one hand and a scroll in the other, over him is a peony scroll and around him several gold ingots. The combination of so many different auspicious symbols: the boy, the cloud-collar, peonies, ingots, on one specimen is very unusual and the pillow seems to be the ideal gift for a newly married couple wishing them happiness, wealth and many children. Gold and silver ingots stylized in the same way are also found on other pillows (Pl. 42:k) and are also seen in Sung paintings, stone engravings, architectural designs etc. and are very common in tomb decorations.[2])

Designs with children which are not merely symbolical but have to be regarded more as genre scenes are frequently found in Tz'u-chou, many of them depicted with great charm and obviously influenced by contemporary paintings where this type of motif was very popular.[3]) As pillow designs we find the children playing in gardens (Pl. 52:a), fishing (Fig. 17:e), flying a kite (Pl. 52:c), riding a hobby-horse (Fig. 17:g) and playing with ducks (Pl. 47:a, 48:b).

Some of the finest designs with the boy motif we find among *Ting yao*, and we have already referred to several of them in connection with other patterns. It seems that on this ware the motif is limited to the moulded variety. We find the boys together with peonies on the bowl Pl. 92:b (Fig. 21:a), and on another similar bowl (Type Ti 49). They are clad in the usual short, open jackets or body-garments which leave the lower part of the body uncovered, they have bracelets around wrists and ankles[4]) and rings in their ears, their positions are extremely acrobatic and carries the thought once more to the relationship with that type of representations. The auspicious meaning of the décor is obvious and is still more so in the designs in which fruits have been added to the composition. The very fine design on the bowl Pl. 83 shows the boys with melons, pomegranates and a third kind of

---

[1]) Paine, *op.cit.* Pl. 10.

[2]) Cp. *Pai sha Sung mu.* Fig. 27.

[3]) The most famous of all painters favouring this motif was Su Han-ch'en, who lived in the 12th century.

[4]) Even if Chinese children also wore this kind of charms to protect them from evil influence, the general appearance of the boys is still surprisingly Indian.

fruit, probably apples. As we have already pointed out, all these symbols are connected with wishes for fertility and puns with the same idea, and are most suitable on wedding presents. The apple sometimes symbolizes peace, and is also known to be used in marriage ceremonies in order to secure a peaceful wedded life and would accordingly be very appropriate in this connection. On another similar bowl the boys are seen with melons and lotus flowers (Pl. 84:a) and in the centre of a dish (Pl. 88:a, Fig. 21:d) we find a single boy climbing in a very fine and detailed lotus scroll. In the latter design, the seed-pod of the lotus with its seeds is also depicted in order to emphasize still more its being a fertility emblem. A design more of the genre type common in Yüan and Ming is found on the dish Pl. 99, which shows two small boys, one of them carrying a lotus bud, chasing a pair of ducks. In the David Foundation is a saucer with moulded decoration of, in the centre, a lotus leaf and surrounding it, five boys each one holding a lotus in his hand.[1])

Apart from the boy designs we also find small toys and figurines representing children in most ceramic wares; they are, as we have already pointed out, particularly common in Ting yao and in the enamelled Tz'u-chou ware. Among the material collected by Palmgren in Ch'ing-ho hsien is a large amount of small figurines and moulds for figurines depicting children.[2])

OTHER HUMAN REPRESENTATIONS

Human representations are very rarely found in Sung ceramics, and it seems that the designs depicting historical and mythological scenes so common in Yüan and Ming had not yet become popular. In tomb paintings and stone carvings genre scenes of different kinds are quite common (cp. Fig. 35:c) and even if the great age of figure-painting had vanished with the fall of the T'ang dynasty, paintings with Taoist and Buddhist deities as well as secular figure scenes were very popular also during Sung.[3])

In *Northern celadon* we find very few examples; we have already mentioned the stand (Pl. 7:f) with strange, gorilla-like men sitting round its foot. It is possible that those figures again have something to do with the wrestling motif which we have discussed above. In a Chinese collection is a Liao *san ts'ai* vase with a related relief design which seems to strengthen this theory.[4])

Another strange celadon specimen is a figure from Yao-chou, in the Peking Palace Museum.[5]) It is 46 cm high and shows a man whose entire body is covered with leaves; in his left hand he holds a vase and in the right a leaf. The statue is

[1]) *David Ting. cat.* No. 188.

[2]) Palmgren, *Sung sherds.*, p. 345.

Cp. also *Chung kuo ku tai tzu i shu hsiao p'in.* Peking 1958.

[3]) Among Palmgren's Ch'ing-ho hsien material are many figures and moulds depicting Buddhist and Taoist figures, warriors, temples etc. (*op.cit.* p. 338–345).

[4]) *Liao tz'u hsüan chi.* Pl. 53.

[5]) *Ku kung po wu yüan ts'ang tz'u hsüan chi.* Pl. 33.

supposed to have come from a temple in Yao-chou dedicated to the god of pharmacy. The figure is said to represent a famous doctor, Shen Shih-miao whose native place was in this region, he was not only a famous doctor but also an expert in pharmacy, and after his death people called him the King of Pharmacy and a temple was built in his honour. The yellowish celadon glaze covering the figure as well as the clay are characteristic of the Yao-chou kiln.

A small crouching figure is also found on the handle of the ewer in Pl. 1:k, and small figurines with human representations are found in Northern celadon as in most other ceramic wares. The Buddhist design of apsaras found on the dish Pl. 10:k (Fig. 41:b) is unique, but patterns of a similar type are well-known from Liao, Sung and Chin tomb decorations.[1])

In *ch'ing-pai* human representations are only found as relief designs on funerary vases (Pl. 30) and in the form of small toys and figurines. During the Yüan dynasty we find a series of very fine Buddhist sculptures in this ware, as we have pointed out earlier (Type Cp 43). Also in *Lung-ch'üan yao* this motif seems to be limited to ceramic sculptures and relief designs, often of religious significance. A fine example of the latter type is the jar Pl. 37:d with Buddhist plaques around the shoulder and a kneeling figure in a niche on the top.

Even in the *Tz'u-chou* ware, which seems ideally suited for designs of this type, human representations, except for children, are very rare. We have already mentioned an unusual vase in Boston (Type Tc 7) with a design of men carrying gourds, surrounded by clouds, probably representing Taoist immortals. In the Philadelphia Museum of Art is an interesting pillow (dated 1179, in the Chin era) decorated with a chess game, with three holy men (*san sheng*). To the left is a Confucian scholar, to the right a Taoist and in the centre a Buddhist priest who is watching the game (Fig. 28:d).[2]) Both these specimens are rare and it seems that this kind of patterns still occupied a rather unimportant place in ceramic art. Another unusual design is found on a pillow of *san ts'ai* type, which shows a garden scene with the drunken poet Li Po seated with bare belly, leaning against a wine jar and surrounded by two attendants.[3])

In the enamelled Tz'u-chou group ceramic sculptures are very common (Pl. 57:e) but the majority of them seem to be slightly later than Sung. A painted enamel design of a standing man is found on a small bowl illustrated in Pl. 57:f. In *Ting yao* human representations seem to be restricted to the ceramic sculptures which have been discussed earlier; Buddhist representations of different kinds are also found in this group.

---

1) *KKHP* 1962:2, Pl. 19:1.

2) Jean Gordon Lee, *A dated Tz'u-chou pillow*. *ACASA* XI:1957.

3) *Los Angeles exh.cat.* No. 252.

DRAGON

The dragon is one of the oldest and most frequently used mythical creatures found in Chinese art, and a recapitulation of the development of this design and its different symbolic meanings would be a tremendous task, which is entirely outside the scope of this study. When we meet the dragon motif in Sung art it had already been in use as a decorative motif for more than two milleniums and several different variants had evolved. In Sung art there are three main types of dragons, two of which are more common and the third one more unusual.

The first one is the *lung* dragon [92], an animal with a scaly serpentine body, four legs with clawed feet and a large head with horns. In Chinese writings it is described as having the horns of a stag, the head of a camel, eyes like a demon, neck like a snake, belly like a sea monster, scales like a carp, claws like an eagle, pads like a tiger and ears like an ox. It usually has a ridge of scales along its back; on each side of the mouth are whiskers, and a beard hangs under its chin. In Sung and earlier this dragon is usually depicted with three claws on each foot, thereafter with four or five.[1]) Since ancient times dragons have been connected with water and rain and consequently have been regarded as symbols of fecundity and fertility. The appearance of a dragon was supposed to be a lucky and favourable event and the creature stands for strength and goodness. Quite early it came to represent the Emperor and the Imperial dignity and authority. In art the constant appurtenance of the dragon is an object which is variously described as *the pearl* or *the jewel*. The significance of this emblem has been much debated; it is sometimes explained as the richness conferred by the fertilizing rains caused by the animal, and sometimes as a significant treasure of the Lord of the Waters who naturally must have many pearls among his possessions. But it has also been identified with the sun and the moon, and it sometimes seems to have been confused with *cintamani* of the Buddhist art, "the jewel that grants every desire". In later ceramics two dragons "fighting for the pearl" is a very common motif, but it is not found in Sung art.

The second main type of dragon is the *ch'ih* [94]; this creature is quite different from the *lung*. Its general appearance is more like a lizard; it usually has a long, thin, bandlike body and a forked tail with curved ends. It is sometimes described as a hydra. The *ch'ih* is sometimes hornless but usually has one or two horns. It was frequently used during the Han dynasty and its appearance during Sung is most likely due to the archaistic interest of the period. The term archaic dragon is also sometimes used for this animal and is quite an adequate term to distinguish it from the *lung*. This type of dragon, the *ch'ih*, did not have the imperial significance of the *lung* and could accordingly be quite freely used for decorative purposes.

The third type we have chosen to call *fish dragon*, because its body is like that

[1]) The name *lung* does later on refer to the five-clawed type, while the dragon with four claws is called *mang* [93]. In this case we have used the word *lung* as a generic term for this type of dragon.

of a fish. It is sometimes provided with large wings. This dragon is very rarely seen in Sung art, but it seems to have been used during a short period from the end of T'ang to the beginning of Sung, and after that it only occurs occassionally until it again becomes popular during Ming. A silver bowl in the Hakutsuru Art Museum is decorated in the bottom with the head of a dragon of this type coming out of the water, where fishes and ducks are swimming around.[1]) A bowl with a similar decoration was exhibited at the MFEA in Stockholm in 1932.[2]) On both these bowls only the heads of the dragons are visible. They are of fish-like appearance, but are provided with strongly marked ears, a crest on the head, round protuberant eyes and a wide-open mouth with a long tongue and sharp teeth. Another bowl in the Hakutsuru Art Museum shows also the body of the dragon, which is altogether like that of a fish.[3]) This type of dragon is also found on Yüeh yao pieces from late T'ang and the 10th century.[4]) A bowl decorated with a pair of such dragons is in the David Foundation (Fig. 11:a). Among the Sung ceramics which we have examined only one piece with similar dragons has been found. They can be seen on the Ting yao dish in Pl. 87:a. The bodies and heads of these two dragons are similar to the earlier described fish dragons, but large wings have been added to the body just below the neck (Fig. 12:c). A mould decorated with a similar dragon is among Palmgren's material from Ch'ing-ho hsien.[5])

Dragons of the *lung* type appear, as we have already stated, very early, but they seem to have assumed the shape we generally associate with this kind of dragon during Sui, when they can be seen, for instance, on bronze mirrors. During T'ang they are also found in various materials, but they do not seem to be more common in the applied arts until the end of the dynasty.[6]) On ceramics the *lung* dragon first appears on *Yüeh yao*. These dragons have a slender, scaly body with back comb, a long tail with straight tip, and as a rule three-cleft feet. The head has a large neck comb, two horns and a grinning mouth with pointed teeth. The dragon is often curled and forms an almost spiral figure (Fig. 11:c–d). A well-known Yüeh yao bowl in the Metropolitan Museum has a very powerful dragon design (Fig. 11:b). The dragons on this bowl are, however, depicted in a more traditional way than those already dealt with; their relationship with the creatures found on T'ang mirrors is obvious. The body of the dragon is very elongated, slender and serpent-like; the scales are only suggested, but the elasticity and strength of the body is extremely well rendered. A characteristic feature, which becomes very common later on, is the loop formed by the tail and one of the hind legs.

The dragon which comes closest to the type common in Yüeh yao is in Sung ceramics found in the *Ting* ware. The *lung* dragon is here found both in the incised

[1]) Gyllensvärd, *op.cit.* Fig. 56:a.

[2]) *Yamanaka and Co. Ltd. Exhibition in the MFEA*, 1932. No. 32.

[3]) Gyllensvärd, *op.cit.* Fig. 56:b.

[4]) Cp. *Yüeh ch'i t'u lu.*

[5]) *Sung sherds.*, p. 363. Also moulds with *lung* dragons were found at the same place.

[6]) Gyllensvärd, *op.cit.*, p. 97.

and in the moulded type, but the motif is rare. A very fine example is seen on the dish Pl. 68 (Fig. 11:e), the dragon is extremely vigorously rendered and we can see here how the dragon-type which became prevalent during the later dynasties is already fully developed. The dish referred to, and a similar one in the David Foundation, are both very close in composition to the Yüeh yao specimens discussed above (Cp. Fig. 11:c–d and e–f). In both cases the dragons are three-cleft, but in the Ting yao examples we can see how the characteristic loop formed by the tail and one of the hind legs has now assumed the shape which hereafter becomes standard, and the pearl or precious jewel placed just above the left fore-leg is also clearly indicated. In the moulded variety of Ting yao we find the motif very similarly rendered but with some minor variations. In this case (Pl. 77) the position of the dragon is the same, but he is turned the other way around (which might just have been originally the result of the use of a mould, which naturally gives a reversed picture) and surrounding him is a band of conventionalized clouds. The dragon in this example is four-cleft, and like most moulded patterns it is very rich in details, the precious jewel is finely executed and has taken the form traditionally used in representations of the *cintamani*. An unusual relief design of a dragon is found round the stem of the lamp in Pl. 58:a.

There are very few intact specimens of Ting yao with dragon designs, but is has been reported that many sherds with this motif have been recovered at the kiln site. But it seems that the motif was very restrictively used. It is possible that already at this time the design was so closely associated with the Imperial Power that it was only allowed for official use. Still more rare than on Ting yao is the dragon motif on *Northern celadon*, and we do not know of any intact specimens with this décor. At the excavation of the Yao-chou kiln, however, several sherds with this design were found (Pl. 10:1) and they were taken by the excavators as evidence of the official status of the kiln. The scarcity of the *lung* dragon motif in general during Sung seems to strengthen the theory that the motif was restricted to the Imperial Court, but how severely this rule was kept we are not able to know.[1])

In designs on *ch'ing-pai* we do not find the characteristic *lung* dragon until the Yüan dynasty,[2]) but then it becomes quite common. Dragons of a similar type are, however, found in relief designs on funeral vases and sometimes in applied functions such as spouts etc., but these dragons are mostly of the *ch'ih* type. Fine examples are, however, found used as a base for pillows towards the end of the dynasty (Pl. 36:a–b).

In *Lung-ch'üan yao*, just as in ch'ing-pai, we do not find the *lung* dragon used as a decorative design during Sung, but only occasionally as an applied ornament.

---

[1]) It seems that the importance of the dragon motif has been somewhat exaggerated, and in all periods after Sung we find dragon-decorated ceramics (even with five-clawed dragons), also of a quality which reveals that they could never have been intended for the Imperial Court. The rules for its use were probably more severely applied on specimens of other materials.

[2]) Cp. *CKc.* No. 570.

The latter type includes many strange specimens which are impossible to assign to any of the main dragon categories (See Type Lc 16). In Yüan, also in this ware, the *lung* dragon becomes very common and is characterized by its position, which gives the impression that it is seated on its hind-legs (Fig. 12:a).

The fact that the *lung* dragon is rare on the *Tz'u-chou yao* is not surprising as the ware never had any official status, but on the contrary it was a typical people's ware. But still we find at least two specimens with dragon designs (Pl. 49:e, h); they are both of a type generally associated with Northern Sung, but at a closer look at least one of the pieces (Pl. 49:h) seems to be later and most probably belongs to the Chin dynasty. The two dragons are very similar in style and they are much more free and "realistic" than any other dragon designs found in Sung ceramics, but this is not surprising as this style seems to be a general tendency in Tz'u-chou specimens. One of the dragons has the usual three claws and the other five, which is uncommon in this period. Stylistically these two pieces are still somewhat of a mystery, but they have obvious similarities with the relief dragon found on the Ting yao specimen in Pl. 58:a (cp. Fig. 12:b).

The *ch'ih* dragon is, as we have already pointed out, a motif which is not found during the preceding T'ang dynasty, but seems to have been adopted during Sung as a result of the archaistic interest which was manifested by the forming of large collections of antiquities of different types and the catalogization and systematization of this material. If this assumption is correct we would not expect the *ch'ih* dragon motif to occur until the latter part of Northern Sung, and we have so far not seen any specimen with this design which is likely to be older than the 12th century.

It is mainly in Ting yao and ch'ing-pai that we find the *ch'ih* dragon, and it is clearly dominating on the first ware. In *Ting yao* we find it used both in the incised and the moulded variety. In the first kind of decoration the dragon is at the beginning very schematically rendered, only the head is a little more detailed and the two horns are clearly visible; it is always seen side-ways from the left and the body forms a C-shaped curve. It still has relationship to the *lung* dragon and we can sometimes see how the hind-leg and the tail form a loop, but the tail is usually split in two parts, each one ending in a spiral. Dragons of this type are often found as the central motif of bowls and dishes (Fig. 13:c, d, f) usually they are combined with other motifs like peonies (Pl. 69) or lotus flowers (Cp. Type Ti 27). More elaborate designs of a similar type are found on specimens which seem to be slightly later. Now the dragon's head is usually seen from above and shows a characteristic three-lobed shape (Fig. 13:e); usually the dragon has only one horn; scroll-work has been added to the dragons' bodies, which gives the design a much richer and more ornamental appearance. Two or more dragons are often combined in the composition (Fig. 13:a–b).

In the moulded variety of Ting yao we find the same dragons but, as is always the case with designs of this kind, they are more detailed and elaborate. We find two dragons richly adorned with attached scroll-work similar to what we have seen in the incised version, as the principal motif of moulded dishes (Pl. 86:b, 87:b), and we also find the dragons in combination with cloud scrolls as border designs (Pl. 86:a). More sketchy types are also found as the central motif of bowls with floral designs, just as we have seen in the incised type (Pl. 92:a).

In *ch'ing-pai* we only find the *ch'ih* dragons in incised patterns and here too it is rare. In one example we can see how the dragons have unusually long serpent-like bodies and their faces are almost human-looking (Pl. 12:k, Fig. 12:e). Dragons of the more common type are seen on Pl. 12:e (Fig. 12:d) and on a similar specimen in the Clark collection,[1]) but even here the faces have the same strange appearance. In both these specimens the dragons are placed opposite to each other in a stiff, almost heraldic arrangement, and in the centre is the pearl stylized as a scroll or flame.

In applied relief and in different practical functions *ch'ih* dragons are quite common in ch'ing-pai. A fine example is a series of cups, the handles of which are formed by *ch'ih* dragons biting over the rim of the vessel (Pl. 28:f–i). The dragons are here of a very characteristic *ch'ih* type similar to what we can find in Han dynasty jades, but the motif strongly resembles the T'ang pottery amphoras where we find a very similar arrangement of the dragons.[2]) We have also seen how in a group of ch'ing-pai ewers from the beginning of Yüan the dragons have been used to form the handles and spouts of the vessels (Pl. 28:a–c).

In Northern celadon and Tz'u-chou yao the *ch'ih* dragon is not used as a decorative motif, and in Lung-ch'üan it is very rarely seen except in applied relief until Yüan. A further exception is a basin in the Palace Museum in Taipei of very thinly potted celadon ware. It has a wide-open mouth and straight, expanding sides, and on the inside are two incised dragons of *ch'ih* type; around the mouth is a key-fret border. The outside has key-fret and petals with carved details.[3]) In Yüan time *ch'ih* dragons are found in that variety of Lung-ch'üan where the design has been left unglazed and appears in red biscuit after firing.[4])

PHOENIX

The auspicious bird known by the Chinese as *feng-huang* [95], but in the West usually called phoenix,[5]) assumes in conformity with the dragon a very important place both in Chinese mythology and in art. *Feng* is really the name of the male

---

[1]) Gray, *op.cit.*Pl. 80.

[2]) *Barlow cat.* Pl. 24:a. Honey, *The ceramic art of China . . .* Pl. 21.

[3]) *Porcelain of the National Palace Museum. Lung-ch'üan ware of the Sung dynasty.* Pl. 19.

[4]) *Chinese Art under the Mongols.* Pl. 80–81. For the *ch'ih* dragon design on a carved lacquer box see the same work Pl. 293.

[5]) The name phoenix is in fact not very appropriate, but since the term has been so generally accepted it is not much use to try to change this practice. We have accordingly used the term phoenix for the *feng-huang* in this paper.

bird and *huang* that of the female. The *feng-huang* is supposed to appear in times of peace and prosperity. It is used as a symbol of the Empress, and like the dragon it was during certain periods forbidden to be used by common people. In the Sung dynasty the phoenix motif is quite common and it does not appear that any strict rules about its use had been issued. A contributary cause seems to have been that the appearance of the *feng-huang* was never so firmly established as that of the dragon, and many different varieties are found, some of them difficult to separate from real birds.

A pair of phoenixes have also been used as marriage symbols in China, and are used in this way, for instance, on T'ang mirrors, the *feng* symbolizing the bridegroom and the *huang* the bride. It is very likely that it is mainly in this capacity that we find the birds used on Sung ceramics.

During the T'ang dynasty the phoenix is a very common motif and from this time it is frequently seen,[1]) for instance, on silver ware. The T'ang phoenix is very characteristic with its powerful head, proud bearing and magnificent tail curling upwards (Fig. 15:i–k). The phoenix generally found in Sung ceramics is quite different in appearance, but it seems that the older type survived in more traditional monuments such as stone carvings for tombs etc.,[2]) and when the bird was used in its capacity of being the emblem of the Southern Qadrant of Heaven.

The development from the T'ang type to the Sung type we can find in this case, as in so many other designs, on *Yüeh yao*. Characteristic features of the phoenixes found on this ware are a high crest on the head, two pointed hornlike projections at the ears, and an upward-curving tuft on the neck. The tail is long and band-like, with volutes and a pointed tip; it is reminiscent of a flame. The wings bend in a very characteristic gentle curve (which is also found in the parrot representations in the same ware), but the details are often highly conventionalized (Fig. 14:f–h). The feathers are merely indicated by parallel lines. The neck is short and has a collar similar in appearance to the neck-tuft. The beak is short and powerful like that of a bird of prey.

In *Northern celadon* the phoenix motif is rare and we only know of two really fine examples. The first is found on the top of a pillow and shows a single bird (Pl. 3:j; Fig. 14 d). The phoenix is depicted in flight with a coiling flower spray in its beak. The head has no crest but only small, upstanding feathers, the neck-tuft is very small, the beak long, thin and pointed and the neck long and S-curved. The tail, which is long and curls gently, is of the flame-like type. The other phoenix which is found on the ewer in Pl. 1:k is of a similar type and also has a floral spray in its beak, but the details are not so clear.

In *ch'ing-pai* we find the phoenix motif in the moulded type, where we can see it in several variations. The phoenix used on this ware usually has a crown-like crest on the head, a prominent neck tuft and two streamer-like feathers coiling

[1]) Gyllensvärd, *op.cit.*, p. 98.

[2]) Cp. *Kao Ku* 1964: 7, p. 351, Fig. 4:3 (Tomb of the Prince of Wei from A.D. 1093).

out from the neck (Fig. 14:a); the tail is no longer band-like but is split into several thin feathers. The design is often found especially on bowls with a moulded décor of floral patterns of different kinds (Pl. 24); the quality of these specimens varies very much from extremely fine examples to very coarse ones, which clearly shows that any restriction on the design to pieces intended for official use was not in existence at this time. The large output of phoenix-decorated ch'ing-pai specimens of this and other types clearly indicates that the ware was intended for general use. Apart from the bowls, we very often find a pair of phoenixes of the same type as design on small boxes; sometimes the phoenixes are depicted alone (Pl. 25:a), sometimes floral sprays are added (Pl. 25:b). Boxes of this kind were probably used as wedding gifts. In this group also the quality is most divergent. A small group of ch'ing-pai specimens executed in a kind of linear relief often has a pair of phoenixes (Pl. 26:b, Fig. 29:a), frequently in combination with sketchy lotus flowers, this type is datable to around 1200. A still later type of phoenix is found in the centre of the bowl Pl. 26:a, those birds have a very short tail and broad flattened wings; and this heavy and inelegant type is typical of Yüan.[1]) It seems that most of the phoenix designs found on ch'ing-pai belong to the Southern Sung period and Yüan.

Phoenixes are also found on funeral vases of ch'ing-pai, and we have also observed that phoenix heads are used on top of ewers preferably at the beginning of Sung and during the preceding centuries (Type Cp. 36).[2])

In *Lung-ch'üan yao* we find phoenixes used as handles of mallet-shaped vases (Pl. 39:1), but otherwise the motif does not seem to be used until Yüan. Nor is it found in Tz'u-chou yao until Yüan, and it is then usually of the same type as the phoenixes found on ch'ing-pai (Fig. 14:b–c).

In the *Ting ware* we only find the phoenix in the moulded variant, but here several different types are used. The most elegant type is undoubtedly the one found on the mould dated 1184 (Fig. 22:a) and on a number of other specimens (Pl. 84:b–c, 85:a, Fig. 22:b). The phoenixes of this type are of a slender kind with a long beak that is straight or very slightly bent. On its head the bird has a thick plume curving backwards. The neck is long and thin and gracefully S-curved, on the under side of the head are small hairs or down which are very characteristic. The wing feathers are carefully drawn, and the tail is long and thin and split into two parts, each ending in a spiral, like those found on the *ch'ih* dragons. A fragment from a mould with this kind of design was also found at the Ting kiln (Fig. 34:12). A second type of phoenix which closely resembles the one we have just described is seen on the dishes Pl. 84:g and 97:a, the only difference is that the birds no longer have the typical long tails but only very short ones. For this reason they are sometimes called not phoenixes but "mandarin ducks". This description, however, is certainly incorrect. If we look closely at the birds we will find that the

[1]) Cp. *Chinese Art under the Mongols*. Pls. 112, 158.

[2]) The development of the phoenix-headed ewers have been treated earlier and we will not repeat it in this context (See: J. Wirgin, *The phoenix motif on Sung ceramics*. 1964, p. 953.). Cp. Fig. 15:a–h.

execution of the head (note the characteristic down under the chin) and the body fully corresponds to that of the earlier described phoenixes, and that only the tail is different. Accordingly it is most probable that these birds too are supposed to represent phoenixes; maybe it is the female bird (*huang*) that is intended here.[1])

Another type of phoenix is found on the dish Pl. 88:b; the head and wings of this bird are similar to the types just mentioned, but the tail is a gently curved, flame-like peacock tail. The bird might be considered to be a peacock, but other representations we have of that bird always show a quite different neck and head, and the tail does not have the flame-like appearance. The dish is closely related to the one in Pl. 84:g in the general arrangement of the design. An unusual phoenix design also found in this ware is the one in Pl. 94:a (Fig. 14:e), which we have already described above (Type Ti 50). The examples given may be sufficient to show the variety of designs of this type found in Ting yao.

In the temmoku ware from *Chi-chou* a pair of phoenixes is a common motif;[2]) they are usually very sketchily depicted and the birds are seen in combination with flowers and butterflies.[3]) Phoenixes of a very similar type are also seen on bronze mirrors during Sung.[4])

LION AND CH'I-LIN

The lion is an animal that is rarely seen in Sung ceramics, though some examples are found. In Sui and T'ang lion designs of different types are very common both on bronze mirrors and on silver specimens, and lions also are often found in the composite floral scrolls on stone carvings from this time. The significance of the lion symbol as it appears in T'ang has been thoroughly penetrated by Cammann,[5]) and it seems that at this time it was mostly a cosmic symbol, but also an emblem found on the marriage mirrors. The lion was not a traditional Chinese symbol but an imported one, and it seems to have been borrowed from two different sources: on the one hand from Western Asia, where it was an important Manichaean symbol; on the other hand from India, where it was associated with Buddhism. The typical T'ang lion[6]) is not found in Chinese ceramics, but is still used in more traditional monuments such as stone carvings on steles.[7]) The few lions we find used in ceramics are of the type specific to China; it is common in later art and is clearly associated with Buddhism. Lions of this type are usually found in pairs as guardians of gates to temples and palaces, the male is usually depicted with a ball and the female

---

1) There were also less spectacular types of phoenixes known as *luan* [96], which later on were used as emblems of the princesses.

2) *Chi-chou yao.* Pl. 19–21, 29.

3) The butterfly is often used as a symbol of longevity and happiness.

4) For an example in the MFEA, see *OCS Sung exh.cat.* No. 229.

5) *The lion and grape patterns on Chinese bronze mirrors. A.A.* 16.1953.

6) Cp. Gyllensvärd, *op.cit.* Fig. 70, p. 117.

7) *Ku tai chuang shih hua wen hsüan chi.* Pl. 72.

with a cub. When the lion is depicted alone he is often seen together with an elaborately embroidered ball with attached ribbons; this motif is usually called "lion pursuing embroidered ball" (*shih tzu kun hsiu ch'iu*) [97]. The ball may represent the Buddhist precious pearl or jewel. Sometimes two lions are seen with the ball between them in exactly the same way as the dragons with the pearl.

On a Tz'u-chou pillow reproduced in the *Pai sha Sung mu*[1]) we find a running lion which carries in his mouth a ribbon attached to an embroidered ball; an almost identical design is found on a pillow in Cambridge, Mass. (Fig. 28:f).[2]) The latter pillow belongs to the group of rectangular Chang pillows which we have not discussed in this paper.

The most interesting lion design we have found in ceramics from this period is the one on the Ting yao dish Pl. 86:a, which we have described above (Type Ti 40:b). Here the lion is still very much in the T'ang tradition, even if it has been rendered in a more three-dimensional and plastic style, and it is also found together with pomegranate scrolls. As we have already pointed out, this traditional motif is still found in Chin stone carvings. On the Ting dish, however, the motif is much more free in its composition and in front of the lion is a most elaborate embroidered ball tied with long ribbons. That the lion and ball motif was used in Chin can also be seen from the decoration in a tomb in Shansi (Fig. 39:b:1). Another Ting dish with the design of a lion among pomegranate scrolls is in the Seattle Art Museum.

Closely related in style to the lion dish (Pl. 86:a) is a dish in the Neave-Hill collection, which we have described as decorated with a *ch'i-lin* (Pl. 85:b). The design of this dish shows an animal with flame-like tail and two horns running with a spray in its mouth among peonies of the palmette-like type. This animal is similar to the lion-like creatures called *suan-i* [99] by Cammann and found in T'ang art.[3]) Two lion-like animals called *suan-i* were found among the stone carvings decorating a 12th-century tomb in Hopei.[4]) The animal on our dish, however, has a head which is more like that of a deer and the legs are certainly not those of a lion; its general appearance is more like the traditional description of the *ch'i-lin* [100].

The *ch'i-lin*[5]) is one of the most auspicious of all Chinese mythical animals, it is the symbol of grandeur, felicity, illustrious offspring and wise administration. It is said to appear only when a king of the highest benevolence sits upon the throne, or when a sage is about to be born. The male is called *ch'i* and the female *lin*. In its general form it is often described as resembling a stag but combines the body of a deer, with the tail of an ox, the forehead of a wolf and the hoofs of a horse. Repre-

[1]) *Op. cit.* Fig. 27:10. Except for the lion the pillow which is decorated in black on a white slip, has a design including ingots and other auspicious objects and carries the inscription *Chen chen tai chi* [98] (Felicitousness for the Residence).

[2]) Paine, *op.cit.* Pl. 27.

[3]) Cp. Gyllensvärd, *op.cit.* Fig. 92:a, p. 147.

[4]) *KKHP* 1962:2, Pl. 23:1–2. In the same tomb was also found a sculpture of a lion.

[5]) It is often named the Chinese unicorn, which is somewhat inappropriate as it is usually depicted with two horns.

sentations of the *ch'i-lin* vary very much; some of them are more like a stag and others are more fantastic and gives the creature the head of a dragon and scales on the body; sometimes the body recalls that of a lion. Although it is one of the oldest of the Chinese mythical creatures it is rarely depicted in art in the earlier periods, but becomes very common during Ming and Ch'ing. The Ting yao dish just mentioned is the only specimen of Sung ceramics we know of with this design.

Sculptures of lions are found in most Sung wares. The excavations at Yao-chou revealed several examples, but otherwise the design is not found in Northern celadon, with one exception. The spout of the ewer in Pl. 1:f is made in the form of a very fine and realistic lion sculpture. In ch'ing-pai we also find sculptures of lions (Pl. 36:c) and lions used as supports of pillows (Pl. 36:d). Among the figurines and moulds from Ch'ing-ho hsien collected by Palmgren are a number of specimens depicting lions and tigers.[1])

TIGER

The tiger is considered to be the "King of beasts" and his forehead often bears the character *wang* (King) when he is depicted in art. The tiger is a symbol of strength and courage and was often used as a military sign. He is also one of the animals of the Four Cardinal Points. Unlike the lion, the tiger is not foreign to China and is not considered a mythical animal in the same way. Realistic representations of tigers are found already in the bronze age. Designs featuring tigers are not very frequent in China during Sung and the dynasties immediately preceding that time, but it seems that the motif was taken up again towards the end of the dynasty and after that it is continuously found in Chinese art.

An interesting design of a more mythical appearance is found on a vase in the Peking Palace Museum which we have referred to above (Type Tc 7), but otherwise the few tiger designs we find in Tz'u-chou, which seems to be the only ware where the design is used, are quite realistic.[2]) The pillow reproduced in Pl. 47:e shows a very free and humorous interpretation of the motif.[3]) Similar tigers are found on other types of Chang pillows of later date.[4])

An interesting group of Tz'u-chou pillows in the shape of tigers it has been possible, thanks to recent excavations, to attribute to the Hao-pi chi kiln in Honan. Pillows of this type are found in several collections (Pl. 52:j–l), they all have the same rather humoristic rendering of the motif which can still be seen in modern Chinese

[1]) *Sung sherds.*, p. 335–337. Cp. also *Chung kuo ku tai tao tzu i shu hsiao p'in*, where several different types of animal figurines are found.

[2]) In Lung-ch'üan yao the motif is taken up during the Yüan dynasty. In the David Foundation is a dish with two tigers in relief in red biscuit.

[3]) The style is very similar to the famous tiger painting in the Daitokuji in Kyoto, attributed to Mu-ch'i. *Chinese Arts of the Sung and Yüan periods.* Tokyo National Museum, 1961. No. 63. Cp. also Pl. 95 in the same catalogue.

[4]) Cp. Paine, *op.cit.* Pl. 30.

representations of the animal. It is interesting to note that this style was already inaugurated during the Sung dynasty.[1])

HSI-NIU

The rhinoceros (*hsi-niu*) which we meet as a design on Sung ceramics has to be included among the mythical animals. There is no attempt at a realistic representation of the animal, but when we do find it, it is clearly used as a legendary motif. Realistic rhinoceros representations are, however, found very early in Chinese art,[2]) and during the bronze age the animal still seems to have been quite frequent in Central and South China, later on it became much more rare but does not seem to have been completely extinguished until the beginning of the Sung dynasty, and might very well have survived still longer in some parts of Yünnan.

At the beginning of the Sung dynasty two different conceptions of the rhinoceros were clearly developed; one realistic, which undoubtedly depicted real animals, and which can be found for instance on T'ang silver ware,[3]) and one mythical, which took its inspiration from literary sources. As the realistic animal does not appear as a design on Sung ceramics we could concentrate on the mythical creature.

In the ancient Chinese texts are mentioned two animals; the *ssu* and the *hsi*, both of which are described as horned animals; in post-Han texts these two terms were undoubtedly used for the rhinoceros, but the question as to whether already in ancient times they referred to a rhinoceros or to a bovine animal led to a bitter quarrel between the scholars Herbert and Lionel Giles on the one side and Berthold Laufer on the other in the early part of the present century.[4]) As a result of this controversy Laufer later on published a lengthy article about the history of the rhinoceros in China,[5]) which is a very valuable but somewhat awkward source of information about the rhinoceros and the use of the rhinoceros horn in China, as well as the different legendary aspects applied to the animal.

We have already seen that the animal we find on Sung ceramics has very little to do with the real rhinoceros, its body is usually more like that of a bovine animal and the horn gives it an appearance which is more related to the unicorn of the Western mythical world. Laufer (*op.cit.*) cites several descriptions of the animals *ssu* and *hsi* from different sources, like the *Erh ya*, and it was undoubtedly from this kind of literary works that the Sung artists got their *hsi-niu* motif. When we

---

[1]) Clay figurines of tigers were also collected by Palmgren in Ch'ing-ho hsien. *Sung sherds*, p. 337.

[2]) The most well-known bronze age example is the rhinoceros-shaped vessel in the Brundage collection (A. G. Wenley, "*A Hsi Tsun from the Avery Brundage collection*". *ACASA*, Vol. VI, 1932) but a very fine example of later date which is still more realistic has been found recently in a Warring States tomb in China (Wen Wu 1965:7, Pl. 1–2).

[3]) Cp. Gyllensvärd, *op.cit.* Fig. 63:b,c.

[4]) Cp. Soame Jenyns, "*The Chinese rhinoceros and Chinese carvings in rhinoceros horn*". *TOCS* 1955–56, p. 31.

[5]) Berthold Laufer, *Chinese clay figures*, Chicago 1914. (p. 73–173, *History of the rhinoceros*).

find the *hsi-niu* in ceramic designs it is usually shown at the shore gazing at the crescent moon in the sky. This motif goes back to an old legend that while the rhinoceros is looking at the moon the peculiar structure within its horn is formed. The rhinoceros horns were sliced to obtain plaques which were used as belt ornaments, and when they were cut, white marks in the shape of a crescent or a star were often found in the horn. The use of such plaques of rhinoceros horn are mentioned both in the *Sung Shih* and the *Chin Shih*.[1])

The motif with the rhinoceros looking at the moon is usually described as "rhinoceros communicating with the sky" and several interesting informative details about the meaning of this design have been gathered by Laufer. In the work *Pen ts'ao shi i* written by Ch'en Ts'ang-k'i, who lived during the first half of the eighth century, the following explanation is given: "There are not two kinds of the rhinoceros, called the land and the water animal. This distinction merely refers to finer and coarser qualities of the horns. As to the rhinoceros 'communicating with the sky', the horn on its skull elongates into a point after a thousand years. It is then adorned, from one end to the other, with white stars, and can exhale a vapour penetrating the sky; in this manner it can communicate with the spirits, break the water and frighten fowl. Hence the epithet communicating with the sky is bestowed on it."[2])

A writer of the second half of the eighth century gives the following statement: "The rhinoceros 'communicating with the sky', during the time of pregnancy beholds the forms of things passing across the sky, and these are reproduced in the horn of the embryo; hence the designation 'communicating with the sky'. When the horn, placed in a water-basin during a moonlight night, reflects the brilliancy of the moon, it is manifest that it is a genuine horn communicating with the sky."[3]) Another source says: "The variety of rhinoceros styled 'communicating with the sky' dislikes its own shadow, and it is in the habit of drinking muddy water."[4])

The above-cited sources may be sufficient to show some of the mythological implications of the *hsi-niu* motif and from where the artists of Sung time received their inspiration. As we can see from these sources, the rhinoceros was associated with water and in later representations of this legendary animal it is often seen living in or running upon the sea. When we find the motif in Sung ceramics the animal is also found surrounded by waves.

In ceramics we find the rhinoceros only in two wares: the *Northern celadon* and the *Ting yao*. We only know of one intact piece with this motif in the former

---

[1]) Under the Chin dynasty the materials employed for official costumes were ranked in the order jade, gold, rhinoceros horn, ivory (*Chin Shih*, Ch. 34 § 3, p. 7; Laufer *op.cit.* p. 142, note 4).

[2]) Laufer, *op.cit.* p. 140.

[3]) Li Sün, in *Hai yao pen ts'ao* (Laufer *op.cit.* p. 147).

[4]) Tuan Ch'eng-shi of the ninth century in the *Yu yang tsa tsu* (Laufer, *op.cit.* p. 144).

ware,[1]) but sherds have been found in Yao-chou (Pl. 9:g). The motif is, however, rather sketchily depicted and no details can be seen. It is interesting to note that the sherds with this design belong to the Chin dynasty.

In Ting yao the design is more common and usually very fine and detailed in the moulding; it is only found in the moulded variety during this time. On the bowl in the Kempe collection (Pl. 92:b, Fig. 21:a) we find the motif in the central panel. The rhinoceros, which is reclining on a small tongue of land surrounded by crested waves, has a bovine body and a short, thick horn on the skull; in the sky is the crescent moon on which the animal is gazing.[2]) On the mould Pl. 93 the animal is again very clearly depicted. In this case the body is more like that of a deer and the horn is more elongated, the surrounding landscape is more full of details, and a band of clouds has been added in the sky. The mould is undoubtedly later than the Ting bowl, but both specimens most likely belong to the Chin dynasty. A Yüan version of the motif can be seen on the incised dish Pl. 84:e, this design is still very close to the earlier one and only has minor differences in the composition. On a Yüan celadon dish of similar shape[3]) we can again find the *hsi-niu*, but this time he is provided with sacred flames springing from his shoulders and flanks, which is typical of the later versions of the motif which are found in Ming and Ch'ing.[4])

The two Ting dishes in Pl. 101 with fluted sides show slightly different versions of the *hsi-niu* motif. In both specimens the animals are almost completely surrounded by waves and clouds, and there is no longer any indication of land. Both animals are definitely stag-like but are individually executed. The crescent moon in the sky is almost concealed among the clouds but it is easily found if we follow the gaze of the animal.

The *hsi-niu* motif is interesting as one of the many motifs which seem to appear for the first time in art during the Sung period. The examples we have found on ceramics all seem to belong to the Chin dynasty, but the motif must have been known in Sung as well and it was most likely Northern Sung literary researches and compilations of ancient texts which made the motif appear in art.

TORTOISE

The tortoise is in China a symbol of longevity, strength and endurance.[5]) It is not very common as a decoration on ceramics. During T'ang it was not very frequent either; it occurs on some silver specimens, but its main use is as a decoration

---

[1]) *China's Beauty*. Pl. 48.

[2]) Sherds with this motif were also found at the Ting kiln (Fig. 32:8).

[3]) *Chinese art under the Mongols*. Pl. 68 b.

[4]) Cp. S. Cammann, *The development of the Mandarin Square, HJAS*, Vol. 8, p. 71, 1944.

[5]) The tortoise encircled by the snake, known by the name "the Black Warrior" is representing the Northern Quadrant. In this capacity it is found in Sung stone carvings together with the three other animals representing the Four Cardinal Points, the dragon, the tiger, and the bird. Cp. *Kao Ku* 1964:7, p. 351, Fig. 4:4.

on mirrors, on which it is often seen as a cord knob. In this position it is very often placed on top of a lotus leaf.[1]) On Sung ceramics we find a decoration which is closely related to that of the mirrors. It is found on specimens of Yüeh yao, Northern celadon and Lung-ch'üan yao. The decoration consists in the centre of a tortoise, usually in applied relief, surrounded by radiating, incised lines which signify the veins of a lotus leaf. The most common specimens bearing this decoration are bowls with leaf-shaped rim (Types Nc 11 and Lc 8) and small dishes; they all apparently belong to Northern Sung. Recently a small dish of this kind was found in a Liao tomb in *Ch'ing Ho Men* in northern China.[2]) Tortoises are also found among Liao sculptures.[3])

The tortoise is on the whole not very common in Chinese art; it is found used as a base for steles and other monuments and on top of seals, but in ceramics and most other types of applied art[4]) it is rare, especially after Yüan.[5])

DEER

There is a large number of different species of Chinese deer,[6]) but that favoured by the artists is the handsome spotted deer or *sika* (*Sika mandarinus*). The deer is believed by the Chinese to live to a very great age, and has therefore become an emblem of long life. It is said to be the only animal that is able to find the sacred fungus of immortality (*ling chih*). A picture of a deer often represents official emolument because of the similar pronunciation—*lu*—of the two words.

During T'ang and the Five Dynasties the deer is a common motif, especially on silver ware, but also on lacquer and ceramics. The deer is often seen in hunting and landscape scenes.[7]) Among the deer found in T'ang is one with a very peculiar horizontal, crown-like antler, which seems to be of Iranian origin. This type of deer is also found in Yüeh yao,[8]) but not in Sung ceramics.

The deer motif is in Sung ceramics mainly found in Tz'u-chou yao, but also in Ting yao. In *Tz'u-chou* we find several representations of the motif on pillows in our Type Tc 6. The finest is perhaps the pillow Pl. 42:k with two noble stags of the spotted type with large antlers; they have floral sprays in their mouths and

[1]) Gyllensvärd, *op.cit.* Fig. 58:f–i., p. 101.

[2]) *KKHP* 1954:8, Pl. 17:3, Fig. 24:3.

[3]) R. Tori, *Illustrations of Archaeology*. Pl. 22.

[4]) A piece of silk on a reliquary in Åbo with decoration of phoenixes, and tortoises with flower vases on their backs has been attributed to late Sung. The tortoises are here of the mythical type. Cp. P. Simmons, *Some recent developments in Chinese textile studies*. *BMFEA*. No. 28, 1956. Fig. 3.

[5]) The tortoise with dragon-like head, found for instance in the capacity of a symbol of the North, was not regarded as an ordinary animal, but as a mythical creature and was still in use during all periods, but the realistic tortoise was usually abandoned because of lewd associations connected with the shape of its head.

[6]) Of the 23 different varieties known in Asia, 19 are found in China.

[7]) Gyllensvärd, *op.cit.* P. 119–120.

[8]) Gyllensvärd, *op.cit.* Fig. 71:c.

the auspicious meaning of the design is further emphasized by the ingots placed under them.[1]) The hinds of the same spotted deer are found on two other pillows in the same group (Pl. 43:b–c) in both cases running in a landscape (Fig. 20:b–c). A fourth pillow of the same kind (Pl. 43:a) shows a reclining deer of a somewhat different kind, the antlers being quite small and bent backwards. Among the cloud-shaped pillows we have one example of a deer design (Pl. 45:l), the deer, which is without horns, has an almost mouse-like face, and is surrounded by clouds which emphasize the celestial character of the animal.

Among the different groups of Chang pillows we have several examples of deer. One pillow of this kind, which has been excavated in China (Fig. 31:e), shows a stag of the spotted deer family, and a fine example of the same species with large antlers is galopping on another pillow type (Pl. 47:b). In our Type Tc 17 several deer-decorated pillows are known; we have here only illustrated two, but earlier we referred to some more. One of them shows a *sika* deer in a landscape carrying a plant in his mouth (Pl. 48:a), the other pillow shows two reclining deer (Pl. 47:l); in both cases they are found together with clouds. On a pillow of *san ts'ai* type is found a stag with an enormous floral spray in his mouth (Pl. 52:i).[2])

In *Ting yao* the deer motif is rare, but an extremely fine example is found on a group of dishes here represented by a specimen in the Victoria & Albert Museum (Pl. 96:a, Fig. 20:a). The design shows two spotted *sika* deer with large antlers among pomegranate scrolls. The general character of the design is like so many Chin-time patterns still very much in the T'ang tradition, but the rendering of the deer is more realistic than those found in earlier representations of this kind. An unusual deer design is the one on the dish in Pl. 102:b, the deer is standing with a floral spray in its mouth and is surrounded by a realistic peony scroll. The deer seems to be wearing a halter.

A Sung silver bowl in the Kempe collection is decorated on the inside with a deer very similar to those found in our Type Tc 17.[3]) In painting of the period the deer motif is also found; among the most well-known examples are the murals from the Liao Imperial mausoleum in *Ch'ing-ling*. The paintings in Ch'ing-ling, which are datable at around 1030, are very fine and realistic, and it is quite possible that it was through Liao influence the deer motif became popular in Sung time. Among a people of hunters like the Liao it is quite natural that this motif should be popular, and we know that even one of their Emperors, Hsing-tsung (1016–1055), was himself a painter of deer.

[1]) A pillow with the design of a running deer surrounded by ingots and other precious symbols is in the Boston Museum of Fine Arts (Paine, *op.cit.*, Pl. 32). The pillow is labelled Northern celadon, but the details of the design and the composition in general do not seem to have anything to do with this ware. It is more likely a type of Tz'u-chou ware.

[2]) A pair of deer of a very strange type is found on a pillow in the Seattle Art Museum (*Los Angeles exh.cat.* No. 241).

[3]) *Chinese Gold & Silver*. No. 138.

OTHER ANIMALS

Other animals than the ones we have already described are rare in Sung ceramics, except for toys and small sculptures, but a few unusual designs are found in Tz'u-chou yao, where they mostly occur on pillows.

In our Type Tc 12 we find two rare designs, one depicts a dancing black bear, the other a cat. The first one (Pl. 45:j) shows the big bear standing on its hind legs leaning against a stick, he is tied with a thick rope to a pole hammered down into the ground. The design apparently depicts a tame bear taught to dance in order to amuse spectators.[1]) This kind of genre pictures is most unusual in ceramics and is a fine example of the new interest in the realistic picturing of the world around us which was new to the Sung time. The other pillow is equally realistic (Pl. 45:k), but the motif is common from painting, it shows a cat with an embroidered ribbon tied around its neck. A very similar painting was found in a Chin dynasty tomb in Shansi,[2]) here too the cat has a ribbon round its neck.

One of our Tz'u-chou pillows shows a running hare (Pl. 46:g) and this motif is already found in Liao ceramics of *san ts'ai* type.[3]) The hare is also found in sgraffito decorated wares from Yüan time (Pl. 55:c).

DUCKS AND OTHER WATER-FOWL

Mandarin ducks and other water-fowl either single or in pairs is a favourite motif in Sung ceramics. The mandarin duck or *yüan-yang* [101] (*Anas galericulata*) is a very beautiful species of duck and a most popular motif of artists, it is usually easy to identify by the wedge-shaped crest jutting out behind the head. A pair of mandarin ducks is one of the most frequent marriage symbols in China. They were chosen as an emblem of conjugal felicity because they were considered to mate for life, and if one of them should die the other would pine away. The goose was also considered to behave in the same way and thus also became a symbol of marital faithfullness.[4])

Ducks and geese are already common motifs in T'ang art, which seems to be partly due to Indian influence; floral scrolls with *hamsa* birds is a well-known Indian motif. As a design on ceramics ducks are rarely seen before the Sung dynasty.

In *Northern celadon* we have several types of designs with this motif. One type shows a large single duck among waves (Pl. 8:c, f); specimens with this design have been found at Yao-chou (Pl. 8:e). In another design we find three ducks swimming

---

[1]) Contemporary writers have described the various and rich spectacles performed by travelling showmen which could be seen on the streets of Hang-chou. Story-tellers, jugglers, acrobats and exhibitors of wild animals are among the entertainers mentioned. (Gernet, *op.cit.*, p. 95, 224).

[2]) *Kao Ku* 1965:7, Pl. 8:11.

[3]) Wirgin, *Some notes on Liao ceramics*. Pl. 13:a.

[4]) Cammann, (*Substance and Symbol* . . . p. 123.) points out that a live goose was a common engagement present by the young man to his future bride.

among lotus flowers (Pl. 10:f), the combination of ducks and lotus flowers is both natural and a very auspicious and appropriate marriage design as well, and many similar designs are found (Pl. 10:g). In one type found both in Lin-ju and in Yao-chou the ducks are standing between large lotus plants (Pl. 10:d–e). A flying goose among lotus flowers and sagittaria is found on a Northern celadon sherd which has been discovered at Fostat (Fig. 24:c).

In *ch'ing-pai* and *Lung-ch'üan yao* duck designs are rarely used, but in the former ware a duck or goose is sometimes seen in the centre of bowls with moulded patterns (Pl. 27:b). In both wares ceramic sculptures of ducks are found; a very fine ch'ing-pai incense-burner in the Art Institute of Chicago[1]) is made in the shape of a lotus flower with a finely sculptured duck as cover, and small boxes with ducks on the cover are quite common.[2])

In *Tz'u-chou yao* ducks and other water-fowl are found in a large number of combinations, especially on the pillows. A pillow of the type which shows the design on a ring-matted ground has a very fine design of a large mandarin duck standing among lotus and sagittaria (Pl. 42:g, Fig. 24:b). Among the fragments found at the kiln site of Tung-ai k'ou several examples of Chang pillows with bird designs were recovered, some of them with flying geese and bamboo (Fig. 31:b). A pillow of the same type with an unusually fine design of a swan is illustrated in Pl. 46:j. Among the cloud-shaped Chang pillows is one with a very lively design of two geese at the waterfront among reeds, which is strikingly similar to paintings of the same time (Pl. 47:c).[3]) On another pillow in the same group a child is chasing a small duck (Pl. 47:a). Similar to the just mentioned pillow with two ducks is another, in the *san ts'ai* group, which also shows a sea-shore with reeds and two ducks, one of them just descending into the water (Colour plate).[4]) Another pillow with *san ts'ai* décor has two large geese or swans swimming among lotus flowers, on the top (Pl. 52:e). This design is very closely related to the dish dated 1112 (discussed under Type Tc 27 above) with a similar motif which in its turn has many parallels among the Liao *san ts'ai* wares.[5])

In the enamel decorated Tz'u-chou ware we also have several examples of designs with mandarin ducks and geese, usually in combination with lotus flowers (Pl. 55:k, 56:k–l).

In *Ting yao* the duck motif is commonly seen both in the incised and in the moulded ware. In the first type a pair of ducks swimming side by side is one of the favourite motifs, the composition varies and the birds are found with sagittaria (Pl. 64:b), with reeds (Pl. 65), with lotus (Pl. 66:b) or with combinations of these

---

1) Koyama, *Chinese ceramics*. Fig. 11.

2) *OCS Sung. exh. cat.* No. 210.

3) Cp. for instance the famous painting with a hundred geese in the Honolulu Academy of Arts.

4) For a similar motif in Sung painting, see, *Chinese Art Treasures, a selected group of objects from the Chinese National Palace Museum* . . . Geneva 1961. Pl. 22.

5) Cp. *OCS Sung exh. cat.* No. 130.

plants (Pl. 66:a, Fig. 8:f), but they are always incised with a few forceful strokes forming an elegant and charming design. The auspicious character of the design is obvious and bowls of this kind were certainly regarded as ideal wedding gifts. Sometimes the birds are placed in panels (Pl. 64:a, Fig. 8:e) and sometimes opposite each other (Fig. 24:a).

In the moulded variety of Ting we find the equivalent to the ducks-among-lotus motif, but, as always in this ware much more detailed; usually the birds are shown against a spiral wave ground (Pl. 90:b). These designs often show several ducks, often in combination with fish (Pl. 89:b), in one case the ducks are alternating with birds that look like egrets or cranes (Pl. 89:a). An unusually fine and detailed design is the one on the bowl Pl. 91:b, which shows a rich lotus scroll combined with other flowers and two birds, one typical mandarin duck and one duck of another type, both very realistically depicted.

Among the white wares, made for Liao, we find a fine early duck design which shows the bird with a large floral spray in its mouth, the character of the pattern is still very much in the traditional T'ang style (Fig. 37:g). The design is found on a square dish of characteristic Liao shape and it is found in several examples, fragments of a dish of this kind have also been recovered from a Liao tomb dated A.D. 1057 (Fig. 37:n).[1])

At the end of Chin and the beginning of Yüan the designs assume a freer character and come closer to painting; veritable landscape scenes are now introduced. One example of this kind is seen in Pl. 97:b, where in the centre of a dish we can see a pond with two mandarin ducks surrounded by insects and a rich variety of different aquatic plants. A similar scene on another dish (Pl. 98) shows a shore landscape with two mandarin ducks and a goose; here too the composition is very rich with lotus, sagittaria and several other plants and a large willow tree. In a garden scene on another dish (Pl. 99) we can see the popular motif of children playing with ducks. The style and composition of these landscape scenes are closely similar to scenes which we will find later on in the blue-and-white porcelain and it seems quite clear that this new style was created during Sung and later on was further developed when a more suitable medium, the underglaze painting, became available.[2])

OTHER BIRDS

Ducks are undoubtedly the birds which are most popular as designs on Sung ceramics, but several other kinds are found, mostly in the Tz'u-chou ware.

In Northern celadon other birds are rarely seen, but on the back of the handle

---

1) Wirgin, *Some notes on Liao ceramics*, p. 28.

2) Cp. Pope, *Fourteenth-century blue-and-white . . .*, Pls 4, 11, 20, 27. Cp. also the central design on our Pl. 89:b and the design found on the inside of a stem-cup in the Oxford Museum of Eastern Art (*Chinese art under the Mongols*, No. 135).

of the ewer Pl. 1:l are small birds of kingfisher type; the design is interesting because of its close similarity with similar birds on Yüeh yao, and is one of many features which show the early character of this particular group of celadon. In ch'ing-pai the bird designs found are mostly so sketchy and dissolved that very little can be learned from them. In the Lung-ch'üan yao birds are mostly found as decorative sculptures on lids of vases and jars (Type Lc 16).

The peacock seems to be closely connected with the phoenix in Chinese art; not only has the *feng-huang* borrowed many of its characteristic features from the peacock, but the birds are also found together and sometimes the peacock seems to be a substitute for the phoenix. Already on some of the marriage mirrors from T'ang the birds are found together or used in similar compositions. When the peacocks are seen in pairs they are most likely a symbol of happy marriage; the bird is also known to signify beauty and dignity. On the Ting yao dish Pl. 79:a we can see four beautiful peacocks among peony scrolls in the outer band, and short-tailed phoenixes in the centre. On the dish in Pl. 100:b, the central motif is a large peacock surrounded by a floral scroll. The design is here very similar to peacocks found in early blue-and-white, where the motif is very common[1]), but a very similar peacock is also found among the wall carvings from a Chin tomb in Shansi dated 1210.[2]) The most beautiful design we know of with peacocks in Ting yao is found on the dish Pl. 96:b (Fig. 21:c). It is decorated in the centre with two peacocks with long magnificent tails; they are surrounded by clouds and in their beaks they hold a long ribbon tied into a bow. That the design in this case is a symbol of happy marriage is obvious.[3])

Of later date is the more genre-like scene found in the dish Fig. 25:a (Pl. 84:h) where a pair of peafowl are depicted in a garden. In those more realistic surroundings the peacock is also found in Tz'u-chou yao. On one pillow belonging to the *san ts'ai* group we can see it with a slender bamboo[4]) and on the back of a pillow in Boston it is found with plants and a garden rock.[5])

The pheasant is also one of the birds from which the *feng-huang* has borrowed certain features, and it seems to be depicted on the pillow in Pl. 52:b. The bird is probably a silver pheasant.

The crane is one of the most popular birds in later Chinese art and one of the favourite symbols of longevity. In Sung ceramics it is, however, very seldom seen. We have already referred to cranes or egrets found together with the ducks on a Ting yao specimen (Pl. 89:a) but otherwise the motif is not often found on this ware, although some sherds with this kind of birds have been found in Ting-chou

---

[1]) Cp. Pope, *Chinese porcelains from the Ardebil shrine*. Pl. 27.

[2]) Wen Wu 1959:6, p. 54, Fig. 18.

[3]) A small Sung silver box in the Kempe collection has a design with two birds with a similar ribbon tied into a bow. (*Chinese Gold & Silver*, Pl. 139).

[4]) For a similar design on Yüan blue-and-white see: *Chinese Art under the Mongols*. Pl. 150.

[5]) Paine, *op.cit.* Pl. 7:c.

(Fig. 32:23). In Tz'u-chou yao we find cranes in the Chang pillow group together with bamboo and reeds (Fig. 31:b, Fig. 26:e) and also on top of a tiger-shaped pillow (Pl. 52:l). Examples are also found in the enamelled group (Type Tc 45).

In Tz'u-chou yao we also find a pillow decorated with a *cock* (Fig. 26:d) and pillows with *quails* (Pl. 42:d). In later Chinese art a pair of quails is a common emblem of conjugal felicity as it was also considered to have the same devotion to its mate as the mandarin duck; the bird is also common in Sung painting.[1])

Parrots are very common in Yüeh yao, but in Sung time we have only found them on one other ware, the Tz'u-chou. Good examples may be seen on top of pillows with ring-matted ground (Pl. 42:e–f, Fig. 26:c), where the birds are quite realistically depicted.

The most common bird motif found on Tz'u-chou yao are small birds of different types perched on a branch. They are found on flowering branches of various kinds, on bare twigs, on bamboo etc. (Pls. 45:i, 46:d–e, 47:d, 48:e, h, 52:k, Fig. 26:a–b), an unusually fine example is the bird watching a butterfly in Pl. 45:i. These bird designs are obviously strongly influenced by contemporary painting, where motifs of this kind were very much in favour, especially from the later part of Northern Sung and onwards.

FISH

The fish motif is extremely common in ceramics and found also in other kinds of art. Like so many other animal symbols, the fish is an auspicious emblem. Due to the similarity in pronunciation of the words for fish and abundance (*yü*) it became a symbol of wealth, and because of its reproductive power it is one of the many emblems of fertility. A pair of fish often symbolizes harmony and connubial bliss. The twin fish used as a Buddhist motif does not seem to have appeared in Sung time.

The favourite fish seems to have been *the carp*, but many other species are found. In T'ang applied arts fishes are sometimes found, but the motif is not particularly common; on some silver objects we can find the motif with two fishes swimming together.[2]) This motif is particularly often found in Sung ceramics, and it is possible that it is inspired from Han bronzes where a pair of fishes is a common motif, for instance, on basins.

The fish motif is found on almost all types of Sung ceramics. The fishes seen on *Northern celadon* are usually quite small and are found three or four together, as can be seen on the incised bowl in Pl. 8:d and the moulded one in Pl. 8:j. A more realistic design with a single fish among water weeds (Pl. 8:g) is almost identical to the decoration on a Ting yao piece with two fishes (Cp Fig. 27:a and b). In *ch'ing-pai* small fishes like those found in Northern celadon are also used in the incised

[1]) *Chinese Arts of the Sung and Yüan periods.* Nos. 29, 32.

[2]) Gyllensvärd, *op.cit.* Fig. 97:1.

type (Pl. 17:a), but larger ones are also found (Type Cp 5). They all have the same split tail-fins as the fishes in the celadon ware. The most common type in this ware is, however, a pair of fishes swimming one over the other in the centre of bowls with the sides divided by radiating ribs (Fig. 29:d:4). In the moulded type a pair of fishes are sometimes also found in the centre of bowls (Type Cp 26), and other fish designs which we have not included here are found towards the end of Sung and the beginning of Yüan.

In the early *Lung-ch'üan yao* we have a few examples of incised designs with the same type of fishes with forked tail, as we have described above (Pl. 39:a) and later incised designs are also found (Pl. 39:b), but the favourite design in this ware is the two applied fishes in the centre of bowls and dishes (Pl. 39:h–i). This design seems to have been in use for a very long time and was produced in enormous quantities.[1]) The relatively stiff arrangement of the fish in this pattern seems to reveal a connection with the earlier mentioned motif found on Han bronzes. Dolphin-like fishes used as handles on mallet-shaped vases is also one of the favourite motifs in this ware (Pl. 39:j, k).

On *Tz'u-chou* pillows fishes, single and in pairs, are found both among the incised and painted wares and in the *san ts'ai* group; some of those designs have been illustrated here (Pl. 46:a, k; see also Type Tc 27) but many more examples could be given. A particularly fine example is a green-glazed pillow in the Tokyo National Museum with a big fish on a ground of overlapping waves.[2]) Also on bowls and jars of Tz'u-chou ware fish designs are found.[3]) The enamel decorated ware also has fish designs (Pl. 56:g).

In *Ting yao* the fish design is most common both in the incised and the moulded type, and we can only give a few examples. Among the incised ware the design with two fishes swimming together in the centre of bowls with ribbed sides (Fig. 32:20, 34:6) is very common and almost identical to the design we have seen on ch'ing-pai. Another fish design which is related to Northern celadon we have already mentioned (Fig. 27:a). Related to the last-mentioned design is that which is usually found on large basins and shows a single large fish among water-weeds (Pl. 67:a, Fig. 8:g).[4]) Small fishes swimming in different directions are found in one type (Pl. 61:e) and a rare dish in the David Foundation[5]) has two small fishes almost hidden among waves. An interesting specimen is also the dish dated 1271 (Pl. 61:f, Fig. 27:c) even if the design is rather coarsely executed.

---

[1]) The *Ko ku yao lun* refers to Lung-ch'üan dishes with a pair of fishes in the bottom. (Bushell's translation of *T'ao Shuo*, p. 45).

[2]) *Sekai* Vol. 10. Pl. 12.

[3]) *Sekai* Vol. 10., Pl. 100, Fig. 102.

[4]) For a later version of this design see: Pope, *Chinese porcelains from the Ardebil shrine*. Pl. 9.

[5]) *David Ting.cat.* No. 176.

In the moulded variety we often find a pair of fishes in the centre of bowls, usually swimming in the same direction[1]) (Pl. 89:a, 91:a, 104:a). Two large carps in a lotus pond are found on the dish in Pl. 79:b. Four fishes among lotus and water-weeds are found in the dish in Pl. 84:d and in the fine and detailed design of ducks and lotus flowers in Pl. 89:b one single small fish can be detected.

[1]) On the dish Pl. 91:b they are, however, swimming, in opposite directions.

A TENTATIVE CHRONOLOGY

The dating of ceramics is often a most difficult task and the wares of the Sung dynasty are no exception to this rule; on the contrary, they are sometimes extremely hard to determine. Two main sources for dating are dated pieces and specimens from datable excavations. Dating is not very common on Sung wares and the dated objects form only a small group, albeit an extremely valuable one. The difficulty with the dated pieces is that we cannot always be sure whether they are genuine or not. We therefore have to be extremely careful with this material and have selected for the purpose of our study only such specimens as even after the most critical examination appear to be authentic. This procedure makes our group of dated objects still smaller, and the total number of pieces that are left is not more than about twenty. Among them only about half of the material is of major importance, notably some moulds.

Nor do the Sung ceramics from datable excavations form a particularly large group, even if the importance of the excavations carried out in China during the last twenty years could not be stressed enough. The Sung tombs in general are not notably rich in ceramic finds, but the material so far excavated has helped us with the dating of several important types. Especially interesting are some tombs datable to Liao and Chin which give us valuable and hitherto unknown information about the ceramic in use during these periods.

Of great importance are, of course, the many new excavations of kiln sites that have taken place in China recently. Thanks to those excavations, the provenience of many ceramic wares have for the first time been revealed, and some older information about kiln sites have either been confirmed or refuted. The question of the kilns has been discussed above under each main type of ware.

Specimens excavated from the two sites of *Chü-lu hsien* and *Ch'ing-ho hsien* in Hopei have often been considered to form an important group among the datable specimens. Both sites were severely damaged by floods which around 1120 are considered to have completely destroyed the two towns. In Chü-lu hsien many different kinds of ceramics have been found, including most notably much cream-coloured porcellanous stoneware; this latter type has become known as Chü-lu hsien ware. The site was first excavated by the Paris dealer L. Wannieck and, later on, by Nils Palmgren,[1] who brought back a large quantity of sherds both from Chü-lu hsien and the nearby Ch'ing-ho hsien; unfortunately the excavation was not very scientifically carried out. There is no indication that there ever was a kiln

[1] *Sung sherds*. Stockholm 1963.

site either at Chü-lu hsien or at Ch'ing-ho hsien, even if some small moulds found at the latter place made Palmgren draw the conclusion that ceramics were produced here. The variety of ceramic wares found at both places is amazing and clearly shows how widely spread the trade must have been at this time. Many of the sherds found are undoubtedly from Northern Sung, but some are definitely later, and unfortunately this rich material is of little help in our attempt to make a closer dating of some Sung types. Some specimens, especially those of the so-called Chü-lu hsien ware, have a very characteristic crazing and staining due to immersion and burial, and those pieces could for good reasons be accepted as Northern Sung, and the majority of the intact vessels which have come from the two sites are also, stylistically, very convincingly of the same period, and could be of help to us in our attempt to work out a dating. But the sherd material must be handled with great caution, and we have not used it to any greater extent in this study.

It is necessary in this connection to lay stress upon how important a factor form is in the dating of Chinese ceramics. This fact was first pointed out by Ingram,[1]) and after that several studies on the subject have been published. A careful study of Sung shapes would no doubt, as we have already stated earlier, be of great interest, but it is neither possible nor justifiable in an investigation of this kind, which is intended to deal mainly with designs. If, however, we were to attempt to draw up a tentative chronology of Sung ceramics it would be necessary to base some of our datings on form. We shall therefore refer quite often in the following to such reasoning.

It is a strange fact that most scholars who have written about Sung ceramics have dealt with the material as if it had been produced by one single state during a certain period. The truth is, as we have seen, that during this period China was divided between at least four different states, *Liao* (907–1125), *Sung* (*Pei Sung* 960–1127, *Nan Sung* 1127–1279) and *Chin* (1115–1234). We have already suggested that each of those states might have produced their own particular style or favoured a certain stylistic trend. We shall accordingly try to divide our material into three main chronological groups which we shall call Northern Sung, Chin and Southern Sung.

The ceramic art of the Liao period has already been discussed in an earlier paper in which we have attempted to show some typical Liao designs and to point out what is characteristic of the Liao style. The often very distinct style of the Liao wares, together with the datable finds made of such specimens, makes it relatively easy to date them. Accordingly it is not necessary in this context to enter upon any further discussion of this material.[2]) We shall, however, use the Liao material for comparative studies.

---

[1]) Sir Herbert Ingram, *Form, an important factor in the dating of early Chinese ceramics. Ethnos* 1946:4.

[2]) The problem which kilns made the Liao wares is not yet solved, and, as we have seen, some of the white wares seem to emanate from Ting-chou. In connection with the designs, however, this problem is of minor importance, and the main point is that the designs favoured by the Liao people are often of very characteristic types, whether they were made by or for the Liaos.

In the following chronology it is not possible or necessary to recall all the different designs we have discussed earlier, we have only tried to select some of the most important ones and to show the relationship between certain groups of designs.

NORTHERN SUNG

The Northern Sung style did not, of course, appear all of a sudden at the beginning of the period, but was gradually developed, and many of its features are found already during the Five Dynasties, and it is not possible to draw a clear distinction between wares made towards the end of that period and those made in early Sung. We shall accordingly include in this group specimens made also during this transitional period.

The importance of the *Yüeh ware* in the development of ceramic decoration from T'ang to Sung has been stressed already before, but it has to be emphasized that the first tendencies to a Sung style in ceramic decoration are found in this ware. It is accordingly natural to turn at first to the celadon group.

In our group of *Early Chekiang celadons* the designs are not so various or elaborate. We find rather sketchy peony scrolls (Pl. 37:g, h, j, l), hanging or horizontal leaves (Pl. 37:e) and overlapping petals (Pl. 37:d, f, g, j) as some of the main motifs. An interesting feature in these designs is that the combing and hatching techniques are already in frequent use. But it is perhaps the shapes of those specimens that are most interesting as an aid to dating. We have already shown that some of the main shapes found here could be dated to the 10th and 11th centuries. An interesting group is formed by the small ewers with a leaf on the shoulder (Pl. 37:j, l) which are matched by a similar one excavated from the 10th century layer in Lung-ch'üan (Fig. 43:a:5). This method of placing an applied leaf on each shoulder of a vessel is often found in Liao and on other wares of T'ang–Sung transition time and can be accepted as a typical feature of the 10th and early 11th centuries.[1])

Another early shape is that found on the vases with tubular attachments on the shoulder or similar arrangements (Pl. 37:a–d) and those of the type seen in Pl. 37:e. Both excavated examples and two vases of Yüeh yao of related shape dated in the *Yüan-feng* era (A.D. 1080) confirm the dating of these specimens.[2]) A very fine early *mei-p'ing* vase from the Ingram collection (Pl. 37:g) gives us valuable information about the shape of this kind of vase in early Sung. The characteristic shaping of the mouth is found also in the vase of slightly different shape in Pl. 37:h.

One of the most interesting groups of celadon from the beginning of Sung is that from *Yao-chou*, which is usually called Tung yao. We have already described

[1]) For Liao specimens with this kind of applied leaves see: *Liao tz'u hsüan chi.* Pl. 35, and Wirgin, *Some notes on Liao ceramics.* Pl. 15.

[2]) One of these vases is in the David Foundation (see our note 2 p. 77) and the other one is in a Japanese collection (*Toso-no seiji,* Pl. 24).

this group at some length and the characteristic design found on it, which we have chosen to call "the bold floral scroll" (Pl. 1:a–h) and also pointed out that the same design is found in Tz'u-chou yao (Pl. 41:a–e). The favourite shapes among specimens in this group are ewers, mostly of the type exemplified by Pl. 1:a–b and Pl. 41:a–b, and a few variants of this form. These shapes are all found in other wares datable to Liao and early Sung.[1] The general character of the bold floral scroll is quite different from the designs found in Yüeh yao, even if many details of the design are clearly influenced by that ware. We have already pointed out earlier the small birds on the back of the handle on the ewer Pl. 1:1, which are obviously copied from the Yüeh ware; and also the treatment of the petals found on the same ewer (Pl. 1:f) shows an influence from the same ware. But for a prototype of the main scroll and the closely connected "conventionalized flower" we have to turn elsewhere. The only possible source for this motif we have been able to find is the design which Gyllensvärd calls "composite baroque sprays" as it is found on a group of silver bowls said to have come from *Pa-lin* in Eastern Mongolia.[2] The similarities between the large luxuriant leaves in the bold floral scroll and those of the silver pattern are striking, and the treatment of the lotus leaf on the ewer in our Pl. 1:e is almost identical to what we can see on a silver bowl of the Pa-lin type in the Kempe collection (Fig. 42:a). Also in the silver pattern we find that strange fruit-like shape which we have called "conventionalized flower" when we meet it on ceramics. The bold floral scroll is much more realistic than the silver design, but it is most probable that it is a development of this design.

We have seen in the *Northern celadon* group how the flower in the bold floral scroll develops into what we have called the conventionalized flower, it could clearly be followed from the rather realistic type in Pl. 1:d, e, g to an intermediate form in Pl. 1:i, to the fully developed conventionalized type of flower in Pl. 1:j. In the last phase of its development in Northern celadon it is usually found together with the scroll we have called "sickle-leaf scroll" (Pl. 2). It would seem that the majority of specimens with this design belong to the Northern Sung dynasty, but it probably continued into early Chin.

The close connection between the "bold floral scroll" and "the conventionalized flower" can be still better seen on the *Tz'u-chou* ware (Fig. 3:13–15), where we often find both designs on the same specimen, as we can see not only on the ewers already referred to (Pl. 41:a–e), but also on some pillows (Pl. 41:g, h, j), and a group of vases of very characteristic form (Pl. 40:i–k). The vases are of a type often found in Liao (Pl. 40:g–h), which again shows the early character of the design.

In *ch'ing-pai* we can also find the conventionalized flower, but here the flower usually assumes a more triangular form when seen from the front, but the side view is very close to the treatment in Tz'u-chou. This triangular flower is rather

[1]) Cp. *Kao Ku* 1965:7, Pl. 10:2–3.

[2]) Gyllensvärd, *op.cit.* Fig. 96:a, e and p. 155, 188.

palmette-like, and it is probably the origin of the palmette-like peony found later on in Ting yao. The similarities between the different types and the possible development from one type to another can be seen in Fig. 3:1–12. The tendency to a palmette-like shape is already found in the Pa-lin silver bowls, where some flowers and clusters of leaves have taken this shape.[1]) A most interesting link between the ceramics of Kiangsi and the Pa-lin bowls is the famous ewer from Chi-chou (Pl. 29:g), the main design of which is composed of a scroll with flowers that have strange acorn-like centres, obviously related to our conventionalized flower (Fig. 42:b).

The earliest type of the conventionalized flower in ch'ing-pai seems to be the one we have illustrated with the vase in Pl. 12:a and the ewer and bowl Pl. 11. We have already shown that the latter piece is datable to the middle of the 11th century by comparison with excavated specimens (Pl. 12:b). The design then becomes more and more dissolved (as we can see in our Types Cp 1 a–c), and it seems that this development took place already during Northern Sung; and it is not likely that the design was in use later than into the early part of the 12th century. Like the sickle-leaf scroll connected with the conventionalized flower in Northern celadon, a similar scroll which we have called "bud tendril" is found with its ch'ing-pai equivalent. Very fine examples of this motif are found on the vase in Honolulu and a similar one in Peking[2]) (Pl. 14; Pl. 12:c). The typical early Sung character of these vases is obvious and they are closely related to the celadon vase in Pl. 37:g (note also the similar use of the hatching technique found on these specimens). The bud tendril is also found on a small ewer Pl. 29:j, which is almost identical to another one in the Kempe coll. (Pl. 29:k) which has the applied leaves on the shoulder which we have shown to be an early feature. The last-mentioned ewer has the body divided by incised lines of the same type as that found on the vase Pl. 12:a, which further shows the close relationship within this group.

Our treatment of the bold floral scroll and the conventionalized flower and the development of these patterns may seem rather detailed, but we find this group of designs one of the most important and typical of the early Sung style and it is also interesting the way it shows not only the link between T'ang and Sung but also the close similarities found between different Sung wares.

We will now return to the *Northern celadon* ware and discuss some other characteristic early types in that ware. Among the different peony designs that we find in this ware we have called one the A-type, and with starting point from this design we are able to distinguish a large group of related specimens. The three ewers with this design illustrated (Pl. 3:a–c) all have the applied leaf on the shoulder and are of a shape with characteristic trumpet-shaped mouth, which we have already seen in Tz'u-chou (Pl. 41:e) and which is also found in Liao. The same shape we also find in the ewer Pl. 4:c, and the design on this ewer once more leads us back

---

[1]) Cp. Gyllensvärd, *op.cit.* Fig. 96:a, e.

[2]) In Liao silver ware we find a scroll motif which is very close to the bud-tendril. Cp. *Wu sheng ch'u t'u tsung yao wen wu chan lan t'u lu,* Pl. 111:1.

to the sickle-leaf scroll. This ewer is obviously related to the one in Pl. 4:a, not only by the sickle-leaf scroll design but both specimens also have the same kind of pointed petals round the neck; also on this ewer we can see the stiff leaves applied on the shoulder. The row of pointed petals round the neck is a feature which we find on several other specimens; we can see it on the two vases Pl. 4:g, i and on the *kundika* vessel in Pl. 3:e. The *kundika* is obviously inspired by a T'ang metal shape, which again supports the early character of this large group.[1])

It is not possible to recapitulate all the Northern celadon designs we have illustrated, but it is necessary to show some more types, all belonging to the same big family we have been discussing, in order to show how close this early Northern Sung group fits together. Our previous discussion had taken us back to the A-type peony, and, if we start out from another specimen in this group, the vase with flower-shaped mouth in Pl. 3:d, it will lead us to other related groups. The most typical design on this vase and other similar ones (Pl. 7:d–e) is the design we have called "serrated petals", and this pattern we can find in its most clear form in the specimens Pl. 7:b, c, f. The lamp or stand in Pl. 7:c is obviously of a very early type; it has earlier been considered to be of Yüeh ware, but we are quite sure that, like most specimens in this fine, early group we are discussing, it is a product of the Yao-chou kiln.[2]) The finest specimen in the lamp group is the famous one formerly in the Sedgwick collection (Pl. 7:f) which by its design on the rim is related to the specimens in our Pl. 4:a–c, and in its shape to several other specimens (Pl. 7:c, i, l; Pl. 4:b and Pl. 3:f). An interesting parallel is also found in Ting yao (Pl. 58:a).

A most interesting feature in this group of Northern celadon is that we find such a variety of designs and forms, and also that we find several very rare and interesting pieces which are obviously not only closely related stylistically but also in the fanciful and elaborate spirit in which they are made (Cp. Pl. 1:k, Pl. 4:b, Pl. 7:f, i, l). The examples given here may be sufficient to give some idea of the early types of designs found in Northern celadon.

To determine which specimens of this ware belong to the latter part of Northern Sung is more difficult, and we are here very dependent on form arguments, but we also have some characteristic features in the designs. The vases in Pl. 5:a–b and the related piece in Pl. 5:c are of a shape that is also found in Yüeh yao, and they would at first seem to be early, but their designs are of a freer type which, we shall see, is characteristic of a later style, and they probably belong to the end of the 11th and the beginning of the 12th centuries.

To the second half of the Northern Sung dynasty we would also like to attribute some other Northern celadon groups. The bottle-shaped vase in Pl. 5:d is still of a characteristic Northern Sung shape, but the elaborate and freer design we find here

[1]) White porcelain vessels of kundika shape have also been found in Liao tombs. Cp. *Wen Wu* 1964:8, p. 52.

[2]) An interesting detail on this specimen is the disc-like ridges around the stem, which are similar to those found around the neck of the Chi-chou ewer (Pl. 29:g).

with the peony type we have called G seems to point at a slightly later date than the first group. Of the same type is the design on the bowl Pl. 5:e, and closely connected with it are also the beehive-shaped peonies found in Pl. 5:g, h, j, and with boys in Pl. 6:a–b. The shape of several of these bowls and the way the design is arranged on them are very similar.[1]) The elaborate bowls in Pl. 4:e, f are also of a related type. The bowl in Pl. 5:k is decorated with the same kind of peony design as we have just mentioned, but it has also a very characteristic peony leaf border framing the main design. The same kind of border is found on the incense-burner Pl. 6:f and the bowls Pl. 6:d–e. The design of these bowls is of a type quite different from the earlier ones, much more free and elegant and more spacious, and their shape is found among specimens which belong to the Chin dynasty. The central peony design of the bowls is the same as we find, for instance, on the two dishes Pl. 4:k–l, which again are of a shape that we associate with the first part of the 12th century. The incense-burner (Pl. 6:f) is related to several others of similar shape (Pl. 6:c, i, l) which are all of a type which we would put at the end of Northern Sung and the beginning of Chin; the design on the lotus decorated piece (Pl. 6:i) is very close to a type that we shall discuss later on and which is typical of Chin.

The dish in Pl. 3:1 is of a certain interest because a similar one has been found in a tomb datable to the end of Northern Sung, and it seems that this somewhat stiffer arrangement with the sprays placed in radiating fields is a slightly later feature than the freer use of the same type of design which we have seen earlier.

Another interesting type is exemplified by the bowls Pl. 8:c, f with ducks on a wave ground; those bowls have a very characteristic shape with their sides slightly lobed. The same shape we find again in the two bowls Pl. 8:g–h, which also have a peculiar tendril border. We would also attribute this type to the beginning of the 12th century. The related wave-designed specimens in Pl. 8:a–b are of a shape datable to the same time. Another type of bowls of characteristic conical shape (Pl. 10:d–e) also seems to belong to this group; they are usually decorated with ducks and lotus. Related is also the dish with boy design in Pl. 10:h.

In the *ch'ing-pai* ware we have already discussed some early types above and compared them with designs on Northern celadon and Tz'u-chou yao. The number of ch'ing-pai designs we are able to date within the Northern Sung dynasty is rather limited, but there are a few types which for different reasons can be referred to this period.

Among the few specimens recovered from early tombs is the vase in Pl. 22:a, which must have been made before 1027. The almost olive-like shape is unusual in this ware, and the deeply carved design is similar to that which we find in the early Chekiang celadons. Unfortunately this piece stands rather isolated and is of little help in dating other specimens, but the vase in Pl. 22:b seems to be a later

[1]) The carving of the petals of the peonies found on these bowls is very similar to a fragment from Yao-chou with the date 1107 (*Ta-kuan*). *Kao Ku* 1959:12, Pl. 7:9.

development of the same shape, the design is related to the bud tendril scroll and the piece is most likely still within the Northern Sung period.

One of the finest designs found in the incised ch'ing-pai group is the swiftly drawn peonies of the type seen in Pl. 21, which are very similar to some Ting yao patterns of Northern Sung date. It seems that this lightly incised type was fully developed at least at the end of the 11th century. A bowl with sketchy bird-designs incised in the same way was found in a tomb datable to 1113 (Fig. 29:b) and helps us to place several designs of the same and similar appearance (cp. Pl. 12:1, Pl. 18:b, Fig. 29:c). One of the bowls with this design which is in the Kempe collection (detail Fig. 29:c) is of a very characteristic shape with a six-foil rim, and this same form we can find in the bowl Pl. 12:d with wave design. The wave design on this and similar specimens (cp. Fig. 4:c) is also quite similar to what we have seen in Northern celadon, and it seems safe to date also this group to around 1100. Slightly later in time and continuing into Southern Sung is the type of wave design seen on the bowl with fishes in Pl. 17:a and the similar one with *ch'ih* dragons in Pl. 12:e.

Waves indicated by long combed bands is a common feature in several wares of Northern Sung time; we can find it both in Northern celadon, Ting yao and ch'ing-pai. The fish-decorated bowl in Pl. 16:b is typical of this group in ch'ing-pai; similar bowls are known from an excavation dated Southern Sung (Fig. 29:d:4), but the type was probably developed earlier, as we can see from similar specimens in Ting yao. To the beginning of the 12th century we would also like to attribute the flower-decorated specimens with combings, found in Pl. 12:g–i. A quite different group which can be definitely dated to the same time is the one with overlapping petal designs on the outside (Pl. 23:d–g); a bowl identical to the one in Pl. 23:d was found in a tomb from 1113 and a ewer of similar shape to the one in Pl. 23:g from a tomb dated around 1100.

An important group which we have not yet discussed is the bowls decorated with more or less dissolved boy figures among flowers. Specimens of this type have been excavated from a well dated to Southern Sung (Fig. 29:d:1), but most specimens found here apparently have to be placed early in the period. If we look at the bowl in Pl. 19:a we can see that the design has close similarities with other types which we have dated to around 1100 (cp. Pl. 22:b) and it seems most likely that this kind of design was developed already during the end of Northern Sung, probably under influence from Northern celadon and then continued into Southern Sung.

There is no group among the ch'ing-pai with moulded designs that we can refer to Northern Sung for stylistic reasons, and we do not know of any datable finds of such specimens.

We have already discussed the designs of the early Chekiang wares above, but there are a few designs found in the more typical *Lung-ch'üan* ware which can also be dated to Northern Sung. One is the incised lotus type found on the bowl in Pl. 38:a, which can be seen on specimens excavated from the Northern Sung layers in Lung-ch'üan; but the type undoubtedly continued during Southern Sung at least in more provincial wares. The bowls with a tortoise in relief on the inside which we have also seen in Northern celadon (Pl. 7:g) is, on the contrary, a type which can definitely be regarded as Northern Sung (Type Lc 8).

Among the rich and varied material found in the *Tz'u-chou* group we have many types which can definitely be dated in the Northern Sung period. We have already discussed the early type in Pl. 41:a–k and Pl. 40:i–k so closely connected with the similar group in Northern celadon. An interesting specimen in this group is the pillow (Pl. 41:g, h, k) which connects this group with the finely incised type illustrated in Pl. 40:l and 41:l, which is also sometimes of identical shape (Pl. 40:k and l) with the first group. On the top of the pillow (Pl. 41:k) is, besides the finely incised design, a panel with a stiff floral spray. This spray is one of the most characteristic motifs during the 11th century and a favourite motif in Liao art (cp. Fig. 37:g–o). We find this motif on many specimens in the early pillow groups which we have illustrated in Pl. 42 and Pl. 43:a–c, with their characteristic ring-matted ground. The date of this interesting group is further confirmed by the pillow dated 1071 in the British Museum (Pl. 42:j). The group also includes specimens of other shapes where we again have the stiff floral spray (Pl. 43:h) and other motifs closely related to those found on the pillows (Pl. 43:d–i). Several shapes found in this group (Pl. 43:h, i) and the one illustrated in Pl. 43:j–l and Pl. 44:a–b are also characteristic of the 11th century. We must in this context again refer to two vases which we have mentioned in our description of this type, one in Boston with Taoist immortals and one in Peking with tigers,[1]) both of which are closely related in shape to the ch'ing-pai vase (Pl. 22:a) datable to the first quarter of the 11th century. It is interesting to note the richness and variety of designs even of very realistic type which is found in this Tz'u-chou group.

A little later in time is the group with designs on a striated ground (Pl. 44:c–i) which as one of its most interesting types has the cloud-shaped pillows. One pillow of this type is recorded to have the date 1103[2]) and several specimens of the type have been discovered from the Chü-lu hsien area and have the characteristic water patina found on inundated objects from this place, which further confirms a date around 1100.

The freely painted and incised designs of the type seen in Pl. 44:j–l and Pl. 45:a–d are closely related to the striated group and the same shapes are found in both types (Cp. Pl. 44:i and Pl. 45:a–b) notably that of the cloud-shaped pillows (Pl. 45:e–f) and both wares have been found in Chü-lu hsien. The cloud-shaped pillows develop into very elaborate types towards the end of Northern Sung (Pl. 45:g–i) and the type undoubtedly continues into Chin where such examples as Pl. 45:j–l, seem to belong.

The sgraffito decorated group is also closely connected with the ones just men-

[1]) *Hoyt.cat.* No. 284; *Ku kung po wu yüan ts'ang tz'u hsüan chi.* Pl. 36.

[2]) Cp. Paine, *op.cit.* No. 29.

tioned. We again find the same shapes, the deep bowls (Pl. 47:g, h, j, k), the bottle-shaped vases (Pl. 49:j–l) and the cloud-shaped pillows (Pl. 46:b–c). Among the finest specimens in this group are the *mei-p'ing* vases and the vases with turned-over lip (Pl. 49:a–h, 50:a–f). This type obviously also continued into Chin and must have been in use for quite a long time. It does not seem to have been any sudden change in style but some specimens are of a character that stylistically fall into the Chin dynasty (Pl. 49:h, Pl. 50:f).

A small group datable on archaeological evidence to around 1100 is formed by pillows of the type seen in Pl. 47:l and 48:a–b.

We know that the *san ts'ai* decoration in the T'ang tradition was popular in Liao and it seems to have been used during the whole of Northern Sung. We have already referred to the duck-decorated dish in the Calmann collection dated 1112,[1]) which shows that the style was still very much the same at the end of Northern Sung as it had been in the earlier part. It is quite natural that this style also was continued by the Chins, and it is accordingly very difficult to know the date of specimens of this kind. The type found in Pl. 51 seems to have begun at the end of Northern Sung[2]) but it includes many specimens which fall into the Chin dynasty, and the same seems to be the case with the oblong pillow group (Pl. 52:a–f) where some specimens have a late Northern Sung character (Pl. 52:e) but the majority have pictorial designs of a later character.

An interesting little group is formed by the tiger pillows (Pl. 52:j–l) which by excavations on the kiln site can be dated to Northern Sung. Their designs found on the top are, however, clearly related to those found in the Chang pillow group and they must be placed not earlier than the 12th century. The Chang pillows we shall discuss later on under Chin as they mainly seem to fall into that period.

The *Ting yao* is undoubtedly one of the most interesting wares regarded on the point of view of design, but also one of the most difficult to date. There are a few dated specimens and some which are datable through other inscriptions but they are all undecorated and of little help. The recent excavations of the kiln site ought to have provided us with reliable information about the date of the main types of this ware, but, as we have already pointed out, the dates given by the excavators are so obviously wrong that we have almost no support at all by this material.

At the beginning of Sung there are a few types with carved designs which are closely related to what we have seen in Tz'u-chou, Northern celadon and Liao wares and which accordingly can be dated on very good reasons. Examples of this type are seen in Pl. 57:g–j and Pl. 58:a–b. The shape of the jar Pl. 57:g and the overlapping petal design on the shoulder completely match with a jar excavated

---

[1]) *OCS Sung exh.* No. 129.

[2]) One pillow of this type was found in a tomb in Loyang datable to the end of Northern Sung (*Kao Ku* 1960:10, p. 12, Fig. 4).

from a Liao tomb.[1]) Moulded designs on white wares from Liao tombs also give us an idea of what the early moulded ware was like, and we can see that it favours stiff floral sprays (Fig. 37:m, o) and flowers related to the conventionalized flower (Fig. 38:d–e).[2]) But early moulded wares are scarce and the majority of Ting yao specimens made during Northern Sung seem to have been undecorated or provided with incised designs.

One of the most beautiful designs found in the incised technique is the one favouring ducks and different water plants (Pl. 64–66). Already Koyama found sherds of this type at the Ting kiln site, but strangely enough no sherds with this type of décor have been published in the recent excavation report. This further strengthens our view that important material from the Ting kilns still are to be expected, and that the material so far excavated gives not only a very limited but also an unreliable source of information.

The stylistic character of the duck design with its typical waves formed by long bands and its finely and lightly incised patterns is obviously closely related with designs we have seen on other wares from the later part of Northern Sung. The same type of carving is seen on the dragon dish Pl. 68 and the fish-decorated specimens Pl. 67 and Fig. 27:a, the similarities between the fish design on Ting yao and the one on Northern celadon from late Northern Sung have already been pointed out (Cp. Fig. 27:a and b).

One of the favourite motifs in Ting yao is the lotus, which we can find in more or less dissolved versions. A fine and detailed type is seen in Pl. 59:a and designs of the same type are recorded from Northern Sung finds.[3]) A little more sketchy type is seen in Pl. 59:b and Pl. 60, and the fully dissolved type can be seen in Fig. 9:a and Pl. 58:c. We find it quite natural to assume that the development has gone from the more realistic type to the dissolved one, but in the Ting excavation report we find the dissolved type already in the material dated Late T'ang and Five Dynasties (Fig. 33:15, 16, 18) and furthermore, we find it on specimens with the sides divided by radiating, raised ribs, a feature which we know is characteristic of the end of Northern Sung (Fig. 33:20). It is our definite opinion that this type of lotus design belongs to the 12th century, and as we have shown earlier, this view is supported by a number of specimens from excavated Chin and Southern Sung sites (Cp. Fig. 29:d:2–3; Fig. 35:a:2; Fig. 35:b). To this group also belongs the mysterious dish in the David Foundation with a Southern Sung date (Fig. 9:a). Peony designs stylistically related to the just-mentioned lotus patterns are found, for instance, on the bowls in Pl. 69, with *ch'ih* dragons in the centre, which we would also refer to the same time.

Several other more or less sketchy designs of peony and lotus are found on speci-

---

[1]) *Kao Ku* 1965:7, Pl. 10:4.

[2]) Cp. Wirgin, *Some notes on Liao ceramics.* Pls. 1–10.

[3]) Cp. *Wen Wu* 1964:8, p. 6, Fig. 1:1.

mens which in their shapes show strong relationship to specimens of Ju yao and Lung-ch'üan yao, and on that account can be placed around the beginning of the 12th century (Pl. 61:a, c, d; Pl. 62).

The mallow-shaped dishes of the type seen in our Fig. 28:e, which have also been found at the Ting kiln site (Fig. 32:19, 25) are related to similar specimens in ch'ing-pai and also seem to be datable to the later part of Northern Sung.

The designs that we have been able to refer to the early and middle part of Northern Sung are rather few, and it would seem that the majority of Ting specimens made during this time were still, like most of the T'ang porcelain, undecorated. Among the undecorated vessels we find many very similar in form to ch'ing-pai and other ceramic wares (Cp Pl. 61:l and Pl. 12:b). Among the moulded wares there are, with the exception of the Liao type already referred to, almost no pieces which we can date to the earlier part of the period. At the end of Northern Sung we find some types, but those we shall discuss in connection with the majority of the moulded wares under Chin.

This short recapitulation of some of the designs used during Northern Sung on different ceramic wares has shown us some general tendencies which might be valuable to sum up before we turn to the next period. We have found that at the beginning of the period strongly carved luxuriant floral scrolls and ornamental petals are among the favourite motifs. Around the middle of the 11th century stiff floral sprays are a common motif, but already at this time surprisingly realistic scenes both of flowers and animals appear, and this style continues into the next period. Combed wave designs in combination with ducks or fishes, and finely incised floral designs, appear towards the end of the period, and a tendency to more sketchy and dissolved designs can also be observed during this time. The variety of patterns found in the Northern Sung period is already very large, and especially the Northern celadon and the Tz'u-chou ware seem to have been of great importance in the creation of new designs.[1])

CHIN

Upon the division between North and South which took place after the fall of the Northern Sung Empire in 1127 some of the main pottery centres came to belong

[1]) There seems to have been a certain influence from Korean ceramics on some of the Northern Sung wares, but it has mostly shown itself in the adoption of certain new shapes and not so much in the designs. Some of the designs found on Korean ceramics are very close to those found in China, but they both seem to go back to the same Liao prototypes (Cp. Gompertz, *Hsü Ching's visit to Korea in 1123*).

It might also be of interest in this context to note a few typical T'ang designs which had already disappeared at the beginning of Sung. The hunting scenes, influenced from Iran and so common on T'ang silver, are not found in Sung art, and in spite of the obvious interest found among the Liaos for animals and hunting they do not seem to have been taken up by the Liaos either. The stiff heraldic use of animals, either single or in pairs, so frequent in T'ang art, is not met with in Northern Sung. The use of the zodiac animals is not found in Sung ceramics, and Buddhist motifs are extremely rare.

to the Chin territory. As we have already stated, it is most likely that many of those kilns continued their work under their new masters. The three main types which we are concerned with in this paper are Northern celadon, Tz'u-chou yao and Ting yao.

In the *Northern celadon* group we have earlier discussed several types which can be dated towards the first part of the 12th century, among those is a special type of bowl with rounded sides and thickened rim. Several specimens of this type have been recovered from Yao-chou, and they are called by the Chinese excavators alternatively Sung and Chin[1]) (Pl. 9:d), but there seems to be little doubt that the latter date is the correct one. The designs on these bowls vary but they all have a very characteristic scroll with rolled-up ends. The most common motif found in the group is lotus scrolls (Pl. 9:a–c), and the same design is also found on the vase Pl. 9:f, which is a rare specimen in this group. Among other motifs found with the same scroll is a sea-star and flowers (Pl. 9:e), boys among flowers (Pl. 9:h) and the rhinoceros gazing at the moon (Pl. 9:g), the last motif is, as we have seen, not known in any Northern Sung specimen. The vase in this group (Pl. 9:f) is related to the vase with lily designs in Pl. 9:i, both specimens have the same peculiar S-shaped scrolls on the shoulder.[2]) The main floral scroll on the latter vase is executed in a free and spacious way, and it is stylistically related to the ewers in Pl. 6:g–h (which also have similar petals round the shoulder as the vase has round the base) but also to the scrolls in the boys-among-flowers design in Pl. 9:j–k. Another type of bowls, which also are of rounded shape with thickened or rolled rim, have small lotus sprays on a wave ground as main design (Pl. 8:l). They are obviously related to the last described scrolls. The most interesting specimen in this group is undoubtedly the one in Pl. 8:i carrying the Chin date 1162, which further seems to confirm our dating of these groups. The described types are the only ones we have found which have a definitely new character, different from the earlier Northern celadon designs, and it might be sufficient to let the ware be represented by this group.

In the *Tz'u-chou* group we have already noted that several Northern Sung types continued into Chin, and this seems to have been particularly the case with the pillows. The most characteristic group of pillows from this time is perhaps the Chang group, and as we have seen in connection with the discussion of the different types within this large group, the dating is difficult, as we have specimens excavated from tombs, dating according to the excavators from Northern Sung to Yüan. It seems, however, quite clear that the majority of the pillows in the groups which we have presented in this study belong to the Chin period. The earliest type seems to be the cloud-shaped pillows (Pl. 47:a–e); they are in shape related to the

[1]) Cp. *China's beauty*, Nos. 36 and 48.

[2]) This most typical S-shaped border is found in exactly the same execution in a wall-painting in a tomb in Shansi from the beginning of Chin, which further seems to support our dating of this design (*Kao Ku* 1965:1, p. 21, Pl. 6:2–5).

leaf-shaped pillows of Northern Sung, and many of the designs are also similar. There is also a striking resemblance to the designs found on the top of the tiger-shaped pillows (Cp. Pl. 47:d and Pl. 52:k). The majority of specimens in the oval and rectangular groups seem to fall in the Chin dynasty (Pl. 46:d–k) and there are none of them which on reliable grounds can be placed as late as Yüan, as they are often dated. There is a tendency to a certain stiffness in some of the designs which we can also find in some patterns on the kidney-shaped pillows of *san ts'ai* type (Pl. 51) which seems to be a characteristic feature of the mature Chin style. Like many pillows in the kidney-shaped group there are several also in the group of rectangular pillows of *san ts'ai* type, which obviously belong to the Chin dynasty (Pl. 52:a–d). Several pillows of this type have very elaborate designs of a pictorial type which is not found in Northern Sung. A characteristic small feature is also the border of stiff bamboo leaves found on the sides of some pillows (Pl. 52:a) and also sometimes on the top (Pl. 52:d). The same type of border is also found on Northern celadon specimens from Chin time and can also be seen in Chin tombs.[1]) The same type of design is also found in the kidney-shaped group (Pl. 51:k).

One style of design which is not found in Northern Sung is the one seen on the specimens in Pl. 54:d–f, with its lofty floral sprays. The ware might be regarded as a provincial variety, but the shapes as well as its relationship with other Chin types make a dating within this time most likely. A related specimen with yellow glaze (Pl. 54:g) and two bowls with the same kind of glaze, one of them datable to Chin (Pl. 54:h–i), show other more unusual types.

At the end of Chin and the beginning of Yüan we find several Tz'u-chou groups which are clearly datable both by excavated specimens and for stylistic reasons. One of these groups is formed by the wine-jars with sketchy designs of leaves, birds and inscriptions (Pl. 53:g–i) and another related with characteristic sketchy leaves (Pl. 53:a–d).

The sgraffito wares from the end of Chin and from Yüan are clearly recognizable both by their characteristic shapes and designs, and the dated jar (Pl. 55:i) in the British Museum also helps us to date one of these groups as late as around 1300. We can see how the tendency to a certain stiffness in the designs which we have already remarked upon becomes more and more accentuated at the end of Chin (Pl. 54:j–l, Pl. 55:a) and turns into very formal and heavy foliage scrolls (Pl. 55:d–f)[2]) and stereotyped and lifeless patterns of other types (Pl. 55:c, h, i).

In the enamelled Tz'u-chou group we have several dated specimens which clearly show that this style was invented by the Chins around 1200. The technique in itself is undoubtedly a major achievement and was to become of great importance later on, but the majority of specimens found are of quite a low quality and must be con-

[1]) *Kao Ku* 1965:1, Pl. 6:7–8.

[2]) This type of foliage scroll can be seen also in Sung stone carvings. Cp. *Ku tai chuang shih hua wen hsüan chi*, Pl. 70.

sidered experimental pieces. Some pieces are of better quality and the colouring is sometimes pleasing, but even in these designs we have a tendency to carelessness and stiffness which we have already found in other wares from the end of the period. The type illustrated in Pl. 55:j–k is clearly datable to around 1200 because of a dated specimen of this type in the Tokyo National Museum, and the types with dotted border and design of characters are likewise datable to the early part of the 13th century both by dated and excavated examples, as we have shown in our earlier discussion of the enamelled group. Of a slightly later date are the specimens in Pl. 56:k–l and Pl. 57:a–d which seem mainly to belong to the Yüan dynasty.

The most controversial group found in Sung ceramics is no doubt the moulded *Ting yao* group. Most experienced scholars who have worked with this problem have found that on stylistic grounds they would like to date the majority of specimens within this group to the second part of Sung. But at the same time the old and, in many quarters, still prevalent idea that the Ting kiln ceased to operate after 1127 has further confused the issue. As we have already explained at some length at different places in the present study, we have found that the main body of moulded Ting specimens were undoubtedly made during Chin. It is not necessary to discuss again all the different reasons we have for this dating, but we will make a short repetition of some of the main designs.

To our help with the dating based on stylistic reasons we have, as we have seen, three very important dated moulds. The first of these and at the same time the most interesting is the David mould dated 1184 (Fig. 22:a),[1]) the second mould is in the British Museum and carries the date 1189 (Fig. 23:a) and the third one in the same collection is dated 1203 (Fig. 23:b). With the aid of these moulds we are able to date a large and interesting group of Ting porcelains.

The David mould is closely related to several phoenix-decorated bowls and dishes (Cp. Fig. 22:a and b, Fig. 23:c), notably the elegant bowls of conical shape with a small flower in the centre (Pl. 84:b–c).[2]) If we now return to the mould (Fig. 22:a) and examine its floral motif, we will find that the flowers are of the characteristic type we have called palmette-like peony, the leaves are elongated and pointed and the leaf-stems are crossing each other in a most typical way. The same kind of flowers we find on the mould dated 1203 (Fig. 23:b). We have seen this floral motif as main design on another group of bowls (Pls. 80–81) which are of the same conical shape as the phoenix bowls and have a similar flower in the centre and a key-fret band near the mouth (Fig. 1:d). The same shape is also found with the boy motif (Pl. 83) and with pomegranate-peonies (Pl. 82). The interesting bowl in Pl. 85:a has both the palmette-like-peonies and the phoenixes just like the David mould,

[1]) Unfortunately the drawing does not show the very characteristic palmette scroll which encloses the design. Cp. *David Ting cat.* Pl. 10, No. 181.

[2]) A mould found at the Ting kiln has the same design of phoenixes and flowers. The mould is apparently intended for one of the characteristic dishes with flattened, horizontal rim. *Kao Ku* 1965:8, Pl. 10:11.

and a very interesting specimen formerly in the Eumorfopoulos collection has two phoenixes on a plate of the same unusual shape as the one seen in Pl. 102:b, which further confirms the late character of the design.[1])

Let us now examine another group of Ting yao pieces which are all more or less related to one another and also to the above-mentioned group. The dish in Pl. 85:b is decorated with a *ch'i-lin* among peony scrolls of the palmette-like type with their characteristic leaves; on the side is an exquisite floral border and above that a key-fret band. The palmette-like peonies are of the same type as we have found on the two moulds and the floral border is very close to the flowers found on the phoenix bowls (Fig. 22:b, Fig. 23:c). The *ch'i-lin* dish is one in a series of similar dishes all of the same characteristic shape and with the designs enclosed by one or two key-fret borders. Very close to the *ch'i-lin* dish is the lion dish in Pl. 86:a, and the two animals are placed in exactly the same way. The scrolls are of the same type but instead of the palmette-like flowers we have pomegranates; we have already seen before how closely connected those two patterns are and how they are all the time interchanged. Round the side of the dish are *ch'ih* dragons and clouds. On another dish (Pl. 86:b) the *ch'ih* dragons are in the centre, and on the side are pomegranate scrolls. Closely related to this group of dishes are also the boy dish in Pl. 88:a, and the dragon dish Pl. 87:a.

The characteristic pomegranate scroll[2]) found in several patterns in the above discussed group is also found in the beautiful deer dishes of the type illustrated in Pl. 96:a, those dishes are of a characteristic shape with flattened rim which seems to be typical of Chin and Yüan.[3]) The composition of the motif on this dish is also very similar to that of the earlier mentioned lion and *ch'i-lin* dishes. One small detail which we find on many specimens in this group is the characteristic small dots that we can see on the bodies of the deer, they are found on the jacket of the boy in Pl. 88:a, on the border dragons in the lion dish (Pl. 86:a), on the tails of the winged dragons (Pl. 87:a). We also find this feature in another specimen, the phoenix dish in Pl. 88:b, which leads us on to other specimens. On this dish we find the dots in the incurved sections of the lobed central panel. The floral border of the dish is very similar to the one found on the *ch'i-lin* dish (Pl. 85:b), and the shape is also the same as found in that group. The new feature in the phoenix dish is the lobed panel enclosing the central motif, which is a typical late arrangement,[4]) we find it again in the dish Pl. 84:g with short-tailed phoenixes. These phoenixes are of exactly the same type as those in the dated mould (Fig. 22:a) with the exception

---

[1]) *GEc*, Vol. III, No. C 171. Now in the British Museum.

[2]) We have discussed the pomegranate scroll and its sources in connection with the principal motifs on p. 177 above.

[3]) A similar shape is already found in Liao ceramics, and the adoption of this form seems to be another example of Chin traditionalism.

[4]) For the use of similar lobed panels enclosing the main motif in Yüan silver cp. *Kao Ku* 1965:6, Pl. 10:2–3.

that the tails of the birds are short; the floral scrolls are also similar to those found on the phoenix bowls (Fig. 22:b), a typical feature is the small round holes found in the leaves.[1]) The shape of the short-tailed phoenix-dish, the panels with stiff prunus flowers and insects, and the central medallion enclosing the main motif are all features which we find in Yüan time. This large group of specimens which we have now discussed on the basis of the moulds from 1184 and 1203 might accordingly, on stylistic grounds, be dated to the second part of Chin and the beginning of Yüan supremacy, approximately from the last quarter of the 12th century to the first half of the 13th century.

The last stage in the development of this type of Ting yao seems to be the more free landscape designs of the type seen in Pl. 84:h (Fig. 25:a), Pls. 97:b, 98 and 99.[2]) The connection between this late group and the preceding one is quite clear and can be shown by transitional specimens and features in the designs. The dish with short-tailed phoenixes in Pl. 97:a has a triangular key-fret on the rim, which is also found in the dish Pl. 84:h that is one of the transitional specimens; another is the beautiful peacock dish in Pl. 96:b, which through its lotus border and the ribbon motif is related to the earlier type, but through its cloud scrolls and the less compact design is closer to the later group (Cp. Pl. 97:b). The dish in Pl. 99, which also belongs to the later type, has a similar arrangement of flowers and insects in panels as in the dish Pl. 84:g, but the scroll work on the garden fence is very close to what we have found on the boy dish in the earlier type (Pl. 88:a).[3]) A still later type which probably marks the end of the traditional Ting yao is the dish in Pl. 100:a with its lotus petal panels in the cavetto, which is of a type seen in underglaze red and blue; it is linked to the dish Pl. 84:g through the scroll designs found on the rim.[4]) The development from one type to another is quite clear in those specimens and they form a most interesting chain of evolution.

Apart from the designs just discussed we have earlier under the different types mentioned some other groups which are also datable to the second part of Chin. Among those are the dishes with chrysanthemum-fluted sides (Pls. 101, 102)[5]) and the richly decorated bowls and dishes of the type seen in Pls. 78–79. Both these

---

[1]) This feature can be seen also in the enamel-painted Tz'u-chou group (Pl. 56:f) and in contemporary paintings, from which no doubt the motif emanates (*Chinese Arts of the Sung and Yüan periods*. Tokyo National Museum. Pl. 43).

[2]) The composition of the motif found on the dish Pl. 98 with the bird coming down from the sky can be seen in contemporary paintings. Cp. *Chinese arts of the Sung and Yüan periods*. Pls. 43, 51.

[3]) The same type of elaborate scroll work can be seen on mural paintings in an earlier mentioned Chin dynasty tomb in Shansi (*Kao Ku* 1965:7, Pl. 7:3–4).

[4]) Exactly the same scroll designs are found in early blue-and-white, a fine example of characteristic eight-lobed shape has been published in the TOCS (Medley, M., Re-grouping 15th century blue-and-white. TOCS 1962–63. Pl. 1:a).

[5]) The garden fence, seen in the design on the dish Pl. 102:a, with its characteristic flower-shaped post tops, can be seen in an almost identical rendering in a mural painting from a Chin tomb in Hopei dated 1195 (*Kao Ku* 1962:12, p. 646. Pl. 6:1).

types are so obviously related to those we have already dealt with that further arguments for their dating should not be necessary.

The Ting yao designs we have just described all belong to the second part of Chin and we have chosen, somewhat irrationally, to discuss those first as we are on firmer ground for the dating of them thanks to the help provided by the dated moulds. The problem of the early moulded ware is more difficult and we must here rely more on purely stylistic reasons.

Among the types which we would like to refer to the first part of the 12th century are the bowls of the type illustrated in Pl. 90:b with ducks on a spiral wave ground. The design found here is quite close to the incised duck designs we have seen earlier and the composition is also different from what we find later on. Of a similar character is the dish Pl. 89:a which is also related to designs found on Northern celadon and to the same group belongs the dish in Pl. 84:d. The later development of the fish design can be seen on the dish in Pl. 89:b.[1])

The lofty peony sprays found on the bowls in Pl. 92, with respectively a *ch'ih* dragon and a rhinoceros gazing at the moon as central motifs are also of a type which is more in the late Northern Sung style and must be dated in the first half of the 12th century. The later development of the interesting rhinoceros motif can be seen on the mould Pl. 93, which again has all the characteristics of the latter part of Chin. The number of moulded specimens of early type which we have shown here are relatively few, but the character of their designs and composition seems quite clear, and several other specimens can be found in different collections, and fragments have also been found at the kiln site (Cp. Fig. 32:1–5, 8–14, 22–24). Typical of this earlier type seems to be a more lofty and spacious type of designs and the division of the interior by radiating ribs into panels. In this paper we have, however, concentrated on the more interesting and complex designs found in the later type, and it has also been our intention to show clearly how the majority of richly decorated moulded specimens belong to Chin and continue into Yüan, where they surely became one of the main sources of inspiration for the later underglaze decorated wares. We would, in line with this, also point out some incised specimens which belong to the same traditition and show that also this ware continued until the Yüan dynasty.

The equivalents to the conical bowls with designs of peonies, phoenixes, boys among floral scrolls etc. in the moulded group, are also found in the incised one, and two examples can be seen in Pl. 61:i–j. One has a lotus design, the other the pomegranate scroll of the same type as we have found in the moulded variety. The pomegranate design is again found on the dishes Pl. 75:a and 73:b. The first dish is of the type with flattened rim which we have already met with in the moulded group and which seems to be characteristic of the latter part of Chin; the second

[1]) The arrangement of the two ducks in the centre of this dish is similar to what we find in early blue-and-white. Cp. *Chinese Art under the Mongols*. Pl. 135.

dish is of a still later shape; characteristic of both is the slightly raised unglazed edge of the rim with which all dishes in this group are provided. On the flat rim of the first dish (Pl. 75:a) is a dissolved scroll border, which is one of the designs often met with in this group. The palmette-like peony so closely connected with the pomegranate one is found on a similar dish (Pl. 75:b). On the flat rim of this dish is a formal palmette scroll, which is one of the main characteristics of this group.[1]) This scroll is a typical T'ang pattern[2]) which was also found in Liao (Cp. Fig. 38:g) and which was revived during Chin and can be found also on silver, sculptures etc. from the Chin—Yüan transition period.[3]) On another similar dish the central design is a peony flower which is a kind of intermediate type between the pomegranate peony and more realistic ones (Pl. 76). A third dish of the same shape and with identical palmette border has a very fine realistic peony in the centre (Pl. 74).

The lotus design which was found on one of the bowls from which we started out in the description of the just discussed group (Pl. 61:i), is also found on dishes of the just described type. One example with the palmette border is seen in Pl. 72:a and another with a key-fret border on the rim in Pl. 61:h. A third dish with the same design is found in Pl. 71, and this dish is closely related to the earlier described pomegranate dish (Pl. 73:b) not only in shape but also by the similar scroll ornaments on the rim; which once more shows how close this group is held together. A fine and unusual specimen with the lotus design is the cup-stand in Pl. 73:a, on this stand we find several examples of the earlier mentioned dissolved scroll border (Cp. Pl. 75:a).[4])

With the help of this border we are able to incorporate the *ch'ih* dragon, which we have already seen in the moulded variety, among the incised designs of Chin date. One example is seen in Pl. 70:a, and another which again is seen on one of

[1]) It is also found in the moulded variety, but it is here slightly more compact. Good examples are found on the David mould (*David Ting cat.* No. 181) and on the bowl Pl. 84:a.

[2]) Cp. Gyllensvärd, *op.cit.* Fig. 77.

[3]) Cp. *Chinese gold and silver in the Carl Kempe collection.* Pl. 140 b. *Chinese Art under the Mongols*, Pls. 18 and 35. The last cited specimen is a silvered bronze cup-stand in the British Museum which is of the same shape as several of the above-mentioned Ting yao dishes with a flattened rim with slightly raised edge. The design on the interior shows floral sprays, including pomegranates. The piece might well be of Chin or very early Yüan date. A similar dish with dissolved scroll border on the flattened rim is in the Kempe collection (*Chinese Gold & silver* . . . Pl. 53 b). This dish is made of gold. Both dishes show the design against a ringmatted ground which seems more typical of Sung and Chin than of Yüan metal wares.

[4]) Cup-stands of this type seem to be one of the favourite utensils during the Sung-Yüan period, and examples can be found in silver, lacquer and ceramics, and they are often reproduced in contemporary paintings. Fine examples can be seen in the carved and painted tomb decorations of the Sung tombs from Pai-sha (*Pai sha Sung mu.* Figs. 22 and 57, Pls. 22, 37, 38, 48). Chin time examples can be seen on a tomb mural from Shansi (*Kao Ku* 1965:7, Pl. 7:3) and a very fine painting from a Yüan tomb from 1265 in Shansi is reproduced in our Fig. 40:b. On this painting we can see the cupstands both stacked one in the other on the table and held in the hand of the servant boy, with a cup placed on it.

the typical dishes with flattened rim is seen in Pl. 61:g. A dish also with *ch'ih* dragons but with a key-fret border on the flat rim is seen in Pl. 70:b (Cp. Pl. 61:h).

This short but compact survey has shown that the same type of designs, motifs and shapes are found both in the moulded and in the incised variety of Ting yao, even if the richness in the first category is not matched in the latter. It seems quite clear that towards the latter part of Chin the moulded variety was the favourite and the incised of minor importance. If the dish in the British Museum dated 1271 (Pl. 61:f) is a typical example of the final phase in the development it shows how badly the workmanship had declined, but it might very well be a more provincial specimen.

The Chin style as we find it in ceramics seems to show two main trends, one realistic and one more traditional. At the beginning of the period we can see how the realistic style of Northern Sung with its interest in flowers, animals and nature continues, and more pictorial designs, obviously inspired by contemporary genre paintings, make their appearance. This style never dies out completely, but towards the end of the period the freshness and spontaneity of the style is deteriorating, and we often find a certain stiffness and lack of vitality in the designs. This style can be best followed in the Tz'u-chou group. Among the new motifs used we can find an increasing use of characters and calligraphic designs in the ceramic decoration.

In Ting yao we find at the beginning of Chin the same type of realistic designs of a lofty and elegant appearance as we have seen at the end of Northern Sung, but towards the second part of the period a more traditional style, clearly inspired by T'ang—Liao prototypes, is introduced, and the two types are then found simultaneously. The most interesting feature is, however, the amazing richness of the designs in the moulded variety and the extremely compact compositions which often completely cover the whole interior of bowls and dishes. The same elaborate and detailed style can also be seen in Chin tombs. Good examples are found in two tombs from Shansi, one dated 1201 and the other 1210, both of which have extremely rich carvings on the interior.[1]) This style seems to have culminated around the beginning of the 13th century, and it is followed by a tendency to more spacious designs often of a pictorial type.

It would be interesting to know to what extent the Ting kiln had official support during the Chin dynasty, the high quality of its products and its preference for certain traditional designs, favoured by the Chins, seem to point to some kind of official status of the kiln.

The marked increase of the ceramic industry during Yüan, and especially the rapid development of painted designs found very shortly after the introduction of the underglaze painting have always been considered something of a mystery. Earlier writers have mostly been of the opinion that the main evolution had already taken place during Sung, and some also like to place the beginning of the under-

---

[1]) *Kao Ku* 1959:5, Pls. 5–6. *Wen Wu* 1959:6, p. 51–54.

glaze blue decoration in that period. During recent years there has been a marked tendency to give much more credit to the Yüan period, and it is now generally considered to have been a very creative period, the achievements of which have been of major importance for the later development of Chinese art, and the significance of the period has perhaps been somewhat too exaggerated; after all, the dynasty ruled for merely a hundred years. The Yüan dynasty was undoubtedly a most important period in the history of Chinese ceramics, and so far there is no evidence that the underglaze blue decoration should have begun earlier, but it seems quite clear that the majority of the designs used in Yüan and the motifs favoured during that period were already found in Sung and Chin.[1]) A careful study of the stone carvings, murals and artefacts found in tombs of Sung and Chin time will most certainly reveal the fact that several types of designs which are now considered typical of Yüan were already in use considerably earlier.

The underglaze painted wares of Yüan were undoubtedly the result of the ceramic achievements of the Kiangsi kilns combined with the decorative motifs developed in the Tz'u-chou and Ting wares. The importance of the Tz'u-chou ware for the later painted designs is obvious and has been pointed out by several authors, but the influence of the Ting yao has been more or less ignored. The survey we have given of the main Ting types during Chin clearly shows the great significance of the Ting ware in its contribution to the later development of the blue-and-white. Both shapes, designs and compositions found in this ware have undoubtedly been of the utmost importance as a source of inspiration for the later Yüan and Ming wares.

SOUTHERN SUNG

The most typical examples we find in the *ch'ing-pai* ware of a style new to the Southern Sung period are discovered in the moulded variety, but there are some types of designs also in the incised type which we have not met with before. As in the Ting yao, the stylistic character of the latter phase of the period is much clearer than the transition between Pei Sung and Nan Sung.

We have already mentioned certain motifs, such as the boys among sketchy flowers, fishes among waves, etc., which began already at the end of Northern Sung and continued during the 12th century. Characteristic of the same time is also the division of bowls and dishes by radiating, raised ribs, and this feature can be found in combination with different motifs (Pl. 12:j, Pl. 16:b, Fig. 29:d:4). The use of

---

[1]) One of the main achievements of the Yüan potters seems to have been the introduction of several new shapes. But also some of those shapes which are considered typical of Yüan can be found in pre-Yüan time. An interesting example is a vase of flattened pear shape with cloud-shaped ears and the characters *fu* and *shou* moulded on the body. This vase which has all the characteristics of a Yüan piece was recovered from a tomb, clearly datable to 1250, of Southern Sung in Kiangsi (*Wen Wu* 1964:4, p. 64, Fig. 1.). Another interesting example is a tomb mural from a Chin tomb dated 1184 which shows a vessel of so-called *kendi* type, which usually also is considered a Yüan shape (*Kao Ku* 1962:4, p. 183, Fig. 4).

the *ch'ih* dragon as a decorative motif also seems to have begun during this time (Pl. 12:e, k). In applied functions we find the *ch'ih* dragon used in a series of very beautiful cups which seem to date from the latter part of the century (Pl. 28:f–i).[1])

Among the characteristic designs of the 13th century are the spiral scrolls of a more or less formal type, usually found on *mei-p'ing* vases and vases with a characteristic flower-shaped mouth (Pl. 22:c–e, g–i). In the same shapes we also find deeply carved composite floral scrolls, sometimes in combination with boys (Pl. 22:f, j–l, Pl. 23:a–c). Some of these specimens are of fine quality and excellent workmanship and show that first-rate pieces were still being made at the end of the period (Pl. 23:b), in spite of the enormous output of the kilns. Besides the more detailed, deeply carved patterns, more cursory incised ones are common, as we have already seen among the spiral scroll decorated specimens (Pl. 22:g–i), and this technique is also used with different dissolved floral motifs, especially lotus flowers, sometimes on vases of the same type (Pl. 18:a), typical of the period, but also on bowls and dishes.

In the moulded variety we find several characteristic designs. One of the favourite motifs usually found on bowls are phoenixes flying among composite floral scrolls. This pattern is often found in a broad band on the inside of the bowl or the dish and in the centre is usually a lotus plant (Pl. 24).[2]) The phoenix bird seems to have been one of the favourite designs of the time, and it is found in many different types. Boxes with a pair of phoenixes as main motif are common (Pl. 25), and they are also frequently found on bowls with a design in a special thread relief technique. In the latter type they are sometimes shown alone (Pl. 26:b) and sometimes in combination with lotus flowers (Fig. 29:a). The other favourite motif in this characteristic ware, which we on the basis of excavated specimens are able to date to around 1200, is a pair of lotus flowers.

Among the motifs that are characteristic of the moulded ch'ing-pai ware are flowers and plants in vases or in trays,[3]) usually found in the radiating panels of round bowls (Pl. 27, Fig. 4:e). Here too the central motif is very often a lotus plant, but sometimes a flying bird. In ceramics the potted plant motif does not seem to appear until Southern Sung and it is mainly used in ch'ing-pai, but the motif is found in tomb stone-carvings already during the end of Northern Sung)[4] and seems to have been very popular in Chin[5]) and Southern Sung.

We also find, arranged the same way as the potted plants, floral sprays of dif-

[1]) The cups are clearly related to a cup in the Severance A. Millikin collection, which is of the beaded type characteristic of early Yüan (*Chinese Art under the Mongols*, Pl. 110).

[2]) The detailed and rich floral designs found on these bowls are very similar to what we have seen in the moulded Ting yao from the same time.

[3]) Potted flowers are occasionally seen also in the enamelled Tz'u-chou group (Cp. Pl. 56:e).

[4]) Very fine examples can be seen in a tomb in Hopei. *KKHP* 1962:2, Pl. 7:4–5.

[5]) A very fine Northern celadon dish with design of potted plants, most proably of Chin date, is in the Nationalmuseum in Copenhagen.

ferent types (Fig. 4:f), and this design continued into the Yüan dynasty and becomes more and more stiff and lifeless. The same development we can also find among the phoenix and composite scroll pattern; the designs are perfect and highly detailed, but hard and mechanical, and the glaze is clear and cold and mostly greenish blue or white in colour.

Among the favourite objects from the ch'ing-pai kilns are boxes of many different forms decorated with floral motifs. Some of them can be dated to the middle of the 12th century (Pl. 31:a), but the type continued during the whole of Southern Sung and was apparently one of the most common export wares. Sherds of boxes of this type with their characteristically ribbed sides (Pl. 32:a–c) have been found in abundant quantities at South East Asian sites. The technique of decoration varies from deeply moulded specimens to those in thin thread relief (Pl. 32:a–b), the latter type seems generally to belong to the end of the period.

The material from the end of Sung and the beginning of Yüan is, as we have already pointed out in our discussion of the different types, very rich, and moulding and thread relief designs of different types are abundant and varying and are found on specimens of new and characteristic shapes (Pls. 33, 34, 28:j–k). Close similarities are found to the contemporary Lung-ch'üan ware. Among the favourite motifs of the period are the chrysanthemum and the prunus. The latter design is often found on a group of vases with scroll-handles which belong to the end of the period (Pl. 23:j–l).[1] Among the applied motifs used at the same time we have illustrated a group of ewers with dragons as handle and spout (Pl. 28:a–c) and similar ones with dragon-spout (Pl. 28:d–e).

The richness of new designs and forms found in the ch'ing-pai wares of the Yüan dynasty and at the very end of Sung is most interesting and can be studied in an abundant material not only from China itself but from the whole of South East Asia. A closer study of this material would no doubt reveal many valuable facts about the later development of the ch'ing-pai ware and the beginning of the blue-and-white. The material will probably also help us with the dating of such materials as lacquer, silver and bronze from Yüan time, which are so far not sufficiently known.

The majority of the Southern Sung *Lung-ch'üan* ware is undecorated or only provided with carved petals or applied ornaments, and it is not until the end of the period that more richly decorated specimens appear. The carved lotus petals found on the outside of dishes and bowls of different shapes are one of the standard motifs of Lung-ch'üan and are found during the whole period in question (Fig. 30:c). Among the applied ornaments two fishes in relief in the centre of bowls and dishes is a motif with the same general use (Pl. 39:h–i). The age of specimens of

[1]) The scroll-handle was, however, used already earlier in ch'ing-pai as can be seen from a vase from a tomb datable to 1128. This vase is of a different shape to those discussed above, but the handles are very similar. (*Kao Ku* 1963:6, p. 344.).

this kind cannot be decided by the designs but has to be judged from the shape of the specimen and the quality of the ware. The Sung celadons are usually of a more porcellanous ware than the thicker and heavier Yüan wares.

Applied fish and phoenix handles is another favourite motif of the time and used during the whole period (Pl. 39:j–l, Fig. 30:c:16).[1]) The use of certain bronze forms which seems to have started already at the beginning of the 12th century is typical of the whole period (Pl. 39:k, Fig. 30:c:17–18).[2])

Among incised designs on Lung-ch'üan yao we find the occasional use of fishes and *ch'ih* dragons and sketchy flowers of different types, and we find one characteristic pattern which is new to the period, the prunus twig with a crescent moon (Pl. 38:b, Pl. 39:c). Wares with thread relief designs of the same type as we have seen in ch'ing-pai are frequent at the later part of the dynasty (Pl. 39:f–g) and especially often found among the wares used for export (Fig. 30:b:4). Among the favourite flowers is also in this ware the chrysanthemum. At the beginning of Yüan more richly decorated specimens become popular, both with moulded and incised designs, and a new technique is that which leaves the applied ornaments unglazed so that they appear in red biscuit after firing. Stamped designs of leaves, seals and different figure motifs also came into use around this time (Pl. 39:e).

As a general judgment we must conclude that the patterns found in Southern Sung are mostly such as we have already seen earlier and only a few new ones such as the prunus motif, the potted plants, and certain other floral motifs as well as the more universal use of the chrysanthemum, the phoenix and the *ch'ih* dragon can be observed. But it is mainly at the latter part of the period, and especially towards the end, that the richer types of designs become more popular. But the two wares we have investigated, the celadon and the ch'ing-pai, are of course, owing to their beautiful glaze and fine quality, ideally suited for undecorated specimens, and it is obvious that these kinds of objects were highly appreciated during the period. Especially is this the case with the Lung-ch'üan yao with its jade-like glaze, where we find some of the finest specimens entirely undecorated, and we know that the Court favoured celadons of this type where form, colour and the more or less accentuated crazing of the glaze were the most important criteria. Many new and beautiful shapes were also invented during the period, some of them, as we have seen, inspired by archaic bronzes.

In the temmoku and other wares from Chi-chou we find among the favourite motifs prunus twigs, prunus flowers, bamboo, scroll-work and various lucky phrases

---

[1]) The curious dolphin-like handles are sometimes also found in silver specimens. Cp. J. J. Smirnoff, *Vostocnoe serebro* (Argenterie Orientale). Petersburg 1909. Pl. 230.

[2]) Also in ch'ing-pai censers of bronze shape are used already at the very beginning of Southern Sung (Cp. *Kao Ku* 1963:6, p. 344).

(Fig. 36).[1]) A characteristic shape found in the white ware from Chi-chou is a jar covered with a lid in the shape of a foliated lotus leaf. This shape is also seen in ch'ing-pai, celadon and early blue-and-white,[2]) as well as in silver.[3])

In the wares imitating Ting yao we also find the moon and the prunus twig as one of the favourite motifs (Pl. 84:i, j, k). It was also one of the most beloved subjects in Southern Sung painting, and probably its allusion to a coming Spring and rejuvenescence held a special message to the people of the languishing Sung Empire.

[1]) Wirgin, *Some ceramic wares from Chi-chou.*

[2]) Wirgin, *op.cit.* Pls. 14–17.

[3]) For silver specimens from Yüan tombs, see *Wen Wu* 1964:12, Pl. 6:2; *Kao Ku* 1965:6, p. 295, Fig. 10:5. Cp. also the jars found on the table in the painting in our. Fig. 40:b.

LIST OF ABBREVIATIONS

AA	The Artibus Asiae. Ascona.
ACASA	Archives of the Chinese Art Society of America. New York.
BCMA	The Bulletin of the Cleveland Museum of Art. Cleveland.
BM	The British Museum. London.
BMFEA	The Bulletin of the Museum of Far Eastern Antiquities. Stockholm.
CKc	Chinese ceramics in the Carl Kempe collection (Gyllensvärd, B.).
FECB	The Far Eastern Ceramic Bulletin. Ann Arbor.
GEc	The George Eumorfopoulos collection. Catalogue. (Hobson, R. L.).
HJAS	Harvard Journal of Asiatic Studies. Cambridge, Mass.
KKHP	The K'ao ku hsüeh pao. Peking.
Kao Ku	The K'ao ku (tung hsün). Peking.
MFA	The Museum of Fine Arts. Boston.
MFEA	The Museum of Far Eastern Antiquities. Stockholm.
OA	The Oriental Art. London.
OCS	The Oriental Ceramic Society. London.
OZ	The Ostasiatische Zeitschrift. Berlin.
ROM	The Royal Ontario Museum. Toronto.
TOCS	The Transactions of the Oriental Ceramic Society. London.
Wen Wu	The Wen wu (ts'an k'ao tzu liao). Peking.
YCHP	The Yen ching hsüeh pao. Peking.

1. 吳越
2. 太平御覽
3. 冊府元龜
4. 考古圖
5. 續考古圖
6. 宣和博古圖
7. 臨汝縣
8. 耀州
9. 東窯
10. 嚴和店
11. 軋花溝
12. 下任村
13. 銅川縣
14. 黃堡鎮
15. 陳爐鎮
16. 上店鎮
17. 立地坡
18. 邠縣
19. 坦齋筆衡
20. 景德鎮陶錄
21. 清河縣
22. 三把蓮
23. 童
24. 吳
25. 上林湖
26. 犀牛
27. 影青
28. 諸蕃志(趙汝适)
29. 青白瓷器
30. 德化
31. 白舍
32. 南豐
33. 菜家合子
34. 麗水縣
35. 雞肋篇(莊季裕)
36. 秘色
37. 大窯
38. 金村
39. 金玉滿堂
40. 河濱遺范(範)
41. 永清窯記
42. 觀台鎮
43. 東艾口村
44. 冶子村
45. 邯鄲市
46. 修武縣
47. 當陽峪
48. 焦作
49. 登封縣
50. 曲河
51. 密縣
52. 窯溝
53. 湯陰縣
54. 鶴壁集
55. 禹縣
56. 扒村
57. 八卦洞
58. 太原市
59. 孟家井
60. 介休縣
61. 洪山鎮
62. 鉅鹿縣
63. 家國永安
64. 清淨忍
65. 張家造
66. 八義
67. 清
68. 曲陽縣
69. 澗磁村
70. 格古要論
71. 永和
72. 尚食局
73. 尚藥局
74. 萱草
75. 奉華

6. 鳳華
7. 聰福
8. 聚秀
9. 禁苑
0. 劉萬立
1. 五王府
2. 東平郡
3. 洛陽牡丹記(歐陽修)
4. 洛陽牡丹記(周叙)
85. 天彭牡丹譜(陸游)
86. 陳州牡丹記(張邦基)
87. 牡丹榮辱志(丘璿)
88. 揚州芍藥譜(王觀)
89. 荷蓮
90. 梅花喜神譜(宋伯仁)
91. 連生貴子
92. 龍
93. 蟒
94. 螭
95. 鳳凰
96. 鸞
97. 獅子滾繡毬
98. 鎮宅大吉
99. 狻猊
100. 麒麟
101. 鴛鴦

BIBLIOGRAPHY

WESTERN LITERATURE

Addis, J. M., *Some ch'ing pai and white wares found in the Philippines.* Manila trade pottery seminar. Introductory notes.

— *A group of underglaze red. TOCS* 1964–66. London 1967.

d'Argencé, R.-Y. Lefebvre, *Chinese ceramics in the Avery Brundage collection.* San Francisco 1967. (*Brundage cat.*)

Ayers, John, *The Baur Collection, Geneva.* Chinese ceramics. Vol. I. Genève 1968. (*Baur cat.*)

— *The Seligman Collection of Oriental Art.* Vol. II. London 1964. (*Seligman cat.*)

— *Some characteristic wares of the Yüan dynasty. TOCS.* 1954–55.

Beurdeley, Michel, *The Chinese collector through the centuries; from Han to the 20th century.* Tokyo 1966.

Boulay, Anthony du, *Chinese Porcelain.* Frankfurt am Main 1963.

Brankston, A. D., *Yüeh ware and the Nine Rocks Kiln. Burlington mag.* No. 73, 1938.

— *An excursion to Ching-te-chen and Chi-an-fu in Kiangsi. TOCS* 1938–39.

Bush, Susan, *"Clearing after snow in the Min mountains" and Chin landscape painting. OA,* Vol. XI. 1965, p. 163.

— *Literati Culture under the Chin. OA,* Vol. XV. 1969, p. 103.

Bushell, S. W., *Description of Chinese pottery and porcelain, being a translation of the T'ao shuo.* Oxford 1910.

Cahill, James, *Chinese painting.* Lausanne 1960.

— *The Art of Southern Sung China.* Asia House. New York 1962.

Cammann, Schuyler, *Substance and symbol in Chinese toggles.* Philadelphia 1962.

— *Types of symbols in Chinese art.* (*Studies in Chinese thought.*) Chicago 1953.

— *Significant patterns on Chinese bronze mirrors. ACASA.* IX. 1955.

— *The development of the Mandarin Square. HJAS.* VIII:2. 1944.

— *The lion and grape patterns on Chinese bronze mirrors. AA.* 16. 1953.

Cheng, Te-k'un, *Archaeological studies in Szechwan.* Cambridge 1957.

Chinese Translations Nos. 1–4. The Victoria & Albert Museum in association with the Oriental Ceramic Society. London 1967–68.

Coomaraswamy, A., *Yaksas,* I–II. Smithsonian Miscellaneous collections. Vol. 80, no. 6. 1928–31.

Cox, Warren E., *The book of pottery and porcelain.* Vol. I. New York 1945.

David, Sir Percival, *Ying ch'ing. OA.* Vol. 1:2, 1955.

— *A commentary on Ju ware. TOCS,* 1936–37. London 1938.

Dexel, Thomas, *Die Formen Chinesischer Keramik.* Thübingen 1955.

Feddersen, Martin, *Chinesisches Kunstgewerbe.* Braunschweig 1955.

Fernald, Helen, *Chinese mortuary pillows in the Royal Ontario Museum. FECB,* Vol. IV:1, 1952. (*Fernald.*)

Figges, Sir John, *A group of decorated lacquer caskets of the Yüan dynasty. TOCS* 1964–66. London 1967.

Fitzgerald, C. P., *China, a short cultural history.* London 1935.

de Flines, E. W. van Orsoy, *Gids voor de Keramische Verzameling, Uitheemse Keramiek.* Batavia 1949.

Franke, O., *Geschichte des Chinesischen Reiches.* IV Band. Berlin 1948.

Fry, R.-Binyon, L., etc., *Chinesische Kunst.* München 1937. (Orig. ed. "*Chinese Art*", London 1935.)

Gernet, Jacques, *Daily life in China on the eve of the Mongol invasion 1250–1276.* London 1962.

Goidsenhoven, J. P. van., *La Ceramique Chinoise.* Bruxelles 1954.

Gompertz, G. St. G. M., *Chinese celadon wares.* London 1958. (*Gompertz.*)

— *Black Koryo ware. OA*, Vol. 3:2, 1950.

— *The "kingfisher celadon" of Koryo. AA*, Vol. 16. 1953.

— *Some notes on Yüeh ware.* I–II. *OA*, Vol. 2:1,3. 1956.

— *Chinese celadon in Tokyo. OA*, Vol. 3:3. 1951.

— *Hsü Ching's visit to Korea in 1123. TOCS.* 1960–62. London 1963.

Gray, Basil, *Early Chinese pottery and porcelain.* London 1953. (*Gray.*)

Gyllensvärd, Bo, *Chinese Gold and Silver in the Carl Kempe collection.* Stockholm 1953. (*Chinese Gold and Silver.*)

— *T'ang Gold and Silver.* Stockholm 1957. BMFEA 29. (*Gyllensvärd.*)

— *Chinese Ceramics in the Carl Kempe collection.* Stockholm 1965. (*CKc.*)

Hansford, S. Howard, *A Glossary of Chinese art and archaeology.* London 1954.

Hardy, S. Yorke, *Illustrated catalogue of Tung, Ju, Kuan, Chün, Kuang-tung & glazed I-hsing ware in the Percival David Foundation of Chinese art.* London 1953.

Heinrich, T. A., *Art treasures in the Royal Ontario Museum.* Toronto 1963.

Hetherington, A. L., *The early ceramic wares of China.* New York 1922.

Hoang, P., *Concordance des Chronologies Néoméniques Chinoise et Européenne.* Shanghai 1910.

Hobson, R. L.—Hetherington, A. L., *The Art of the Chinese Potter.* London 1923.

Hobson—Rackham—King, *Chinese ceramics in private collections.* London 1931. (*Private.*)

Hobson, R. L., *Chinese pottery and porcelain.* Vol. I. London 1915.

— *Chinese art.* London 1927 (revised ed. 1952).

— *Catalogue of Chinese pottery and porcelain in the collection of Sir Percival David.* London 1934.

— *Handbook of the pottery and porcelain of the Far East in the Department of Oriental Antiquities, British Museum.* London 1948. (*BM Handbook.*)

— *The George Eumorfopoulos collection; Catalogue of the Chinese, Corean and Persian pottery and porcelain.* Vol. I–VI. London 1925–28. (*GEc.*)

— *Notes on a visit to Hangchow. TOCS* 1935–36.

— *Chinese porcelain from Fostat. Burlington mag.* Vol. 61, 1932.

— *A dish of Yüeh ware. Burlington mag.* Vol. 63, 1933.

— *The exhibition of Chinese art.* I—The Ceramics. *Burlington mag.* Jan. 1936.

— *Yüeh ware and Northern celadon. TOCS* 1936–37.

— *Chinese, Corean and Japanese potteries.* New York 1941.

Hochstadter, W., *Early Chinese ceramics in the Buffalo Museum of Science.* New York 1946. (*Hochstadter.*)

Hollis, H. C., *More Sung dynasty stoneware. BCMA.*1949.

Honey, W. B., *The ceramic art of China and other countries of the Far East.* London 1945.

— *Corean pottery.* London 1947.

Ingram, Sir H., *Form, an important factor in the dating of early Chinese ceramics. Ethnos* 1946:4.

Jenyns, R. Soame, *Chinese Art. The Minor Arts II.* Fribourg 1965.

— *The Chinese rhinoceros and carvings in rhinoceros horn. TOCS* 1954–55.

Karlbeck, O., *Notes on the wares from the Chiao Tso potteries. Ethnos*, Vol. 8, No. 3, 1943.

Karlgren, Bernhard, *Kina.* Världshistoria utgiven av Sven Tunberg och S. E. Bring. Stockholm 1928.

Klein, D., *Die frühen Seidengewebe auf der China-Ausstellung in London. OZ*, Neue Folge 1936.

Kuo, Pao-ch'ang—Ferguson, John C., *Noted porcelains of successive dynasties with comments and illustrations, by Hsiang Yüan-pien.* Peiping 1931.

Koyama, Fujio, *Liao pottery wares. TOCS* 1962-63. London 1964.

— *On the discovery of the ruins of Ting yao. ACASA*, Vol. 3, 1948–49.

— *The Yüeh-chou yao celadon excavated in Japan. AA*, Vol. 14, 1951.

Lane, A., *Sung wares and the Saljug pottery of* — *Persia. TOCS*, 1946–47. London 1948.

Laufer, Berthold, *Chinese clay figures.* Part I. Chicago 1914. Field Museum of Natural History. Publication 177.

Le Coq, A. von, *Chotscho.* Berlin 1913.

Lee, Jean Gordon, *A dated Tz'u-chou pillow. ACASA* XI. 1957.

Lee, Sherman E., *A history of Far Eastern art.* New York 1964.

— *Sung ceramics in the light of recent Japanese research. AA*, Vol. 11, 1948.

— *Two early Chinese ivories. AA*, Vol. 16, 1953.

Lee, Sherman E.—Ho, Wai-Kam, *Chinese art under the Mongols: The Yüan dynasty.* Cleveland 1968. (*Chinese art under the Mongols.*)

Lessing, F., *Ueber die Symbolsprache in der Chinesischen Kunst. Sinica* 9–10. 1934–35.

Leth, A., *Chinese art.* Copenhagen 1953.

Li, H. L., *The garden flowers of China.* New York 1959.

Lin, Yutang, *The Gay Genius.* The life and times of Su Tungpo. New York 1947.

— *The importance of understanding.* Cleveland and New York 1960.

— *The Chinese theory of art.* London 1967.

Lindberg, G., *Hsing-yao and Ting-yao. BMFEA*, No. 25, 1953.

Lion-Goldschmidt, Daisy, *Arts de la Chine.* Bronze-Jade-Sculpture-Céramique. Fribourg 1960.

Locsin, Cecilia Y., *A group of white wares from Te-hua.*

— *A group of painted wares from Chi-chou and some related wares excavated in the Philippines.*

— *Lead-glazed wares excavated in the Philippines.* Manilla trade pottery seminar. Introductory notes.

Locsin, Leandro and Cecilia, *Oriental ceramics discovered in the Philippines.* Tokyo 1967.

Lovell, Hin-Cheung, *Illustrated catalogue of Ting yao and related white wares in the Percival David Foundation of Chinese art.* London 1964. (*David Ting cat.*)

Medcalf, C. J. B., *Hsiang-hu and the identity of Ying-ch'ing. OA*, Vol. 1:1.

Medley, M., *Illustrated catalogue of porcelains decorated in underglaze blue and copper red in the Percival David Foundation of Chinese art.* London 1963.

— *Re-grouping 15th century blue and white. TOCS* 1962–63. London 1964.

Needham, J., *Science and civilization in China.* Vol. I. Cambridge 1954.

Newton, Isaac, *Chinese ceramic wares from Hunan. FECB* Vol. X, 1958.

Ozaki, N., *Chinese Literature on Ceramics, OA* III: 1. (Spring 1957.)

Paine, R. T., *Chinese ceramic pillows. FECB*, Vol. 7:3, 1955. (*Paine.*)

Palmgren, Nils, *Sung sherds.* Stockholm 1963.

— *Selected Chinese antiquities from the collection of Gustaf Adolf Crown Prince of Sweden.* Stockholm 1948.

Plumer, James Marshall, *The Ting-yao kiln-sites:* Koyama's significant discoveries. *ACASA*, III, 1948–49.

— *Saggars of Sung.* II. *OA*, Vol. 1:2. 1955.

Poor, Robert, *Notes on the Sung dynasty archaeological catalogs. ACASA* XIX, 1965.

Pope, John A., *Fourteenth-century blue and white. A group of Chinese porcelains in the Topkapu Sarayi Müzesi, Istanbul.* Freer Gallery of Art, Occasional papers, Vol. 2:1. Washington 1952.

— *Chinese porcelains from the Ardebil shrine.* Washington 1956.

Rackham, B., *Catalogue of the Le Blond collection of Corean pottery.* London 1918.

Reidemeister, L., *Keramische Funde aus Jehol und die Lohan von I-chou. OZ*, Vol. 13, 1937.

— *Das Yüeh-yao. OZ*, Vol. 15–16. 1939-40.

Rücker-Embden, O., *Chinesische Frühkeramik.* Leipzig 1922.

Sayer, Geoffrey R., *Ching-te-chen T'ao-lu.* London 1951.

— *T'ao ya.* London 1959.

Shirae, S,—Cox, W. E., *Hsiang-hu and the identity of ying-ch'ing. OA*, Vol. 2:2. 1949.

Sickman, Laurence, *Chinese silver of the Yüan dynasty. ACASA*, XI, 1957.

Sickman, L.—Soper, A., *The art and architecture of China.* London 1956.

Sirén, Osvald, *Kinas konst under tre årtusenden.* 1–2. Stockholm 1942–43.

— *Chinese painting.* Leading masters and principles. London 1956–58.

— *The Chinese on the art of painting.* New York 1963.

— *Kinas trädgårdar.* Stockholm 1948–50.

Simmons, P., *Some recent developments in Chinese textile studies. BMFEA* 28, 1956.

Smirnoff, J. J., *Vostocnoe serebro* (Argenterie Orientale). Petersburg 1909.

Sommarström, Bo, *Archaeological researches in the Edsen-Gol region, Inner Mongolia.* Part I. Stockholm 1956.

Speiser, Werner, *Die Kunst Ostasiens.* Berlin 1956.

Stein, M. A., *Serindia.* 1–5. Oxford 1921.

— *The thousand Buddhas.* London 1921.

Sullivan, Michael, *Chinese ceramics, bronzes and jades in the collection of Sir Alan and Lady Barlow.* London 1963. (*Barlow cat.*)

— *Notes on Chinese export wares in Southeast Asia. TOCS* 1960–62. London 1963.

Tomita, K.—Ch'iu, K'ai-ming, *Chinese leather wine bottles and their ceramic imitations. OA*, Vol. 1:3.

Torii, R., *Sculptured stone tombs of the Liao dynasty.* Peking. 1942.

— *Chio-ti of the Khitans. YCHP*, No. 29, 1941.

Tregear, Mary (coordinated by), *Arts of China. Neolithic cultures to the T'ang dynasty. Recent discoveries.* Tokyo 1968.

Tregear, Mary, *Guide to the Chinese ceramics in the department of Eastern art, Ashmolean Museum.* Oxford 1966.

— *Early Chinese green wares in the collection of the Ashmolean Museum Oxford. OA*, 13:1, 1967.

Trubner, Henry, *Royal Ontario Museum. The Far Eastern collection.* Toronto 1968.

— *Two examples of Ch'ing-pai porcelain in the Royal Ontario Museum. ACASA* XVII, 1963.

— *Tz'u-chou and Honan temmoku. AA*, Vol. 15. 1952.

Ulei, *Mongolian wrestling. China Pictorial.* 1957:10.

Vasselot, J. J. M., *La Ceramique Chinoise. Musée du Louvre.* Vol. 1. Paris. 1922.

Visser, H. F. E., *Asiatic art in private collections of Holland and Belgium.* Amsterdam 1947.

Wheatley, Paul, *Geographical notes on some commodities involved in Sung maritime trade. Journal of the Malayan Branch Royal Asiatic Society.* Vol. 32:2. 1959.

Williams, C. A. S., *Outlines of Chinese Symbolism.* Peiping 1931.

Wirgin, Jan C., *Some notes on Liao ceramics. BMFEA* 32, 1960.

— *Some ceramic wares from Chi-chou. BMFEA* 34, 1962.

— *The phoenix motif on Sung ceramics* (Festskrift tillägnad Carl Kempe 80 år). Stockholm 1964.

Wittfogel, K.—Feng, Chin Sheng, *History of Chinese society. Liao.* Philadelphia 1949.

Yamashita, T., *A Kitan variety of Sung pottery discovered in Jehol.* Monumenta Serica. Vol. 2, 1937.

Zimmermann, E., *Chinesische Porzellan.* I–II. Leipzig 1923.

CATALOGUES

Benaki Museum. Catalogue of the Chinese pottery and porcelain. *Athens* 1939.

Die Sammlung des Herrn Dr. Otto Burchard, Berlin. Auktionsleitung: Paul Cassirer und Hugo Helbing. *Berlin* 1928.

Ausstellung Chinesischer Kunst. *Berlin* 1929.

C. B. Hoyt Collection, Memorial exhibition. Museum of Fine Arts, *Boston* 1952. (*Hoyt cat.*)

Exhibition of Chinese ceramics lent by Mr. and Mrs. Eugene Bernat. MFA, *Boston* 1947.

City Art Gallery Bristol. The Schiller collection. *Bristol* 1948.

Handbook of the Department of Oriental art. The Art Institute of *Chicago* 1933.

Kinas kunst i svensk og dansk eje. Det Danske Kunstindustrimuseum. *Copenhagen* 1950.

Chinese Ceramics. Municipal Gallery of Modern Art. Parnell Square, *Dublin* 1967.

Chinese Art Treasures. A selected group of objects from the Chinese National Palace Museum and The Chinese National Central Museum, Taichung, Taiwan. Exhibited in the United States 1961–62. *Geneva* 1961.

Gammal kinesisk konst. Helsingfors konsthall. *Helsinki* 1956.

Chinesische Keramik. Museum für Ostasiatische Kunst. *Köln* 1965.

Illustrated catalogue of early Chinese pottery and porcelain. Burlington Fine Arts Club. *London* 1910.

The Chinese exhibition. A commemorative catalogue of the international exhibition of Chinese art, Royal Academy of Arts. *London* 1936.

Celadon wares. Illustrated catalogue of an exhibition held by the OCS. *London* 1948.

Loan exhibition of the arts of the T'ang dynasty. OCS. *London* 1955.

The arts of the Sung dynasty. TOCS 1959–60. *London* 1960. (*OCS Sung exh. cat.*)

Chinese ceramics from the prehistoric period through Ch'ien Lung. A loan exhibition from collections in America and Japan. Los Angeles County Museum. *Los Angeles* 1952. (*Los Angeles exh. cat.*)

Chinese ceramics of the Sung dynasty. The Currier Gallery of Art. *Manchester*, New Hampshire. 1959.

Illustrated catalogue of Chinese Government exhibits for the International Exhibition of Art in London. Vol. II, Porcelain, *Nanking* 1936.

Exhibition of Chinese ceramics in the collection of the Museum Yamato Bunkakan. *Nara* 1961.

The Metropolitan Museum of Art. Exhibition of early Chinese pottery and sculpture. *New York* 1916.

The Sunglin collection of Chinese art and archaeology. Peking. Catalogue of an exhibition. *New York* 1930.

Collection of Chinese and other Far Eastern art. Assembled by Yamanaka & Company Inc. *New York* 1943.

Select specimens of archaeological collections in the Ryojun Government collection. *Port Arthur* 1935.

A loan exhibition of Chinese Art. Singapore Art Society. *Singapore* 1952.

A loan exhibition of Chinese art. Early periods. Singapore Art Society. *Singapore* 1954.

Nordlig Sung keramik ur svenska samlingar. Nationalmuseum. *Stockholm* 1949.

Sung—Ming. MFEA exhibition catalogue no. 3, *Stockholm* 1965.

Chinese art from the Collection of H. M. King Gustaf VI Adolf of Sweden. MFEA Exh. cat. No. 7, *Stockholm* 1967.

Kina som hobby. Gustaf Hilleströms samling. MFEA Exh. cat. No. 8. *Stockholm* 1968.

Porcelain of the National Palace Museum, *Taipei*. Hong Kong 1961–62.
Ju ware of the Sung dynasty.
Chün ware of the Sung dynasty.
Kuan ware of the Sung dynasty.
Kuan ware of the Southern Sung dynasty. I–II.
Ko ware of the Sung dynasty. I–II.
Lung-ch'üan ware of the Sung dynasty.

Illustrated catalogue of old oriental ceramics donated by Mr. Yokogawa. Tokyo National Museum. *Tokyo* 1953. (*Yokogawa cat.*)

China's beauty of 2000 years. Exhibition of ceramics and rubbed copies of inscriptions in Sian. *Tokyo* 1965. (*China's beauty.*)

Chinese arts of the Sung and Yüan periods. Tokyo National Museum. *Tokyo* 1961.

To-so mei do ten. *Tokyo* 1964.

Chinese Art. Catalogue. *Venezia* 1954. (*Venezia exh. cat.*)

JAPANESE LITERATURE

Choyokaku kansho. (Collection of old textile fabrics.) Tokyo c. 1890.

Hayashiya, S.—Hasebe, G., *Chinese ceramics.* Tokyo 1966.

Kobayashi, T., *Toyo toji kanshoroku chugoku hen* (Far Eastern pottery and stoneware). Tokyo 1949.

Koyama, Fujio, *Chinese ceramics.* One hundred masterpieces from collections in Japan, England, France and America. Tokyo 1960. (*Koyama.*)

— *Post-war discoveries of T'ang and Sung kiln sites.* 1962.

– *So ji.* Tokyo 1943.
– *The Southern and Northern styles of Chinese ceramics.* The *Bijutsu Kenkyu*, No. 143, Vol. 4. Tokyo 1947.
– *Ting yao bowls with golden designs.* The *Bijutsu Kenkyu.* No. 109. Tokyo 1941.
Mayuyama, Junkichi, *Chinese ceramics in the West.* Tokyo 1960. (*Mayuyama.*)
Sekai Toji Zenshu. Vol. 9, Sui and T'ang. Tokyo 1956. Vol. 10, Sung and Liao. Tokyo 1955.
Tamura, J.—Kobayashi, Y., *Tombs and mural paintings of Ch'ing-ling, Liao Imperial masuoleums of the 11th century A.D. in Eastern Mongolia.* Vol. I–II. Kyoto 1952–53.
Toji Zenshu (Ed. Koyama, Fujio).
Vol. 10. Toso-no seiji. Tokyo 1957.
Vol. 12. Toso-no hakuji. Tokyo 1959.
Vol. 13. So-no jishu yo. Tokyo 1961.
Vol. 14. Ryo-no toji. Tokyo 1960.
Tokiwa, D.—Sekino, T., *Buddhist monuments in China.* 1–5. Tokyo 1926–38.

CHINESE LITERATURE

CHI CHOU YAO. Peking 1958. 吉州窯

CHING - TE CHEN T´AO TZ´U CHIH KAO. Peking 1959. 景德鎮陶瓷史稿

CHUNG KUO CHIH WU T´U CHIEN. Shanghai 1960. 中國植物圖鑑

CHUNG KUO CH´ING TZ´U SHIH LÜEH. Shanghai 1957. 中國青瓷史略

CHUNG KUO KU TAI T´AO TZ´U I SHU HSIAO PIN. Peking 1958. 中國古代陶瓷藝術小品

CHUNG KUO KU WEN WU. Peking 1962. 中國古文物

CHUNG KUO LI TAI MING HUA CHI. Peking 1959. 中國歷代名畫集

CHUNG KUO TZ´U CH´I TI FA MING. Shanghai 1956. 中國瓷器的發明

CH´ÜAN KUO CHI PEN CHIEN SHE KUNG CH´ENG CHUNG CH´U T´U WEN WU CHAN LAN T´U LU. Shanghai 1956. 全國基本建設工程中出土文物展覽圖録

HSIN CHUNG KUO TI K´AO KU SHOU HU. Peking 1961. 新中國的考古收獲

KIANGSU SHENG CH´U T´U WEN WU HSÜAN CHI. Peking 1963. 江蘇省出土文物選集

KU KUNG PO WU YÜAN TS´ANG TZ´U HSÜAN CHI. Peking 1962. 故宮博物院藏瓷選集

KU TAI CHUANG SHIH HUA WEN HSÜAN CHI. Hsian 1953. 古代裝飾花紋選集

KUANG CHOU HSI TS´UN KU YAO I CHIH. Peking 1958. 廣州西村古窯遺址

LIANG SUNG MING HUA TS´E. Peking 1963. 兩宋名畫册

LIAO TZ´U HSÜAN CHI. Peking 1961. 遼瓷選集

NAN T´ANG ERH LING FA HSÜEH PAO KAO. Nanking 1957. 南唐二陵發掘報告

NEI MENG KU CH´U T´U WEN WU HSÜAN CHI. Peking 1963. 內蒙古出土文物選集

PAI SHA SUNG MU. Peking 1957. 白沙宋墓

SUNG TAI MIN CHIEN T´AO TZ´U WEN YANG. Shanghai 1960. 宋代民間陶瓷紋樣

SUNG TAI PEI FANG MIN CHIEN TZ´U CH´I. Peking 1955. 宋代北方民間瓷器

T'ANG SUNG T'AO TZ'U WEN YANG CHI. Peking 1959. 唐宋陶瓷紋樣集

T'ANG SUNG T'UNG CHING. Peking 1958. 唐宋銅鏡

T'ANG SUNG YÜAN MING CH'ING HUA HSÜAN. Shanghai 1960. 唐宋元明清畫選

WU SHENG CH'U T'U TSUNG YAO WEN WU CHAN LAN T'U LU. Peking 1958. 五省出土重要文物展覽圖錄

YAO TZ'U T'U LU. Peking 1956. 耀瓷圖錄

YÜEH CH'I T'U LU. Shanghai 1937. 越器圖錄

CHINESE PERIODICALS

K'AO KU

1959:1 p.47 赤峯大窩鋪發現一座遼墓

1959:5 p.222 山西省文管會侯馬工作站工作的總收獲

1959:5 p.242 河南安陽西郊唐宋墓的發掘

1959:6 p.318 江蘇南部宋墓記略

1959:7 p.350 河北石家莊市趙陵鋪鎮古墓清理簡報

1959:7 p.369 河北邢台發現宋墓和冶鐵遺址

1959:8 p.430 四川東山灌溉渠宋代遺址及古墓清理簡報

1959:11 p.622 湖北地區古墓葬的主要特點

1959:12 p.671 陝西銅川宋代窯址

1959:12 p.690 洛陽澗西金墓清理記

1960:2 p.15 遼寧省建平、新民的三座遼墓（馮永謙）

1960:2 p.29 錦西大臥鋪遼金時代畫象石墓（雁羽）

K'AO KU

1960:2 p.34 錦西西孤山遼蕭孝忠墓清理簡報（雁羽）

1960:2 p.43 遼寧綏中縣城後村金元遺址（王增新）

1960:3 p.39 河南鶴壁市古煤礦遺址調查簡報

1960:4 p.56 廣州沙河雙燕崗發現元墓

1960:7 p.57 山西孝義下吐京和梁家莊金元墓發掘簡報

1960:10 p.10 洛陽澗濱仰韶、殷文化遺址和宋墓清理

1960:10 p.37 山西大同郊區五座遼壁畫墓

1961:3 p.148 長沙東郊楊家山發現南宋墓

1961:12 p.681 山西侯馬金墓發掘簡報

1962:1 p.31 黑龍江蘭西縣發現金代文物

1962:4 p.182 遼寧朝陽金代壁畫墓

1962:5 p.246 北京南郊遼趙德鈞墓

1962:6 p.312 耀州瓷窯分析研究（王家廣）

1962:8 p.414 廣東惠陽白馬山古瓷窯調查記（曾廣億）

1962:8 p.418 上海宋墓（黃宣佩）

1962:10 p.535 龍泉溪口青瓷窯址調查紀略（金祖明）

1962:12 p.646 河北新城縣北場村金時立愛和時豐墓發掘記

1963:1 p.54 福建閩侯硋油宋代瓷窯調查

1963:2 p.71 河南鞏縣石家莊古墓葬發掘簡報

1963:3 p.140 北京出土的遼、金時代鐵器

1963:6 p.343 南京中華門外宋墓

1963:6 p.344 南京市郊區龍潭宋墓

1963:10 p.576 江西南昌朱姑橋元墓

K'AO KU

1964:2 p.79 吉林懷德秦家屯古城調查記（陳相偉）

1964:5 p.237 武昌卓刀泉兩座南宋墓葬的清理

1964:5 p.242 遼寧喀左縣大城子元代石槨墓（徐英章）

1964:7 p.349 宋魏王趙頵夫妻合葬墓（周到）

1964:7 p.370 江西撫州發現元代合葬墓

1964:11 p.558 浙江紹興繆家橋宋井發掘簡報

1964:11 p.561 江西永新北宋劉沆墓發掘報告

1964:11 p.564 河南鞏縣宋陵調查（郭湖生，戚德耀，李裕淦）

1965:1 p.21 湖北麻城北宋石室墓清理簡報（王善才，陳恒樹）

1965:1 p.25 山西太原郊區宋、金、元代磚墓（戴尊德）

1965:1 p.46 河南新安趙峪村發現金代遺物

1965:3 p.157 溫州西郭出土北宋瓷質碑銘

1965:5 p.236 浙江金華青瓷窰址調查（張翔）

1965:6 p.287 廣東出土的古代陶罈續介

1965:6 p.289 蘇州吳張士誠母曹氏墓清理簡報

1965:7 p.352 山西長治李村溝壁畫墓清理（王秀生）

1965:7 p.374 內蒙古科右前旗白辛屯古墓古城的調查

1965:8 p.394 河北曲陽縣澗磁村定窰遺址調查與試掘

1965:8 p.428 河南鞏縣稍柴清理一座宋墓

1965:10 p.507 河北曲陽澗磁村發掘的唐宋墓葬

1965:10 p.511 陝西漢中市王道池村宋墓清理（王玉清）

1965:11 p.571 江西南城，清江和永修的宋墓（薛堯）

1965:12 p.643 內蒙古巴林左旗出土北宋銀鋌（李逸友）

K'AO KU HSÜEH PAO

1954:2 (No.8) p.163 義縣清河門遼墓發掘報告(李文信)

1956:3 (No.13) p.1 赤峰縣大營子遼墓發掘報告

1959:3 (No.25) p.107 浙江餘姚青瓷窯址調查報告(金祖明)

1962:2 (No.30) p.31 河北井陘縣柿莊宋墓發掘報告

WEN WU

1951:2 p.46 汝窯的我見(陳萬里)

1951:2 p.53 禹州之行(陳萬里)

1952:1 p.56 調查平原、河北二省古代窯址報告(陳萬里)

1953:9 p.91 邢越二窯及定窯(陳萬里)

1954:4 p.44 談當陽峪窯(陳萬里)

1955:4 p.72 我對於耀瓷的初步認識(陳萬里)

1955:4 p.75 耀窯摭遺(商劍青)

1956:7 p.17 略談三年來武漢市的文物保護與發現(藍蔚)

1956:7 p.36 湯陰縣鶴壁古瓷窯遺址(楊寶順)

1956:8 frontispiece 河南安陽及陝西略陽出土的宋代瓷器

1956:8 back cover 湖南長沙發現的幾件宋代瓷器

1956:11 p.15 我對於遼墓出土幾件瓷器的意見(陳萬里)

1956:12 p.39 陝西丹鳳縣商雒鎮宋墓清理簡報

1956:12 p.55 汝窯址調查簡報

1957:10 p.57 鶴壁集印象(陳萬里)

1958:2 p.10 遼瓷簡述(李文信)

WEN WU

1958:2	p.32	同安縣汀溪水庫古瓷窑調查記
1958:2	p.36	光澤茅店宋代瓷窑址(曾凡)
1958:2	p.38	川西古代瓷器調查記(徐鵬章)
1958:3	p.65	合肥西郊南唐墓清理簡報
1958:5	p.49	山西忻縣北宋墓清理簡報(馮文海)
1958:5	p.52	鄭州南關外北宋磚室墓
1958:5	p.72	伊盟郡王旗發現黑釉刻花瓶
1958:6	p.57	西安曲江池西村元墓清理簡報
1958:8	p.42	余姚窑瓷器探討(王士倫)
1958:10	p.32	汝窑址的調查與嚴和店的發掘
1958:10	p.36	山西介休洪山鎮宋代瓷窑址介紹(吳連城)
1958:11	p.75	河南方城鹽店莊村宋墓
1959:6	p.22	定瓷的裝飾藝術(梁之, 張守智)
1959:6	p.50	侯馬金代董氏墓介紹
1959:6	p.57	侯馬的一座帶壁畫宋墓(萬新民)
1959:6	p.59	觀台窑址發掘報告
1959:6	p.62	福建省最近發現的古代窑址
1959:7	p.63	昭盟巴林左旗林東鎮金墓(李逸友)
1959:7	p.67	瓷器淺說(馮先銘)
1959:8	p.72	瓷器淺說(馮先銘)
1959:10	p.44	建國以來對於古代窑址的調查(陳萬里)

1959:10 p.85 高安、清江發現兩座宋墓

1959:11 p.19 江蘇吳縣元墓清理簡報

1962:3 p.59 閩侯縣懷安村的一座宋墓

1962:10 p.34 山西省大同市元代馮道真、王青墓清理簡報

1963:1 p.27 浙江省龍泉青瓷窰址調查發掘的主要收獲

1963:1 p.43 記五代吳越國的另一官窰（汪濟英）

1963:5 p.42 上京款大晟南呂編鐘（李文信）

1963:5 p.45 淮安宋墓出土的漆器（羅宗真）

1963:6 p.26 中國歷代燒制瓷器的成就與特點（陳萬里）

1964:2 p.54 河南省密縣、登封唐宋窰址調查簡報

1964:3 p.47 河南密縣、登封唐宋古窰址調查（馮先銘）

1964:4 p.63 江西出土的幾件宋瓷

1964:8 p.1 河南省鶴壁集瓷窰遺址發掘簡報

1964:8 p.15 河南省臨汝縣宋代汝窰遺址調查（馮先銘）

1964:8 p.27 河南省禹縣古窰址調查記略（葉喆民）

1964:8 p.37 磁州窰遺址調查（李輝柄）

1964:8 p.49 順義縣遼淨光舍利塔基清理簡報

1964:9 p.46 孟家井瓷窰遺址（楊芝榮）

1964:12 p.52 江蘇無錫市元墓中出土一批文物

1965:2 p.19 廣東博羅、揭陽、澄邊古瓷窰調查（曾廣億）

1965:2 p.36 記1964年在故宮博物院舉辦的"古代藝術展覽"中的瓷器（馮先銘）

1965:9 p.26 新中國陶瓷考古的主要收獲（馮先銘）

1965:10 p.46 安徽鳳台"連城"遺址內發現一批唐——元時代的文物

1966:5 p.56 武漢市十里舖北宋墓出土漆器等文物

FIGURE INDEX

FIGURE 1.

a) Detail from the Northern celadon ewer Pl. 1:j.
b) Mould, Pl. 2:b.
c) Northern celadon bowl. Pl. 2:g.
d) Ting yao bowl. *Wen Wu* 1959:6, p. 23.
e) Northern celadon ewer and bowl, Pl. 2:h and Pl. 4:c.
f) Detail from a N. celadon dish, Pl. 3:1.

FIGURE 2.

a) N. celadon dish, Pl. 3:i.
b) Detail from the front of the N. celadon pillow Pl. 3:j.
c) N. celadon dish, Pl. 3:k.
d) N. celadon bowl. Hetherington coll.
e) N. celadon bowl. Tokyo National Museum.
f) N. celadon vase. Winkworth collection.

FIGURE 3.

1–15 details of conventionalized flowers.
1) Tz'u-chou yao. 2) N. celadon. 3) Tz'u-chou yao. 4) N. celadon. 5) Ch'ing-pai. 6) Ting yao. 7) N. celadon. 8) Ch'ing-pai. 9) Ch'ing-pai. 10) N. celadon. 11) Ting yao. 12) Ch'ing-pai. 13–15) Tz'u-chou. 16) Detail from the Ting yao bowl Pl. 94:a. 17) Detail from a Ting yao bowl with moulded design.

FIGURE 4.

Ch'ing-pai specimens from the Kempe collection.
a) CKc 550. b) 543. c) 541. d) 539. e) 565. f) 576.

FIGURE 5.

a) Detail from a Ting yao dish. David Foundation (No. 175).
b) Detail from a Ting yao bowl, Mrs. Alfred Clark coll.
c) Detail from a Tz'u-chou vase, Pl. 49:1.
d) Detail from a Tz'u-chou pillow. Pl. 45:h.

FIGURE 6.

a) Design on the Tz'u-chou pillow Pl. 44:f.
b) Design on the Tz'u-chou pillow Pl. 44:e.
c) Detail from the Tz'u-chou basin Pl. 44:h.
d) Design on a Tz'u-chou pillow. Museum of Fine Arts, Boston (*Paine* No. 10).

FIGURE 7.

a) Design on the N. celadon bowl Pl. 5:h.
b) Design on the Tz'u-chou pillow Pl. 45:g.
c) Design on the Tz'u-chou pillow Pl. 52:h.
d) Design on the Tz'u-chou vase Pl. 44:k.
e) Design on the Tz'u-chou pillow Pl. 42:c.
f) Design on the Tz'u-chou bowl Pl. 56:b.

FIGURE 8.

Designs on Ting yao specimens in the Kempe collection.
a) CKc 417. b) 468. c) 413. d) 466. e) 456. f) 415. g) 416.

FIGURE 9.

a) Design from a Ting yao dish in the David Foundation (No. 184).
b) Design from a Ting yao dish Pl. 59:a.
c) Design from a Ting yao dish Pl. 61:h.
d) Design from a N. celadon bowl. (*Rücker-Embden* Pl. 14:a).

FIGURE 10.

a) Northern celadon vase Pl. 9:f.
b) Northern celadon dish Pl. 10:i.
c) Tz'u-chou pillow Pl. 42:h.

FIGURE 11.

a) Detail from a Yüeh yao bowl. David Foundation.
b) Detail from a Yüeh yao bowl. The Metropolitan Museum of Art.
c)–d) Yüeh yao sherds, after *Yüeh ch'i t'u lu.*
e) Ting yao dish, Pl 68.
f) Design from a Ting yao dish. David Foundation (No. 159).

FIGURE 12.

a) Detail from a Lung-ch'üan basin. Yüan. David Foundation.
b) Detail from the Tz'u-chou vase Pl. 49:e.
c) Detail from the Ting yao dish Pl. 87:a.
d) Detail from the ch'ing-pai bowl Pl. 12:e.
e) Detail from the ch'ing-pai bowl Pl. 12:k.

FIGURE 13.

a) Detail from the Ting yao dish Pl. 61:g.
b) Detail from the Ting yao dish Pl. 70:a.
c) Detail from a Ting yao dish. The British Museum.
d) Detail from the Ting yao dish Pl. 69:a.
e) Detail from the Ting yao dish Pl. 70:b.
f) Detail from a Ting yao dish. Carl Kempe collection (CKc 452).

FIGURE 14.

a) Detail from the ch'ing-pai box Pl. 25:a.
b) Detail from a Tz'u-chou vase. Yüan. (Hobson-Hetherington, *The Art of the Chinese potter*, Pl. 82.)
c) Detail from a Tz'u-chou vase. Yüan.
d) Detail from the top of the pillow Pl. 3:j.
e) Details from the Ting yao bowl Pl. 94:a.
f) Yüeh yao sherd. From *Yüeh ch'i t'u lu.*
g) Detail from a Yüeh yao dish. (Hobson, "*A dish of Yüeh ware*", *Burl. Mag.* 63, 1933.)
h) Yüeh yao sherd. From *Yüeh ch'i t'u lu.*

FIGURE 15.

a) Green glazed ewer. 10th cent. Winkworth coll. (*Venezia exh. cat.* No. 335).
b) Detail from the ch'ing-pai ewer Pl. 29:f.
c) Detail of a Ting type ewer. Corean coll.
d) Detail of white porcelain vase. T'ang. Minneapolis Institute of Arts.
e) Detail of the vase Pl. 29:g.
f) Detail of a ewer, Ting type. (*Eumorfopoulos cat.* Vol. III, C 239. Pl. 39).
g) Ch'ing-pai ewer Pl. 29:h.
h) Mural painting from Chotscho. (*Chotscho* Pl. 15).
i)–k) T'ang phoenixes after Gyllensvärd *op.cit.* Fig. 57:i–k.

FIGURE 16.

a) Detail of a mural painting (Stein, *The thousand Buddhas*, Pl. XLVI).
b) Mural painting from Temple T', Chotscho (*Chotscho*, Pl. 8).
c) Prayer sheet from Ch'in-fo-tung, dated 947 (Stein, *Serindia*, Pl. C).
d) Detail from a Northern celadon bowl (*Rücker-Embden*, Pl. 43).
e) Detail of compound cloth. Seattle Art Museum.

FIGURE 17.

a) Design from a ch'ing-pai bowl. Coll. H. M. the King of Sweden.
b) Design from the ch'ing-pai bowl Pl. 19:b.
c) Architectural design.
d) Design from the ch'ing-pai bowl Pl. 20:b.
e) Design on top of Chang type Tz'u-chou pillow (*Wen Wu* 1965:2. Pl. 4).
f) Design on Tz'u-chou pillow. Heeramaneck coll. (*Cox* 383).
g) Design on Tz'u-chou pillow. Heeramaneck coll. (*Cox* 389).
h) Detail from a silver bowl. Art Institute of Chicago (*Gyllensvärd* Fig. 82:f).

FIGURE 18.

a) Design on a Sung bronze mirror. Cammann coll. (*ACASA*, Vol. IX, 1955, p. 62).
b) Design on a Ming bronze mirror. MFEA.
c) Liao ceramic pot. (R. Torii, *Chio-ti of the Khitans*).
d) Detail from the top of a ch'ing-pai pillow. Victoria & Albert Museum.
e) Detail from the Northern celadon bowl Pl. 9:j.
f) Detail from the Lung-ch'üan dish Pl. 39:e.
g) Fragment of Northern celadon bowl (Sommarström *op.cit.* Pl. 24:12).

FIGURE 19.

a) Detail from the side of a Tz'u-chou pillow. Museum of Fine Arts, Boston (*Paine* Pl. 10).
b) Design on the Tz'u-chou pillow Pl. 52:c.
c) Design on the Tz'u-chou pillow Pl. 52:f.
d) Design on the Tz'u-chou pillow Pl. 47:a.
e) Design on the Tz'u-chou pillow Pl. 42:1.
f) Design on the Ting yao bowl Pl. 84:a.
g) Design on the ch'ing-pai bowl Pl. 19:a.

FIGURE 20.

a) Design on the Ting yao dish Pl. 96:a.
b) Design on the Tz'u-chou pillow Pl. 43:b.
c) Design on the Tz'u-chou pillow Pl. 43:c.
d) Detail from the Tz'u-chou pillow Pl. 42:k.

FIGURE 21.

Designs from Ting yao specimens in the Kempe collection.
a) CKc 457. b) 455. c) 458. d) 461. e) 408. f) 460.

FIGURE 22.

a) Design on a mould for Ting yao, dated 1184. David Foundation (No. 181).
b) Design from the Ting yao bowl Pl. 84:b.

FIGURE 23.

a) Design on a mould for Ting yao dated 1189 and detail of same. The British Museum.
b) Detail of design on a mould for Ting yao dated 1203. The British Museum.
c) Detail from the Ting yao bowl Pl. 84: c.

FIGURE 24.

a) Design on a Ting yao dish (Koyama, *So-ji*, Pl. 11).
b) Design from the Tz'u-chou pillow Pl. 42:g.
c) Fragment of a Northern celadon dish (Hobson, *Chinese porcelain from Fostat*).

FIGURE 25.

a) Design on the Ting yao dish Pl. 84:h.
b) Tz'u-chou yao fragment from Chiao-tso.
c) Design on the Tz'u-chou pillow Pl. 45:i.

FIGURE 26.

a) Design from a Tz'u-chou pillow. Museum of Fine Arts, Boston (*Paine* No. 20).
b) Design from the Tz'u-chou pillow Pl. 46:d.
c) Design from the Tz'u-chou pillow Pl. 42:e.
d) Design from a Tz'u-chou pillow. Japanese coll. (After Kobayashi *op.cit.*).
e) Design from a Tz'u-chou pillow. Japanese coll. (After Kobayashi *op.cit.*).

FIGURE 27.

a) Design on a Ting yao bowl. (*Wen Wu* 1959:6, p. 23).
b) Design on the Northern celadon bowl Pl. 8:g.
c) Design on the Ting yao dish Pl. 61:f.

FIGURE 28.

a) Ting type vessel in basket shape. National Palace Museum, Taipei.
b) Ting type vessel in basket shape. National Palace Museum, Taipei.
c) Cup-stand of Tz'u-chou yao. Warren E. Cox coll.
d) Design on Tz'u-chou pillow. Dated 1179 (Chin). Philadelphia Museum of Art.
e) Design on a Ting yao dish. Carl Kempe coll. (CKc 355).
f) Design from a Tz'u-chou pillow. Richard B. Hobart coll. (*Paine* No. 38).

FIGURE 29.

a) Ch'ing-pai bowl from a tomb in Hupeh dated 1213 (*Kao Ku* 1964:5, p. 239).
b) Ch'ing-pai bowl from a tomb in Hupeh dated 1113 (*Kao Ku* 1965:1, p. 23).
c) Detail from a ch'ing-pai bowl in the Kempe collection (CKc 542).
d) Ceramics excavated in the Chekiang province and tentatively dated to S. Sung (*Kao Ku* 1964:11, p. 559).

FIGURE 30.

Ceramics excavated in Lung-ch'üan hsien (*Kao Ku* 1962:10, p. 536–538).
a) Northern Sung vessels.
b) Yüan vessels.
c) Southern Sung vessels.

FIGURE 31.

a) Tz'u-chou sherds from Kuan-t'ai (*Wen Wu* 1964:8, Pl. 6:2).
b) Tz'u-chou sherds from Tung-ai k'ou (*Wen Wu* 1964:8, Pl. 6:4).
c) Northern celadon sherds from Yao-chou (*Kao Ku* 1959:12, p. 673).
d) Tz'u-chou tiger pillow from Hao-pi chi (*Wen Wu* 1964:8, Pl.2).
e) Tz'u-chou pillow from a tomb in Hopei (*Kao Ku* 1959:7, p. 369).

FIGURE 32. — FIGURE 34.

Sherds etc. excavated at the Ting yao site in Chien-tz'u ts'un, Hopei.
(*Kao Ku* 1965:8, p. 397, p. 403, p. 407).

FIGURE 35.

a) Ceramics from a Chin tomb dated 1184 (*Kao Ku* 1962:4, p. 185).
b) White porcelain from a Chin tomb (*Wen Wu* 1959:7, p. 64).
c) Wall carving in a Northern Sung tomb in Honan (*Kao Ku* 1965:8, p. 428).
d) Inscriptions on Ting yao (*Wen Wu* 1959:7, p. 71).

FIGURE 36.

Designs on temmoku bowls from Chi-chou (*Chi chou yao*. Pls. 23–25).

FIGURE 37.

a) Liao phoenix-head vase, green glaze (*KKHP* No. 8, 1954, p. 177, Fig. 10:4).
b) Liao phoenix-head vase (*Sekai* 10; Fig. 185:1).
c) Liao vase, white porcelain (*KKHP* No. 8, 1954, p. 170, Fig. 4:3).
d) Liao vase, white porcelain (*KKHP* No. 13, Pl. 6:3).
e) Liao vase, white porcelain (*Sekai* 10; Fig. 171).
f) The Tz'u-chou vase Pl. 40:j.
g) Liao white porcelain dish. Carl Kempe collection (CKc 390).
h) Detail from a square three-coloured Liao dish (*Sekai* 10; Pl. 139 lower).
i) Detail from the dish g above.
j) Detail from a three-coloured Liao bowl (*Sekai* 10; Fig. 195).
k) Detail from a Tz'u-chou yao plate.
l) Detail from the vase Fig. 38:b.
m) Detail from a white Liao dish. Coll. H. M. the King of Sweden.
n) Fragments of white porcelain dish. From Ching Ho Men.
o) White porcelain bowl with peony design. From tomb no. 3 in Ta Yin Tzu (*KKHP* 1956:3, Pl. 7:4).
p) Detail from a triangular white porcelain dish. Liao. Carl Kempe coll. (CKc 390).

FIGURE 38.

a) Vase with black sgraffito design. Liao. (*Eumorfopoulos cat.* III, C 397).
b) Detail from a *mei-p'ing* vase, black sgraffito design. Liao (*Sekai* 10; Pl. 137).
c) Bowls, three-coloured ware. Liao (*Sekai* 10; Fig. 195).
d) Detail from the dish Fig. 37:g.
e) Detail from a white porcelain jar (*KKHP* No. 8, 1954, Fig. 24: 2).
f)–h) Liao stone engravings. From Tamura-Kobayashi, *Tombs and mural paintings of Ch'ing-ling.*

FIGURE 39.

a) Bronze mirror from a tomb in Hupeh, datable to 1113 (*Kao Ku* 1965:1, p. 23).
b) Design on bricks from a tomb in Shansi. Chin. (*Kao Ku* 1965:7, p. 355).

FIGURE 40.

a) Inscriptions on pillow fragments from Tung-ai k'ou.
b) Tomb mural from a Yüan tomb (datable to 1265) in Shansi (*Wen Wu* 1962:10).

FIGURE 41.

a) Ting yao bowl with dragon design. Seligman coll. (*Cat.* no. D 76).
b) Northern celadon dish with apsaras. Seligman coll. (*Cat.* no. D 148).

FIGURE 42.

a) Lotus spray. Detail from a silver bowl in the Kempe collection (CKc 115).
b) Drawing of the Chi-chou ewer Pl. 29:g.
c) Southern Sung ceramics excavated in Chekiang (*Kao Ku* 1964:11, p. 558).
d) Design on side of pillows from Tung-ai k'ou.

FIGURE 43.

a) Ceramics excavated at Lung-ch'üan (*Wen Wu* 1963:1, p. 32).
b) Celadon sherd from Ta-yao.

PLATE INDEX

PLATE 1.

Northern celadon.

a) Ewer. H: 19.7 cm. Museum of Fine Arts, Boston (*Hoyt* no. 229).
b) Ewer. H: 18,5 cm. Japanese collection.
c) Ewer. H: 14 cm. The Royal Ontario Museum, Toronto.
d) Ewer. Mukden Museum.
e) Ewer. H: 8½″. Formerly in the coll. of Lord Cunliffe.
f) Ewer. H: 7⅜″. The Cleveland Museum of Art, Purchase from the J. H. Wade Fund.
g) Covered jar. H: 10.6 cm. *Yao tz'u t'u lu.* Part 1. Pl. 4.
h) Jar. From Yao-chou. *Kao Ku* 1959:12, Pl. 7:11.
i) Jar. H: 12.2 cm. The Royal Ontario Museum, Toronto.
j) Ewer. H: 9″. A. Brundage coll. M. H. de Young Memorial Museum, San Francisco.
k) Ewer. H: 21 cm. The Metropolitan Museum of Art, New York.
l) Detail of f above.

PLATE 2.

Northern celadon.

a) Bowl D: 4⅞″. Coll. Sir. Alan and Lady Barlow.
b) Clay mould. The British Museum, London.
c) Bowl. D: 7¼″. The Victoria & Albert Museum, London.
d) Bowl. D: 11 cm. Collection F. Vannotti, Lugano.
e) Covered bowl. D: 4½″. Coll. Sir Alan and Lady Barlow.
f) Covered bowl. Japanese collection.
g) Bowl. D: 7″. Formerly Oppenheim coll.
h) Bowl. D: 5.9″. The National Museum, Tokyo.
i) Basin. *Yao tz'u t'u lu.* Part 1. Pl. 20.
j) Dish. D: 20.5 cm. The Royal Ontario Museum, Toronto.
k) Dish. D: 19.3 cm. Lin-ju hsien, Yen-ho tien yao.
l) Jar. Japanese collection.

PLATE 3.

Northern celadon.

a) Ewer. H: 25.5 cm. Collections Baur (No. A 24).
b) Ewer. H: 9¾″. A. Brundage coll. M. H. de Young Memorial Museum.
c) Ewer. H: 8.7″. The British Museum.
d) Jar. H: 4½″. The Buffalo Museum of Science.
e) *Kundika*, sprinkler. H: 21.8 cm. The Museum of Fine Arts, Boston (*Hoyt* 231).
f) Lamp. H: 8.7 cm. Carl Kempe coll. (CKc 87).
g) Bowl. D: 13 cm. The Royal Ontario Museum, Toronto.
h) Bowl from Yao-chou. *Kao Ku* 1959:12, Pl. 7:10.

i) Bowl. D: 20.7 cm. Fitzwilliam Museum, Cambridge.
j) Pillow. H: 10.6 cm. Japanese collection.
k) Bowl. Japanese collection.
l) Dish. D: 10 cm. Carl Kempe coll. (CKc 68).

PLATE 4.

Northern celadon.
a) Ewer. H: 29.5 cm. The Royal Ontario Museum, Toronto.
b) Ceremonial bowl and stand. H: 9.1; H: 12.5 cm. The Museum of Fine Arts, Boston (*Hoyt* 232).
c) Ewer. H: 11.4″. Tokyo National Museum.
d) Bowl. *Yao tz'u t'u lu*. Part 1. Pl. 16.
e) Bowl. D: 17 cm. Coll. Mrs. Alfred Clark.
f) Bowl. Formerly Messrs. Barling, London.
g) Vase. H: 10.6″. Coll. M. Calmann.
h) Vase. H: 29.8 cm. Tokyo National Museum.
i) Vase. H: 22.1 cm. Japanese collection.
j) Box. D: 18 cm. Sir Percival David Foundation.
k) Dish. D: 18 cm. Collections Baur (No. A 25).
l) Dish. D: 20.5 cm. The Royal Ontario Museum, Toronto.

PLATE 5.

Northern celadon.
a) Vase. H: 7 13/16″. Seattle Art Museum.
b) Vase. H: 17.2 cm. *Yao tz'u t'u lu*. Part 2, Pl. 4.
c) Vase. *Toso-no seiji*. Pl. 2.
d) Vase. H: 17 cm. Japanese collection.
e) Bowl. Bristol City Art Gallery.
f) Fragment of box, from Yao-chou. *Kao Ku* 1959:12, Pl. 7:2.
g) Dish. D: 7¾″. Coll. Sir Alan and Lady Barlow.
h) Bowl. D: 15.1 cm. Japanese collection.
i) Fragment from Yao-chou. *Kao Ku* 1959:12, Pl. 7:7.
j) Bowl. D: 5.7″. Mrs. Walter Sedgwick coll.
k) Bowl. D: 6½″.
l) Bowl. D: 7″. Coll. Sir Alan and Lady Barlow.

PLATE 6.

Northern celadon.
a) Dish. D: 6¼″. Victoria & Albert Museum.
b) Bowl. D: 6″. The Metropolitan Museum.
c) Incense-burner. H: 15.4 cm. *Yao tz'u t'u lu*. Part 2. Pl. 5.
d) Bowl. D: 19 cm. Collections Baur (No. A 27).
e) Dish. D: 7¼″. Coll. Sir Alan and Lady Barlow.
f) Incense-burner. Tokyo National Museum.
g) Ewer. H: 10 cm. The Royal Ontario Museum, Toronto.
h) Ewer. H: 8.7 cm. *Yao tz'u t'u lu*. Part 2, Pl. 3.
i) Incense-burner. H: 6⅞″. A. Brundage coll. M. H. de Young Memorial Museum.
j) Bowl. D: 12.8 cm. From Yao-chou.
k) Bowl. D: 5¾″. Bristol City Art Gallery.
l) Incence-burner. H: 11.8 cm. The Royal Ontario Museum, Toronto.

PLATE 7.

Northern celadon.

a) Bowl. D: 12.7 cm. The Royal Ontario Museum, Toronto.
b) Jar. H: 10 cm. Japanese collection.
c) Stand. H: 5″. Nasli Heeramaneck coll.
d) Jar. *Toso-no seiji* Pl. 33.
e) Jar. H: 5.5 cm. *Yao tz'u t'u lu.* Part 2, Pl. 1.
f) Stand. H: 7 1/2″. Formerly Sedgwick collection.
g) Bowl. D: 4 1/2″. Seligman collection.
h) Bowl. Collection Eugene Bernat.
i) Stand from Yao-chou. *Kao Ku* 1959:12. Pl. 7:13.
j) Bowl. D: 7.7″. Coll. M. Calmann.
k) Bowl. Art Institute of Chicago.
l) Stand. H: 7″. A. Brundage coll. M. H. de Young Memorial Museum.

PLATE 8.

Northern celadon.

a) Dish. *Sekai* Vol. 10. Fig. 18.
b) Fragment from Yao-chou. *Kao Ku* 1959:12, Pl. 7:1.
c) Bowl. D: 17.2 cm. Seligman coll.
d) Bowl. D: 11.7 cm. Seligman coll.
e) Fragment from Yao-chou. *Kao Ku* 1959:12, Pl. 7:6.
f) Bowl. D: 6 5/8″. Victoria & Albert Museum.
g) Bowl. D: 5.6″. The British Museum.
h) Bowl. D: 12.5 cm. Collections Baur (No. A 26).
i) Bowl. dated 1162, Chin. D: 8 1/8″. Coll. Nasli Heeramaneck.
j) Bowl. D: 3.8″. Sir Percival David Foundation.
k) Bowl. D: 5.5″. Coll. Lt.-Col. & Mrs. W.B.R. Neave-Hill, London.
l) Bowl. D: 13.8 cm. MFEA.

PLATE 9.

Northern celadon.

a) Bowl. D. 7.3″. Formerly Eumorfopoulos coll.
b) Bowl. D: 19 cm. *Rücker-Embden*, Pl. 14 a.
c) Bowl. Tokyo National Museum.
d) Bowl from Yao-chou. D: 18.6 cm.
e) Bowl. D: 21 cm. Japanese collection.
f) Vase. H: 31 cm. Museum Yamato Bunkakan.
g) Sherd from Yao-chou.
h) Sherd from Yao-chou. *Kao Ku* 1959:12, Pl. 7:5.
i) Vase. H: 9.25″. Victoria & Albert Museum.
j) Bowl. D: 4 3/4″. Seligman coll.
k) Bowl.
l) Bowl. D: 15.5 cm. Japanese collection.

PLATE 10.

Northern celadon.

a) Pillow. L: 28 cm. Museum of Fine Arts, Boston. (*Hoyt* 233).
b) Cup. Coll. Terada, Kyoto.
c) Cup and stand. *Yao tz'u t'u lu.* Part 1, Pl. 3.

d) Bowl. D. 10.6 cm. Carl Kempe coll. (CKc 78).
e) Bowl. D: 11 cm. Coll. H. M. the King of Sweden.
f) Dish. D: 14 cm. Seligman coll.
g) Saucer. D: 6.4″. Formerly Eumorfopoulos coll.
h) Bowl. D: $6\frac{1}{8}$″. Coll. Sir Alan and Lady Barlow.
i) Dish. D: 7.7″. Sir Percival David Foundation.
j) Dish. D: 19.6 cm. Seligman coll.
k) Dish. D: 16.5 cm. Seligman coll.
l) Sherd from Yao-chou. *Kao Ku* 1959:12, Pl. 7:4.

PLATE 11.

Ch'ing-pai ewer with basin. H: 21.2, H: 12.4 cm. Museum of Fine Arts, Boston (*Hoyt* 380).

PLATE 12.

Ch'ing-pai.
a) Vase. H: $12\frac{7}{8}$″. The British Museum.
b) Ewer, from a N. Sung tomb in Kiangsi. *Kao Ku* 1965:11, Pl. 9:3.
c) Vase. H: 26.8 cm. Peking Palace Museum.
d) Bowl. D: 12.4 cm. Seligman coll.
e) Bowl. D: $8\frac{1}{2}$″. R. Bruce coll.
f) Dish. D: 20.3 cm. Hakone Art Museum.
g) Dish. D: 18 cm. Seligman coll.
h) Dish. D: 7.5″. Coll. J. C. Thomson.
i) Bowl. D: $7\frac{5}{8}$″. Coll Sir Alan and Lady Barlow.
j) Dish. *Toso-no hakuji.* Pl. 55.
k) Bowl. D: $4\frac{1}{4}$″. Bristol City Art Gallery.
l) Bowl. D: $7\,^{1}/_{7}$″. Coll. Sir Alan and Lady Barlow.

PLATE 13.

Ch'ing-pai.
a) Bowl. D: 17.5 cm. Carl Kempe coll. (CKc 543).
b) Bowl. D: 18 cm. Museum of Fine Arts, Boston.

PLATE 14.

Ch'ing-pai vase. Honolulu Academy of Arts, Honolulu.

PLATE 15.

Ch'ing pai.
a) Box with two covers. H: 7.6 cm. Carl Kempe coll. (CKc 550).
b) Box. D: 12 cm. MFEA.

PLATE 16.

Ch'ing-pai.
a) Bowl. D: 18.5 cm. MFEA.
b) Bowl. Coll. O. Falkman.

PLATE 17.

Ch'ing-pai.
a) Bowl. D: $7\frac{1}{2}$ cm. City Art Gallery, Bristol.
b) Dish. D: 14.8 cm. Carl Kempe coll. (CKc 547).

PLATE 18.

Ch'ing-pai.

a) Vase. H: 15 cm. MFEA.

b) Bowl. Coll. R. Hultmark.

PLATE 19.

Ch'ing-pai.

a) Bowl. D: 19.7 cm. Museum of Fine Arts, Boston (*Hoyt* 368).

b) Bowl. Röhsska Konstslöjdmuseet, Gothenburg.

PLATE 20.

Ch'ing-pai.

a) Bowl. D: 7 ½″. The Cleveland Museum of Art, The Charles W. Harkness Endowment Fund.

b) Bowl. Coll. J. Hellner.

PLATE 21.

Ch'ing-pai.

a) Bowl. D: 7¾″. City Art Gallery, Bristol.

b) Bowl. D: 19.5 cm. MFEA.

PLATE 22.

Ch'ing-pai.

a) Vase from a tomb in Nanking dated 1027. H: 37 cm.

b) Vase. H: 13⅜″. City Art Gallery, Bristol.

c) Vase. H: 9.7″. The British Museum.

d) Vase. H: 76 cm. Danzan Jinja.

e) Vase. Metropolitan Museum of Art.

f) Vase. H: 29 cm. Japanese coll.

g) Vase. H: 28.5 cm. Collections Baur (No. A 123).

h) Vase from a Yüan tomb in Ssuch'uan. *Ch'üan kuo chi pen* . . . Pl. 253.

i) Vase. Royal Scottish Museum, Edinburgh.

j) Vase. H: 29.2 cm. The Royal Ontario Museum, Toronto.

k) Vase. H: 42 cm. Art Institute of Chicago.

l) Vase. H: 39 cm. Japanese collection.

PLATE 23.

Ch'ing-pai.

a) Ewer. H: 24 cm. Musée Guimet, Paris.

b) Cup. H: 20.3 cm. Mr. and Mrs. Frederick M. Mayer.

c) Ewer. Japanese collection.

d) Cup. D: 13 cm. Carl Kempe coll. (CKc 528).

e) Jar and cover. H: 7 cm. Carl Kempe coll. (CKc 527).

f) Incense-burner. H: 10.2 cm. Japanese collection.

g) Ewer. H: 18 cm. Japanese collection.

h) Stem-cup. H: 6″. Sir Harry and Lady Garner.

i) Stem-cup. H: 5¼″. Honolulu Academy of Arts.

j) Vase. H: 17.5 cm. MFEA.

k) Vase. H: 16.9 cm. Philadelphia Museum of Art.

l) Vase. From a Yüan tomb in Ssuch'uan. *Ch'üan kuo chi pen* . . . Pl. 254:3.

PLATE 24.

Ch'ing pai.

a) Bowl. D: 18 cm. MFEA.

b) Bowl. D: 18 cm. MFEA.

PLATE 25.

Ch'ing-pai.

a) Box. D: 9.5 cm. Carl Kempe coll. (CKc 551 a).

b) Box. D: 9.8 cm. Carl Kempe coll. (CKc 551 b).

PLATE 26.

Ch'ing-pai.

a) Bowl. D: 17.7 cm. Carl Kempe collection (CKc 563).

b) Bowl. Formerly O. Karlbeck coll.

PLATE 27.

Ch'ing-pai.

a) Bowl, one of a pair. D: 18.6 cm. Carl Kempe coll. (CKc 565).

b) Bowl. D: 18 cm. MFEA.

PLATE 28.

Ch'ing-pai.

a) Ewer. H: 12.7 cm. The British Museum.

b) Ewer. H: 10.5 cm. Carl Kempe coll. (CKc 569).

c) Ewer, from a Yüan tomb in Ssuch'uan. *Ch'üan kuo chi pen* . . . Pl. 254:1.

d) Miniature ewer. H: 4.4 cm. Carl Kempe collection (CKc 523).

e) Ewer. *Toso-no hakuji*. Pl. 50.

f) Cup. H: 7.5 cm. Carl Kempe coll. (CKc 533).

g) Cup. H: 3⅛″. Fitzwilliam Museum, Cambridge.

h) Cup. Honolulu Academy of Arts.

i) Cup. H: 3″. Coll. Sir Alan and Lady Barlow.

j) Ewer. H: 7″. Honolulu Academy of Arts.

k) Miniature ewer. H: 5.8 cm. Carl Kempe coll. (CKc 522).

l) Incense-burner. H: 5¼″. A. Brundage coll. M. H. de Young Memorial Museum.

PLATE 29.

Ch'ing-pai.

a) Incense-burner. H: 8 cm. Carl Kempe coll. (CKc 557).

b) Incense-burner. H: 3″. Coll. Sir Alan and Lady Barlow.

c) Incense-burner. H: 3.7″. Coll. Mrs. Leopold Dreyfus.

d) Vase. H: 25.4 cm. The British Museum.

e) Vase. H: 7″. Mrs. Alfred Clark.

f) Miniature ewer. H: 11.5 cm. Carl Kempe coll. (CKc 517).

g) Ewer. Chi-chou ware. H: 34.3 cm. The British Museum.

h) Ewer. H: 14″. The Brooklyn Museum.

i) Vase. H: 15⅜″. Cleveland Museum of Art, Mr. and Mrs. Severance A. Millikin collection.

j) Ewer. H: 15.5 cm. Japanese collection.

k) Ewer. H: 9.8 cm. Carl Kempe coll. (CKc 524).

l) Ewer. H: 21.9 cm. The Royal Ontario Museum. Toronto.

PLATE 30.

Ch'ing-pai.

a) Funeral vase. H: 73 cm. MFEA.

b) Funeral vase. H: 65 cm. MFEA.

PLATE 31.

Ch'ing-pai.

a) Box and cover, with inside tray. D: 6 cm. MFEA.

b) Box. D: 6 cm. Carl Kempe coll. (CKc 556).

c) Box. Olive-coloured glaze. D: 6.9 cm. Carl Kempe coll. (CKc 555).

PLATE 32.

Ch'ing-pai.

a) Box. D: 6 cm. MFEA.

b) Box. D: 6.3 cm. Carl Kempe coll. (CKc 554).

c) Box. D: 8.3 cm. Carl Kempe coll. (CKc 553).

d) Box. D: 7.3 cm. MFEA.

PLATE 33.

Ch'ing-pai.

a) Vase. H: 18 cm. MFEA.

b) Ewer. H: 3 1/2". Honolulu Academy of Arts.

PLATE 34.

Ch'ing-pai, vase. H: 21 cm. Carl Kempe coll. (CKc 571).

PLATE 35.

Ch'ing-pai.

a) Granary model. H: 9.2 cm. Carl Kempe coll. (CKc 514).

b) Ewer. H: 15 cm. Carl Kempe coll. (CKc 564).

PLATE 36.

Ch'ing-pai.

a) Pillow. L: 17.5 cm. Peking Palace Museum.

b) Stand. L: 15 cm. Carl Kempe coll. (CKc 516).

c) Lion figure. L: 7". The Royal Ontario Museum, Toronto.

d) Pillow. L: 17.6 cm. Museum of Fine Arts. Boston.

PLATE 37.

Lung-ch'üan yao.

a) Vase. H: 26.1 cm. Seligman collection.

b) Vase from Lung-ch'üan. H: 20.3 cm.

c) Vase. The British Museum.

d) Vase. Honolulu Academy of Arts.

e) Vase. Art Gallery and Museum, Glasgow. Burrell collection.

f) Vase. H: 9 3/4". Coll. Mrs. Alfred Clark.

g) Vase. H: 10 5/8". The Museum of Eastern Art, Oxford. Ingram coll.

h) Vase. H: 19.7 cm. The Royal Ontario Museum, Toronto.

i) Jar. H: 4.3". Seligman collection.

j) Ewer. H: 13.3 cm. Seligman collection.

k) Ewer. H: 6 1/2". Honolulu Academy of Arts.

l) Ewer. H: 6 5/8". Coll. Sir Alan and Lady Barlow.

PLATE 38.

Lung-ch'üan yao.

a) Bowl. D: 16.4 cm. Coll. Carl Kempe (CKc 123).

b) Bowl. Coll. Eugene Bernat.

PLATE 39.

Lung-ch'üan yao.

a) Box. D: 8.2 cm. Seligman coll.

b) Bowl. D: 5 1/8". City Art Gallery, Bristol.

c) Bowl. D: 5". Rijksmuseum, Amsterdam.

d) Box. D: 4.3". Formerly Eumorfopoulos collection.

e) Bowl. D: 11 cm. Carl Kempe coll. (CKc 139).

f) Box. D: 8 cm. Carl Kempe coll. (CKc 130).

g) Vase. H: 5 5/8". Coll. Sir Alan and Lady Barlow.

h) Bowl. D: 20.8 cm. National Palace Museum, Taipei.

i) Bowl. D: 13.5 cm. National Palace Museum, Taipei.

j) Vase. H: 9". Iwasaki collection.

k) Vase. Japanese collection.

l) Vase. H: 12.1". Bishamon do Temple.

PLATE 40.

a–f) Lung-ch'üan yao.

a) Vase. H: 10 1/8". Coll. Mrs. Alfred Clark.

b) Vase. H: 9 1/2". A. Brundage coll. M. H. de Young Memorial Museum.

c) Vase. D: 4 1/2". Coll. Sir Alan and Lady Barlow.

d) Vase. Tokyo National Museum.

e) Vase. H: 25.2 cm. Japanese collection.

f) Vase. H: 24 cm. Carl Kempe coll. (CKc 101).

g) Vase. H: 40 cm. Liao white ware.

h–l) Tz'u-chou yao.

h) Vase. H: 36 cm. Private coll.

i) Vase. H: 42.8 cm. Museum of Fine Arts, Boston.

j) Vase. H: 40 cm. Freer Gallery of Art, Washington.

k) Vase. H: 17 1/4". The Minneapolis Institute of Arts.

l) Vase. H: 41.3 cm. The Cleveland Museum of Art.

PLATE 41.

Tz'u-chou yao.

a) Ewer. H: 20.2 cm. Tokyo National Museum.

b) Ewer. H: 6 7/8". The Cleveland Museum of Art, J. H. Wade Fund.

c) Ewer. H: 5". The British Museum.

d) Ewer. H: 15.5 cm. The Museum Yamato Bunkakan.

e) Ewer. H: 17 cm. The Royal Ontario Museum, Toronto.

f) Jar. H: 13.5 cm. Freer Gallery of Art.

g) Pillow. D: 17.9 cm. The Art Institute of Chicago. Lucy Maud Buckingham Coll.

h) Back of g above.

i) Ewer. Japanese collection.

j) Pillow. D: 16.5 cm. The Museum Yamato Bunkakan.

k) Top of g above.

l) Vase. H: 12". The Buffalo Museum of Science.

PLATE 42.

Tz'u-chou pillows.

a) H: 8.8 cm. From Teng-feng hsien.
b) Gustaf Hilleström collection, Stockholm.
c) L: 8.5″. The Royal Ontario Museum, Toronto.
d) L: 16.9 cm. Seligman collection.
e) L: 20.5 cm. Wellesley College Art Museum.
f) L: 17 cm. From Mi hsien.
g) L: 25.8 cm. Museum of Fine Arts, Boston.
h) L: 29.5 cm. Formerly Rücker-Embden collection.
i) Vassar College, N.Y.
j) L: 8.7″. The British Museum. Dated 1071.
k) L: 16.2 cm. The Victoria & Albert Museum.
l) L: 10.5″. The Royal Ontario Museum, Toronto.

PLATE 43.

Tz'u-chou yao.

a) Pillow. L: 20.7 cm. Seligman collection.
b) Pillow. L: 16.2 cm. Museum of Fine Arts, Boston.
c) Pillow. L: 7.7″. Formerly Lord Cunliffe collection.
d) Vase. H: 37.5 cm. Seligman collection.
e) Vase. H: 15″. The Victoria & Albert Museum.
f) Vase. H: 16½″. Warren E. Cox.
g) Vase. H: 10⅜″. Formerly Alexander collection.
h) Ewer. H: 7″. Hetherington coll.
i) Ewer. *Sung tai pei fang*. Pl. 18.
j) Vase. City Art Museum of St. Louis.
k) Vase. H: 13.5 cm. Museum of Fine Arts, Boston (*Hoyt* 285).
l) Vase. H: 13.7″. Captain Dugald Malcolm coll.

PLATE 44.

Tz'u-chou yao.

a) Vase. H: 22 cm. From Ch'ing-ho hsien.
b) Vase. H: 13″. City Art Gallery, Bristol.
c) Fragment of pillow from Kuan-t'ai.
d) Pillow. L: 11.9″. The Royal Ontario Museum, Toronto.
e) Pillow. L: 12″. The Royal Ontario Museum, Toronto.
f) Pillow. L: 30.3 cm. Museum of Fine Arts, Boston.
g) Dish. D: 8.1″. Coll. Sir Alan and Lady Barlow.
h) Basin. D: 37 cm. H. M. the King of Sweden.
i) Jar. D: 5.1″. Coll. Mrs. Alfred Clark.
j) Vase. H: 18 cm. From Ch'ing-ho hsien.
k) Vase. H: 26.1 cm. Japanese collection.
l) Vase. Collection unknown.

PLATE 45.

Tz'u-chou yao.

a) Jar. H: 17 cm. From Ch'ing-ho hsien.
b) Jar. H: 16.2 cm. Japanese collection.
c) Jar. H: 4½″. Coll. Sir Alan and Lady Barlow.

d) Vase. H: 23 cm. From Ch'ing-ho hsien.
e) Pillow. Japanese collection.
f) Pillow. Japanese collection.
g) Pillow. D: 30.3 cm. Coll. Iwasaki.
h) Pillow. D: 29.7 cm. Tokyo National Museum.
i) Pillow. D: 34.8 cm. Museum of Fine Arts, Boston.
j) Pillow. D: 31.5 cm. The British Museum.
k) Pillow. Formerly Private Swedish coll.
l) Pillow. D: 11 5/8". A. Brundage collection. M. H. de Young Memorial Museum.

PLATE 46.

Tz'u-chou pillows.
a) D: 29 cm. The Museum Yamato Bunkakan.
b) Private collection, Sweden.
c) Japanese collection.
d) D: 25.1 cm. Museum of Fine Arts, Boston.
e) From a Sung tomb in Honan.
f) Japanese collection.
g) Japanese collection.
h) Japanese collection.
i) Japanese collection.
j) Honolulu Academy of Arts.
k) D: 38.7 cm. The Art Institute of Chicago. Gift of Russell Tyson.
l) Japanese collection.

PLATE 47.

Tz'u-chou yao.
a) Pillow D: 13.75". The Royal Ontario Museum, Toronto.
b) Pillow. D: 12 1/2". The Cleveland Museum of Art, Gift of Mrs. Langdon Warner.
c) Pillow. D: 31 cm. MFEA.
d) Pillow. Japanese collection.
e) Pillow. D: 12 5/8". Coll. Mr. & Mrs. James M. Plumer.
f) Pillow. L: 10.5". The Royal Ontario Museum, Toronto.
g) Bowl. H: 15.6 cm. Seligman collection.
h) Bowl. *Sung tai pei fang*, Pl. 10.
i) Pillow. L: 27.1 cm. Museum of Fine Arts, Boston.
j) Bowl. Japanese collection.
k) Bowl. H: 15.4 cm. The Metropolitan Museum of Art.
l) Pillow, from a tomb in Hopei. *KKHP* 1962:2, Pl. 25:3.

PLATE 48.

Tz'u-chou yao.
a) Pillow. Japanese collection.
b) Pillow. D: 8 3/4". Coll. Nasli Heeramaneck.
c) Pillow. L: 18. 5 cm. MFEA.
d) Pillow. L: 43.8 cm. C. Adrian Rübel collection.
e) Pillow. L: 17". The Cleveland Museum of Art. Edward L. Whittemore Fund.
f) Pillow. L: 18.5 cm. Dated 1119. Museum of Fine Arts, Boston.
g) Pillow. Japanese collection.
h) Pillow. L: 44 cm. Japanese collection.

i) Jar. H: 11.2 cm. Carl Kempe coll. (CKc 270).
j) Cup. D: 12.2 cm. From Teng-feng hsien.
k) Jar. H: 13.3 cm. Carl Kempe collection (CKc 276).
l) Jar. *Sung tai pei fang*, Pl. 13.

PLATE 49.

Tz'u-chou yao.
a) Vase. H: 19½″. A. Brundage collection. M. H. de Young Memorial Museum.
b) Vase. The Metropolitan Museum of Art.
c) Vase. H: 39.3 cm. The British Museum.
d) Vase. H: 43.4 cm. Japanese collection.
e) Vase. H: 40.6 cm. Hakutsuru Art Museum.
f) Vase. H: 54.5 cm. Japanese collection.
g) Vase. Private collection, France.
h) Vase. H: 57 cm. William Rockhill Nelson Gallery of Art.
i) Jar. H: 24.3 cm. Japanese collection.
j) Vase. H: 19.4 cm. Japanese collection.
k) Vase: H: 19.4 cm. Japanese collection.
l) Vase. H: 19 cm. Japanese collection.

PLATE 50.

Tz'u-chou yao.
a) Vase. H: 31.3 cm. City Art Museum, St. Louis.
b) Vase. H: 22.6 cm. Freer Gallery of Art, Washington.
c) Vase. H: 11½″. Fitzwilliam Museum, Cambridge.
d) Vase. H: 32 cm. Messrs. C. T. Loo.
e) Vase. H: 33 cm. Japanese collection.
f) Vase. Formerly C. T. Loo, New York.
g) Vase. *Sung tai pei fang*, Pl. 16.
h) Jar. *Sung tai pei fang*, Pl. 15.
i) Brush-bath. D: 7⅞″. Coll. Mr. & Mrs. Frederick M. Mayer, New York.
j) Pillow. Japanese collection.
k) Pillow. D: 13″. Coll. Captain Dugald Malcolm.
l) Pillow. Japanese collection.

PLATE 51.

Tz'u-chou pillows.
a) Japanese collection.
b) D: 10¼″. The Buffalo Museum of Science.
c) L: 37 cm. Collections Baur (No. A 80).
d) L: 40 cm. Japanese collection.
e) L: 12″. The Royal Ontario Museum, Toronto.
f) L: 13″. The Royal Ontario Museum, Toronto.
g) Japanese collection.
h) Japanese collection.
i) Japanese collection.
j) Private collection, Sweden.
k) Japanese collection.
l) L: 30.4 cm. C. Adrian Rübel collection.

PLATE 52.

Tz'u-chou pillows.

a) Freer Gallery of Art, Washington.
b) The British Museum.
c) L: 32.7 cm. C. Adrian Rübel collection.
d) L: 29.7 cm. Museum of Fine Arts, Boston.
e) L: 19″. Captain Dugald Malcolm coll.
f) L: 15″. The Buffalo Museum of Science.
g) L: 33 cm. H. M. the King of Sweden.
h) L: 34.7 cm. Museum of Fine Arts, Boston.
i) L: 11½″. Honolulu Academy of Arts.
j) L: 35.6 cm. The Art Institute of Chicago, Gift of Russell Tyson.
k) L: 15″. A. Brundage collection, M. H. de Young Memorial Museum.
l) Tokyo National Museum.

PLATE 53.

Tz'u-chou yao.

a) Vase. H: 25 cm. From Pa-ts'un, Yü hsien, Honan.
b) Vase. H: 24 cm. H. M. the King of Sweden.
c) Vase. From Pa-ts'un.
d) Vase. Private coll., U.S.A.
e) Stand. D: 13 cm. H. M. the King of Sweden.
f) Pillow. L: 17.7 cm. Dated 1336. C. Adrian Rübel collection.
g) Wine-jar. H: 27 cm. The British Museum.
h) Wine-jar. From a Chin tomb in Liao Ning.
i) Wine-jar. H: 23.5 cm. Seligman collection.
j) Jar. H: 10.5 cm. Seligman collection.
k) Jar. H: 11″. Captain Dugald Malcolm coll.
l) Vase. Tokyo National Museum.

PLATE 54.

Tz'u-chou yao.

a) Jar (H: 11 cm) and vase (H: 24 cm). From Ch'ing-ho hsien.
b) Ewer. H: 23 cm. J. Hellner collection.
c) Ewer. Japanese collection.
d) Vase. H: 41.2 cm. Japanese collection.
e) Vase. H: 14.8″. The British Museum.
f) Vase. Musée Guimet, Paris.
g) Vase. H: 43 cm. Japanese collection.
h) Bowl. D: 19.9 cm. Japanese collection.
i) Bowl. D: 17.5 cm. From Yao-chou.
j) Vase. Art Institute of Chicago.
k) Jar. *Sung tai pei fang*, Pl. 29.
l) Vase. Musée Cernuschi, Paris.

PLATE 55.

Tz'u-chou yao.

a) Vase. H: 34 cm. Seligman collection.
b) Jar. H: 51.3 cm. MFEA.
c) Jar. Tokyo National Museum.

d) Vase. Honolulu Academy of Arts.
e) Jar. Private collection, Sweden.
f) Jar. Private collection, Sweden.
g) Jar. Formerly Eumorfopoulos collection.
h) Vase. Formerly Eumorfopoulos collection.
i) Vase. H: 27.3 cm. Dated 1305. The British Museum.
j) Bowl. D: 15.2 cm. Japanese collection.
k) Bowl. D: 15.5 cm. Japanese collection.
l) Bowl. D: 14.7 cm. MFEA.

PLATE 56.

Tz'u-chou enamelled ware.
a) Bowl. D: 15.2 cm. Japanese collection.
b) Bowl. D: 15.3 cm. Japanese collection.
c) Dish. D: 17 cm. Collections Baur (No. A 81).
d) Bowl. D: 15.7 cm. Fitzwilliam Museum, Cambridge.
e) Bowl. The British Museum.
f) Bowl. D: 15.7 cm. The Art Institute of Chicago.
g) Bowl. Coll. Eugene Bernat.
h) Bowl. D: 12.5 cm. Japanese collection.
i) Bowl. D: 13.5 cm. Japanese collection.
j) Bowl. Honolulu Academy of Arts.
k) Saucer dish. D: 8½″. Seligman coll.
l) Bowl. D: 8.9 cm. Seattle Art Museum, Thomas D. Stimson Memorial Collection.

PLATE 57.

a–f) Tz'u-chou enamelled ware.
a) Bowl. D: 6⅜″. Cleveland Museum of Art, Mrs. A. Dean Perry collection.
b) Vase. Formerly Eumorfopoulos collection.
c) Vase. H: 19.7 cm. MFEA.
d) Covered bowl. H: 10 cm. MFEA.
e) Figurine. H: 7¾″. Cleveland Museum of Art, John L. Severance Fund.
f) Bowl. D: 10.3 cm. Carl Kempe collection (CKc 280).
g–l) Ting yao.
g) Jar. H: 12 cm. Japanese collection.
h) Covered jar. H: 15.5 cm. Sir Percival David Foundation (No. 193).
i) Ewer. H: 18 cm. Collection M. Calmann, Paris.
j) Ewer. H: 19 cm. Formerly Rücker-Embden collection.
k) Covered jar. D: 4.7″. Mrs. Alfred Clark collection.
l) Dish. D: 26 cm. Formerly Rücker-Embden collection.

PLATE 58.

Ting yao.
a) Incence-burner. H: 16 cm. Carl Kempe coll. (CKc. 417).
b) Vase. H: 5⅜″. City Art Gallery, Bristol.
c) Bowl. Ex. Heeramaneck Coll. New York.

PLATE 59.

Ting yao.
a) Bowl. N. Lundgren coll., Stockholm.
b) Bowl. J. Hellner coll.

PLATE 60.

Ting yao.
Bowl. D: 21.5 cm. MFEA, Stockholm.

PLATE 61.

Ting yao.
a) Vase. H: 27.3 cm. Percival David Foundation (No. 103).
b) Vase. H: 36.3 cm. Percival David Foundation (No. 101).
c) Vase. H: 10⅜″. Coll. Sir Alan and Lady Barlow (No. C 178).
d) Basin. D: 25.1 cm. Percival David Foundation (No. 102).
e) Dish. D: 6″. Fitzwilliam Museum, Cambridge.
f) Dish, dated 1271. D: 7¾″. The British Museum.
g) Dish. Inscribed *feng-hua.* D: 21 cm. Percival David Foundation (No. 116).
h) Dish. Tokyo National Museum.
i) Bowl. D: 21 cm. (*China's beauty of 2000 years,* No. 81).
j) Bowl. D: 19.5 cm. Collections Baur (No. A 10).
k) Dish. D: 20.2 cm. Percival David Foundation (No. 166).
l) Ewer. Japanese collection.

PLATE 62.

Ting yao.
a) Bowl. D: 17.3 cm. Carl Kempe coll. (CKc. 411).
b) Dish. D: 22.7 cm. Carl Kempe coll. (CKc. 466).

PLATE 63.

Ting yao.
a) Bowl. D: 25.8 cm. Carl Kempe coll. (CKc. 409).
b) Bowl. D: 16.7 cm. Museum of Fine Arts, Boston (*Hoyt* 254).

PLATE 64.

Ting yao.
a) Dish. D: 20 cm. Carl Kempe coll. (CKc. 456).
b) Dish. Ex. coll. Holmes.

PLATE 65.

Ting yao. Bowl. Museum of Fine Arts, Boston.

PLATE 66.

Ting yao.
a) Dish. D: 21.5 cm. Carl Kempe coll. (CKc. 415).
b) Dish. J. Hellner coll.

PLATE 67.

Ting yao.
a)—b) Basin. D: 28.3 cm. Carl Kempe coll. (CKc. 416).

PLATE 68.

Ting yao. Dish. D: 30 cm. Carl Kempe coll. (CKc. 412).

PLATE 69.

Ting yao.
a) Bowl. D: 22.8 cm. Carl Kempe coll. (CKc. 408).
b) Dish. J. Hellner coll.

PLATE 70.

Ting yao.
a) Bowl. Ex. coll. Yawe.
b) Dish. D: 8 7/8″. Ex. coll. Yawe.

PLATE 71.

Ting yao. Dish. D: 26.2 cm. Freer Gallery of Art, Washington D.C.

PLATE 72.

Ting yao.
a) Dish. D: 25.7 cm. Museum of Fine Arts, Boston (*Hoyt* 255).
b) Dish. D: 11.5 cm. Carl Kempe coll. (CKc. 467).

PLATE 73.

Ting yao.
a) Cup-stand. J. Hellner coll.
b) Dish. Private coll., the Hague.

PLATE 74.

Ting yao. Dish. D: 10 1/2″. William Rockhill Nelson Gallery of Art. Kansas City.

PLATE 75.

Ting yao.
a) Dish. D: 26.5 cm. Carl Kempe coll. (CKc. 455).
b) Dish. J. Hellner collection.

PLATE 76.

Ting yao. Dish. D: 20.8 cm. The British Museum.

PLATE 77.

Ting yao. Dish. Collection Eugene Bernat. Milton, Mass.

PLATE 78.

Ting yao.
a) Plate. D: 30.2 cm. Percival David Foundation (No. 164).
b) Plate. D: 11 7/8″. The Cleveland Museum of Art. Gift of Ralph King.

PLATE 79.

Ting yao.
a) Dish. D: 29.1 cm. Freer Gallery of Art.
b) Dish. D: 30.4 cm. Freer Gallery of Art.

PLATE 80.

Ting yao.
a) Bowl. D: 5 1/2″. Victoria & Albert Museum, London.
b) Bowl. D: 7″. Formerly C. T. Loo, New York.

PLATE 81.

Ting yao. Bowl. D: 6 1/8″. Honolulu Academy of Arts.

PLATE 82.

Ting yao.
a) Bowl. D: 8 1/8″. Victoria & Albert Museum.
b) Bowl. Museum of Eastern Art, Oxford.

PLATE 83.

Ting yao. Bowl. D: 21.5 cm. MFEA, Stockholm.

PLATE 84.

Ting yao and Ting type.
a) Bowl. D: 8 3/8″. The British Museum.
b) Bowl. D: 7″. The British Museum.
c) Bowl. D: 7″. Percival David Foundation (No. 108).
d) Dish. D: 7 1/2″. Fitzwilliam Museum, Cambridge.
e) Dish. D: 10 1/8″. The British Museum.
f) Covered bowl. Dated 1162. H: 5″. The British Museum.
g) Dish. D: 21.6 cm. Japanese collection.
h) Dish. D: 21.5 cm. Percival David Foundation (No. 161).
i) Bowl. D: 5 1/8″. Coll. Eugene Bernat, Milton, Mass.
j) Bowl. D: 10 3/8″. Formerly coll. I. Yvey, San Francisco.
k) Bowl. Coll. unknown.
l) Pillow. H: 6″. L: 7 1/2″. A. Brundage collection. M. H. de Young Memorial Museum, San Francisco.

PLATE 85.

Ting yao.
a) Dish. Museum of Eastern Art, Oxford.
b) Dish. Coll. Lt-Col. and Mrs. W.B.R. Neave-Hill, London.

PLATE 86.

Ting yao.
a) Dish. D: 7″. Percival David Foundation (No. 115).
b) Dish. Museum of Eastern Art, Oxford.

PLATE 87.

Ting yao.
a) Dish. D: 6 3/4″. Malcolm coll. London.
b) Dish. D: 6 1/4″. Seligman collection (No. D 76).

PLATE 88.

Ting yao.
a) Dish. D: 17 cm. Carl Kempe coll. (CKc. 461).
b) Dish. The British Museum.

PLATE 89.

Ting yao.
a) Bowl. D: 7 1/8". Victoria & Albert Museum.
b) Dish. D: 18.8 cm. Freer Gallery of Art.

PLATE 90.

Ting yao.
a) Bowl. Brown glaze. D: 16 cm. Carl Kempe coll. (CKc. 421).
b) Bowl. Honolulu Academy of Arts. Honolulu.

PLATE 91.

Ting yao.
a) Dish. D: 6 3/4". Malcolm collection. London.
b) Bowl. D: 6 3/8". The Cleveland Museum of Art, Gift of Mr. and Mrs. Ralph King.

PLATE 92.

Ting yao.
a) Bowl. D: 8". Seattle Art Museum.
b) Bowl. D: 20.8 cm. Carl Kempe coll. (CKc. 457).

PLATE 93.

Pottery mould. D: 22.9 cm. Freer Gallery of Art.

PLATE 94.

Ting yao.
a) Bowl. Coll. Mrs. N. Lundgren, Stockholm.
b) Dish. D: 6 1/8". Victoria & Albert Museum. London.

PLATE 95.

Ting yao.
a) Bowl. D: 10". The Cleveland Museum of Art, The Fanny Tewksbury King coll.
b) Dish. Coll. Mr. and Mrs. S. Nydell, Gothenburg, Sweden.

PLATE 96.

Ting yao.
a) Dish. D: 8 1/4". Victoria & Albert Museum.
b) Dish. D: 20.7 cm. Carl Kempe coll. (CKc. 458).

PLATE 97.

Ting yao.
a) Dish. D: 20.5 cm. Carl Kempe coll. (CKc. 460).
b) Dish. Coll. Edward T. Chow.

PLATE 98.

Ting yao. Dish. D: 11.4". Percival David Foundation (No. 171).

PLATE 99.

Ting yao. Dish. D: 8.7″. Percival David Foundation (No. 117).

PLATE 100.

Ting yao.
a) Dish. The Museum of Eastern Art, Oxford.
b) Dish. D: 8⅞″. Ex. coll. C. T. Loo, New York.

PLATE 101.

Ting yao.
a) Dish. Royal Scottish Museum, Edinburgh.
b) Dish. Museum of Eastern Art, Oxford.

PLATE 102.

Ting yao.
a) Dish. D: 5″.
b) Dish. Coll. Lt-Col. & Mrs. W.B.R. Neave-Hill, London.

PLATE 103.

Ting yao.
a) Dish. D: 10.3 cm. Coll. Carl Kempe (CKc. 462).
b) Dish. Victoria & Albert Museum.

PLATE 104.

Ting yao.
a) Dish. D: 3¾″. Honolulu Academy of Arts.
b) Bowl. D: 4⅞″. Seattle Art Museum.

CROSS INDEX FROM PLATES TO TYPES

Plate no.		Date	Type	Page
Pl. 1	a–i	Early Northern Sung	Nc 1	22
	j–l	Northern Sung	Nc 2	24
Pl. 2	a–l	Northern Sung	Nc 2	24
Pl. 3	a–h	Early Northern Sung	Nc 3 a	27
	i–k	Early Northern Sung	Nc 3 b	28
	l	Early Northern Sung	Nc 3 c	29
Pl. 4	a–c	Early Northern Sung	Nc 3 c	29
	d–f	Early Northern Sung	Nc 3 d	29
	g–j	Early Northern Sung	Nc 3 e	30
	k–l	Late Northern Sung	Nc 3 f	30
Pl. 5	a–b	Late Northern Sung	Nc 3 f	30
	d–e	Northern Sung	Nc 3 g	31
	f–j	Late Northern Sung	Nc 4	31
	k	Late Northern Sung	Nc 5	31
	l	Late Northern Sung	Nc 6	32
Pl. 6	a–b	Late Northern Sung	Nc 6	32
	c	Late Northern Sung—Chin	—	32
	d–f	Late Northern Sung—Chin	Nc 7	32
	g–h	Chin	Nc 8	32
	i	Late Northern Sung—Chin	—	32
	j–k	Northern Sung	Nc 9	33
	l	Northern Sung—Chin	Nc 34	42
Pl. 7	a	Northern Sung	Nc 9	33
	b–f	Early Northern Sung	Nc 10	34
	g	Northern Sung	Nc 11	35
	h	Northern Sung	Nc 36	43
	i	Early Northern Sung	Nc 10	34
	j–k	Northern Sung	Nc 12	35
	l	Early Northern Sung	—	34
Pl. 8	a–b	Northern Sung	Nc 13	35
	c	Northern Sung	Nc 14	36
	d	Northern Sung	Nc 15	36
	e–f	Northern Sung	Nc 14	36
	g–h	Late Northern Sung	Nc 16	36
	i	Chin	Nc 17	37
	j	Northern Sung	Nc 18	38
	k	Late Northern Sung	Nc 19	38
	l	Chin	Nc 17	37
Pl. 9	a–d	Chin	Nc 20	38
	e	Chin	Nc 21	39
	f	Chin	Nc 20	38
	g	Chin	Nc 22	39
	h	Chin	Nc 23	40
	i	Chin	Nc 25	40
	j–k	Chin	Nc 27	40
	l	Chin	Nc 25	40
Pl. 10	a	Late Northern Sung	Nc 26	40
	b–c	Northern Sung	Nc 35	43
	d–e	Late Northern Sung	Nc 28	41
	f–g	Late Northern Sung—Chin	Nc 29	41
	h	Late Northern Sung	Nc 30	41
	i	Late Northern Sung—Chin	Nc 31	42
	j	Late Northern Sung	Nc 32	42
	k	Northern Sung	Nc 33	42
	l	Northern Sung	Nc 37	43
Pl. 11		Early Northern Sung	Cp 1 A	50

Plate no.		Date	Type	Page
Pl. 12	a	Early Northern Sung	Cp 1 A	50
	b	Tomb dated 1057	—	50
	c	Northern Sung	Cp 2	51
	d	Northern Sung	Cp 3	52
	e	Late Northern Sung—Southern Sung	Cp 7	53
	f	Late Northern Sung—Southern Sung	Cp 8	53
	g–i	Late Northern Sung—Southern Sung	Cp 9	54
	j	Southern Sung	Cp 17	57
	k	Late Northern Sung—Southern Sung	Cp 11	55
	l	Northern Sung	Cp 12	55
Pl. 13	a	Northern Sung	Cp 1 B	51
	b	Northern Sung	Cp 1 C	51
Pl. 14		Northern Sung	Cp 2	51
Pl. 15	a–b	Northern Sung	Cp 2	51
Pl. 16	a	Late Northern Sung	Cp 4	52
	b	Late Northern Sung—Southern Sung	Cp 5	52
Pl. 17	a	Late Northern Sung—Southern Sung	Cp 6	53
	b	Late Northern Sung—Southern Sung	Cp 9	54
Pl. 18	a	Southern Sung	Cp 10	54
	b	Northern Sung	Cp 13	55
Pl. 19	a–b	12th century	Cp 14	56
Pl. 20	a–b	12th century	Cp 15	56
Pl. 21	a–b	Northern Sung	Cp 16	57
Pl. 22	a	Tomb dated 1027	—	58
	b	Northern Sung	Cp 18	58
	c–e	Southern Sung—Yüan	Cp 19	58
	f	Southern Sung—Yüan	Cp 20	59
	g–i	Southern Sung—Yüan	Cp 19	58
	j–l	Southern Sung—Yüan	Cp 20	59
Pl. 23	a–c	Southern Sung—Yüan	Cp 20	59
	d–g	Northern Sung	Cp 21	59
	h–i	Northern Sung	Cp 22	60
	j–l	Southern Sung—Yüan	Cp 31	64
Pl. 24	a–b	Southern Sung	Cp 24	61
Pl. 25	a–b	Southern Sung	Cp 25	61
Pl. 26	a	Southern Sung—Yüan	Cp 26	62
	b	Southern Sung, c. 1200	Cp 27	62
Pl. 27	a–b	Southern Sung	Cp 28	63
Pl. 28	a–e	Yüan	Cp 32	65
	f–i	Southern Sung	Cp 33	65
	j–k	Southern Sung—Yüan	Cp 34	66
	l	Northern Sung	Cp 35	66
Pl. 29	a–e	Northern Sung	Cp 32	65
	f–i	Five Dynasties—Early Northern Sung	Cp 36	67
	j	Northern Sung	Cp 2	51
	k–l	Early Northern Sung	Cp 37	67
Pl. 30	a–b	Southern Sung-Yüan	Cp 38	67
Pl. 31	a–c	Southern Sung	Cp 40	68
Pl. 32	a–d	Southern Sung—Yüan	Cp 41	69
Pl. 33	a–b	Southern Sung—Yüan	Cp 41	69
Pl. 34		Southern Sung—Yüan	Cp 42	70
Pl. 35	a	Southern Sung—Yüan	Cp 39	68
	b	Yüan	—	71
Pl. 36	a–d	Southern Sung	Cp 43	70
Pl. 37	a–d	Five Dynasties—Early Northern Sung	Lc 1	77
	e–f	Early Northern Sung	Lc 2	78
	g–h	Early Northern Sung	Lc 3	78
	i	Northern Sung	Lc 5	79
	j–l	Five Dynasties—Early Northern Sung	Lc 4	79

Plate no.		Date	Type	Page
Pl. 38	a	Northern Sung	Lc 6	80
	b	Southern Sung	Lc 10	82
Pl. 39	a	Northern Sung	Lc 7	81
	b	Southern Sung	Lc 7	81
	c	Southern Sung	Lc 10	82
	d	Southern Sung	Lc 11	82
	e	Southern Sung—Yüan	Lc 12	82
	f–g	Southern Sung—Yüan	Lc 13	83
	h–i	Southern Sung—Yüan	Lc 14	83
	j–l	Southern Sung	Lc 15	84
Pl. 40	a–f	Southern Sung	Lc 16	84
	g–h	Liao	—	91
	i–k	Early Northern Sung	Tc 3	91
	l	Early Northern Sung	Tc 2	90
Pl. 41	a–k	Early Northern Sung	Tc 1	89
	(k)–l	Early Northern Sung	Tc 2	90
Pl. 42	a–h	Northern Sung, 11th century	Tc 5	92
	i–l	Northern Sung, 11th century	Tc 6	93
Pl. 43	a–c	Northern Sung, 11th century	Tc 6	93
	d–i	Northern Sung, 11th century	Tc 7	93
	j–l	Northern Sung, 11th century	Tc 8	94
Pl. 44	a–b	Northern Sung, 11th century	Tc 8	94
	c–f	Northern Sung, 11th—Early 12th century	Tc 9	95
	g–i	Northern Sung, 11th—Early 12th century	Tc 10	96
	j–l	Northern Sung, 11th—Early 12th century	Tc 11	97
Pl. 45	a–d	Northern Sung, 11th—Early 12th century	Tc 11	97
	e–l	Late Northern Sung—Chin	Tc 12	97
Pl. 46	a–c	Late Northern Sung—Chin	Tc 12	97
	d–f	Late Northern Sung—Chin	Tc 13	98
	g–j (k)	Late Northern Sung—Chin	Tc 14	99
	l	Late Northern Sung—Chin	Tc 15	100
Pl. 47	a–e	Late Northern Sung—Chin	Tc 15	100
	f	Late Northern Sung—Chin	Tc 16	101
	g–h	Late Northern Sung—Chin	Tc 20	103
	i	Late Northern Sung—Chin	Tc 16	101
	j–k	Late Northern Sung—Chin	Tc 20	103
	l	Late Northern Sung	Tc 17	101
Pl. 48	a–b	Late Northern Sung	Tc 17	101
	c	Northern Sung, 11th—Early 12th century	Tc 18	102
	d–e	Northern Sung	Tc 19	103
	f	Northern Sung, 11th—Early 12th century	Tc 18	102
	g–h	Northern Sung	Tc 19	103
	i	Northern Sung	Tc 34	114
	j	Northern Sung	Tc 33	114
	k	Northern Sung	Tc 35	114
	l	Northern Sung	Tc 4	91
Pl. 49	a–l	Northen Sung—Chin	Tc 21	104
Pl. 50	a–b	Late Northern Sung—Chin	Tc 22	105
	c–f	Late Northern Sung—Chin	Tc 23	106
	g–h	Northern Sung	Tc 24	106
	i–l	Late Northern Sung	Tc 25	107
Pl. 51	a–l	Late Northern Sung—Chin	Tc 26	108
Pl. 52	a–f	Late Northern Sung—Chin	Tc 27	109
	g–i	Late Northern Sung—Chin	Tc 28	110
	j–l	Late Northern Sung—Chin	Tc 29	111
Pl. 53	a–e	Yüan	Tc 30	111
	f	Dated 1336	—	112
	g–i	Chin—Yüan	Tc 31	112
	j–l	Northern Sung	Tc 32	113

Plate no.		Date	Type	Page
Pl. 54	a–c	Northern Sung	Tc 32	113
	d–f	Chin	Tc 36	115
	g	Chin	Tc 37	115
	h–i	Chin	Tc 38	116
	j–k	Yüan	Tc 39	116
	l	Yüan	Tc 40	117
Pl. 55	a–h	Yüan	Tc 40	117
	i	Dated 1305	Tc 40	117
	j–k	Chin, c. 1200	Tc 41	118
	l	Chin	Tc 42	118
Pl. 56	a–e	Chin	Tc 42	118
	f–j	Chin, c. 1200	Tc 43	119
	k	Chin—Yüan	Tc 44	120
	l	Chin—Yüan	Tc 45	120
Pl. 57	a	Chin—Yüan	Tc 45	120
	b–c	Chin—Yüan	Tc 46	121
	d	Chin—Yüan	Tc 45	120
	e (f)	Chin—Yüan	Tc 47	121
	g–h	Early Northern Sung	Ti 1	129
	i–j	Early Northern Sung	Ti 2	130
	k	Late Northern Sung–Chin	Ti 9	133
	l	Late Northern Sung—Chin	Ti 10	133
Pl. 58	a	Early Northern Sung	Ti 1	129
	b	Early Northern Sung	Ti 2	130
	c	Early 12th century	Ti 5	131
Pl. 59	a	Northern Sung	Ti 7	132
	b	Northern Sung	Ti 8	132
Pl. 60		Northern Sung	Ti 8	132
Pl. 61	a	Late Northern Sung	Ti 11	134
	b–c	Late Northern Sung	Ti 13	134
	d	Late Northern Sung	Ti 14	135
	e	Chin	Ti 23	137
	f	Dated 1271	Ti 25	138
	g	Chin	Ti 28	139
	h–i	Chin	Ti 29	140
	j	Chin	Ti 31	142
	k	Northern Sung	Ti 32	143
	l	Northern Sung	—	219
Pl. 62	a	Late Northern Sung	Ti 11	134
	b	Late Northern Sung	Ti 12	134
Pl. 63	a	Late Northern Sung	Ti 12	134
	b	Late Northern Sung	Ti 15	135
Pl. 64	a	Northern Sung	Ti 16	135
	b	Northern Sung	Ti 17	135
Pl. 65		Northern Sung	Ti 18	136
Pl. 66	a	Northern Sung	Ti 19	136
	b	Northern Sung	Ti 20	136
Pl. 67		Late Northern Sung	Ti 21	136
Pl. 68		Northern Sung	Ti 26	138
Pl. 69	a–b	Late Northern Sung—Chin	Ti 27	138
Pl. 70	a–b	Chin	Ti 28	139
Pl. 71		Chin	Ti 29	140
Pl. 72	a–b	Chin	Ti 29	140
Pl. 73	a	Chin	Ti 29	140
	b	Chin	Ti 31	142
Pl. 74		Chin	Ti 30	141
Pl. 75	a–b	Chin	Ti 31	142
Pl. 76		Chin	Ti 31	142
Pl. 77		Late Northern Sung	Ti 33	143

Plate no.		Date	Type	Page
Pl. 78	a–b	Chin	Ti 34	143
Pl. 79	a–b	Chin	Ti 34	143
Pl. 80	a–b	Chin	Ti 35	145
Pl. 81		Chin	Ti 35	145
Pl. 82	a–b	Chin	Ti 36	145
Pl. 83		Chin	Ti 37	146
Pl. 84	a	Chin	Ti 37	146
	b–c	Chin	Ti 38	146
	d	12th century	Ti 43	150
	e	Yüan	Ti 48	152
	f	Chin	Ti 53	154
	g–h	Chin—Yüan	Ti 55	156
	i–k	Late Chin—Yüan	—	161
	l		—	161
Pl. 85	a	Chin	Ti 39	148
	b	Chin	Ti 40	148
Pl. 86	a–b	Chin	Ti 40	148
Pl. 87	a–b	Chin	Ti 40	148
Pl. 88	a	Chin	Ti 41	149
	b	Chin	Ti 42	149
Pl. 89	a–b	12th century	Ti 43	150
Pl. 90	a	12th century	Ti 43	150
	b	12th century	Ti 44	151
Pl. 91	a–b	Chin	Ti 45	151
Pl. 92	a	Chin	Ti 47	152
	b	Chin	Ti 48	152
Pl. 93		Chin—Yüan	Ti 48	152
Pl. 94	a	Chin	Ti 50	153
	b	Chin	Ti 51	154
Pl. 95	a	Chin	Ti 52	154
	b	Chin	Ti 54	155
Pl. 96	a–b	Chin	Ti 54	155
Pl. 97	a–b	Chin	Ti 54	155
Pl. 98		Chin	Ti 54	155
Pl. 99		Chin—Yüan	Ti 55	156
Pl. 100	a	Yüan	Ti 56	157
	b	Chin—Yüan	Ti 57	157
Pl. 101	a–b	Chin—Yüan	Ti 58	158
Pl. 102	a	Chin	Ti 59	158
	b	Chin	Ti 60	158
Pl. 103	a–b	Chin	Ti 62	159
Pl. 104	a–b	Chin—Yüan	Ti 62	159

CORRIGENDA

Page 21	line 16 Kao Ku 1959:8 *read* Kao Ku 1959:12.
Page 31	Type: Nc 4 line 12 (Pl. 4:j) *read* (Pl. 5:j).
Page 236	Figges *read* Figgess.
Page 251	Figure 16. c) Ch'in-fo-tung *read* Ch'ien-fo-tung
Page 255	Plate 2. l) Japanese collection *read* The Metropolitan Museum of Art, New York.
Page 268	Plate 66. b) J.Hellner coll. *read* Lundgren coll. M.F.E.A.

Fig. 1

Fig. 2

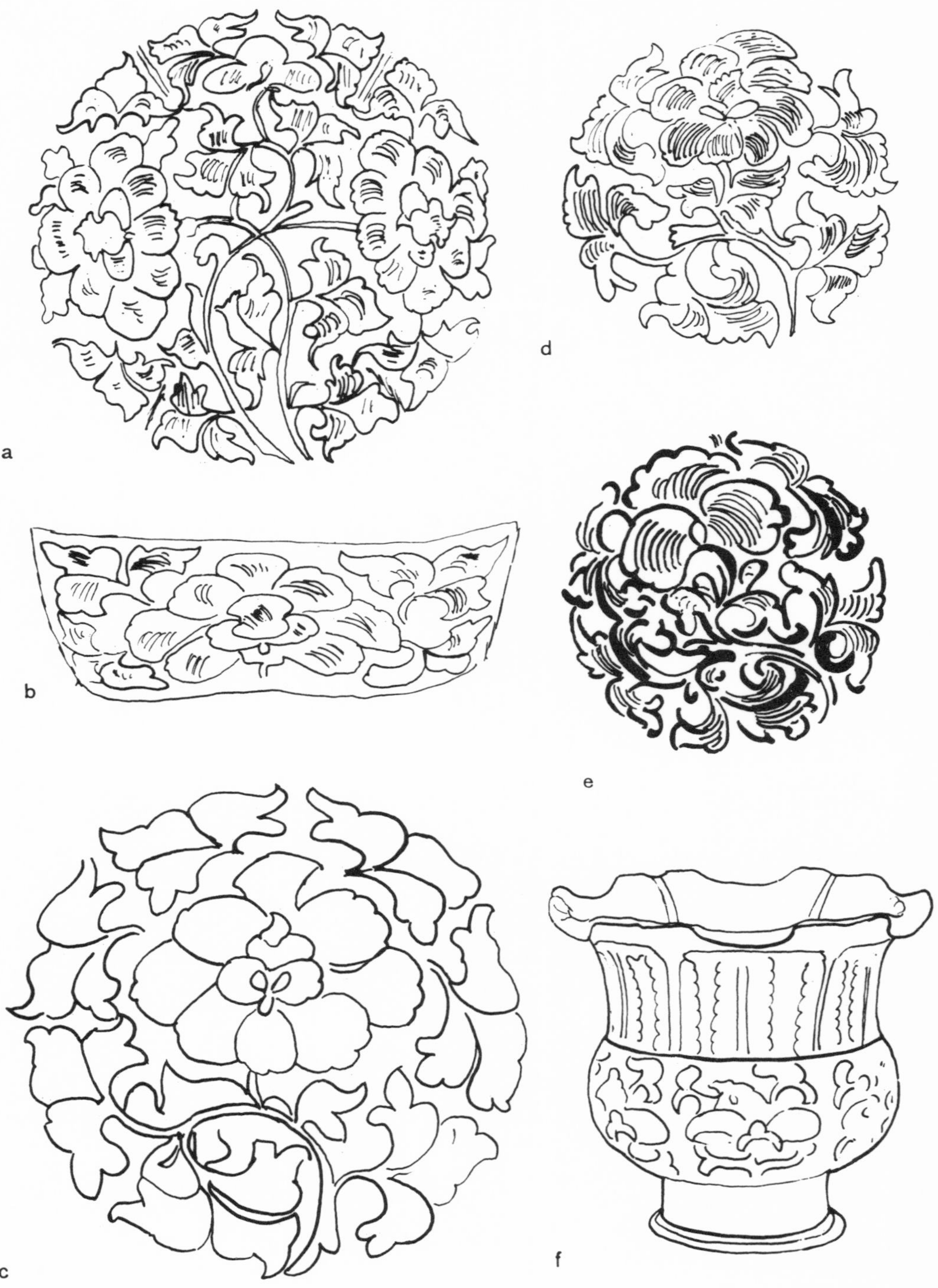

Fig. 3

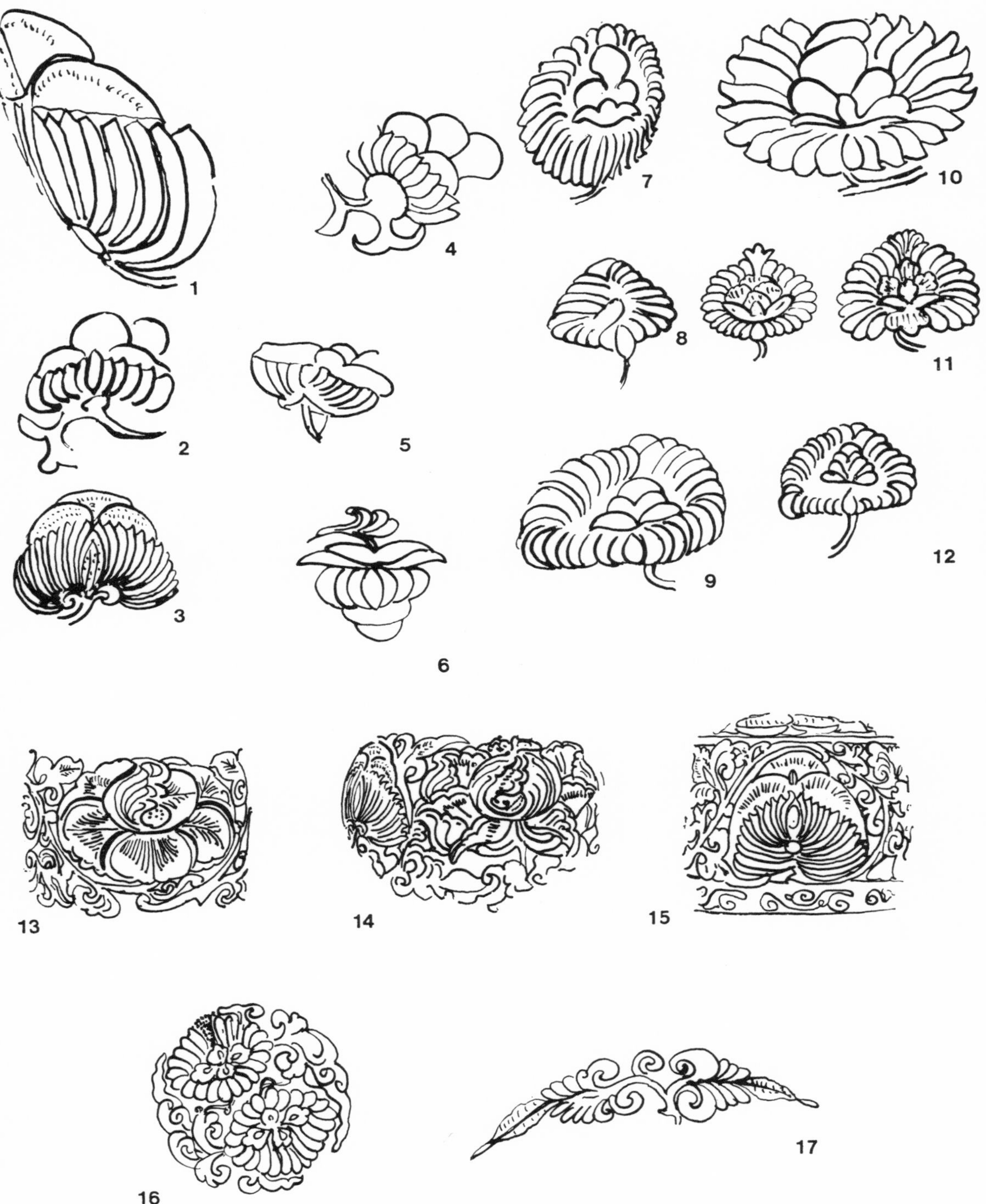

Fig. 4

Fig. 5

Fig. 6

Fig. 7

Fig. 8

a

b

c

d

e

f

g

Fig. 9

Fig. 10

Fig. 11

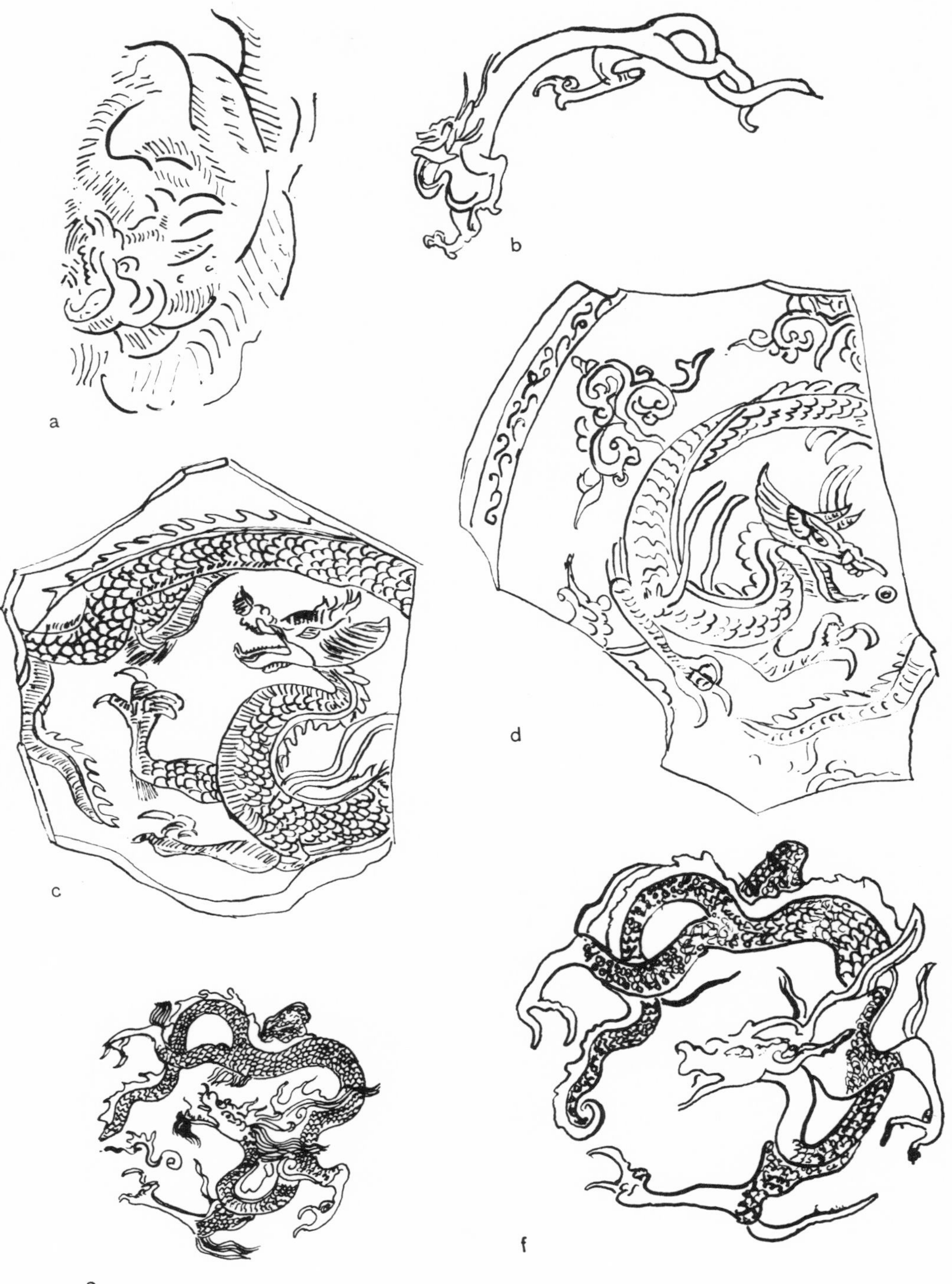

Fig. 12

Fig. 13

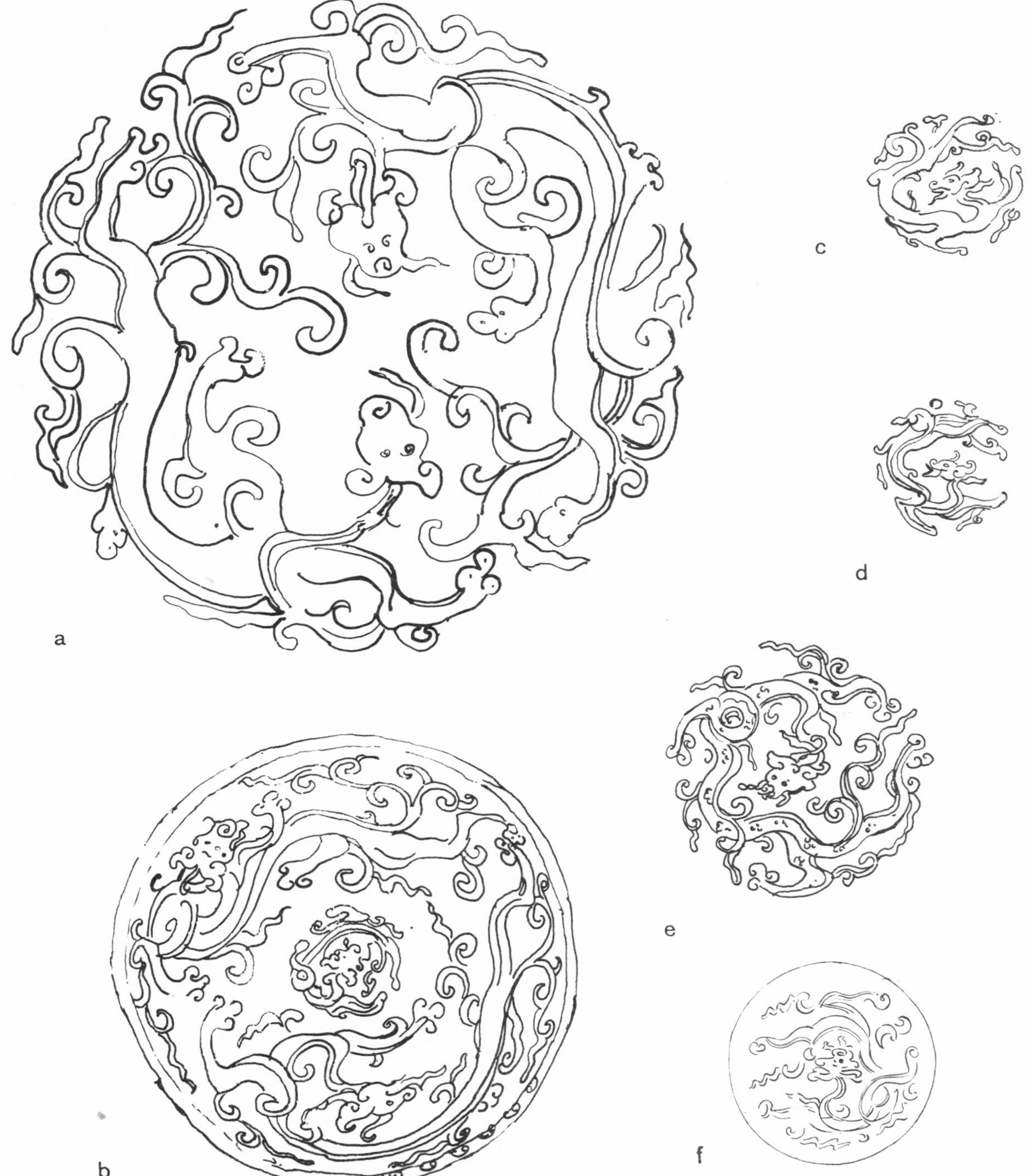

Fig. 14

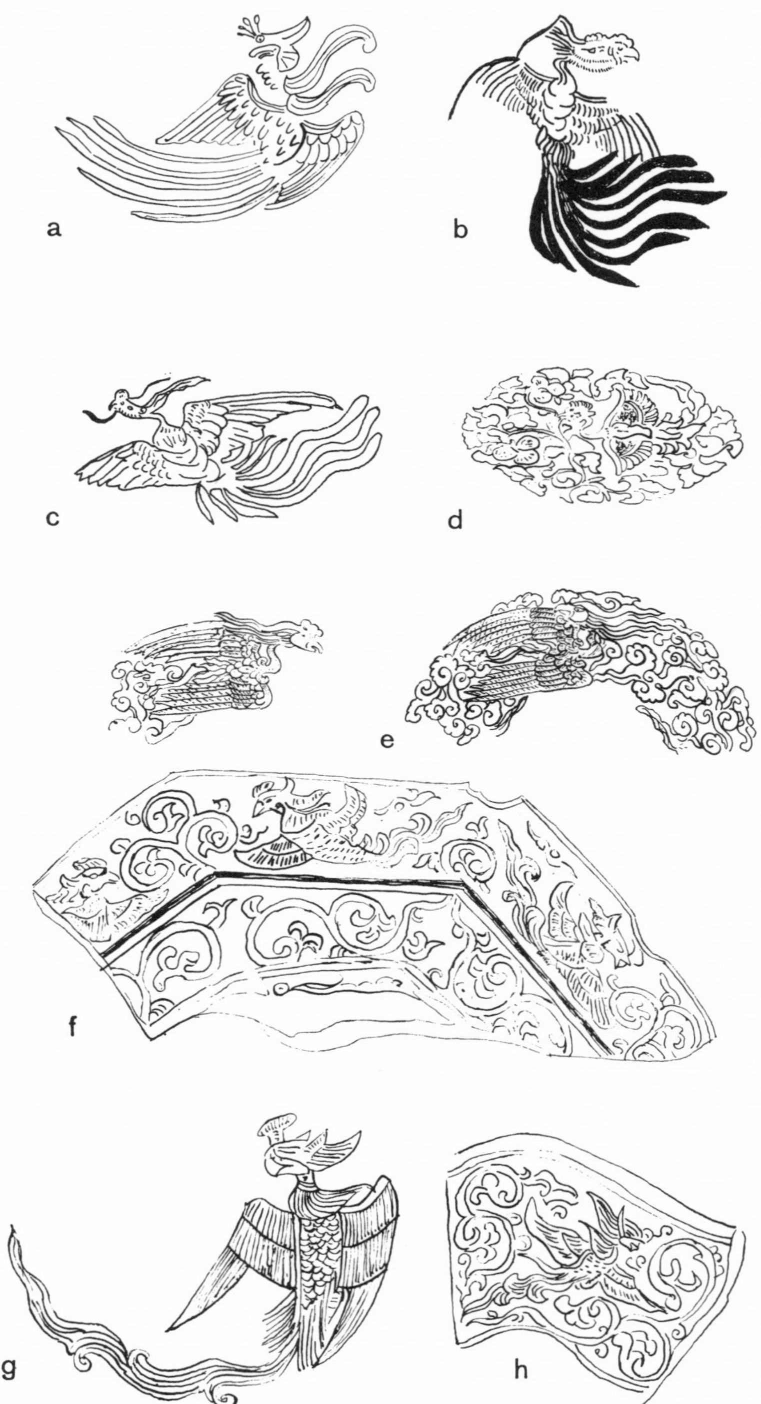

Fig. 15

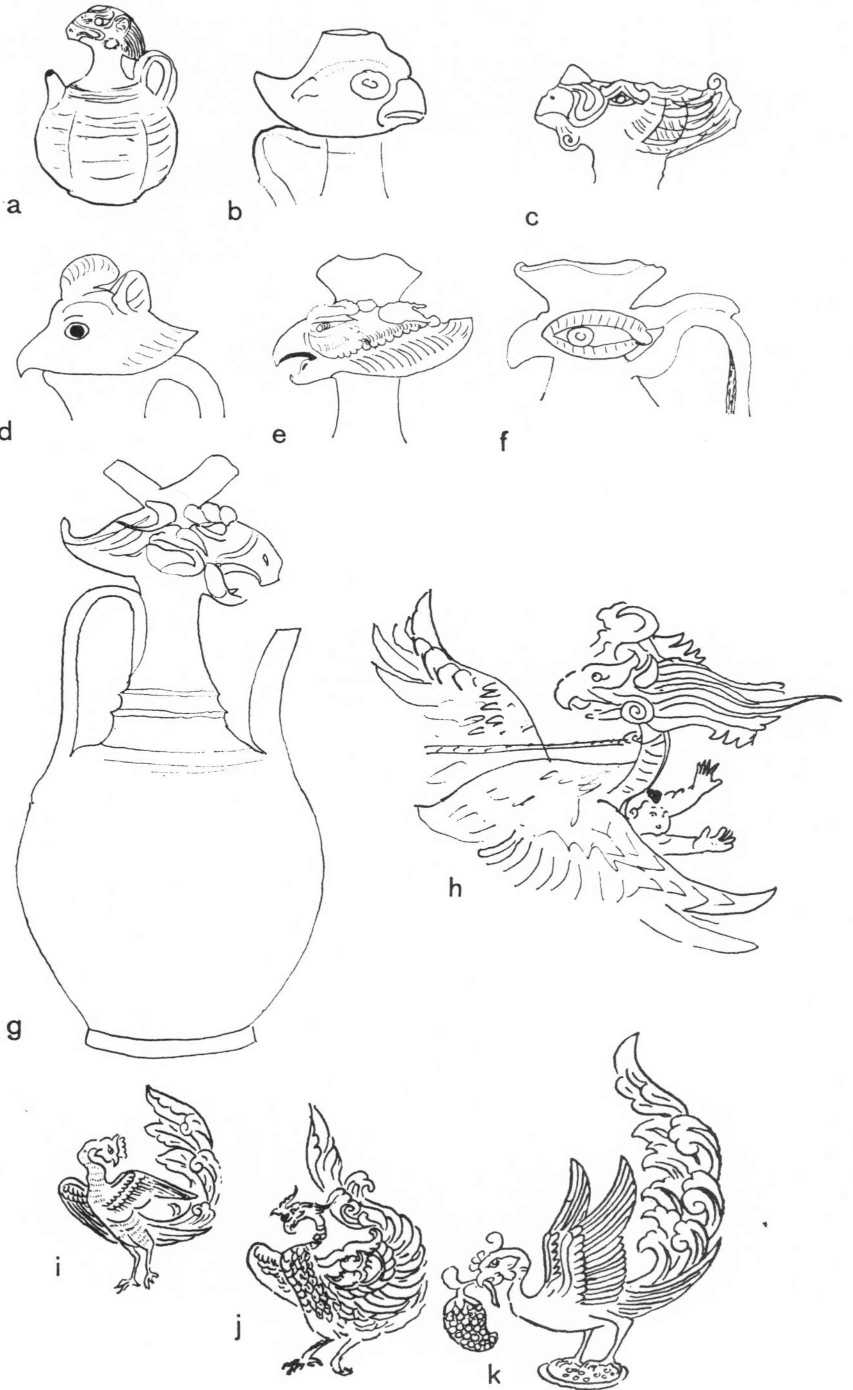

Fig. 16

Fig. 17

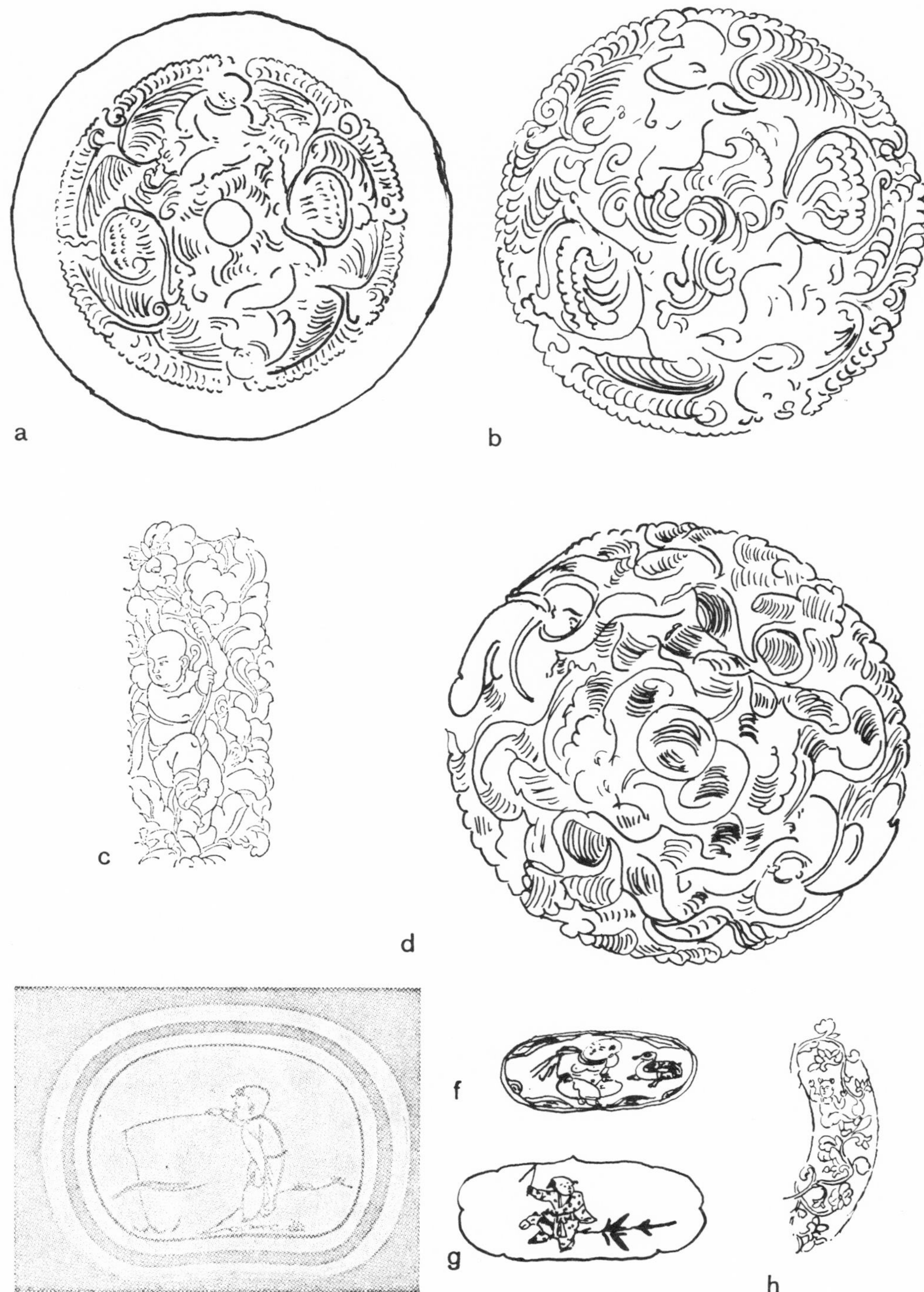

Fig. 18

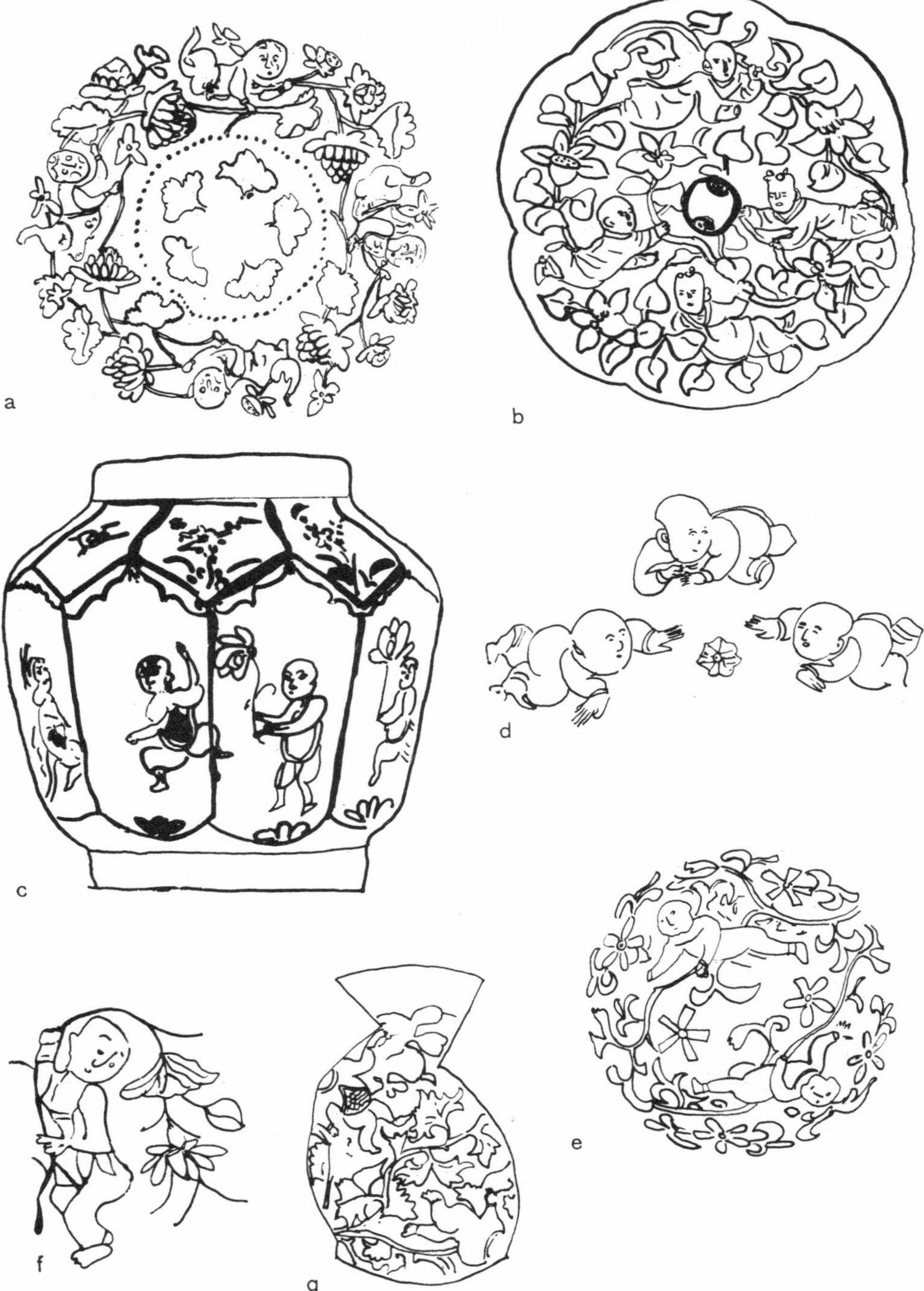

a
b
c
d
e
f
g

Fig. 20

Fig. 21

Fig. 22

Fig. 23

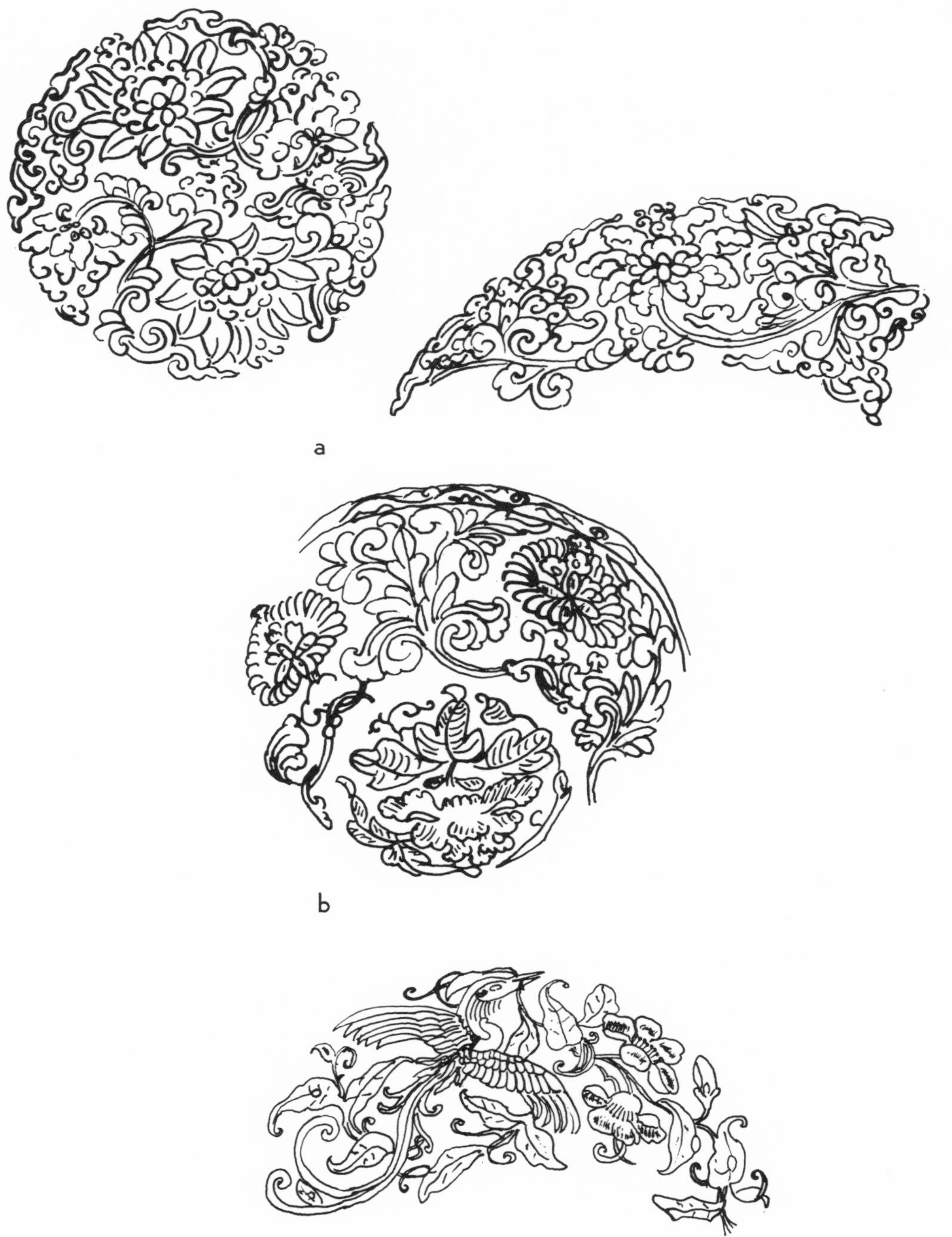

a

b

c

Fig. 24

a

b

c

Fig. 26

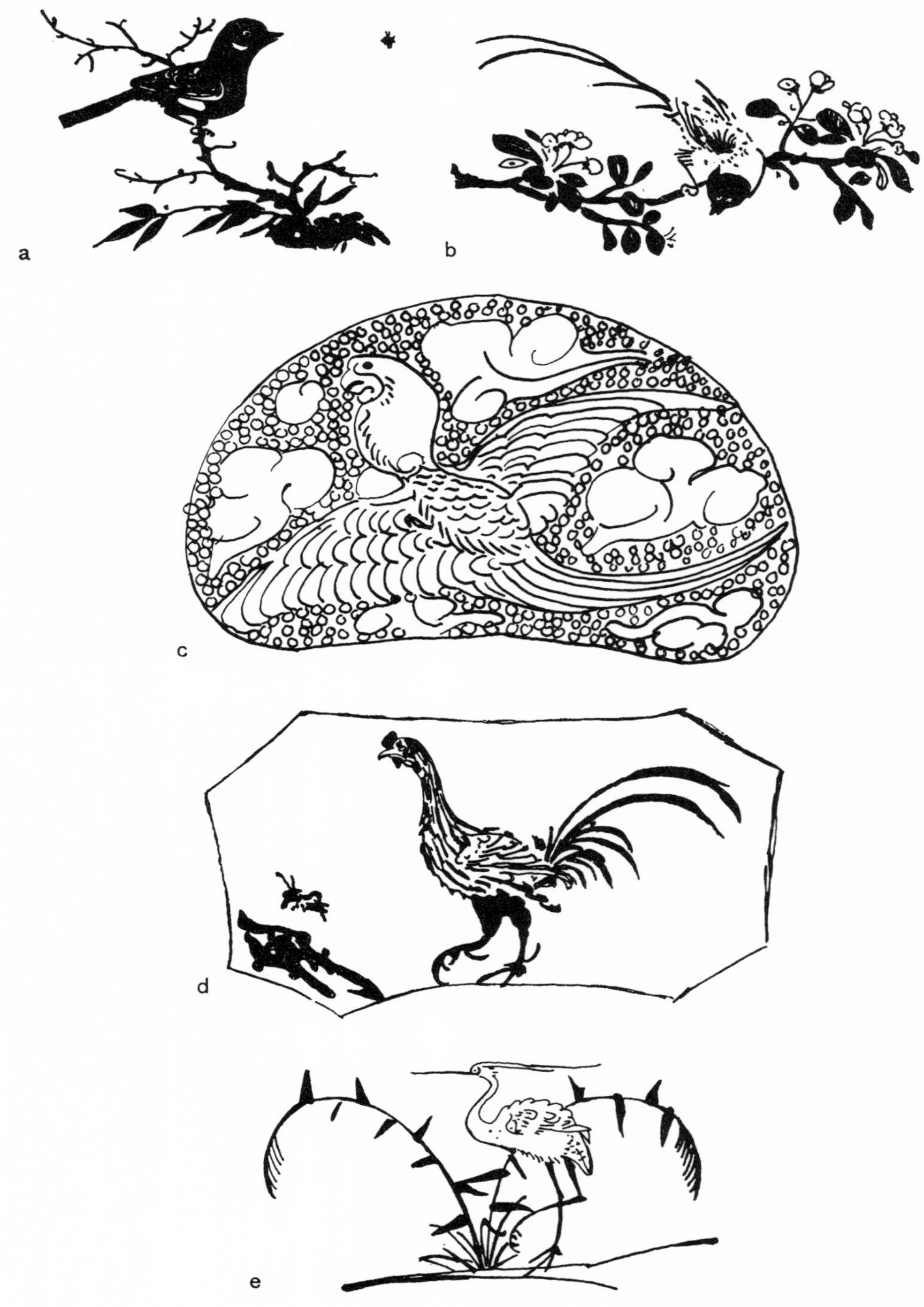

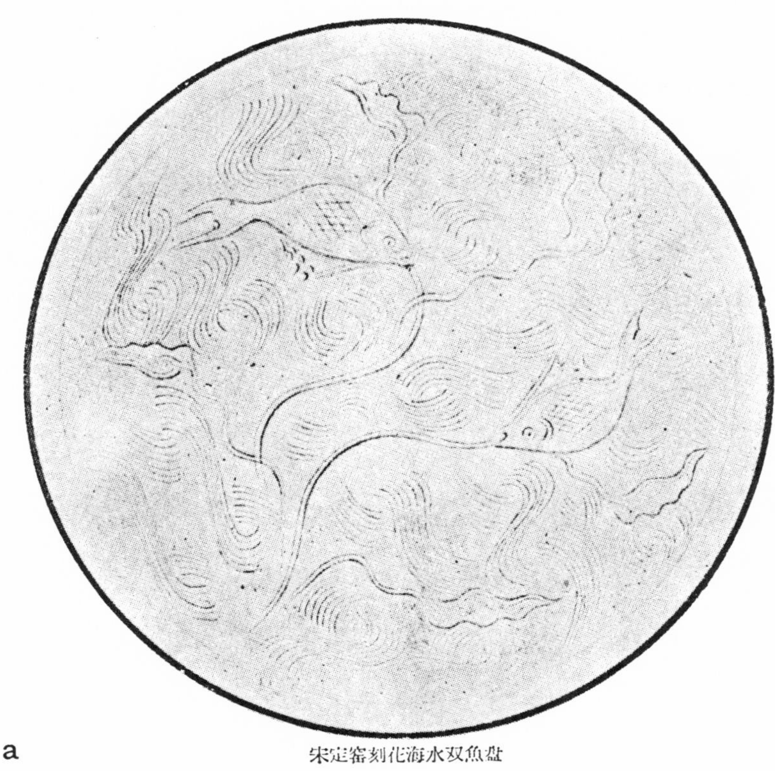

a 宋定窑刻花海水双魚盘

b

c

Fig. 28

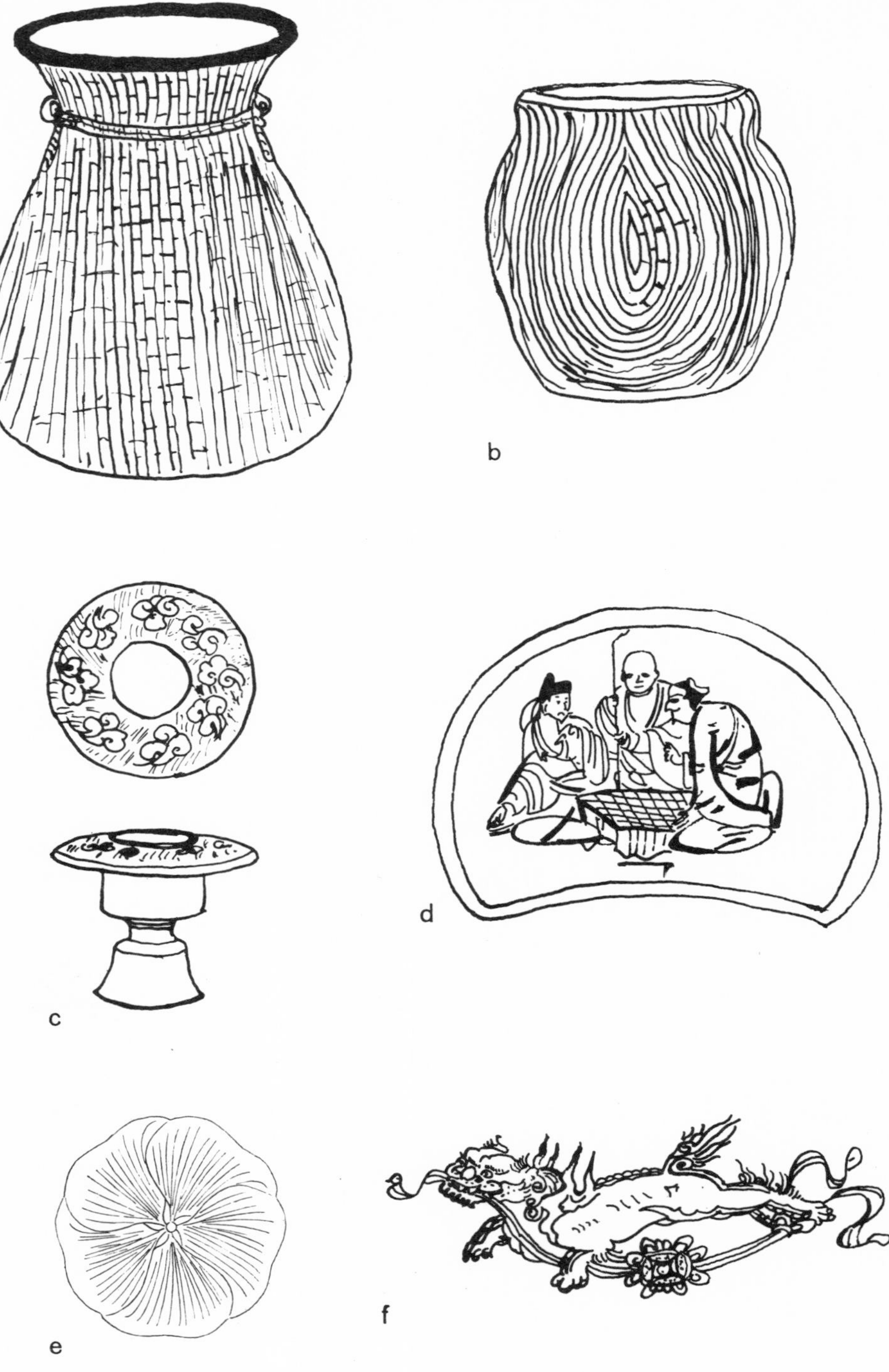

Fig. 29

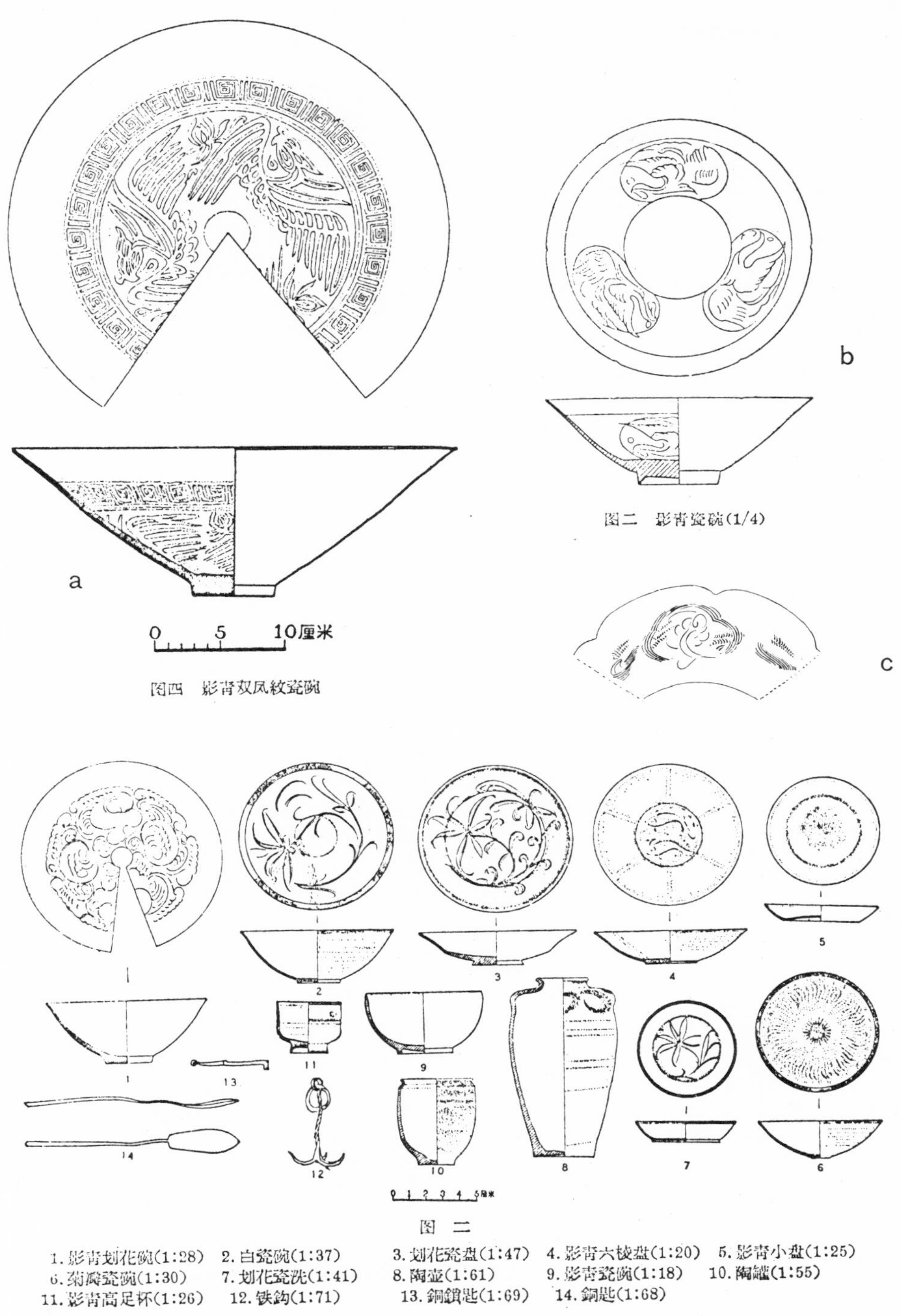

图 二

1. 影青划花碗(1:28) 2. 白瓷碗(1:37) 3. 划花瓷盘(1:47) 4. 影青六棱盘(1:20) 5. 影青小盘(1:25)
6. 菊瓣瓷碗(1:30) 7. 划花瓷洗(1:41) 8. 陶壶(1:61) 9. 影青瓷碗(1:18) 10. 陶罐(1:55)
11. 影青高足杯(1:26) 12. 铁鉤(1:71) 13. 銅鎖匙(1:69) 14. 銅匙(1:68)

Fig. 30

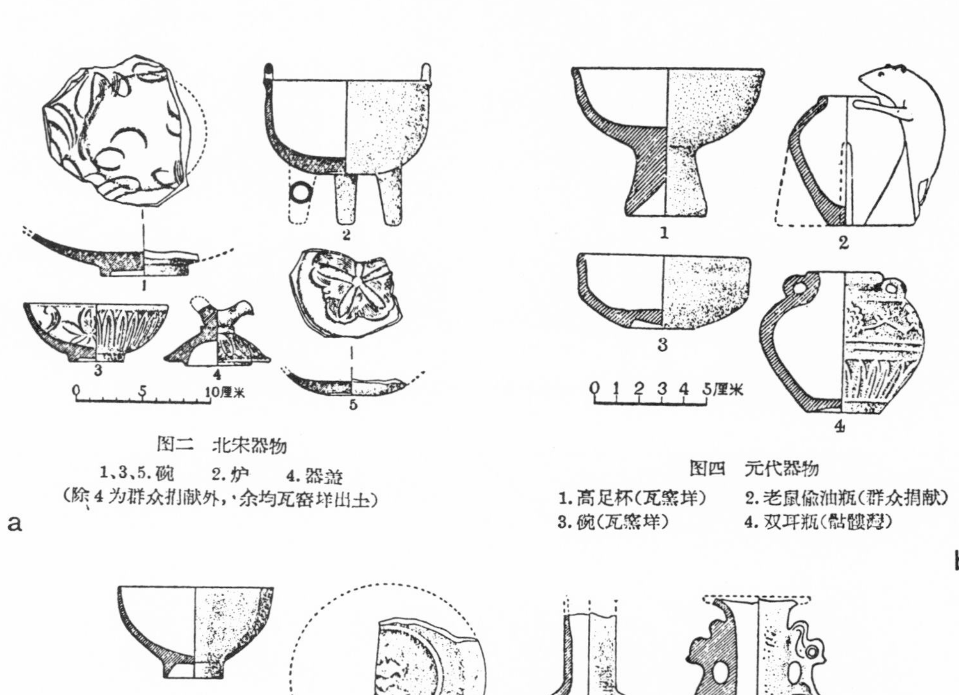

图二　北宋器物

1、3、5.碗　2.炉　4.器盖

(除4为群众捐献外，余均瓦窑垟出土)

a

图四　元代器物

1.高足杯(瓦窯垟)　2.老鼠偷油瓶(群众捐献)

3.碗(瓦窯垟)　4.双耳瓶(骷髅湖)

b

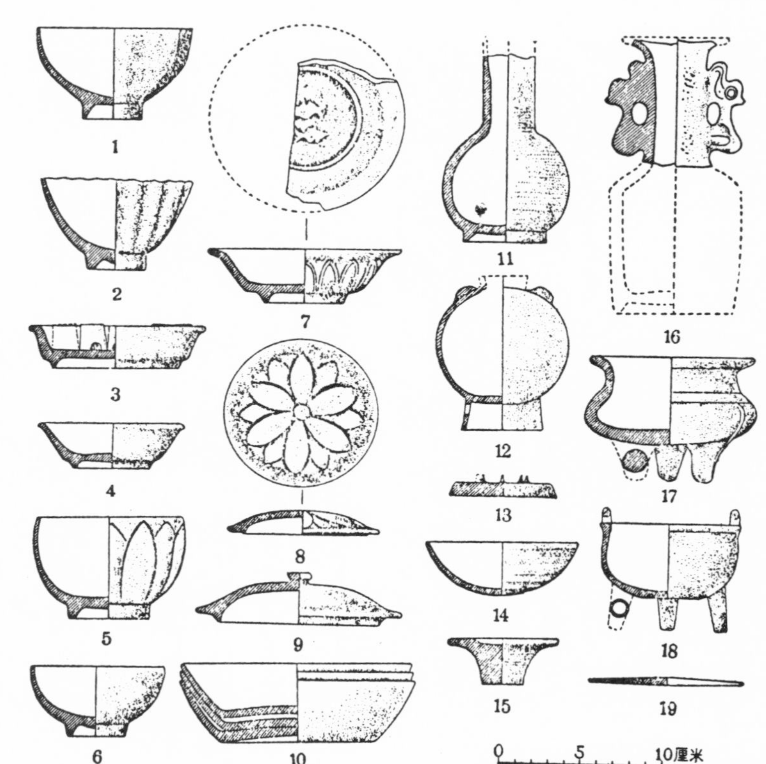

图三　南宋器物

1、2、4—6.碗　3.灯　7、10.洗　8—9.盖　11.长颈瓶　12.扁壶
13—15、19.窯具　16.凤耳瓶　17、18.炉 (5.旻下，7.骷髅湖，11.群众捐献，14、17.李家山，余均瓦窑垟出土)

c

Fig. 31

a

b

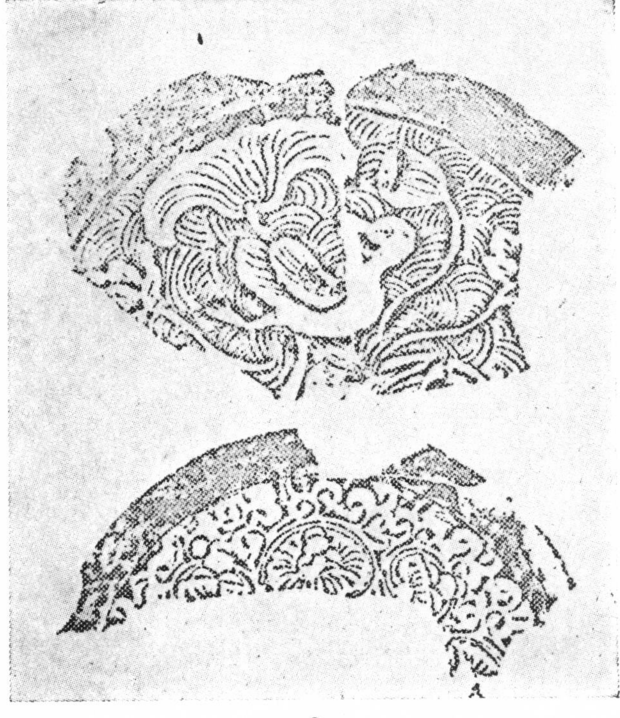

c

d

e

Fig. 32

图二　北宋瓷器上的印花和刻花紋飾摹本（1/4）

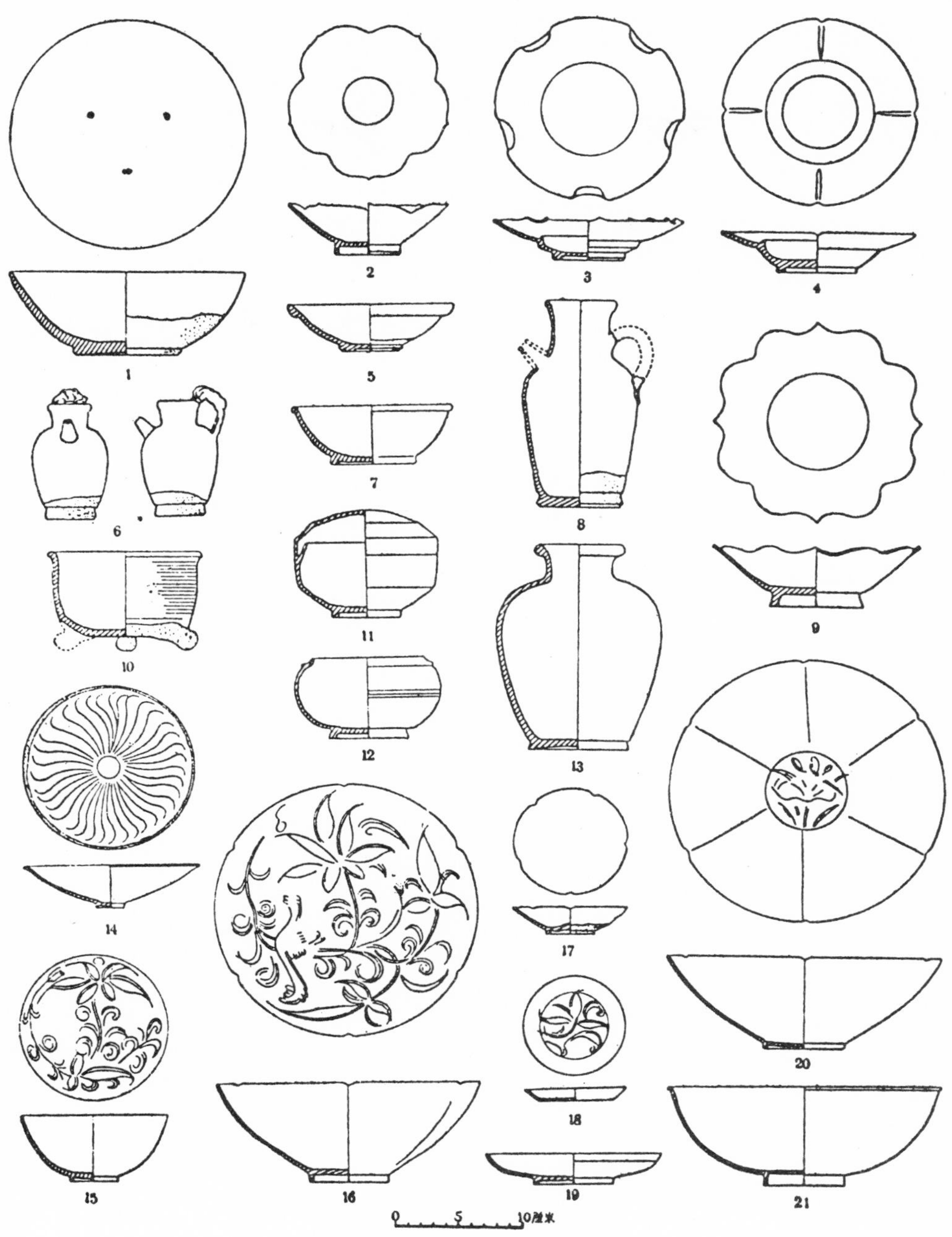

图七 采集遗物

1、5、7、21. 碗(963、001、927、929) 2、9、19. 盘(925、005、919) 3、4. 托盘(928、002) 6、8. 注壶(932、003) 10. 三足炉(964) 11. 奁盒(006) 12. 罐(926) 13. 瓶(949) 14. 划花碗(923) 15、16、20. 刻花碗(007、942、962) 17、18. 碟(924、920)

Fig. 34

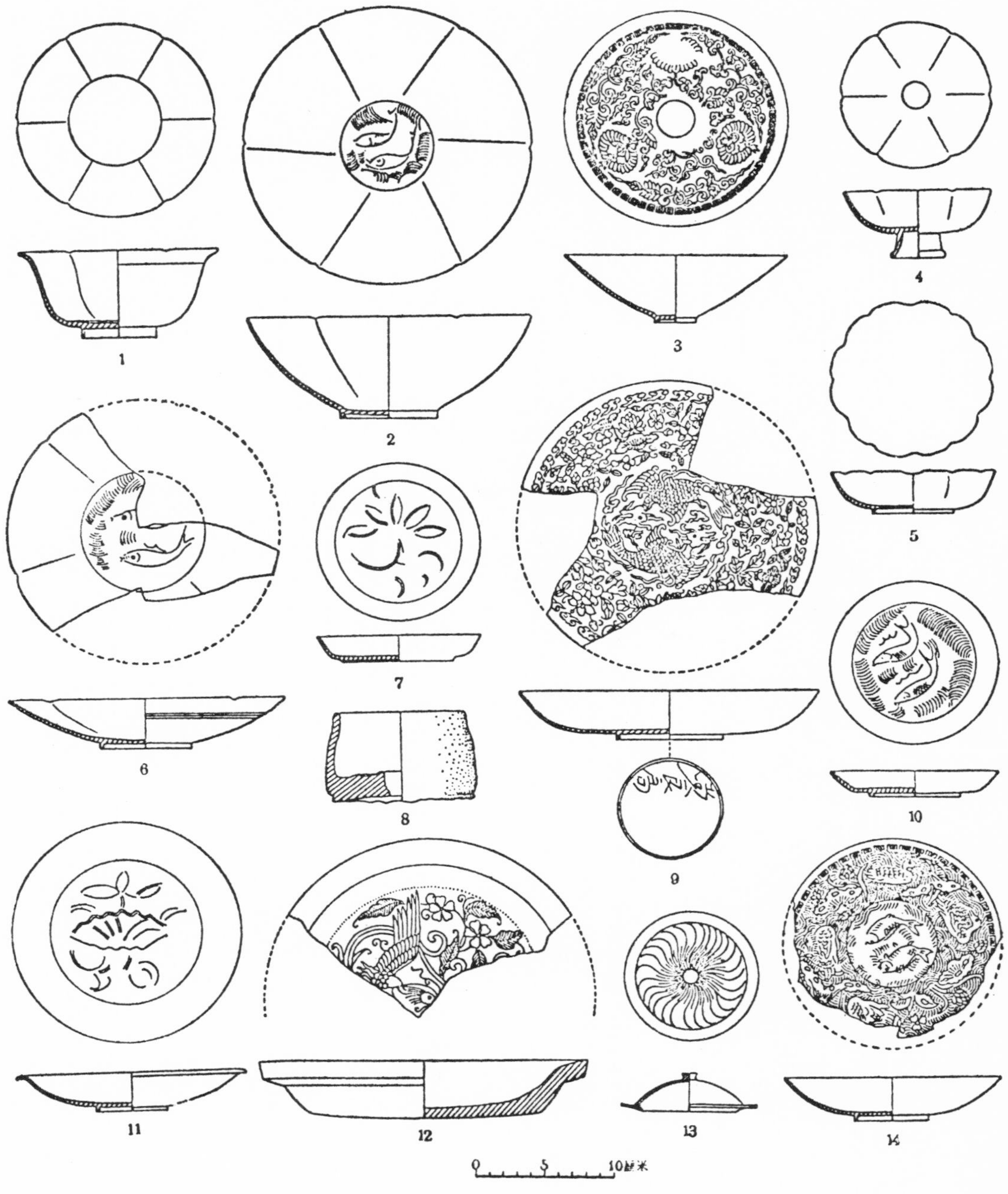

图 一〇

1—4.碗(T7①:10、T9①:8、T11①:5、T4①:9) 5—7、9—11、14.盘(T9①:12、T6①:1、T6①:4、T9①:10、T9①:4、T12①:5、T7①:9) 8.匣钵(T9①:15) 12.印花盘残模(T6①:12) 13.器盖(T9①:14)

Fig. 35

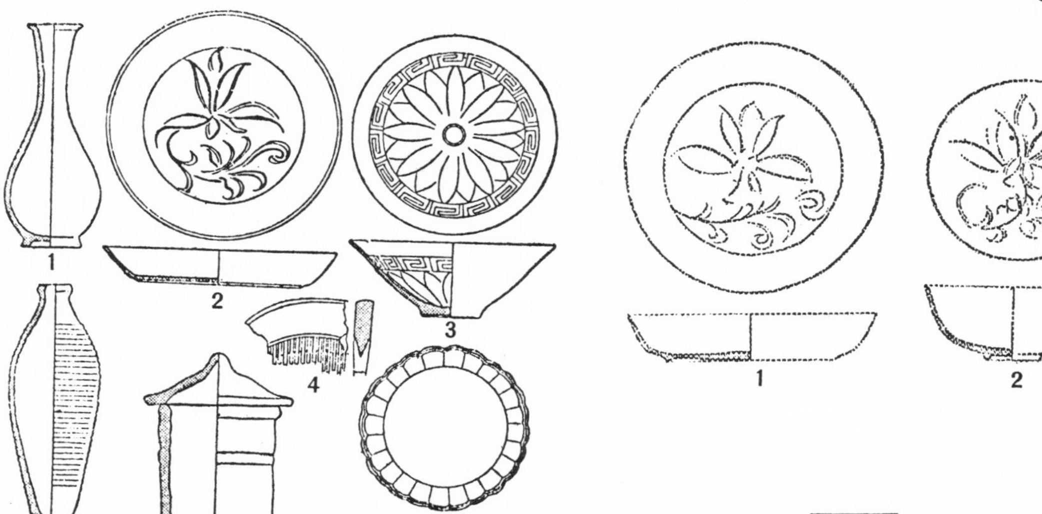

b

图 八

1. 翠綠釉長頸陶瓶 2. 白瓷碟 3. 影青印花小瓷碗
4. 骨梳子 5. 灰綠釉鸡腿罈 6. 骨灰罐 7. 影青瓷碟

(1、6 为1/8, 4为1/2, 5为1/16, 余均1/4)

a

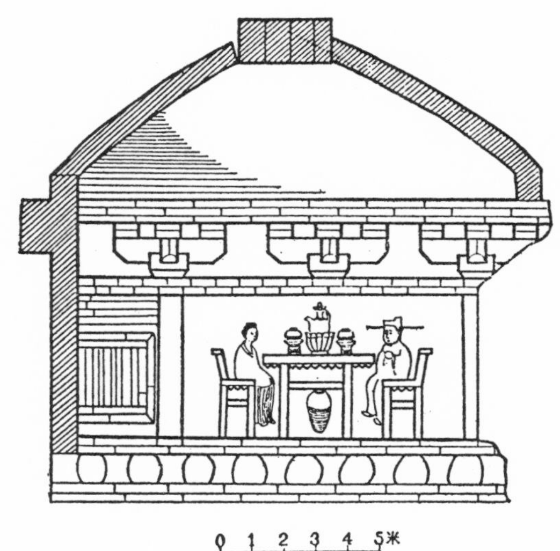

c

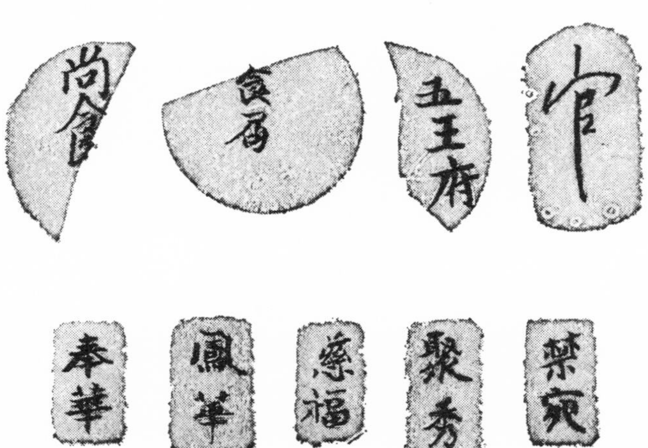

插图3 宋 定 窑 銘 文 拓 本

d

Fig. 36

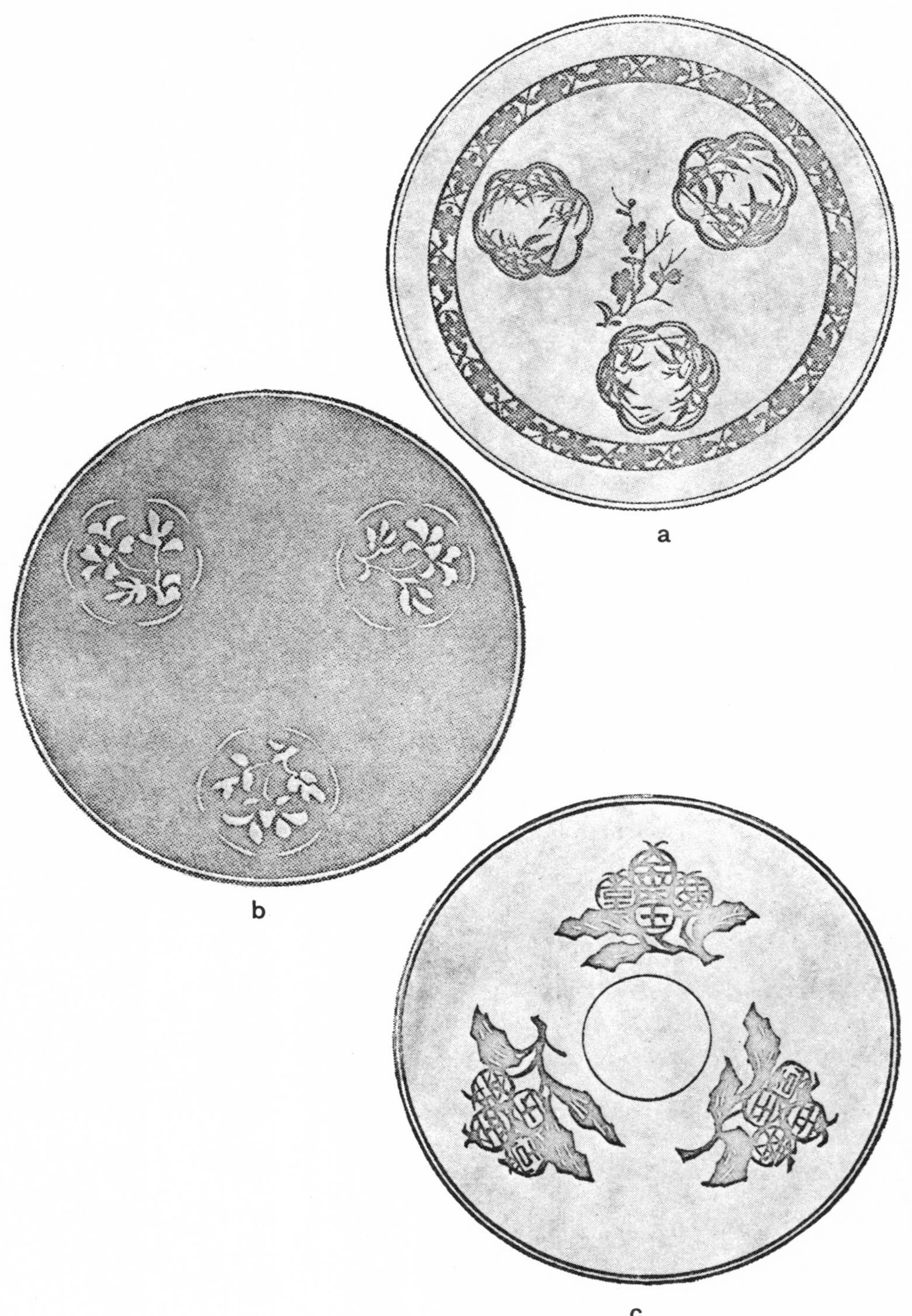

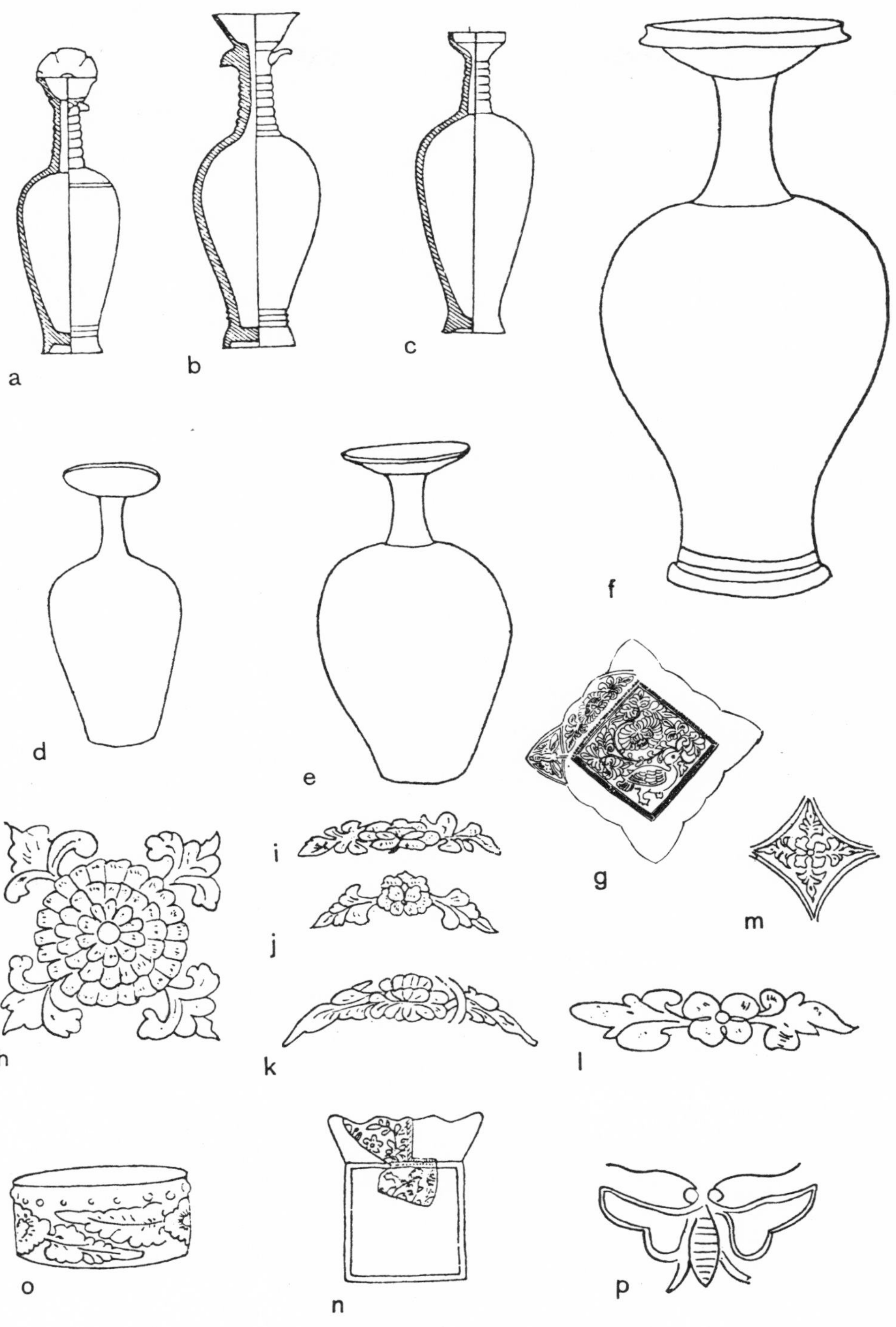
a
b
c
f
d
e
g
i
j
m
h
k
l
o
n
p

Fig. 38

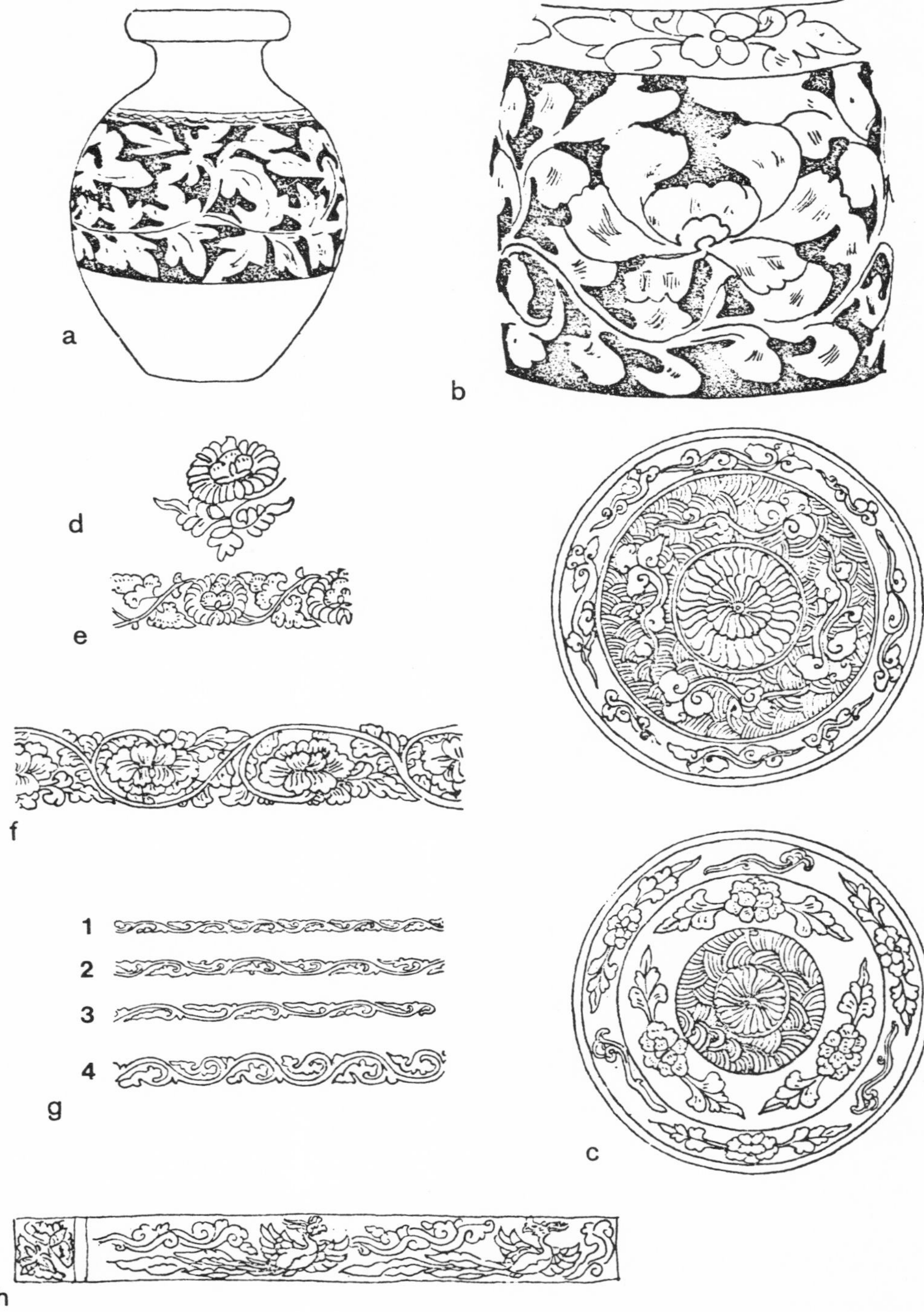

Fig. 39

a

图四　大型芙蓉花銅鏡(1/4)

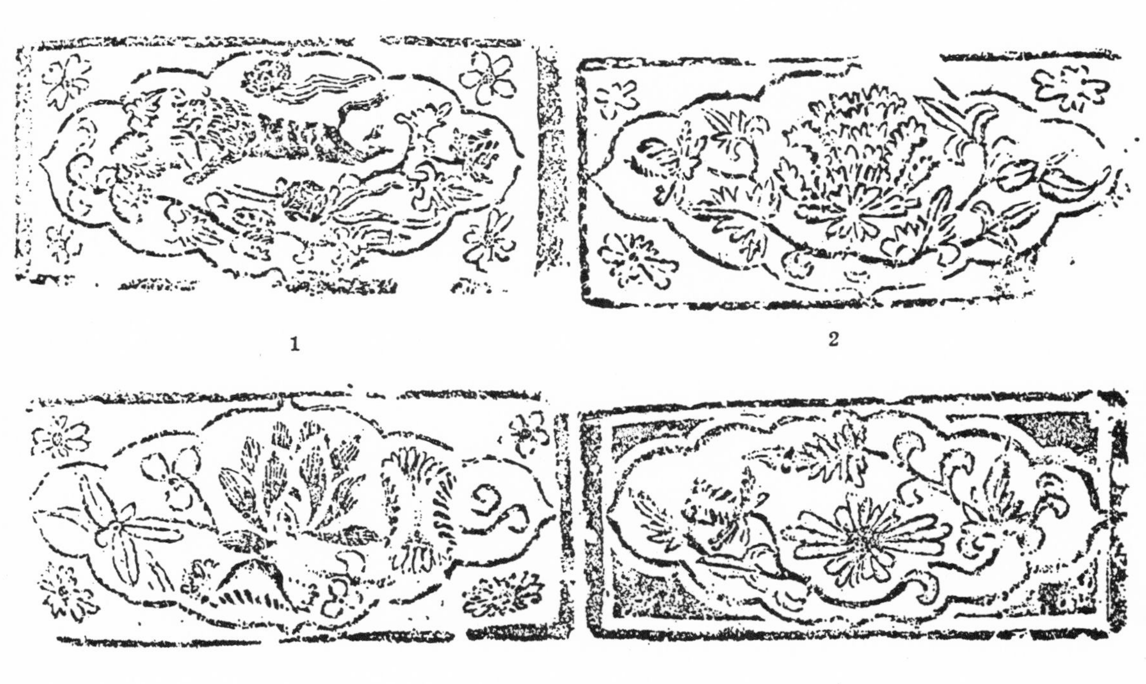

b

图四　北壁須弥座上束腰花磚紋飾拓本（約2/9）
1. 獅子　2. 牡丹　3. 荷花　4. 菊花

Fig. 40

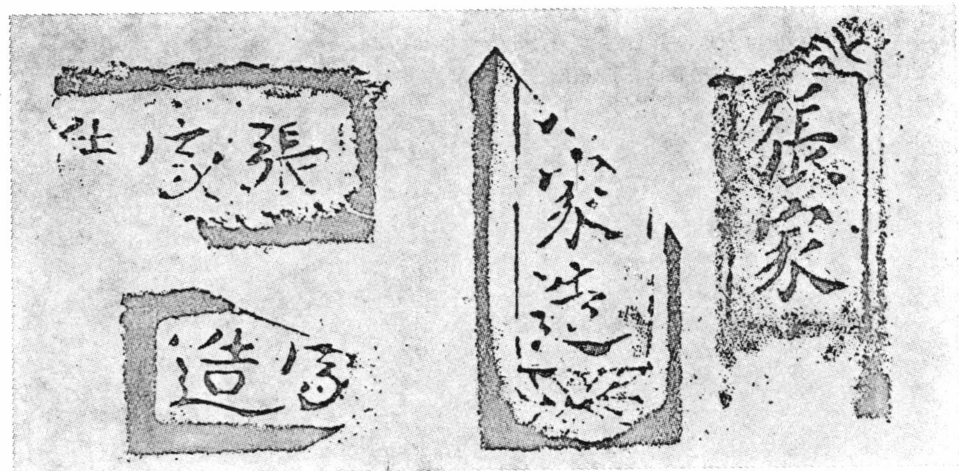

图二四　东艾口"张家造"枕款

a

b

Fig. 41

a

b

Fig. 42

a

b

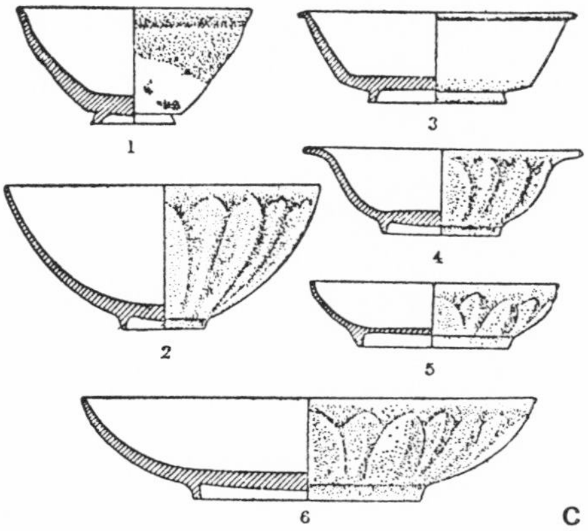

c

图一 1.黑釉瓷碗(1:15) 2.青瓷莲瓣碗(1:4) 3.青瓷洗(1:8) 4.青瓷洗(1:2) 5.青瓷莲瓣盘(1:1) 6.青瓷莲瓣盘(1:6)

d

Fig. 43

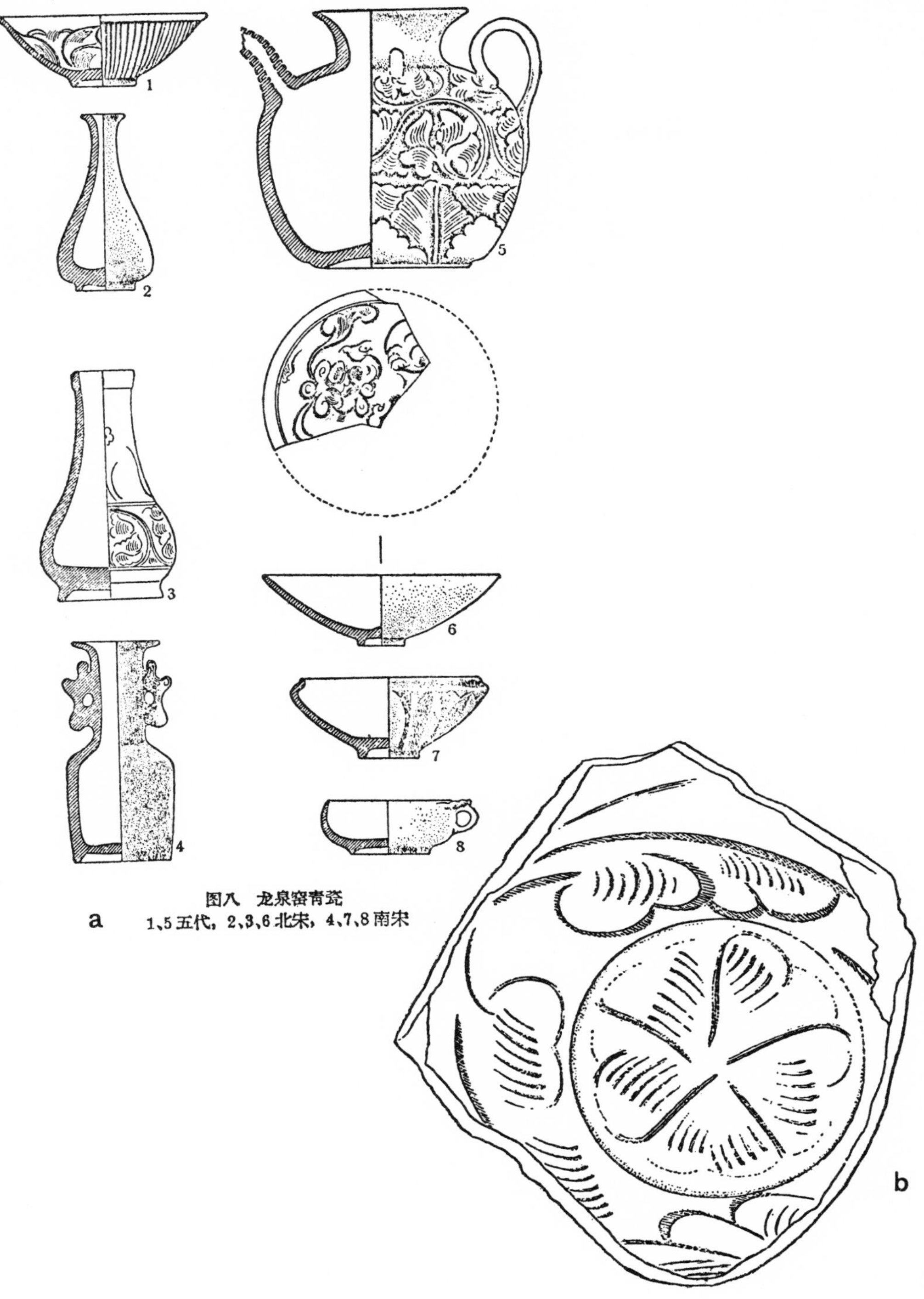

图八　龙泉窑青瓷

a　1、5 五代，2、3、6 北宋，4、7、8 南宋

b

a b c

d e f

g h i

j k l

Pl. 2

a b c

d e f

g h i

j k l

a b c

d e f

g h i

j k l

Pl. 4

a b c
d e f
g h i
j k l

a b c

d e f

g h i

j k l

Pl. 6

a

b

c

d

e

f

g

h

i

j

k

l

a b c

d e f

g h i

j k l

Pl. 8

a b c d e f g h i j k l

a b c

d e f

g h i

j k l

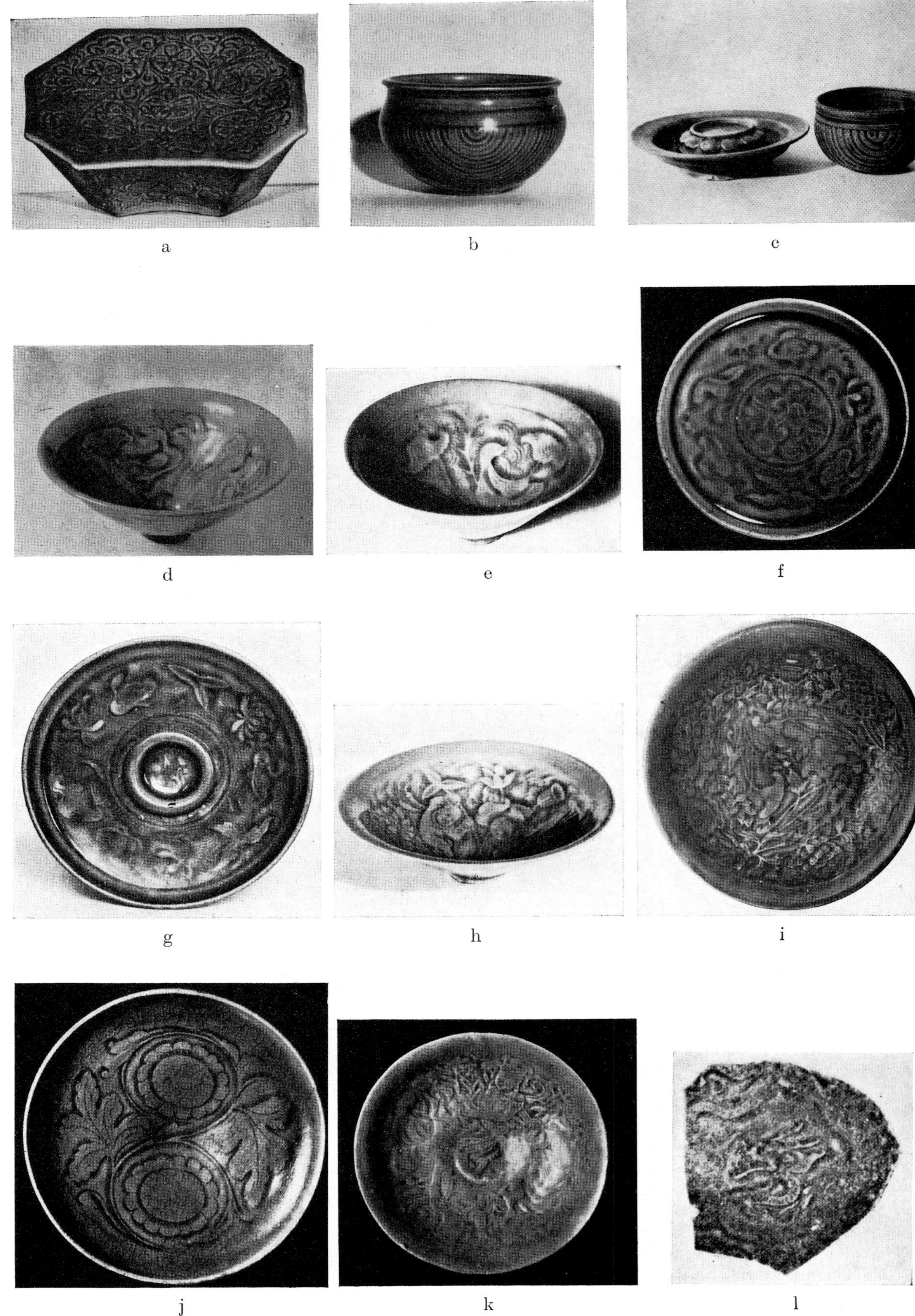

a b c

d e f

g h i

j k l

a b c d e f g h i j k l

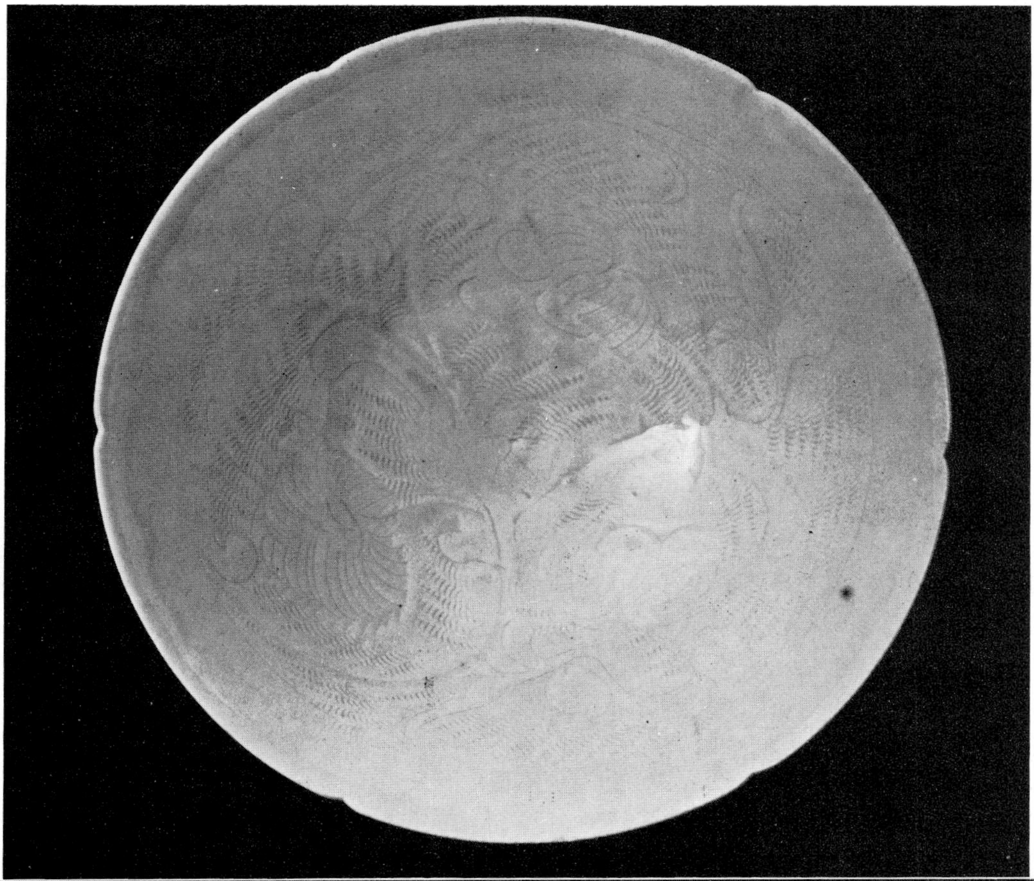

a

b

Pl. 14

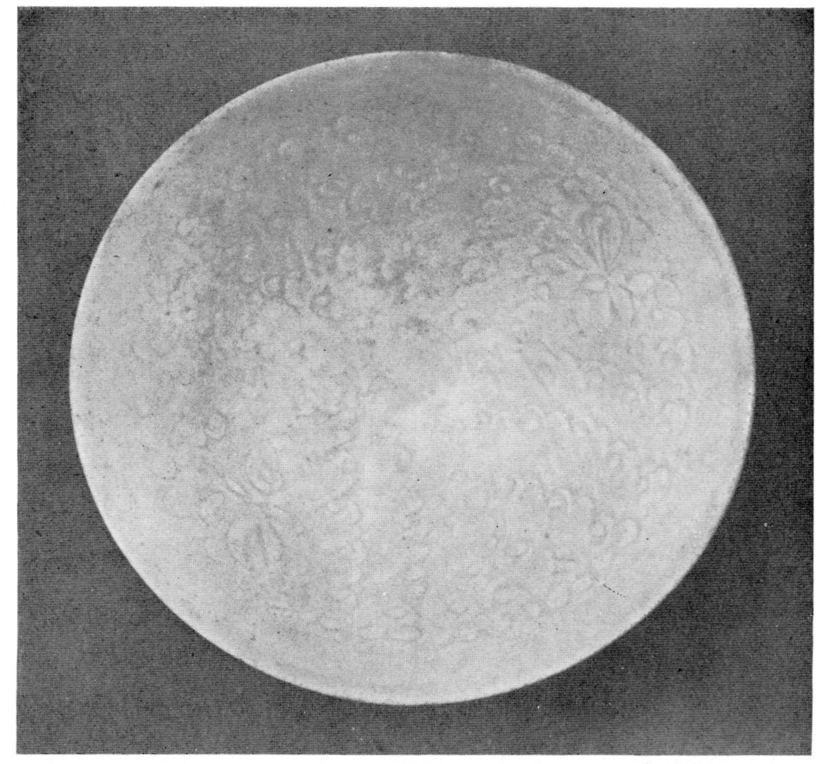

a

b

a

b

a

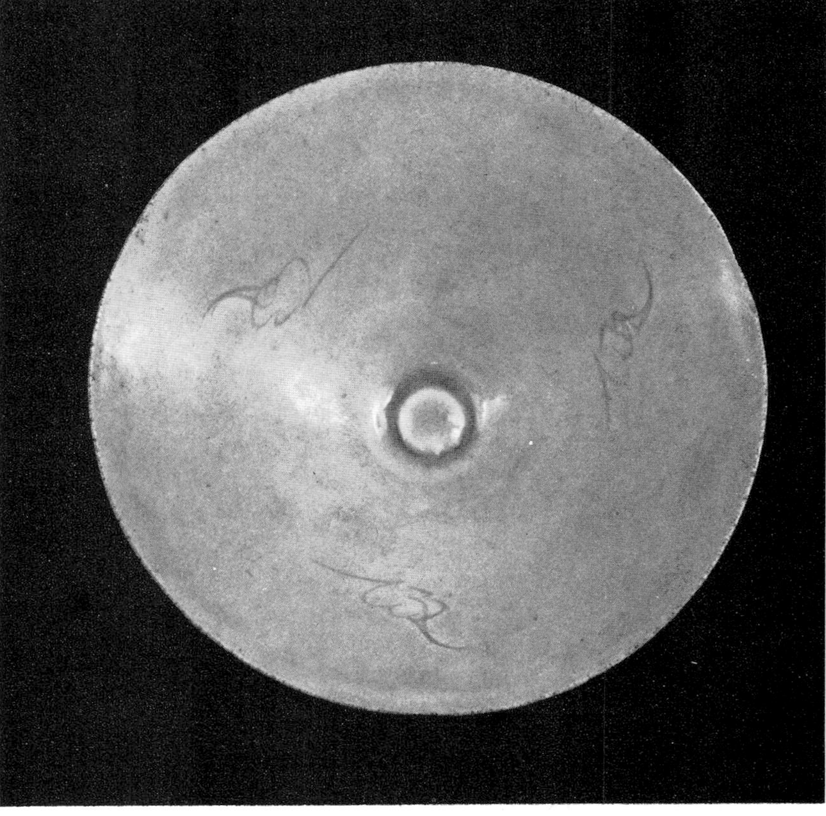

b

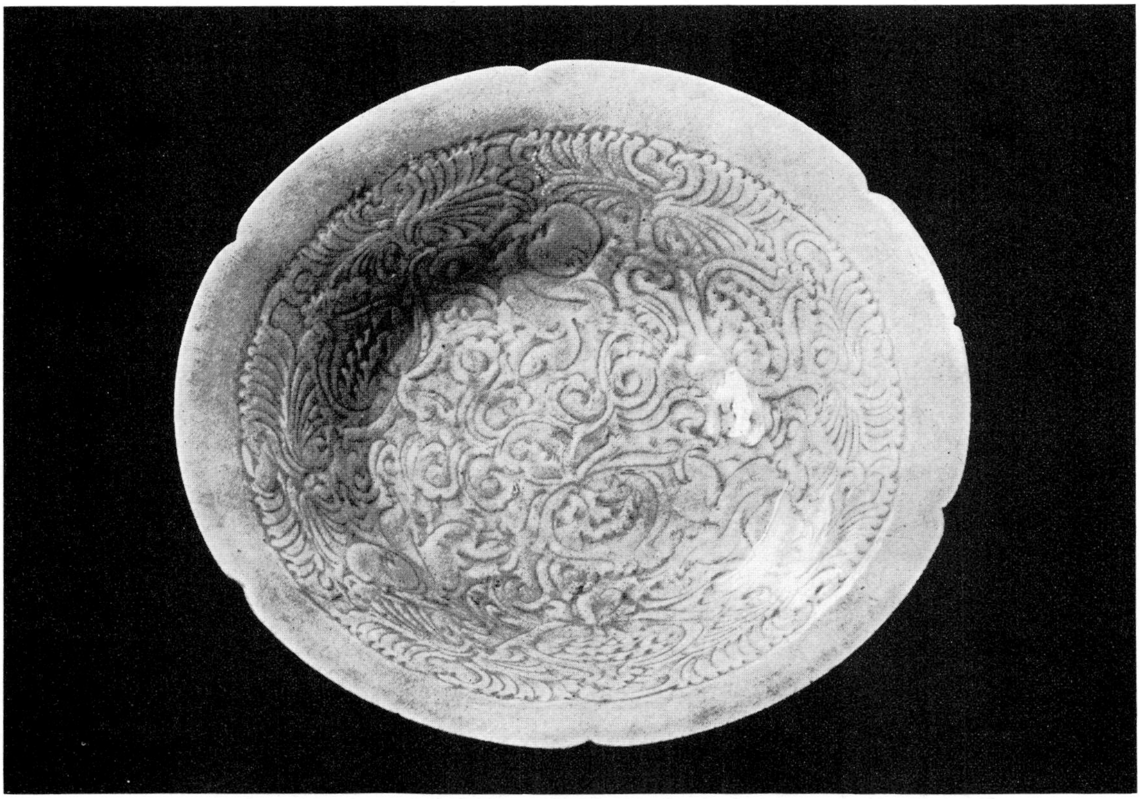

a

b

a

b

a

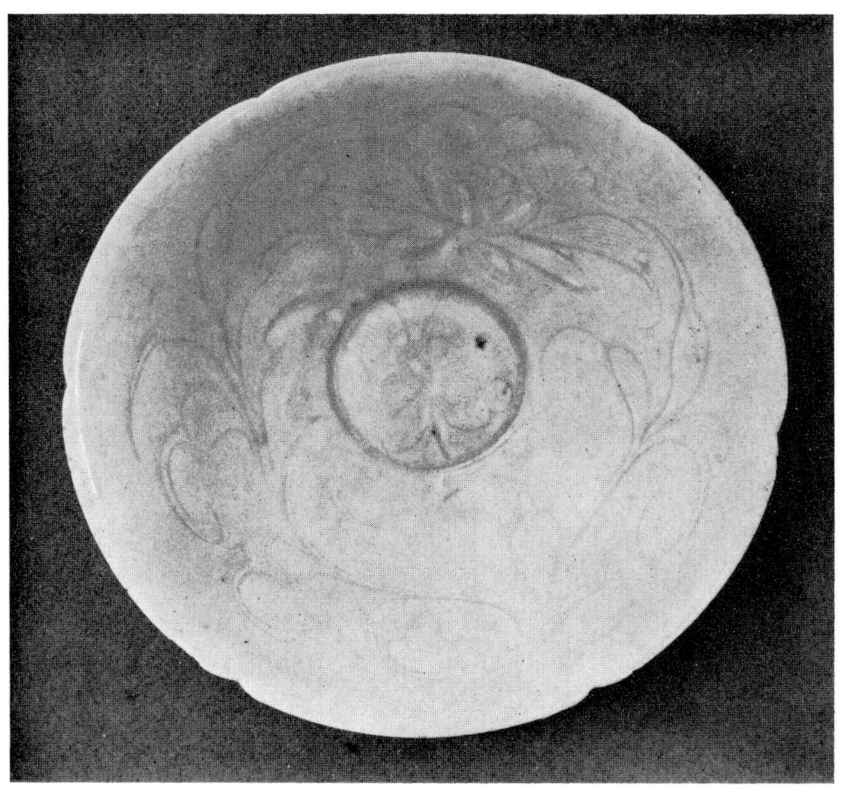

b

a b c

d e f

g h i

j k l

a b c

d e f

g h i

j k l

a

b

a

b

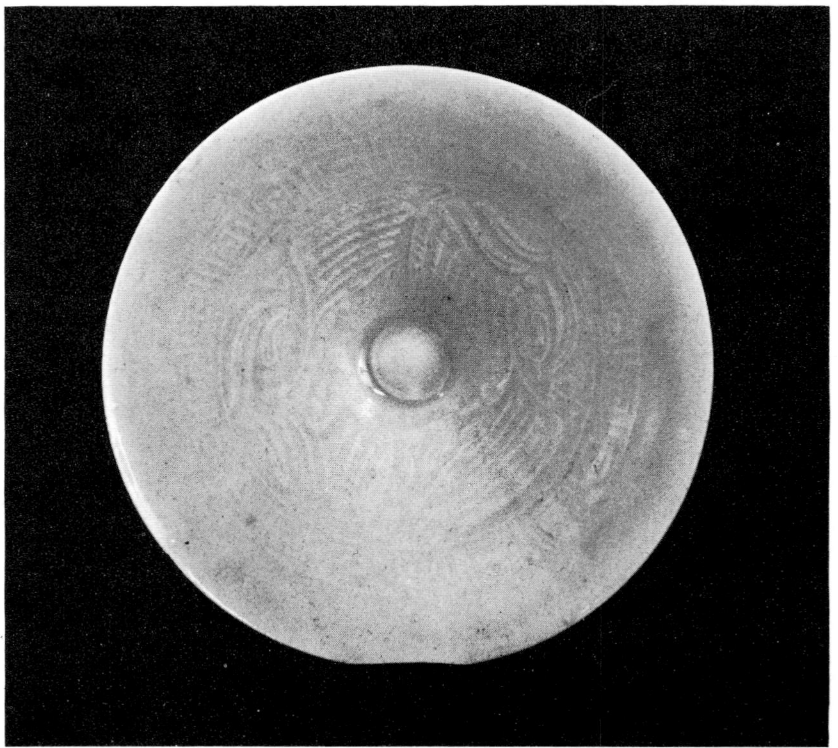

b

a

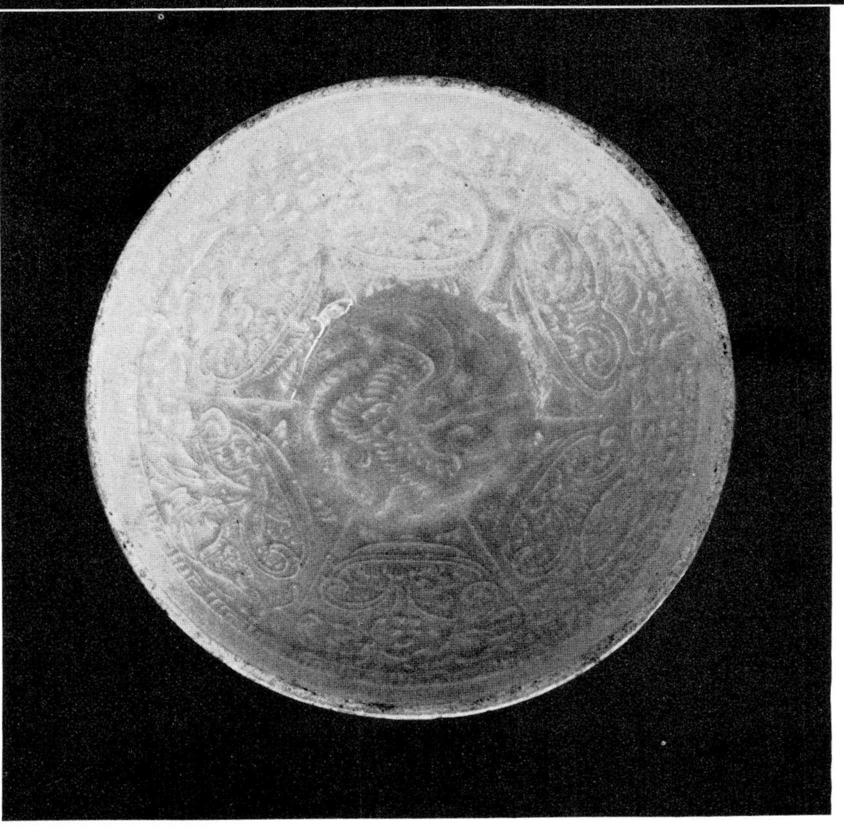

b

a
b
c
d
e
f
g
h
i
j
k
l

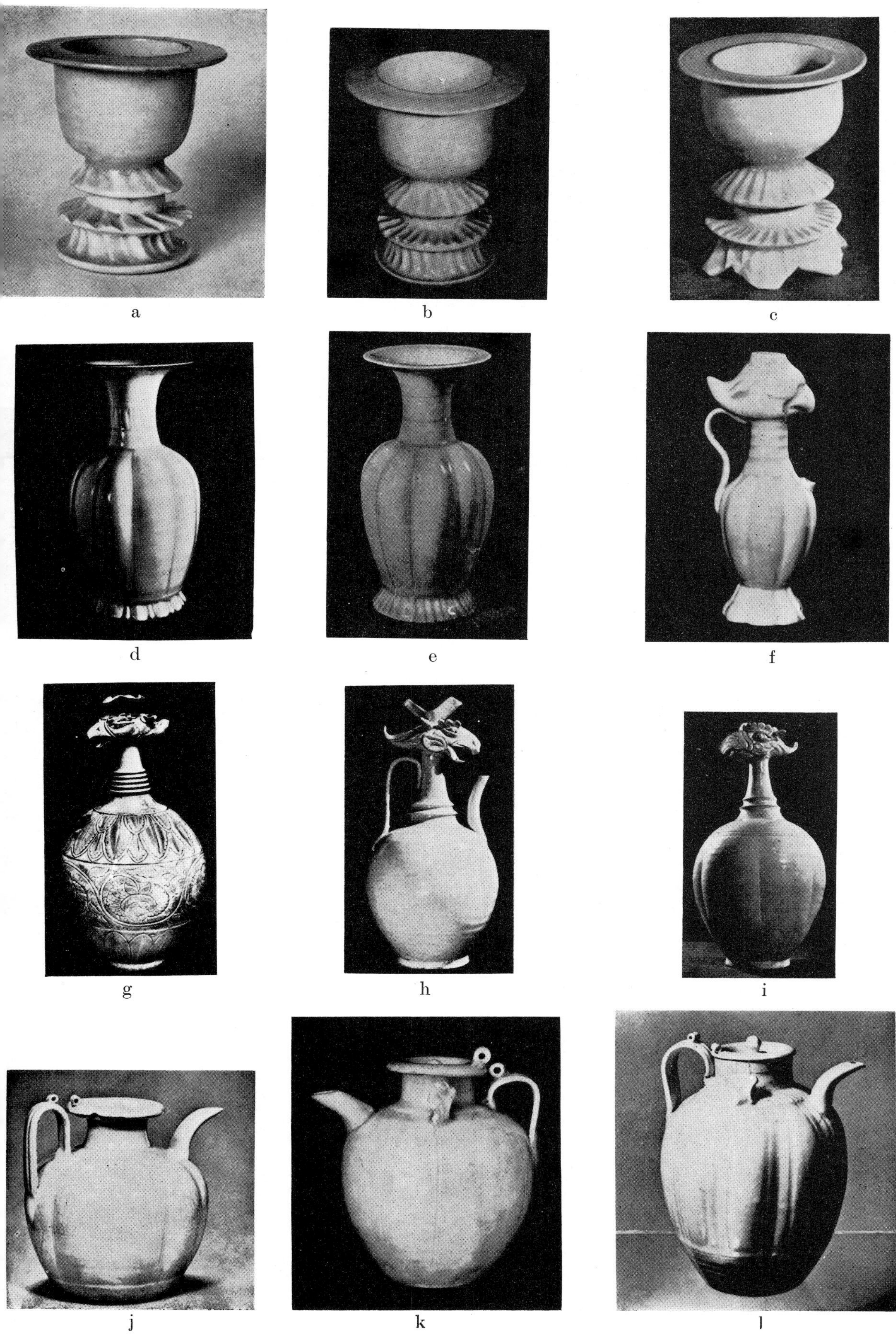

a b c d e f g h i j k l

a

b

a

b

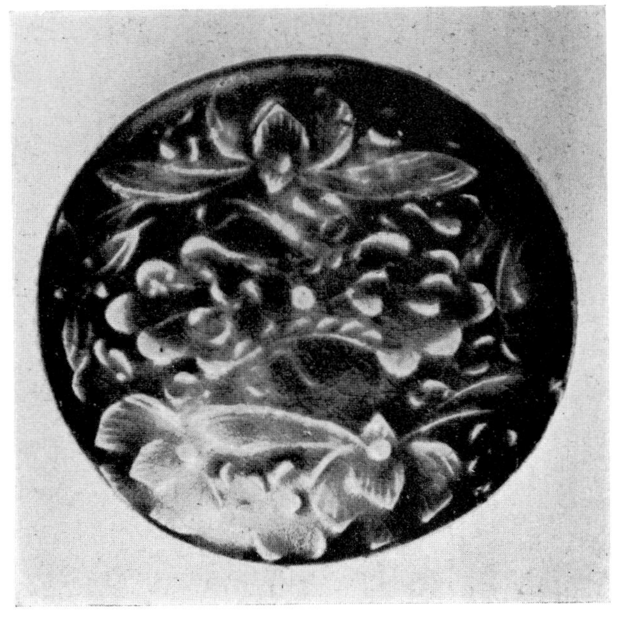

c

a

b

c

a

b

a

b

a

b

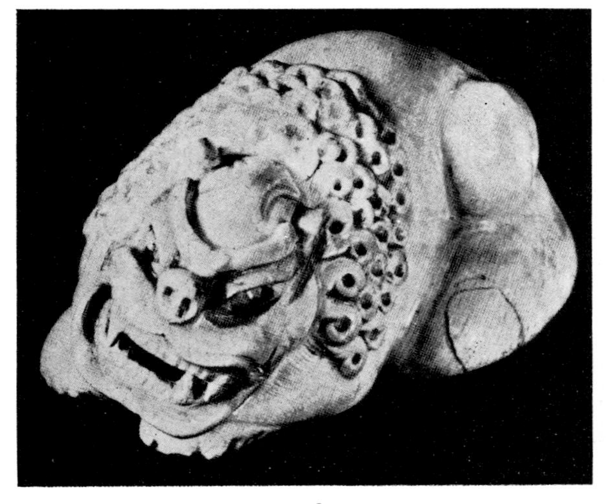

c

d

a b c

d e f

g h i

j k l

a

b

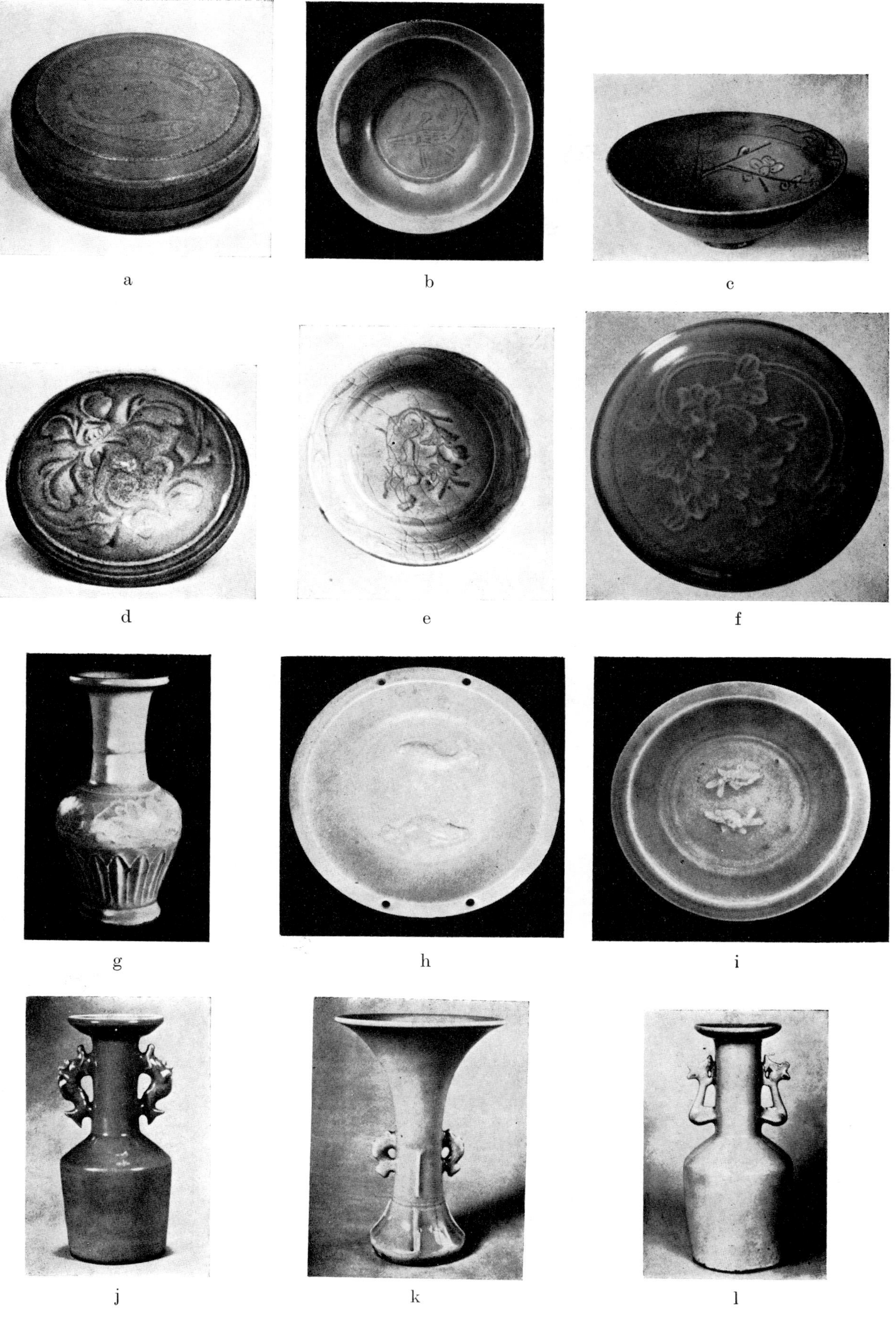

a b c

d e f

g h i

j k l

Pl. 40

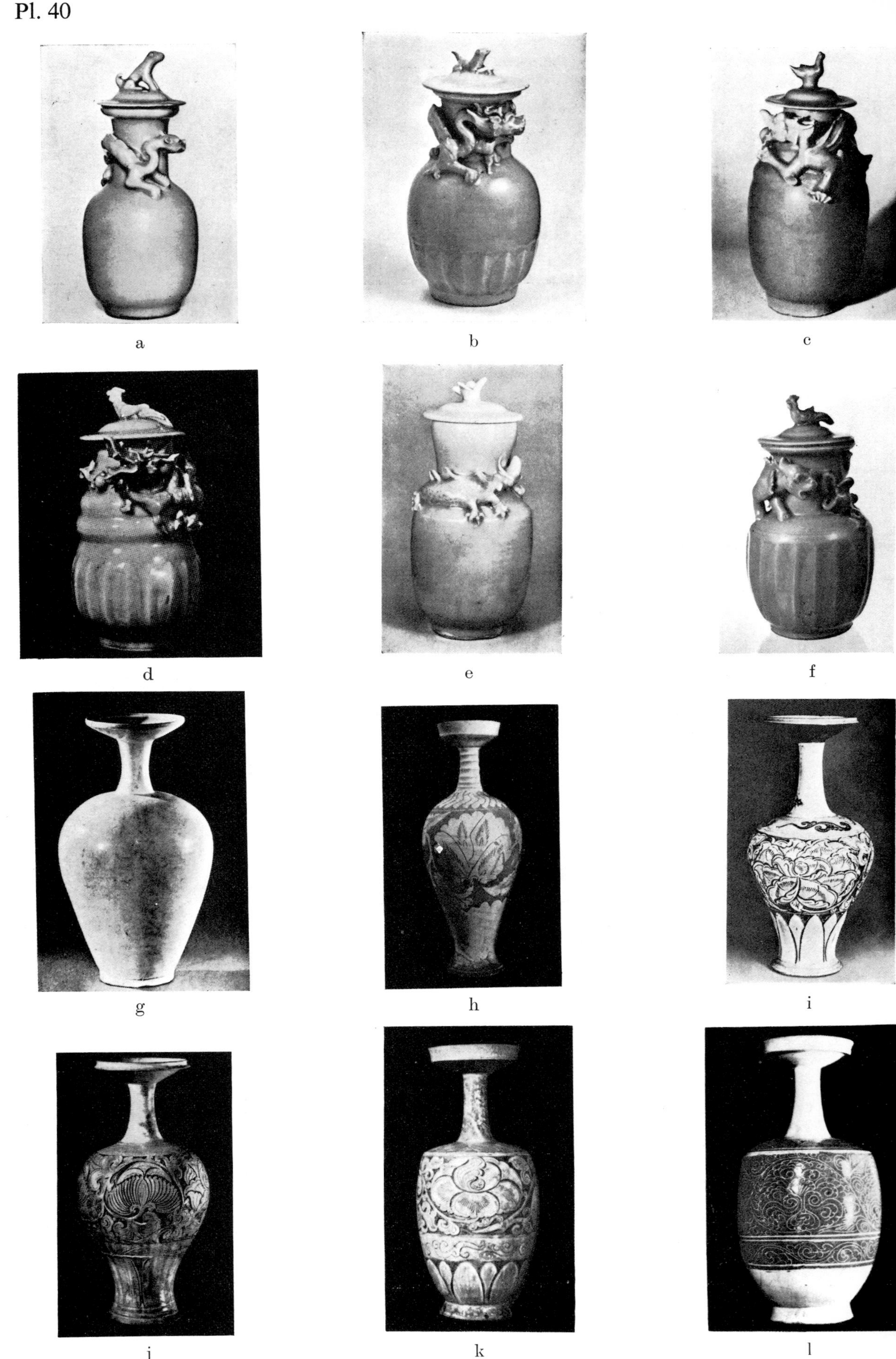

a b c

d e f

g h i

j k l

a b c

d e f

g h i

j k l

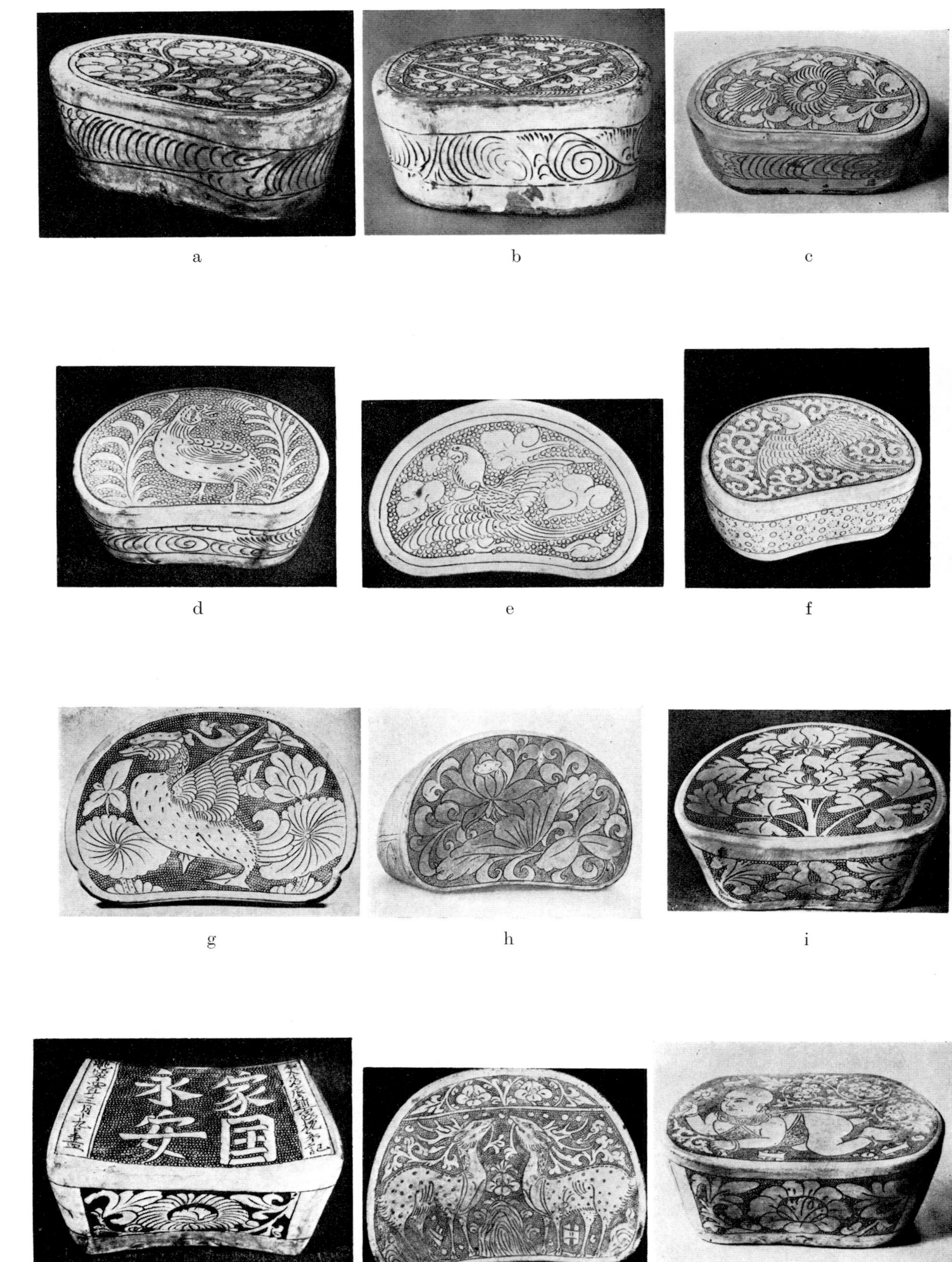

a b c

d e f

g h i

j k l

Pl. 43

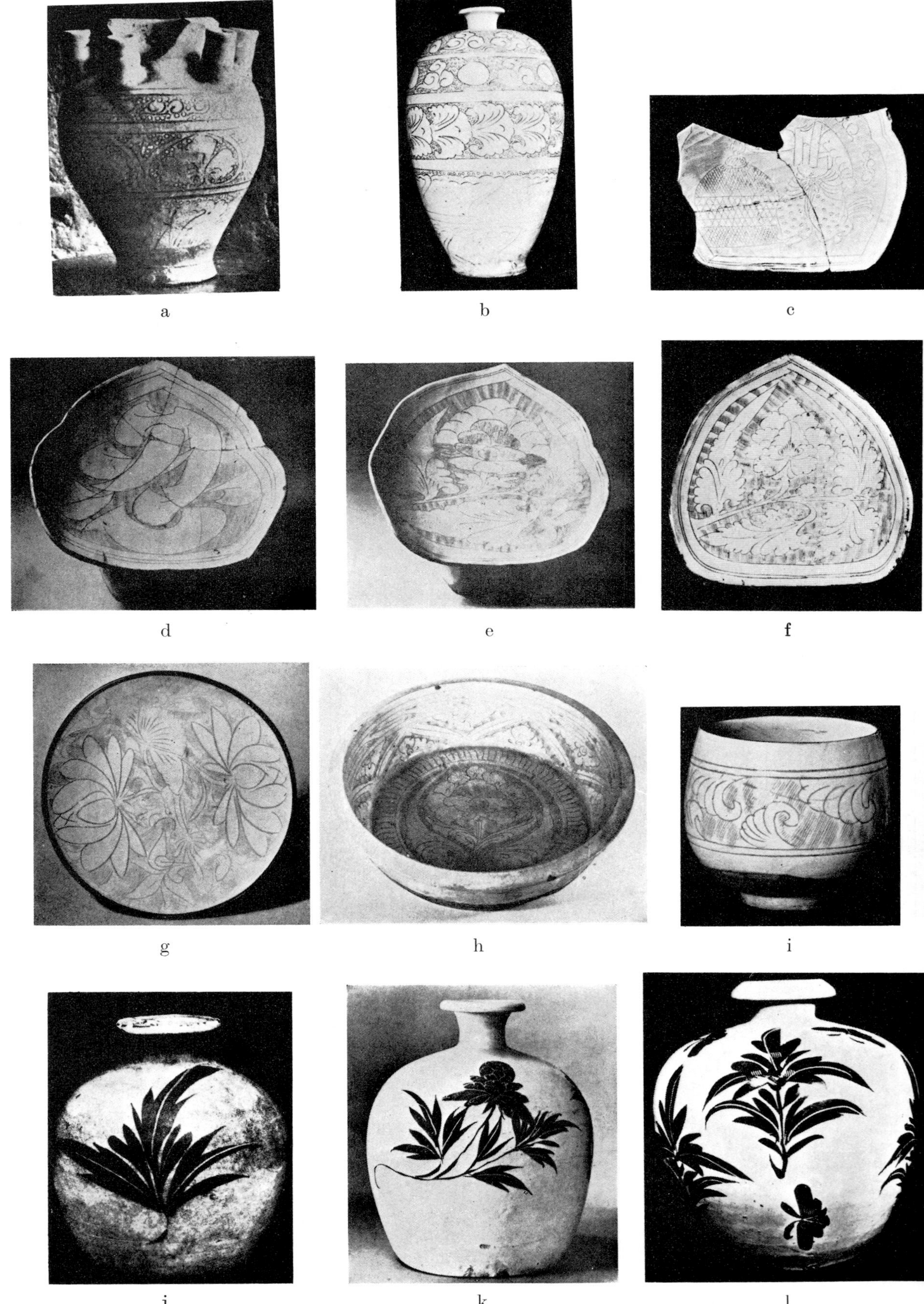

a b c

d e f

g h i

j k l

a b c

d e f

g h i

j k l

a b c

d e f

g h i

j k l

a b c

d e f

g h i

j k l

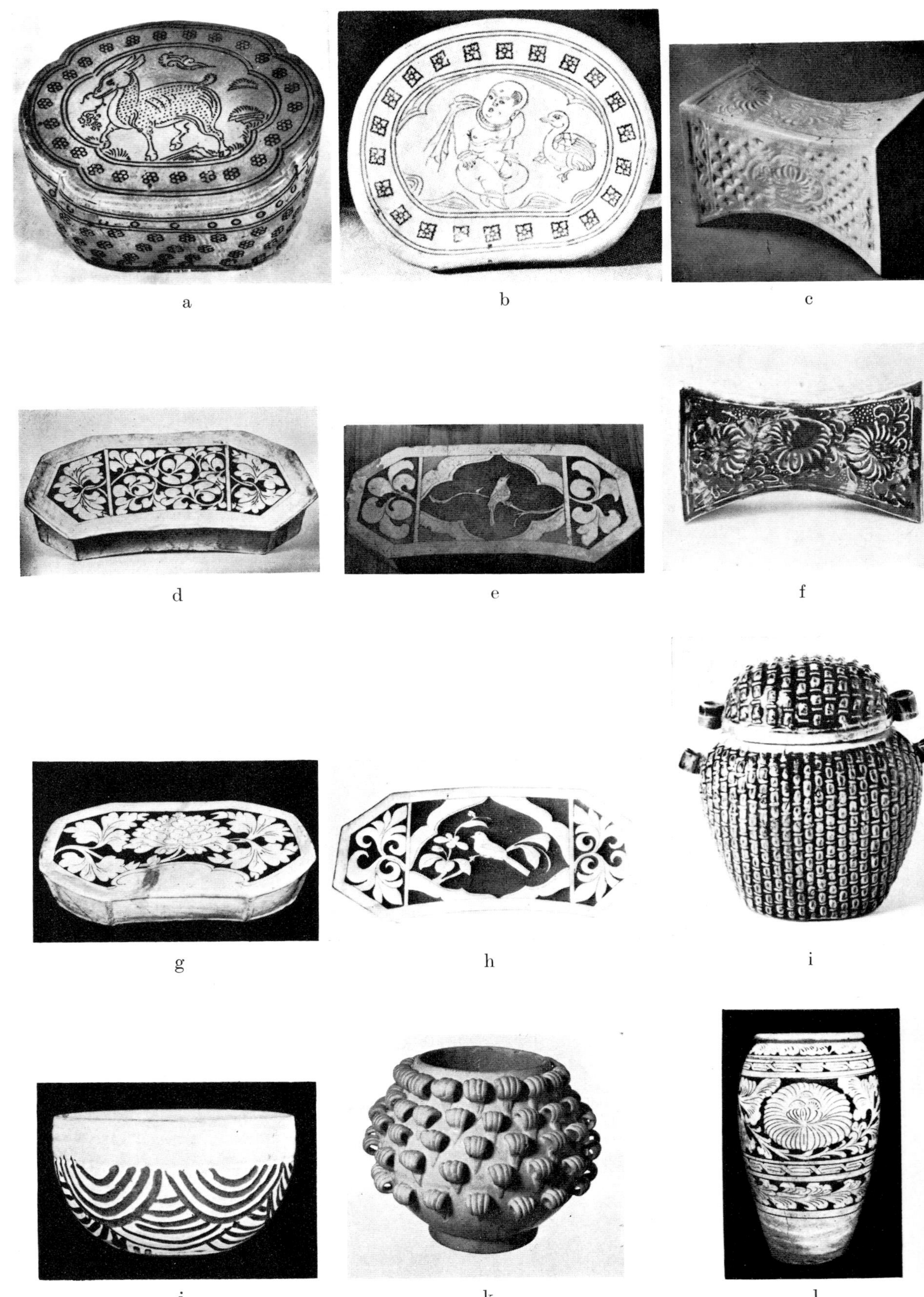

a b c

d e f

g h i

j k l

a b c

d e f

g h i

j k l

a b c

d e f

g h i

j k l

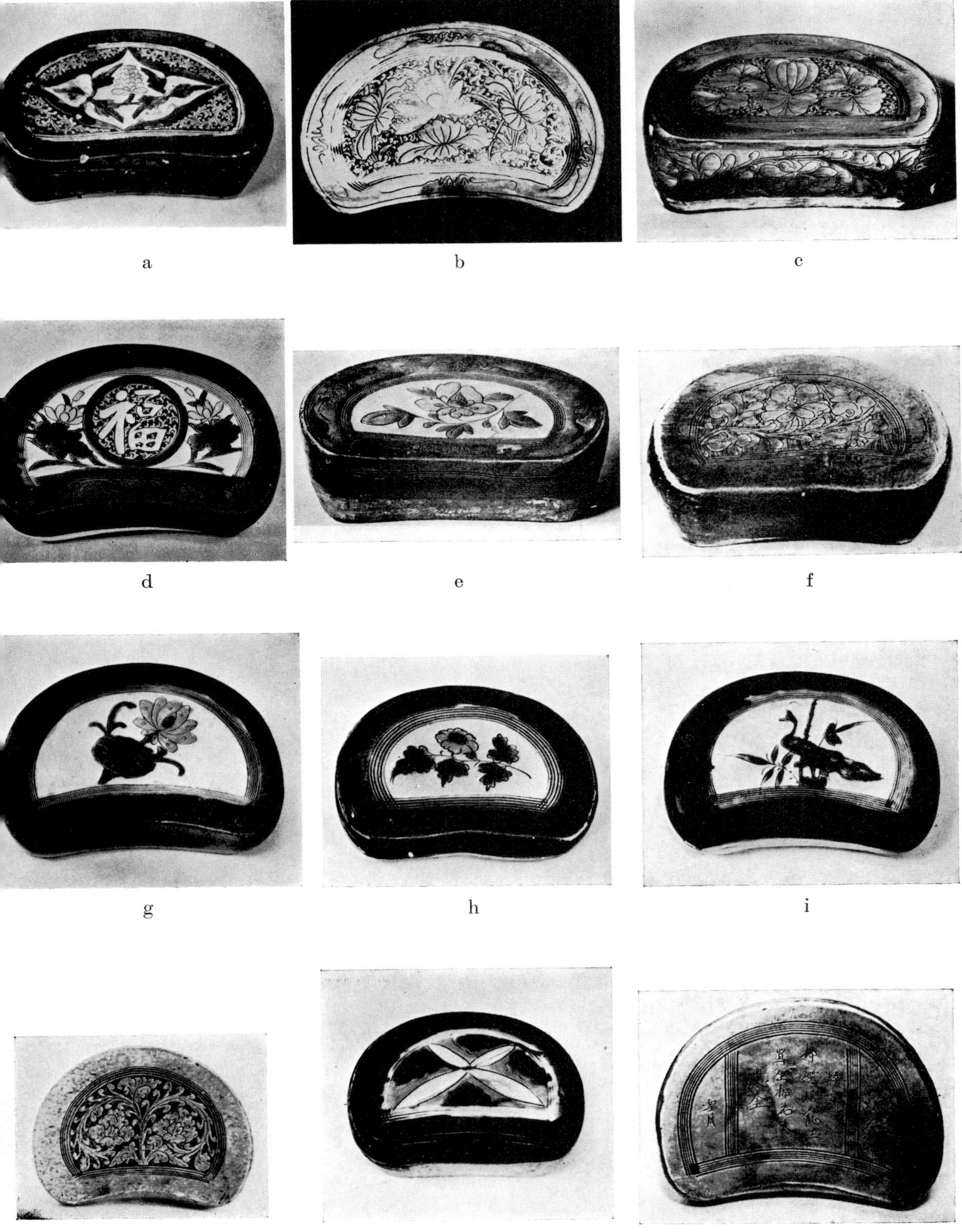

a b c

d e f

g h i

j k l

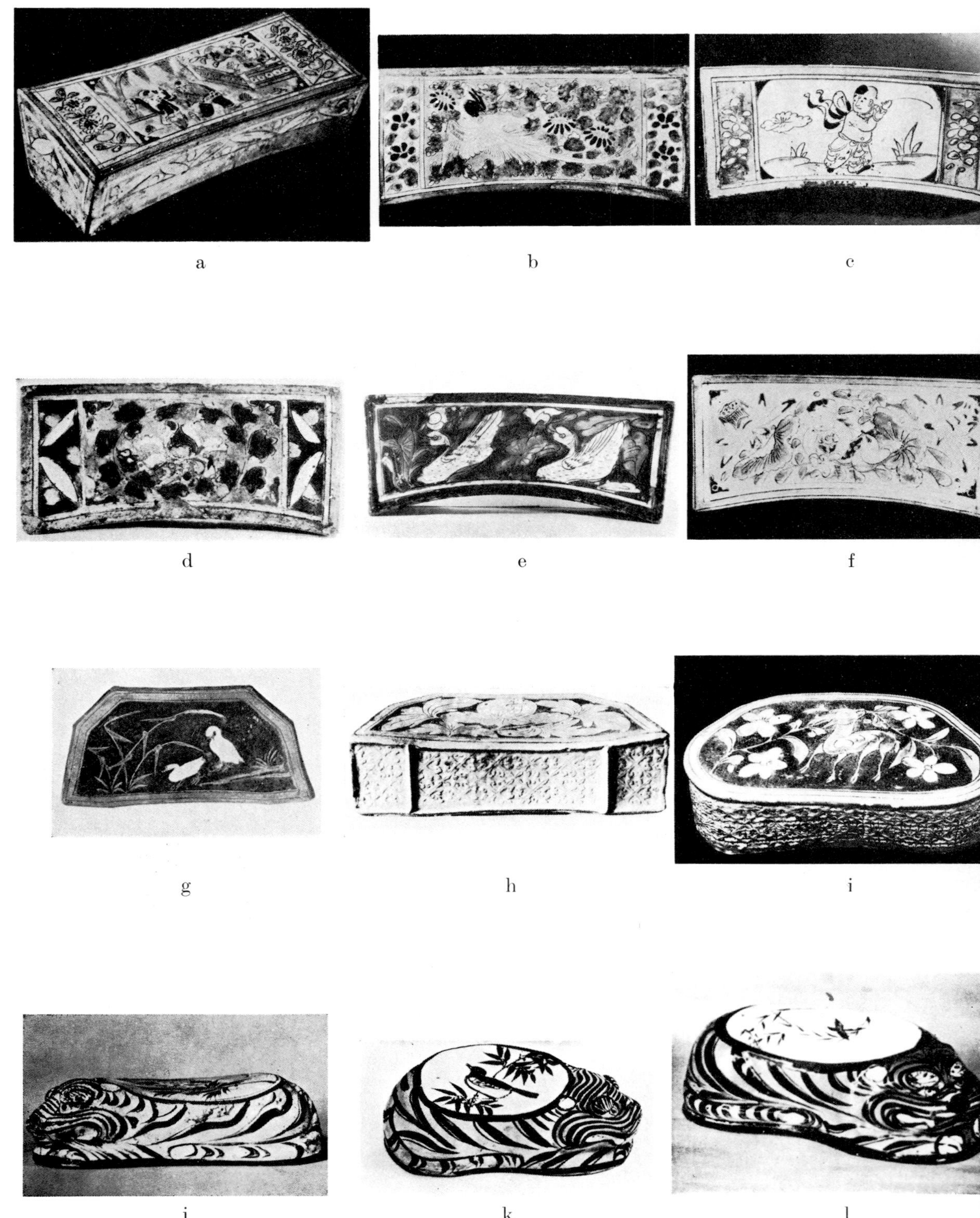

a b c

d e f

g h i

j k l

a
b
c
d
e
f
g
h
i
j
k
l

Pl. 54

a b c

d e f

g h i

j k l

a b c

d e f

g h i

j k l

Pl. 56

a b c

d e f

g h i

j k l

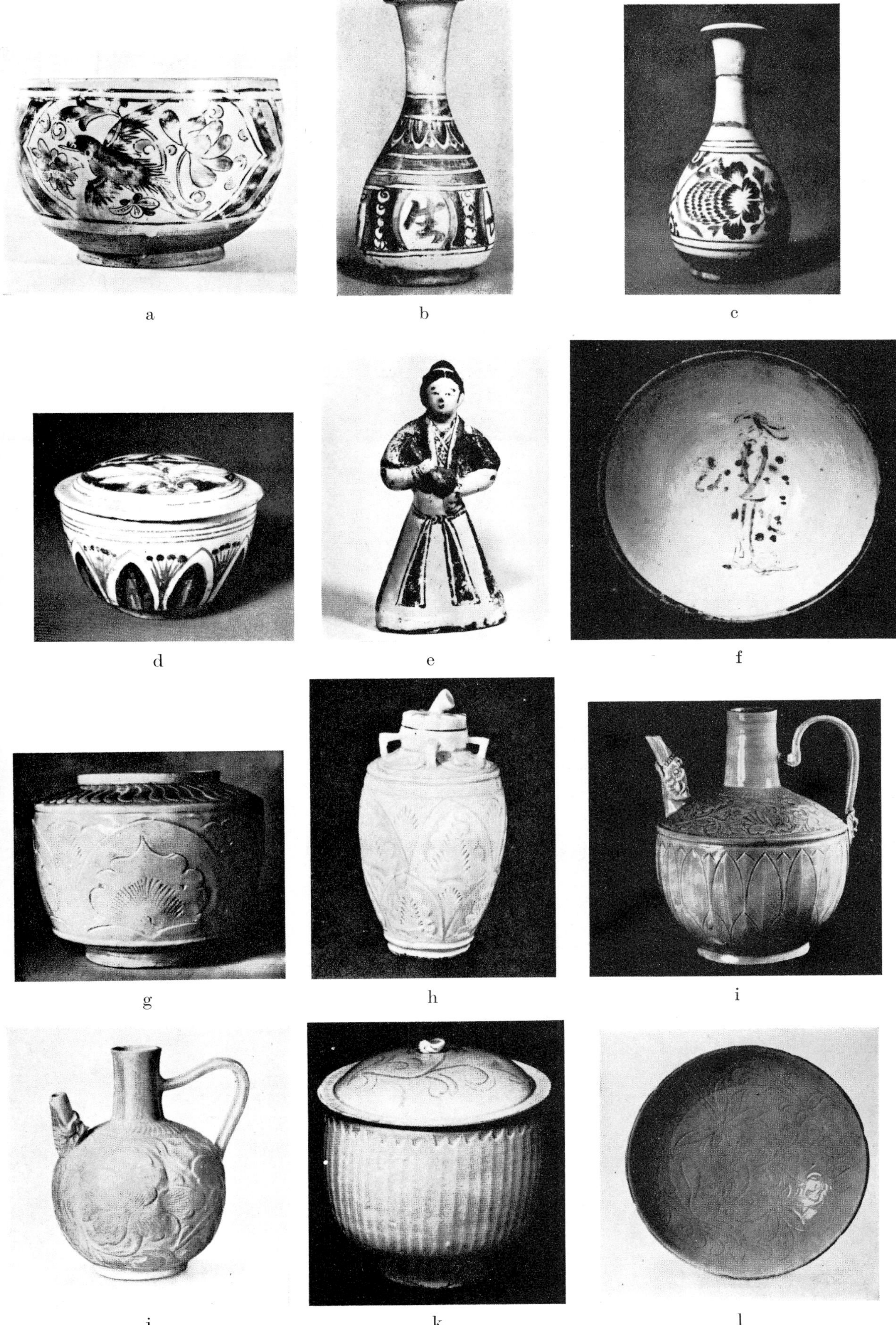

a b c

d e f

g h i

j k l

a

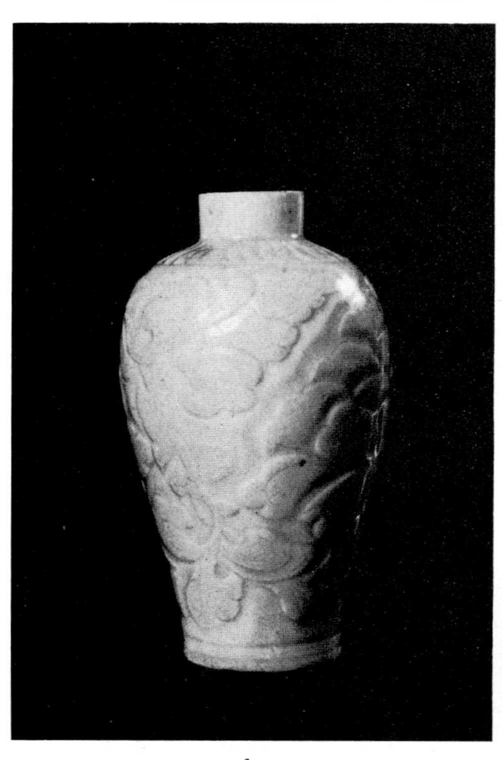

b

c

a

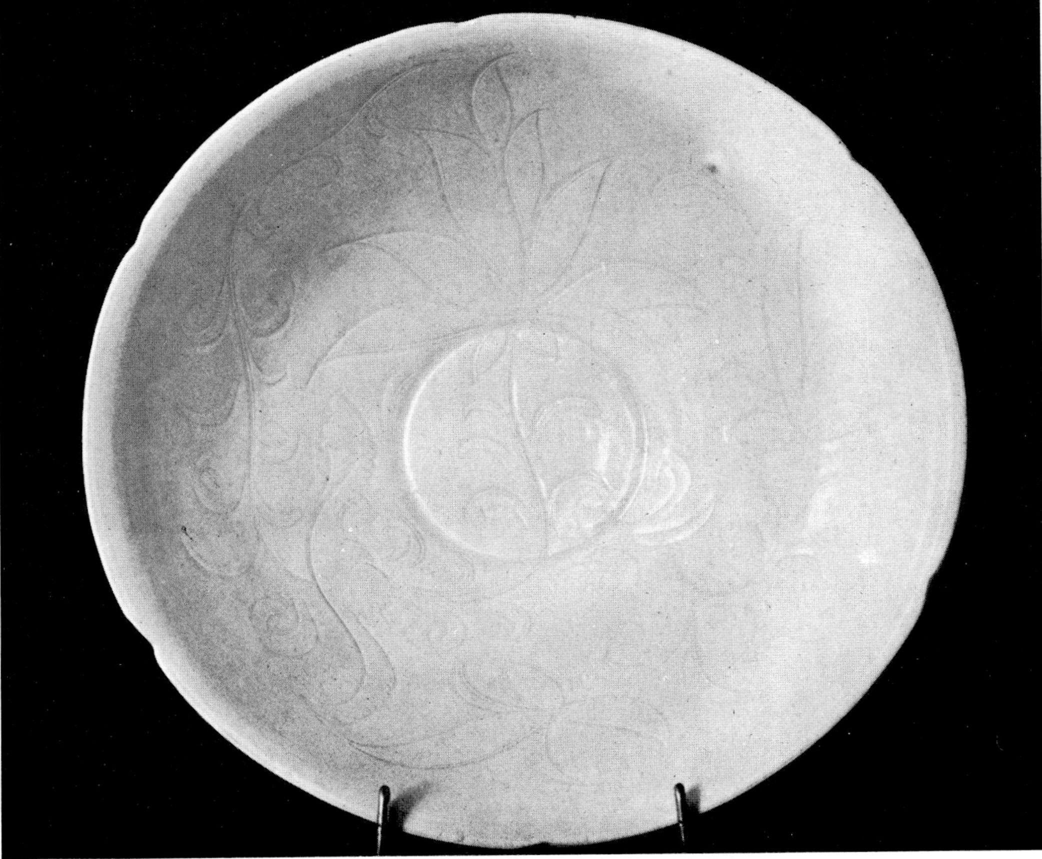

b

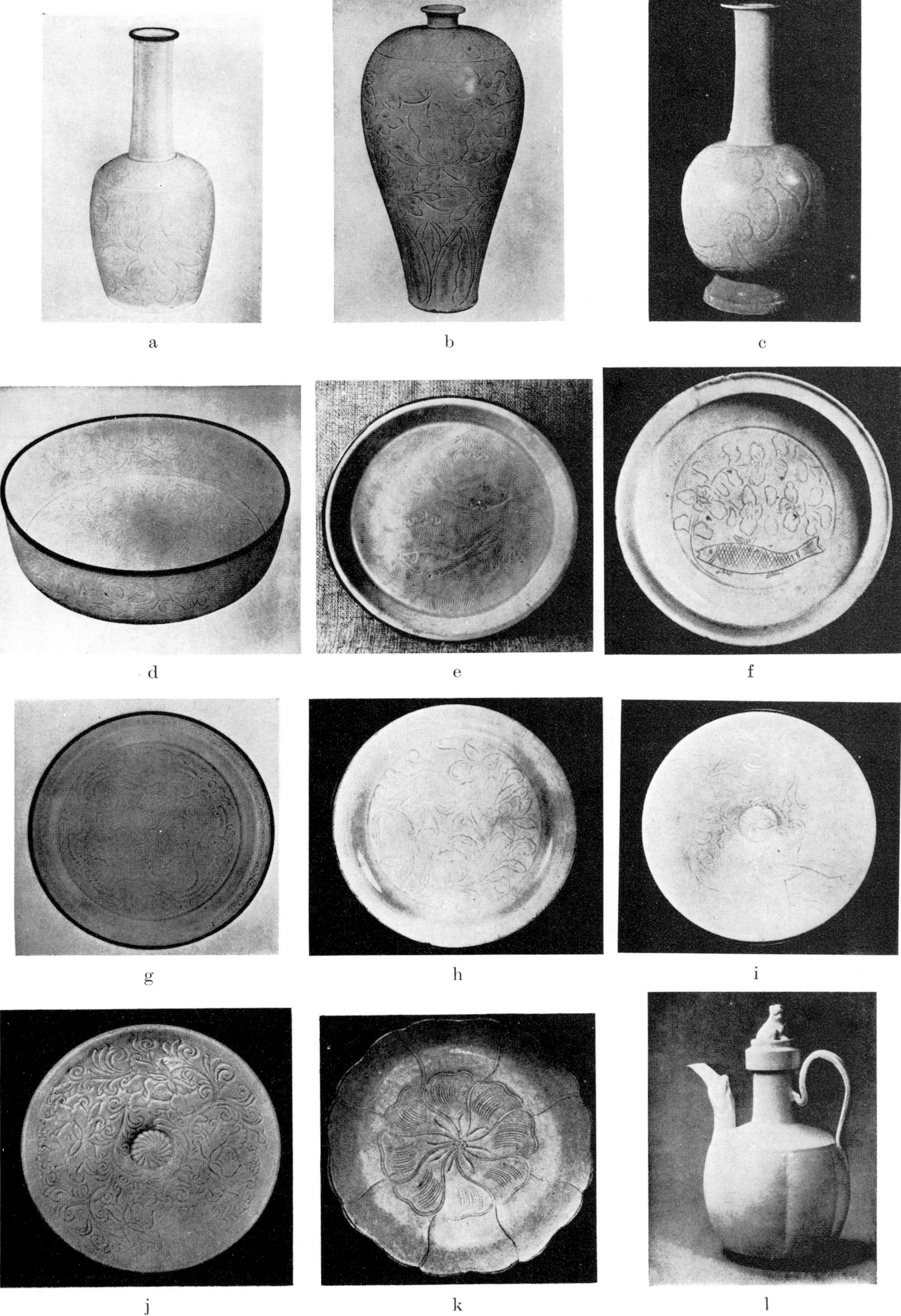

a b c

d e f

g h i

j k l

Pl. 62

a

b

a

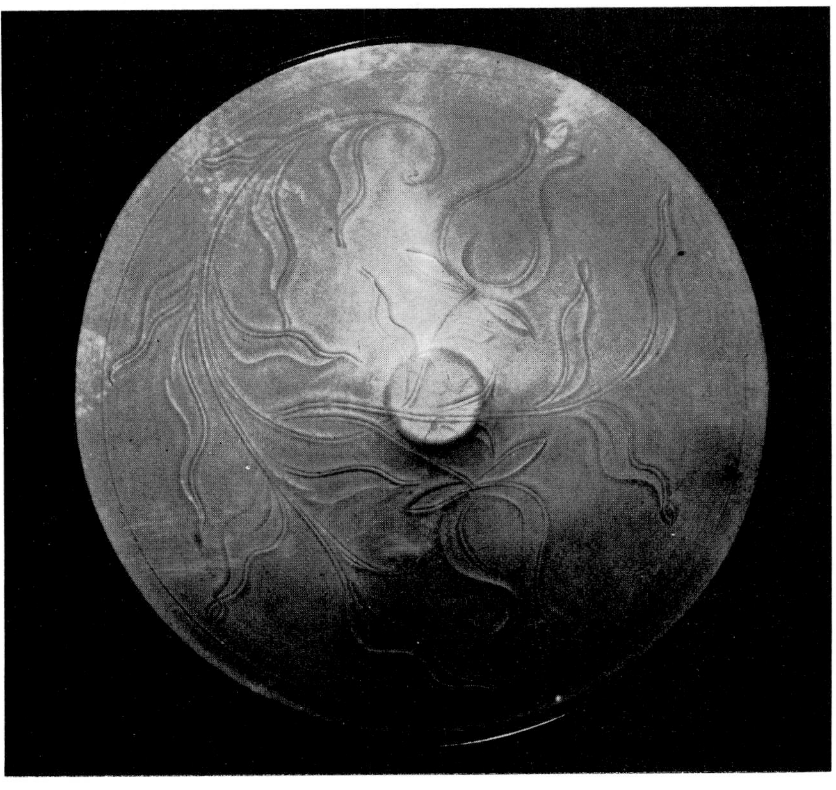

b

a

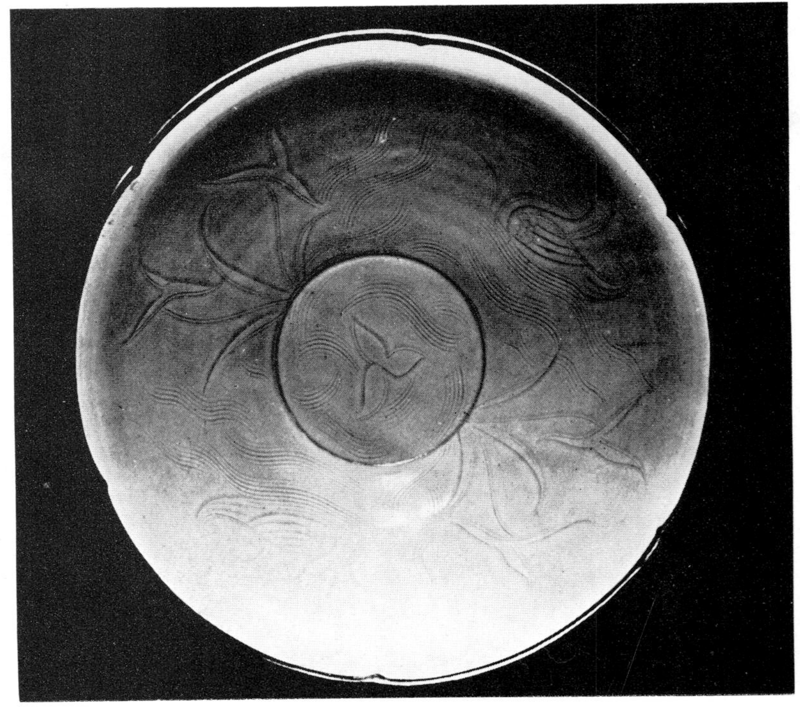

b

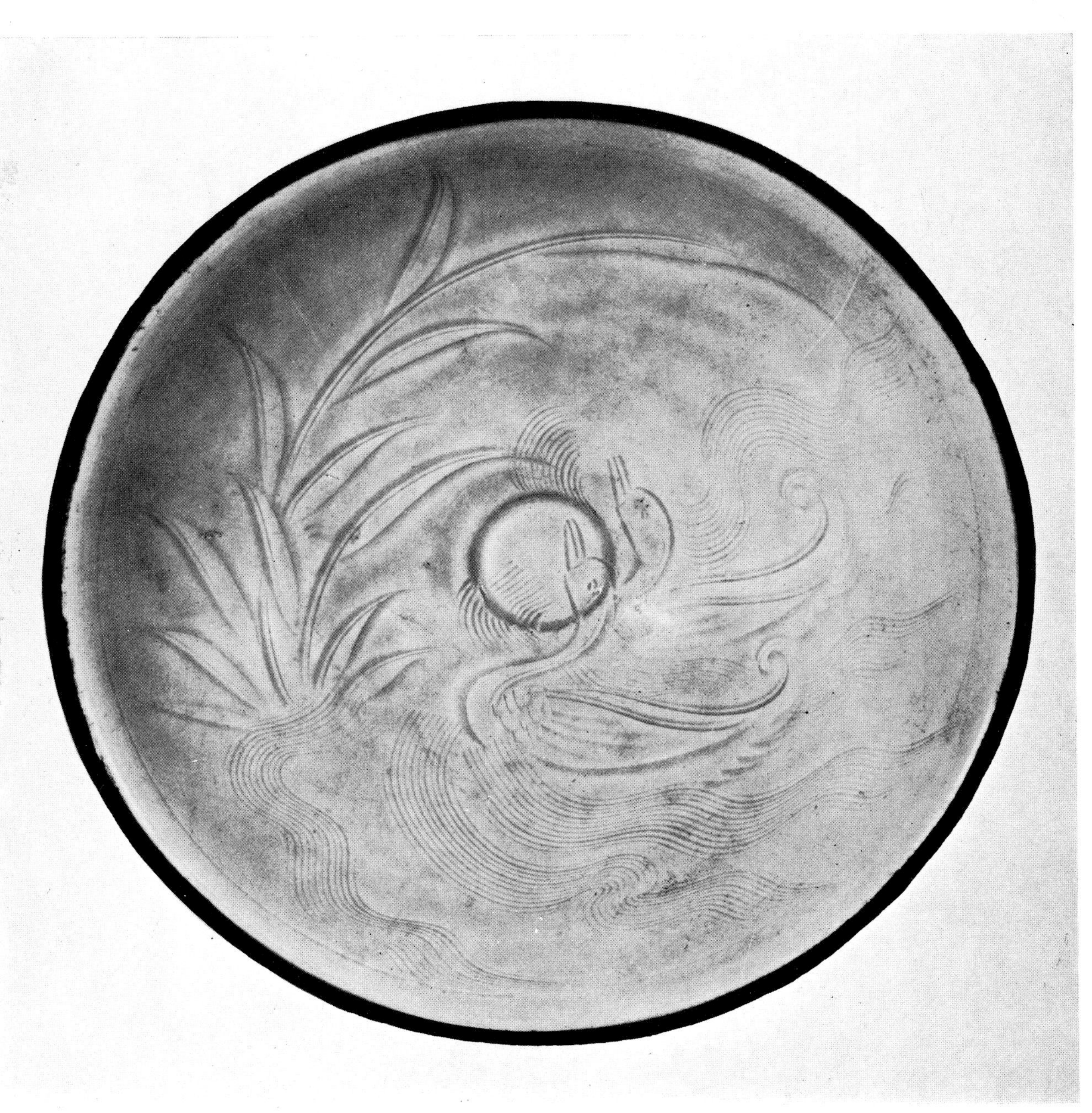

a

b

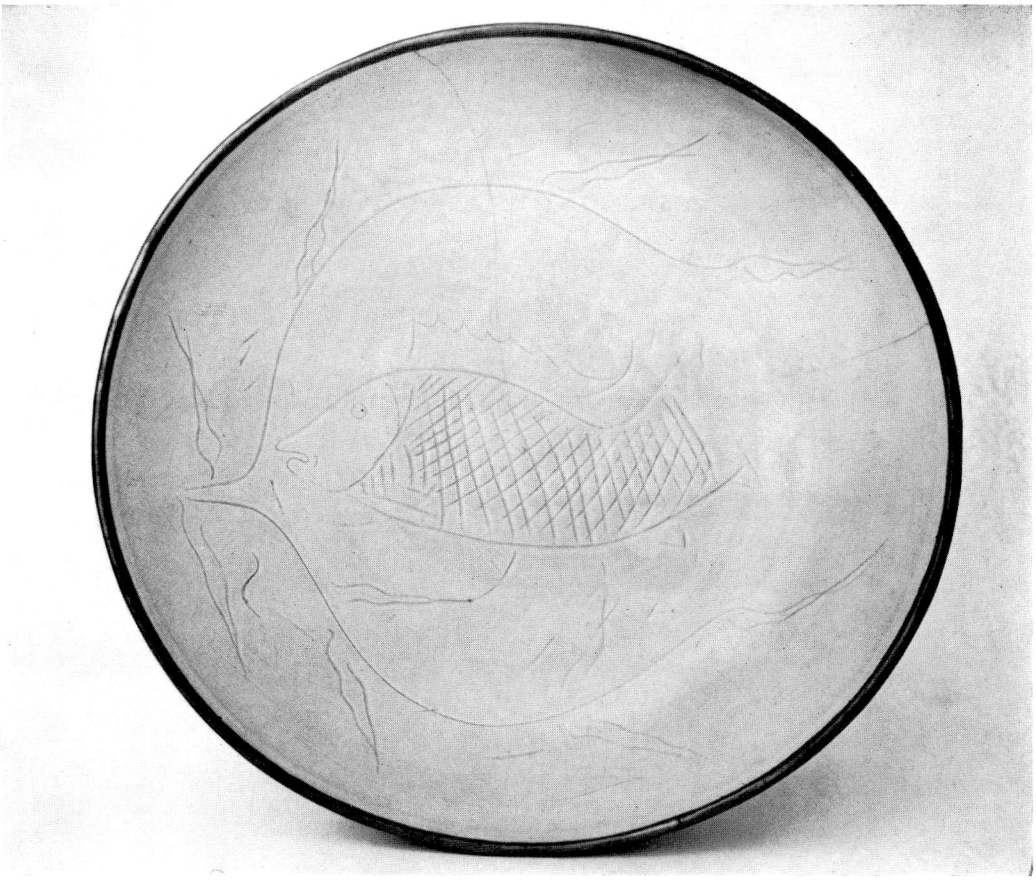

a

b

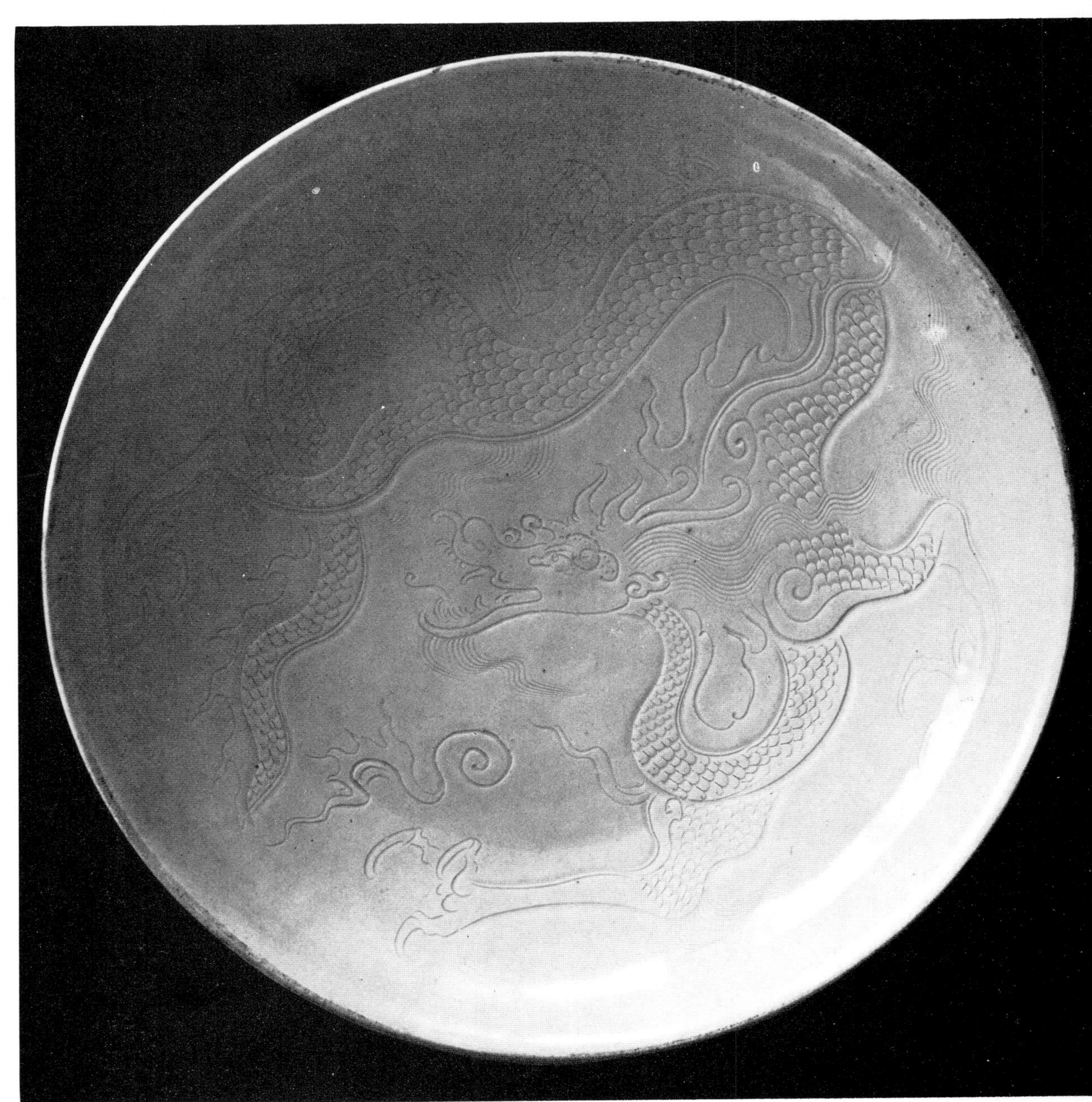

a

b

a

b

a

b

a

b

a

b

a

b

a

b

a

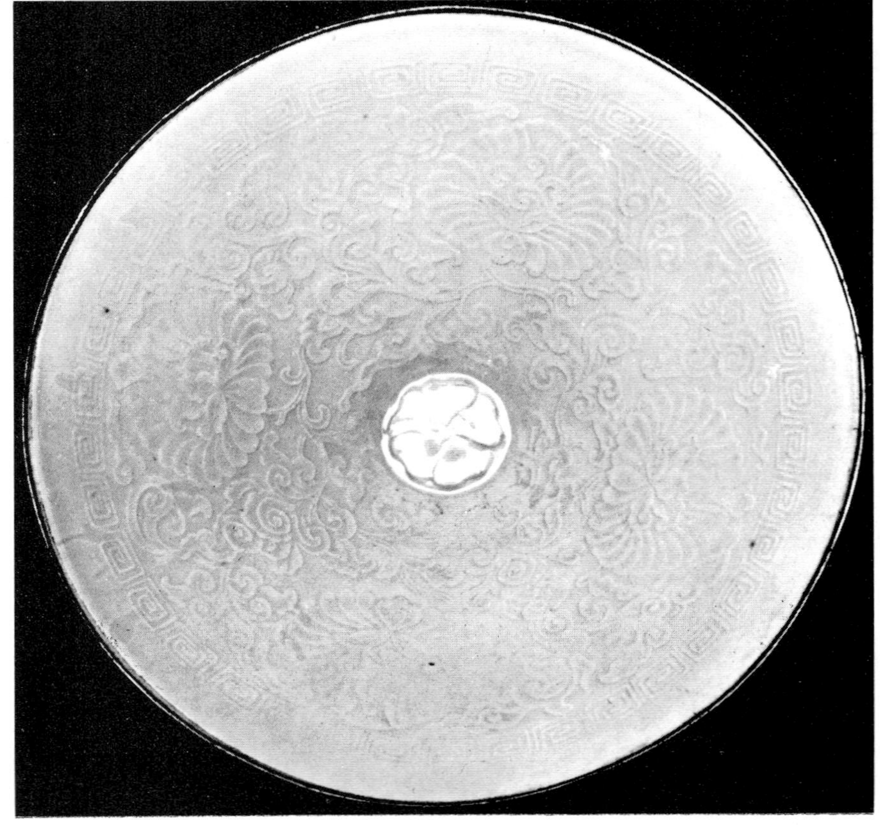

b

a

b

a b c

d e f

g h i

j k l

a

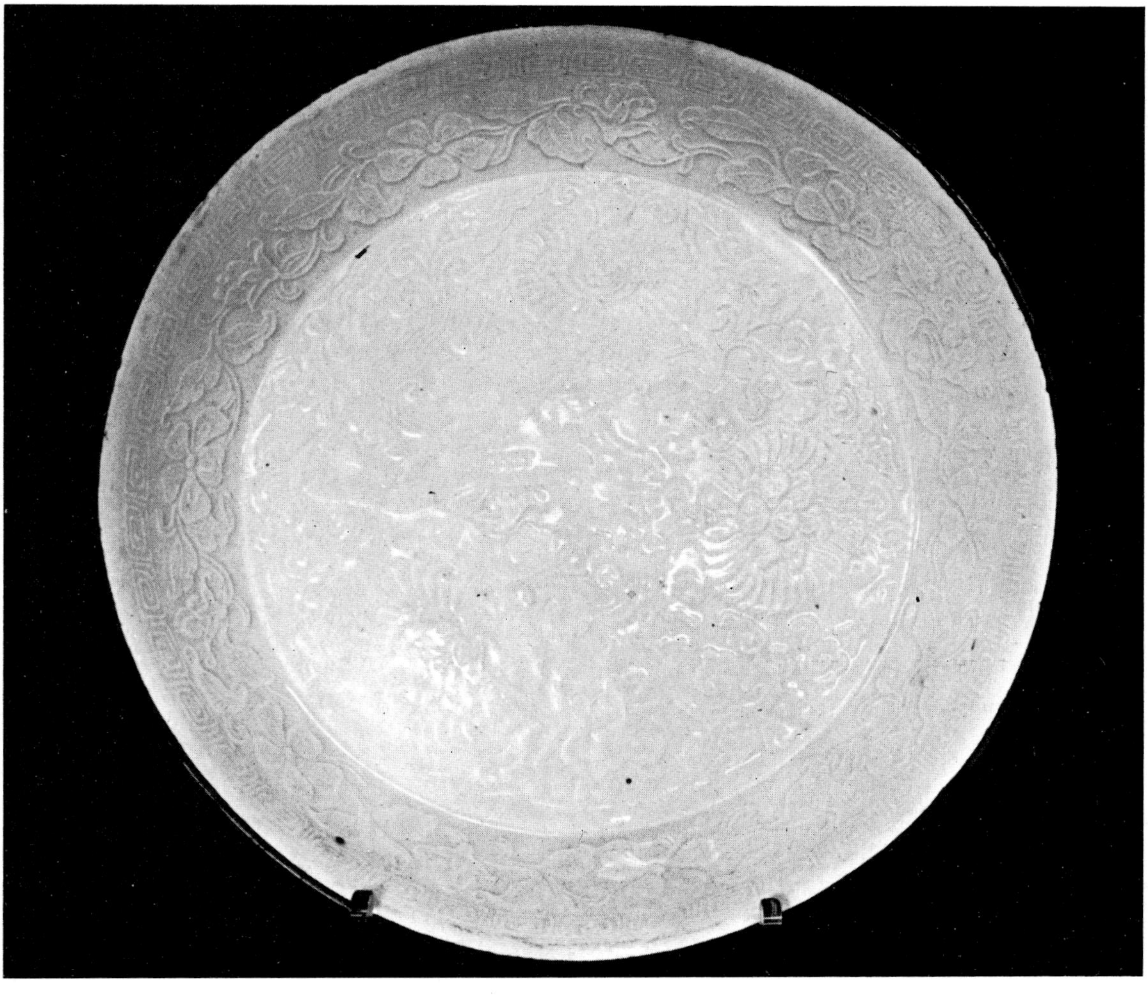

b

a

b

a

b

a

b

a

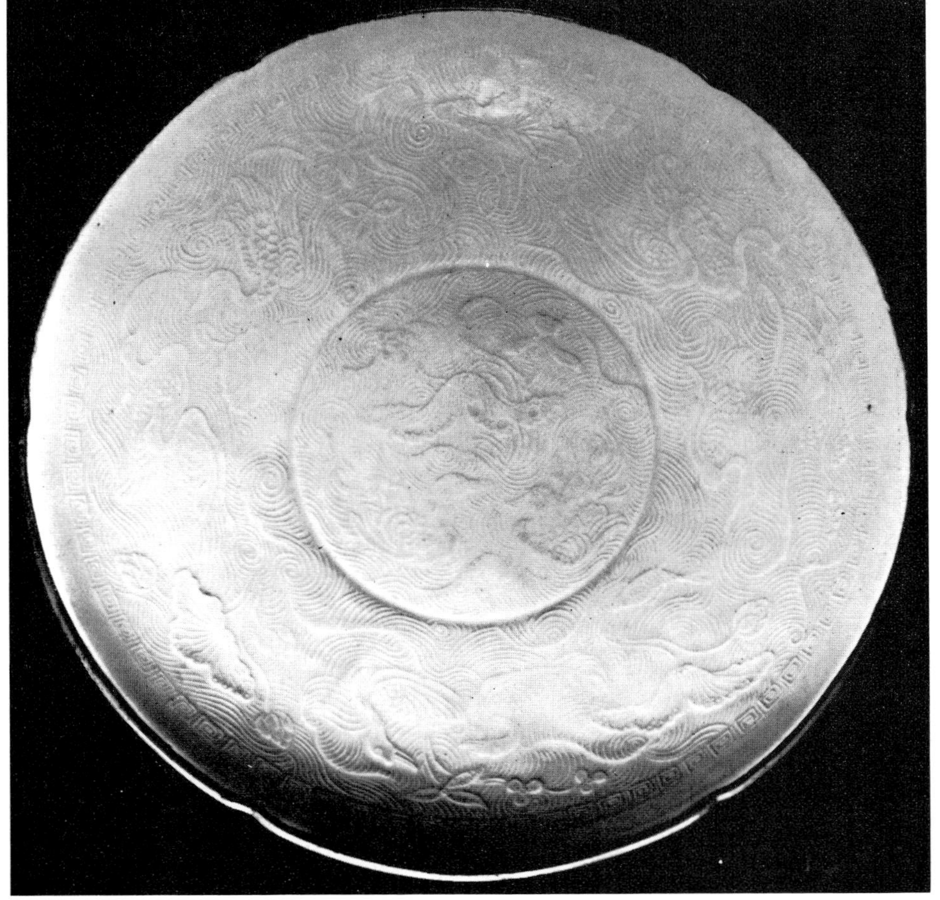

b

a

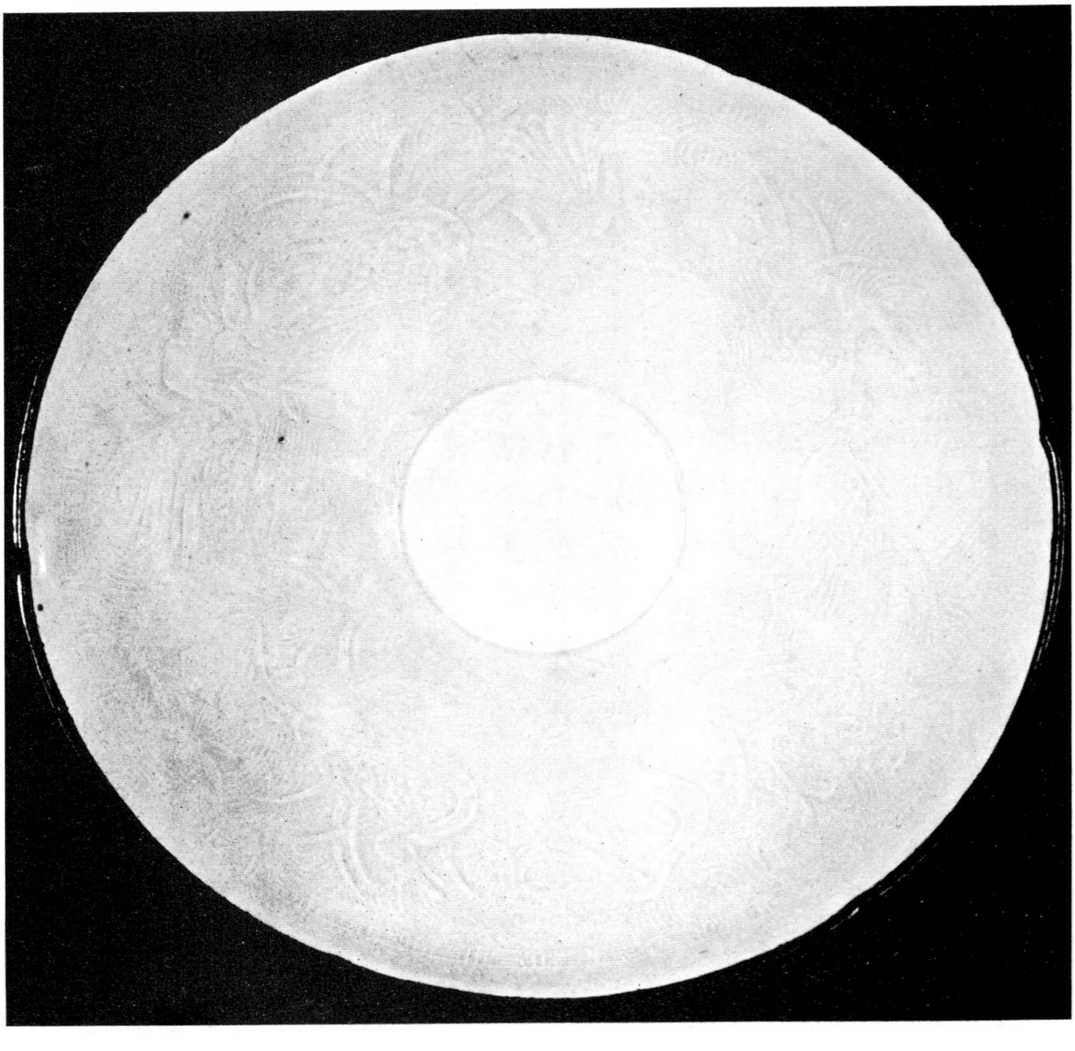

b

a

b

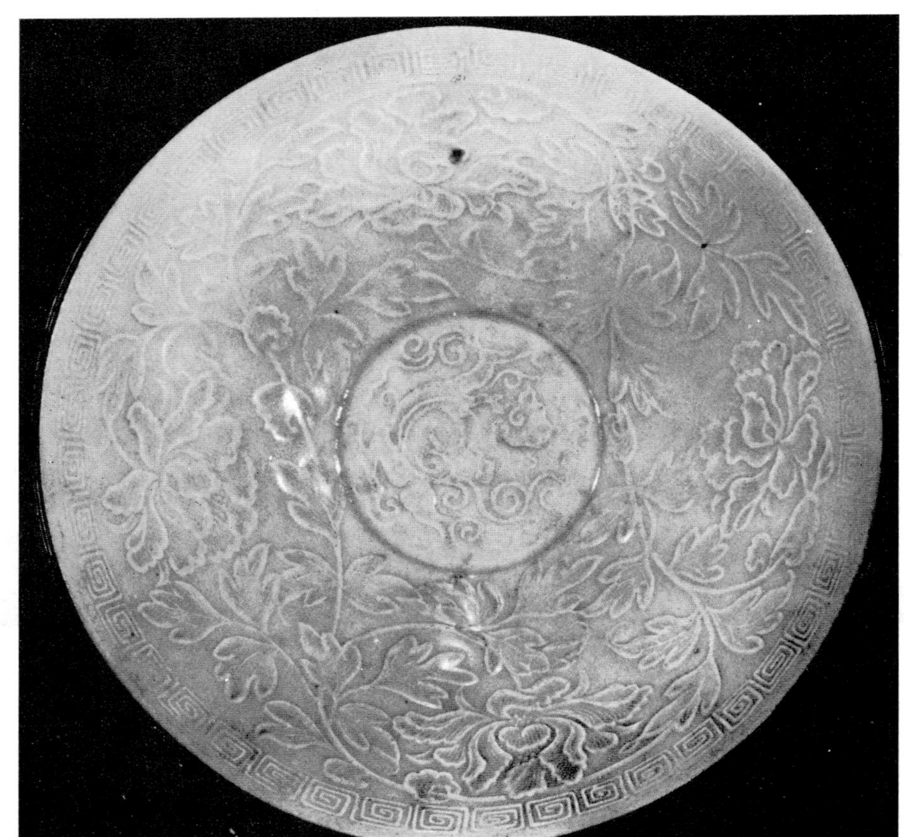

a

b

a

b

a

b

a

b

a

b

Pl. 98

a

b

a

b

a

b

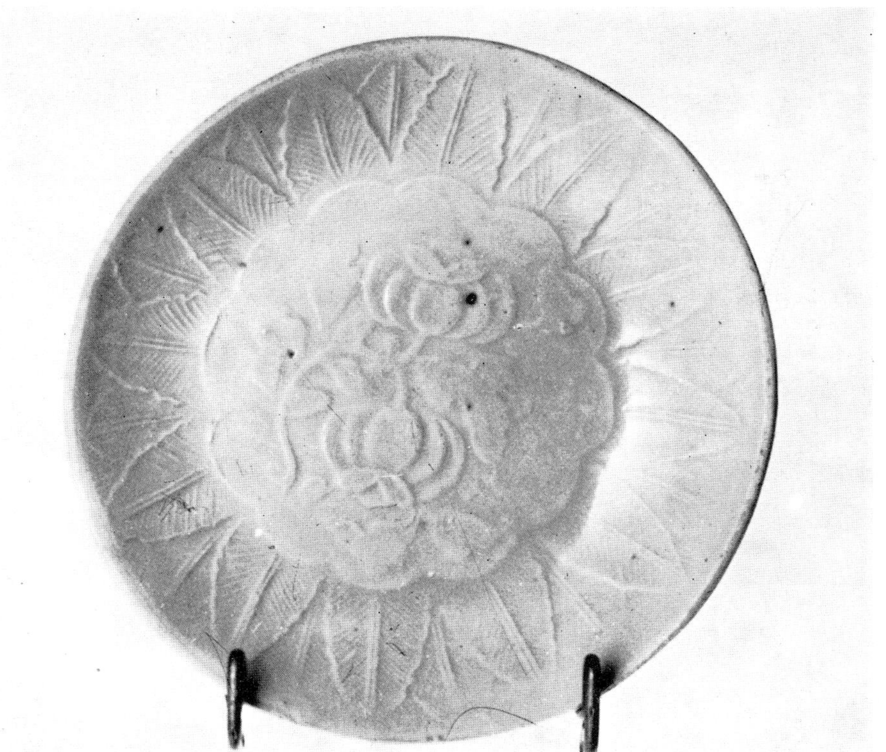

a

b

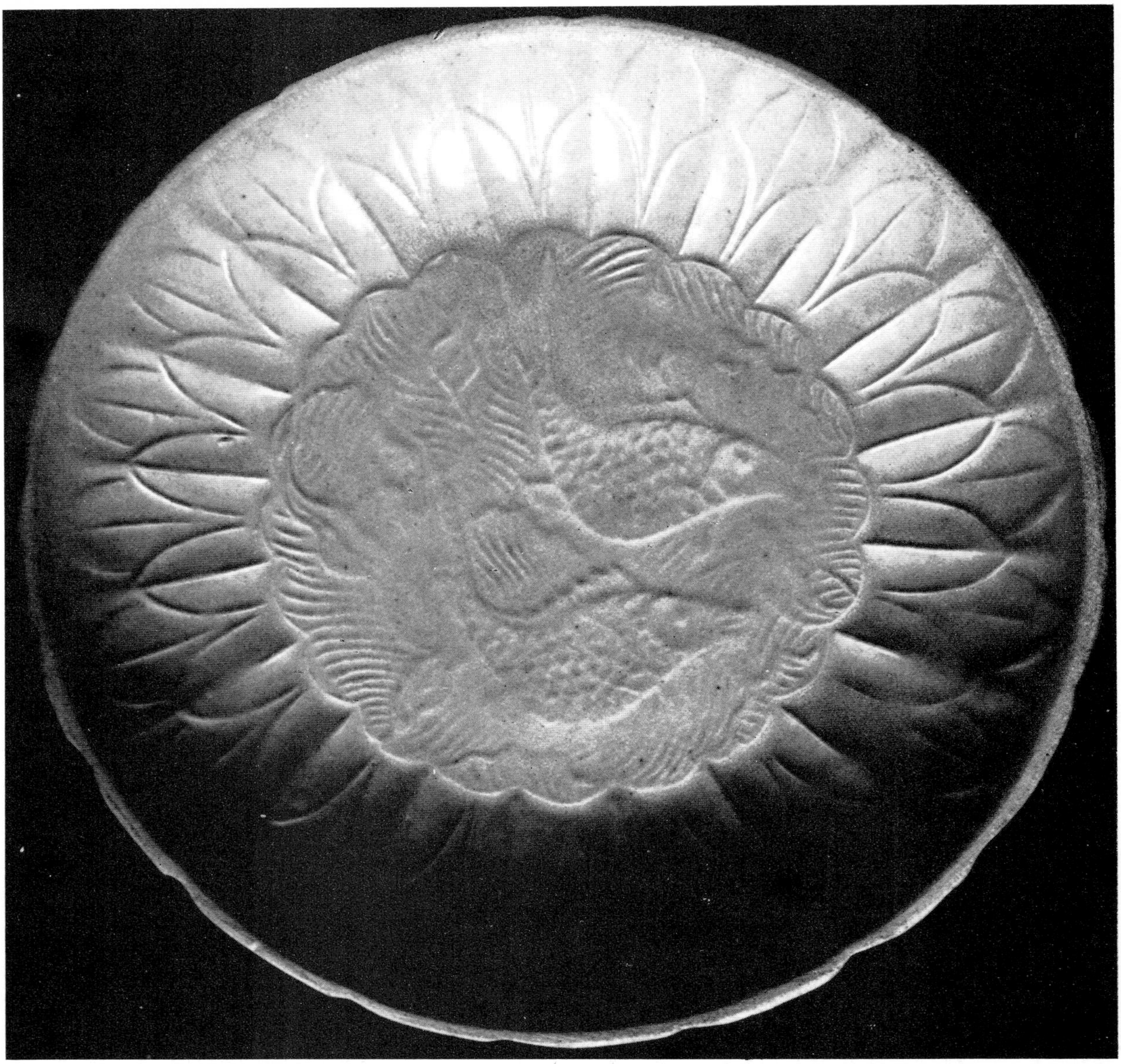

a

b

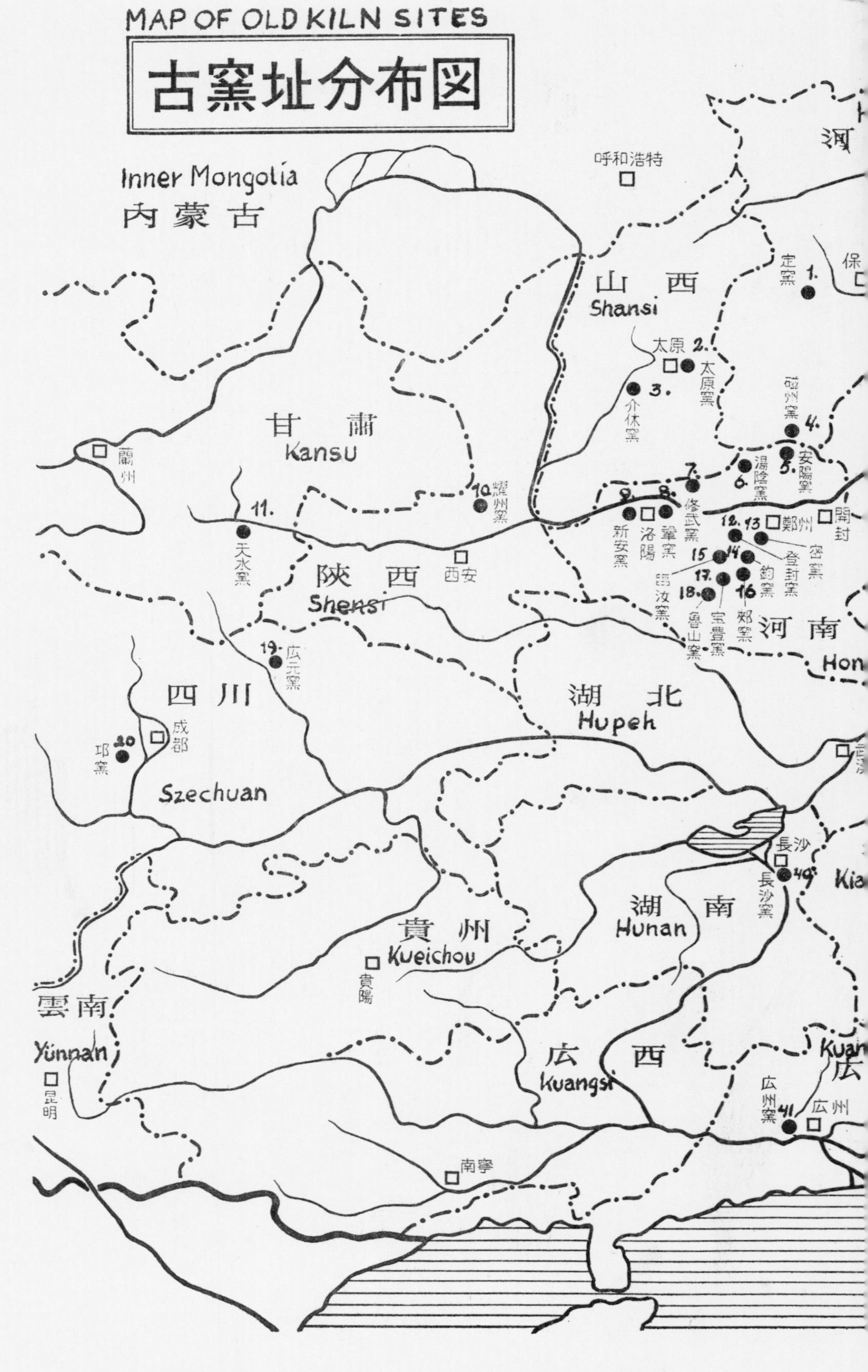

MAP OF OLD KILN SITES
古窯址分布図
Inner Mongolia
内蒙古
呼和浩特
山西
Shansi
1.
定窯
2.
太原
太原窯
3.
介休窯
4.
磁州窯
5.
安陽窯
6.
湯陰窯
7.
修武窯
8.
鞏窯
9.
新安窯
洛陽
10.
耀州窯
11.
天水窯
甘粛
Kansu
蘭州
陝西
Shensi
西安
鄭州
開封
12.
登封窯
13.
密窯
14.
鈞窯
15.
臨汝窯
16.
郟窯
17.
宝豊窯
18.
魯山窯
河南
19.
広元窯
四川
Szechuan
20.
邛窯
成都
湖北
Hupeh
長沙
49.
長沙窯
湖南
Hunan
貴州
Kueichou
貴陽
雲南
Yünnan
昆明
広西
Kuangsi
41.
広州窯
広州
南寧